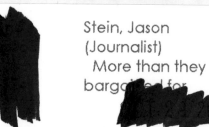

Stein, Jason
(Journalist)
More than they
bargained for

BARGAINED FOR

DATE DUE

MORE THAN THEY
BARGAINED FOR

Scott Walker,
Unions,
and the Fight for Wisconsin

Jason Stein *and* Patrick Marley

THE UNIVERSITY OF WISCONSIN PRESS

The University of Wisconsin Press
1930 Monroe Street, 3rd Floor
Madison, Wisconsin 53711-2059
uwpress.wisc.edu

3 Henrietta Street
London WC2E 8LU, England
eurospanbookstore.com

Printed in the United States of America

Library of Congress Cataloging-in-Publication Data

Stein, Jason, journalist.
More than they bargained for : Scott Walker, unions, and the fight for Wisconsin /
Jason Stein and Patrick Marley.
p. cm.
Includes bibliographical references and index.
ISBN 978-0-299-29384-0 (pbk. : alk. paper) — ISBN 978-0-299-29383-3 (e-book)
1. Labor movement—Wisconsin—History—21st century. 2. Protest movements—
Wisconsin—History—21st century. 3. Collective bargaining—Government
employees—Wisconsin. 4. Wisconsin—Politics and government—21st century.
I. Marley, Patrick, journalist. II. Title.
HD8083.W6S74 2013
322′.209775—dc23
2012040563

To Amanda, Zane, and Xavier
And to Denise and Elsa
Omnia vincit amor; et nos cedamus amori.

—VIRGIL, *Eclogues* Book Ten

Democracy isn't pretty all the time.

—JEFF FITZGERALD, Speaker of the Wisconsin Assembly,
February 18, 2011

Contents

Illustrations

Acknowledgments

More people helped us in the writing of this book than we could ever adequately thank. We thank the editors at the University of Wisconsin Press as well as the ones at the *Milwaukee Journal Sentinel* who not only allowed but encouraged us to write this book: Marty Kaiser, George Stanley, Tom Koetting, Gary Krentz, Mike Juley, Becky Lang, Eric Aspenson, and especially Mike Mulvey, who edited a nonstop stream of web posts and daily stories during the height of the protests. We are also indebted to our fellow reporters who contributed so much to both this book and the *Journal Sentinel*'s coverage of this extraordinary time in Wisconsin, particularly Daniel Bice, Lee Bergquist, Bill Glauber, Dave Umhoefer, Craig Gilbert, Don Walker, and Emma Roller. We were also helped greatly by a number of other reporters at the paper, including Steve Schultze, Tom Kertscher, Jim Nelson, Amy Hetzner, Erin Richards, Tom Tolan, Ben Poston, Larry Sandler, John Schmid, Rick Romell, Sharif Durhams, Karen Herzog, Cary Spivak, Kathleen Gallagher, Mark Johnson, Crocker Stephenson, Thomas Content, Bruce Vielmetti, Laurel Walker, Mike Johnson, Guy Boulton, Jim Stingl, Annysa Johnson, and Alison Bauter. The photographers and videographers who camped out at the Capitol with us brought the story to life in a way that we couldn't, and for that we offer a hearty thanks to Mike De Sisti, Gary Porter, Tom Lynn, Mark Hoffman, Michael Sears, Bill Schulz, Kristyna Wentz-Graff, and Rick Wood. We also appreciate the efforts of graphic artists Lou Saldivar and Enrique Rodriguez, as well as all the copy editors who improved our work on never-ending deadlines. Those who share the Capitol press room with us are more like colleagues than competitors, and we wish to thank them, too, particularly Scott Bauer and Todd Richmond of the Associated Press; Mary Spicuzza and Clay Barbour of the *Wisconsin State Journal*; Gwyn and Trevor Guenther of the Wheeler Report; Jessica VanEgeren of the *Capital Times*; Jessica Arp of WISC-TV; Steven Walters of the WisconsinEye Public Affairs Network; Greg Neumann of WKOW-TV; Zac Schultz of Wisconsin Public Television; Shawn Johnson of Wisconsin Public Radio; Bob Hague, Jackie Johnson, and Andrew Beckett of the Wisconsin Radio Network; JR Ross and Greg Bump of WisPolitics.com; and our many other fellow journalists. Dick Wheeler—dean of the statehouse press corps, founder of the Wheeler Report, and now namesake of the Capitol press room—helped us learn enough legislative procedure to follow the machinations at work in the passing of Act 10, and we miss him greatly. WisconsinEye's archived footage of legislative sessions, committee hearings, and other events was tremendously helpful in writing this book, and we thank the network for what it makes freely available to the public.

We are grateful for the cooperation of those we write about: elected officials of both parties, their aides, demonstrators and labor leaders, and conservative groups. Particularly helpful were the staff at the legislative service agencies. We also thank those who read and commented on the manuscript, including Stacy Forster Benedict, Steven Walters, Chris Reynolds, the UW Press reviewers, and our *Journal Sentinel* colleagues. We are particularly grateful to the staff of the UW Press for believing in this project.

Last and most important, Jason thanks Amanda, Zane, Xavier, and family and Patrick thanks Denise, Elsa, and family for their support, understanding, and patience during the longest two years in Wisconsin politics.

Actors in the Events

Scott Walker, GOP governor of Wisconsin, formerly Milwaukee County executive

Scott Fitzgerald, GOP Senate majority leader, formerly Senate minority leader

Jeff Fitzgerald, GOP Assembly speaker, formerly Assembly minority leader, brother to Scott

Mike Ellis, GOP Senate president

Jim Doyle, former Democratic governor

Tom Barrett, mayor of Milwaukee, Walker's 2010 Democratic opponent for governor and 2012 recall candidate for governor

Kathleen Falk, former Dane County executive and 2012 Democratic recall candidate for governor

Rebecca Kleefisch, GOP lieutenant governor

J.B. Van Hollen, GOP attorney general

Mark Miller, Democratic Senate minority leader

Peter Barca, Democratic Assembly minority leader

Representative Robin Vos, GOP co-chairman of the Joint Finance Committee

Senator Alberta Darling, GOP co-chairwoman of the Joint Finance Committee

Dale Schultz, Republican senator

Tim Cullen, Democratic senator

Glenn Grothman, Republican senator

Bob Jauch, Democratic senator

Brett Hulsey, Democratic representative

Keith Gilkes, chief of staff to Governor Walker; manager of the 2010
  campaign and the 2012 recall

Eric Schutt, deputy chief of staff to Governor Walker, later chief of staff

Mike Huebsch, Walker's secretary of administration, former GOP
  Assembly speaker

Jenni Dye, demonstrator and Twitter addict, later Dane County Board
  supervisor

Michael Brown, founder of the recall group United Wisconsin

Maryann Sumi, Dane County judge overseeing lawsuit over Walker's
  Act 10 union measure

John Albert, Dane County judge overseeing lawsuit over access to the
  Capitol

Ismael Ozanne, Democratic district attorney in Dane County

John Chisholm, Democratic district attorney in Milwaukee County

David Prosser, Wisconsin Supreme Court justice

Ann Walsh Bradley, Wisconsin Supreme Court justice

Tim Russell, deputy chief of staff to Walker when he was Milwaukee
  County executive

Kelly Rindfleisch, deputy chief of staff to Walker when he was Milwaukee
  County executive, following Russell

Charles Tubbs, chief of the Capitol Police

Susan Riseling, chief of the University of Wisconsin–Madison police

Mary Bell, president of the Wisconsin Education Association Council

Marty Beil, executive director of the Wisconsin State Employees Union

Chronology

April 28, 2009—Milwaukee County Executive Scott Walker officially declares his candidacy for governor as a Republican.

May 2010—Darlene Wink resigns from Walker's county executive office after the *Milwaukee Journal Sentinel* reports that she repeatedly posted online comments on political stories during work hours. Separately, Milwaukee County district attorney John Chisholm converts an investigation into missing money from a veterans fund into a secret John Doe probe that will reach into numerous other areas.

November 1, 2010—Investigators seize material from Walker's campaign and county executive offices.

November 2, 2010—Walker defeats Milwaukee Mayor Tom Barrett, becoming Wisconsin's forty-fifth governor. His fellow Republicans take control of the Legislature from Democrats.

December 3, 2010—The Walker administration prepares a bill eliminating some aspects of collective bargaining for public workers.

December 15, 2010—Democrats hold a lame-duck session to try to pass labor contracts before Walker takes office, but it comes one vote shy of passing the Senate because two Democrats vote against it.

February 11, 2011—Walker formally announces his plan for repealing collective bargaining for most public employees.

February 14, 2011—The first large protest begins at the Capitol, after small ones over the weekend.

February 15, 2011—A massive protest occurs. The Legislature's Joint
Finance Committee begins a hearing on the bill, and opponents try to
stall it with nonstop testimony.

February 16, 2011—The hearing continues until 3 a.m., when Republicans
end it. Democrats start their own hearing, which runs into the next
week. Police keep the Capitol open overnight, setting a precedent that
allows protesters to camp in the building for weeks. Madison schools
close because many teachers call in sick to protest. In a late-night
meeting, the Finance Committee approves the bill and sends it to the
Senate and Assembly.

February 17, 2011—Senate Democrats leave Wisconsin to prevent
Republicans from passing the bill. Madison schools remain closed, and
some other school districts follow suit.

February 18, 2011—With the Senate unable to act, Assembly Republicans
briefly take up the bill without Democrats on the floor but then delay
the vote to another day. Public-sector unions announce they would agree
to monetary concessions in exchange for keeping their collective
bargaining ability.

February 19, 2011—Protests continue, with Tea Party supporters holding a
smaller counterprotest alongside Walker's opponents at the Capitol.

February 22, 2011—The Assembly begins what is likely the longest
legislative debate in state history on the bill. A recall effort—the first of
many on both sides—is filed against Democratic Senator Jim Holperin
of Conover. The liberal blogger Ian Murphy, posing as billionaire
industrialist David Koch, speaks by phone with Walker for twenty
minutes.

February 23, 2011—Murphy releases audio of his prank phone call. Debate
in the Assembly continues for a second day.

February 25, 2011—The Assembly passes the collective bargaining changes
after more than sixty-one hours of debate.

February 26, 2011—Senate Democrats secretly meet with public-sector
union leaders at the Illinois Education Association office in Libertyville,
including the incoming head of the national teachers union.

February 28, 2011—The Walker administration sharply limits access to the
statehouse and requires visitors to go through metal detectors. Unions
file a lawsuit in Dane County Circuit Court in an attempt to open up the

building. Senate Majority Leader Scott Fitzgerald meets with Jauch and fellow Democratic Senator Tim Cullen in Kenosha in an effort to get them to return.

March 1, 2011—Walker gives his budget address. First Judge Daniel Moeser and then later Judge John Albert order broader access to the Capitol while the union suit continues, but Walker's administration keeps limits in place.

March 2, 2011—Jauch, Cullen, and Senate Minority Leader Mark Miller meet with top Walker aides to further discuss changes to the bill that would bring Democrats back to Wisconsin.

March 3, 2011—Judge Albert orders the Walker administration to remove unauthorized people and material from the Capitol and then restore access to the building. Senate Republicans vote to find their Democratic colleagues in contempt of the Senate.

March 4, 2011—Walker sends layoff notices to 1,500 state employees.

March 6, 2011—Jauch and Cullen again meet with Walker aides, coming near to finalizing a proposal the two Democrats can take to their skeptical caucus.

March 7, 2011—The public is granted freer access to the Capitol but not as much as had been available before Walker's bill. Miller sends Walker a letter asking to negotiate along the border, drawing rebukes from Republicans in talks with Jauch and Cullen. The talks effectively end.

March 9, 2011—Shortly after 4 p.m., Senate Republicans order a conference committee to meet at 6 p.m. to approve a revised version of the bill that could pass without the presence of the Democrats. The committee passes the bill amid fierce objections from Democrats that the meeting violates the state's open meetings law, and the Senate endorses it eighteen to one shortly thereafter with all Democrats absent. Protesters flood the Capitol.

March 10, 2011—The Assembly passes the bill fifty-three to forty-two. Assembly Minority Leader Peter Barca and others file formal complaints alleging the conference committee violated the open meetings law.

March 11, 2011—Walker signs the bill, which becomes known as Wisconsin 2011 Act 10.

March 12, 2011—Senate Democrats return to Madison to cheers from crowds on the Capitol lawn.

March 16, 2011—Acting on Barca's complaint, Dane County District Attorney Ismael Ozanne files a court challenge alleging the conference committee violated the open meetings law.

March 18, 2011—Dane County Circuit Judge Maryann Sumi issues a temporary restraining order blocking implementation of Act 10.

March 25, 2011—At the urging of Scott Fitzgerald, the state Legislative Reference Bureau publishes Act 10 despite the restraining order.

March 29 and 31, 2011—Sumi issues a pair of rulings stating that the restraining order is still in effect, including one that says the law has not yet been published despite the Legislative Reference Bureau's action.

April 5, 2011—Wisconsin Supreme Court Justice David Prosser narrowly wins re-election in a race focusing on Act 10.

April 7, 2011—Walker's administration asks the state Supreme Court to take the case on Act 10.

April 11, 2011—As part of the John Doe probe, the railroad executive William Gardner is charged with illegally funneling money to Walker's campaign. Separately, Walker spokesman Cullen Werwie and others are granted immunity for other aspects of the investigation.

June 13, 2011—Six of the Supreme Court's seven justices argue over when the decision on Act 10 will be released. Justice Ann Walsh Bradley confronts Prosser face to face in an attempt to get him to leave her office. In what he says is a defensive reflex, he puts his hands on her neck.

June 14, 2011—In a four to three ruling, the Supreme Court finds the open meetings law largely does not apply to the Legislature and reinstates Act 10.

July and August 2011—Nine recall elections are held over Act 10, against six Republican senators and three Democratic senators. The challengers unseat two Republicans, narrowing the GOP Senate majority to seventeen seats to the Democrats' sixteen.

August 18, 2011—Two union locals sue over Act 10 in Dane County.

September 14, 2011—Federal Bureau of Investigation agents raid the Madison home of Cindy Archer, Walker's former administration secretary in Milwaukee County and, until a month earlier, his deputy administration secretary as governor.

October 8, 2011—Labor leaders meet with Jim Messina, manager of
President Barack Obama's campaign, and Mike Tate, chairman of the
Wisconsin Democratic Party, to discuss a Walker recall.

November 15, 2011—Recall petition drives begin against Walker, Lieutenant
Governor Rebecca Kleefisch, and four Republican state senators.

December 15, 2011—Walker's campaign sues the state Government
Accountability Board, saying it doesn't plan to do enough to root out
fraudulent and duplicate recall signatures. The litigation ultimately leads
the board to enter all the names into a database, delaying the signature
verification process by weeks.

January 5, 2012—Separate embezzlement charges are issued against two
former Walker associates: Tim Russell, Walker's former deputy chief of
staff and housing director at the county; and Kevin Kavanaugh, a Walker
appointee to a veterans board.

January 17, 2012—Petitions are filed to recall Walker and the others.

January 26, 2012—Kelly Rindfleisch, another former deputy chief of staff to
Walker at the county, is charged with four felonies for misconduct in
office for working on the lieutenant governor campaign of Brett Davis
while on the county clock. Wink is charged with two misdemeanors for
raising money for Walker on county time; she reaches a plea deal.

March 30, 2012—The Accountability Board determines enough signatures
have been filed to hold all recalls. Despite union efforts to keep him out
of the race, Tom Barrett announces he will run for governor, creating a
four-way Democratic primary. Also, a federal judge rules parts of Act 10
are unconstitutional, while upholding major aspects of the law.

May 8, 2012—Barrett handily wins the Democratic primary.

June 5, 2012—Walker wins the recall election by a bigger margin than in
2010, making him the first governor in the country's history to prevail in
a recall election. Democrats take the Senate.

August 11, 2012—Presumptive Republican presidential nominee Mitt
Romney picks Congressman Paul Ryan of Janesville, a Walker ally, as
his running mate, briefly causing the polls in the presidential race in
Wisconsin to tighten.

September 14, 2012—Dane County Circuit Judge Juan Colás issues a
decision striking down significant portions of Act 10 as unconstitutional

for municipal, county, and school workers. Attorney General J.B. Van
Hollen immediately appeals.

October 11, 2012—Rindfleisch pleads guilty to felony misconduct in office.

October 12, 2012—A jury finds Kavanaugh guilty of stealing more than
$51,000 intended to help veterans.

November 6, 2012—In spite of Walker's recent recall win and Ryan's
presence on the ballot, President Barack Obama carries Wisconsin, as
does Democratic U.S. Senate candidate Tammy Baldwin. Republicans
retake the state Senate.

November 19, 2012—Rindfleisch is sentenced to six months in jail and
three years of probation. The judge stays the sentence while she appeals
earlier rulings.

November 29, 2012—Russell pleads guilty to felony embezzlement.

January 18, 2013—A federal appeals court panel upholds Act 10 in its
entirety, reversing the March 2012 decision that had struck down parts
of the law. Unions keep their attention on the state courts, where parts of
Act 10 remain on hold because of Judge Colás's decision.

January 22, 2013—A Milwaukee County judge sentences Russell to two
years in prison and five years of probation.

MORE THAN THEY
BARGAINED FOR

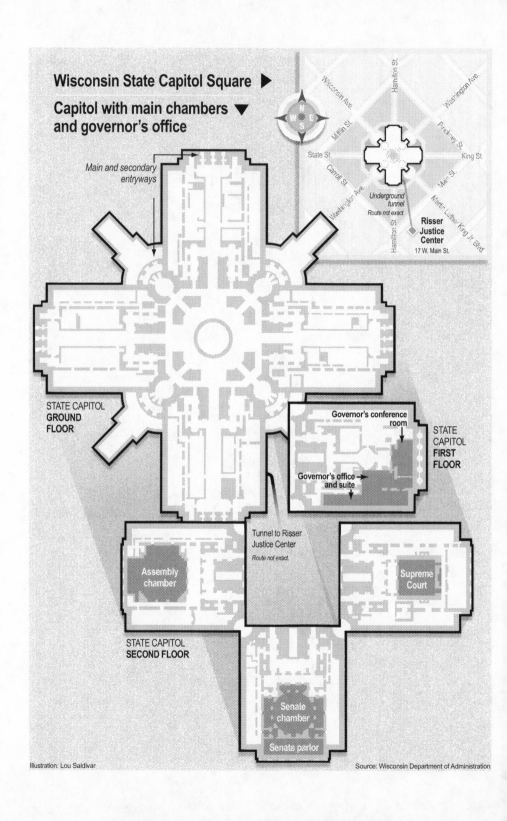

Wisconsin State Capitol Square ▶

Capitol with main chambers ▼
and governor's office

Main and secondary
entryways

Wisconsin Ave.
Hamilton St
Washington Ave.
Mifflin St.
Pinckney St.
State St.
King St.
Carroll St.
Main St.
Washington Ave.
Martin Luther King Jr. Blvd.
Hamilton St.

Underground
tunnel
Route not exact.

Risser
Justice
Center
17 W. Main St.

STATE CAPITOL
**GROUND
FLOOR**

Governor's conference
room

STATE
CAPITOL
**FIRST
FLOOR**

Governor's office
and suite

Tunnel to Risser
Justice Center
Route not exact.

Assembly
chamber

Supreme
Court

STATE CAPITOL
SECOND FLOOR

Senate
chamber

Senate parlor

Illustration: Lou Saldivar

Source: Wisconsin Department of Administration

I

"Put Up or Shut Up"

THE TELEVISION CAMERAS WERE ROLLING in the top-floor hearing room of Wisconsin's Capitol, and every Republican was smiling for them. The members of the GOP's newly elected majority in the state Senate whooped and applauded as Scott Kevin Walker, a trim figure of medium height in a dark suit and red tie, took a triumphant turn through the room. The governor-elect had thinning hair but a youthful face and energy. He had celebrated his forty-third birthday just two days before, on November 2, 2010—the same day he'd won the election. His potential at that moment seemed enormous. A former lawmaker himself, Walker had left the statehouse for more than eight years to serve as the elected executive of Milwaukee County, and now he was returning in style as the first Republican to win the governor's race in Wisconsin in a dozen years. He got backslapping hugs from the male senators and a kiss from one of the women. He shook the hand of every senator, leaning in close to say a few words to some. "There's too many people to meet," Walker joked.

Boosted by a national wave, the Republican Party had taken control of all of state government in a complete flip, something not seen in Wisconsin since 1938. Republicans didn't just win back the governorship and both houses of the Legislature; they seized sizable majorities and stunned the Democrats by defeating both the Assembly speaker and Senate majority leader—the top lawmakers in each house. In the Senate especially, the win had been impressive, overcoming Democrats' hopes even late into the campaign that they could hold onto that house. The GOP's gains in Wisconsin that November outstripped those in almost any other state, putting Walker and other Badger

3

State Republicans in the vanguard of a national conservative movement gaining ground in other states like Ohio and New Jersey. Wisconsin was more than just a bright spot for the national GOP; it was a beacon and would be so for the next two years. Wisconsin became the leader among statehouses, in Congress, and in the national Republican Party, as the country took a more conservative approach to meeting its financial challenges.

The Republican senators and Walker were meeting in one of the most striking statehouses in the country. Just a few feet shorter than the nation's Capitol and with the largest dome in the United States, the Wisconsin Capitol is a stately 284 feet 9 inches of white granite rising from the isthmus separating Madison's two largest lakes. The building is laid out in the form of a giant X whose two sets of paired wings measure 483 feet 9 inches long apiece. Ornamented with carved oak, intricate mosaics, stained-glass skylights, and dozens of varieties of stone, it provided a grand setting for the intense events that would soon sweep through it. Begun in 1906 to replace an earlier building destroyed by fire, the Capitol had been built by Progressive-era politicians as a kind of temple of democracy, and it had been reinvested with that grandeur by a $159 million, fourteen-year restoration completed in 2002. This is a building to make those who enter it—whether a governor-elect or an anonymous citizen—reflect on the high purpose that lies or ought to lie at the heart of politics.

Just before Walker entered the Senate Republican caucus room, the senators finished electing their leaders. As majority leader, they had chosen Scott Fitzgerald, a short, stocky retired lieutenant colonel in the U.S. Army Reserve whose silver hair made him appear older than his forty-six years. Fitzgerald had served as minority leader for the Republicans for the past four years and had overseen their return to power in his house. Now, by a unanimous ballot, his colleagues picked Fitzgerald to guide them through what would turn out to be the most divisive and bizarre year and a half in state politics since the turbulent 1960s—a period that stands out not just in the history of Wisconsin but in that of the United States. Fitzgerald was by no means a novice for this task; he had a sense of the way political power could be preserved for decades or lost overnight. He was part of an influential political family in Dodge County, where his father was elected sheriff as a Republican before going on to serve as a U.S. marshal. Fitzgerald had represented the area for sixteen years as its senator, and his younger brother Jeff was taking over as speaker of the Assembly. The brothers laid claim to the two most powerful positions in state government after the one held by Walker himself; they were the ones who would now have the biggest say in determining which bills would pass their houses and go to Walker for his signature. Yet Scott Fitzgerald had known defeat in politics. In September 2004 he had been chosen for this same job as Senate majority leader. Less than two months later, a moderate GOP senator deposed him, leaving Fitzgerald with the lesson—delivered often in state Capitols but rarely so abruptly—that nothing and no one in politics is permanent. The senator who had carried out that coup, Dale Schultz, sat a few seats away now. A massive man with sandy hair, Schultz had the easy demeanor of someone who was careful to keep his size from intimidating others. His soft-spoken manner didn't keep him from bucking his party, though. Schultz had managed to represent a rural district west of Madison for decades because he kept to the political center. But doing so in the coming months would be a challenge unlike any a sitting senator had seen.

The senators made one other key choice before Walker entered the room—installing as Senate president Mike Ellis of Neenah, a veteran lawmaker who was, in spite of his customary boots, even shorter than Fitzgerald. The sixty-nine-year-old Ellis was a politician quite literally from a different era, a former school teacher who was one of the Capitol's legendary fixtures. When Ellis was first elected to the Legislature in 1970, Scott Walker was just three years old. An irascible, irreverent figure with a toupee so obvious even he poked fun at it, Ellis had a deep knowledge about the institution of the Senate and the workings of the state budget. He was the son of a union paper mill worker, and although Ellis had long been a fiscal hawk, he was also seen as a relative moderate in what was suddenly a very conservative majority. Ellis, for instance, had taken such past stands as seeking a system of public financing for political campaigns. Chomping nicotine gum and swearing at friends and enemies alike, he was one of the old boys held over from the days when the Senate was their exclusive club, when Republicans and Democrats gathered after hours at the Avenue Bar.

In the midst of electing other, largely ceremonial, leaders following the vote for Ellis, the signal came that Walker had arrived for a bit of pomp—the meeting between the incoming governor and his new Senate majority. Fitzgerald announced as Walker entered to shouts and clapping, "I would like everyone to please welcome the governor-elect of the state of Wisconsin."

After touring the room, Walker took a seat at a table before the GOP senators as if he were there to give committee testimony. In seven and a half minutes, he laid out his plan for the senators and the state to put Wisconsin's ailing economy and its citizens back to work by cutting taxes and bureaucracy.

Like other Rust Belt states, Wisconsin had been socked by the recession. Companies like General Motors had closed factories while iconic firms like Harley-Davidson had forced concessions from their union workers. Since 2007 the state had lost 140,000 more jobs than it had created. Wisconsin was somewhat better off than the rest of the country—the state's unemployment rate was high at 7.6 percent but still well below the national rate of 9.8 percent. Yet the situation in Wisconsin seemed bleak because of the sense that manufacturing, the state's swamped flagship, had been tossing jobs overboard. Wisconsin still had a greater share of workers employed in the manufacturing sector than any other state except Indiana, but that sector had seen more than a quarter of its jobs—150,000 in total—disappear over the last decade, with a huge chunk of them lost in 2009 alone. Conservatives made much of the fact that by late 2009, government workers in the state outnumbered workers employed in manufacturing for the first time in more than fifty years. As the recession broke in 2008 and good employers such as manufacturers shut their doors, many thousands of formerly well-paid workers found themselves in a bleak labor market, often with nothing more than their high school diplomas. The same uncertainty that prevailed in private households hung over the state budget itself, which had a projected shortfall of more than $3 billion over the next two and a half years, including a smaller, short-term potential deficit that would have to be dealt with in the coming months. The state's spending on health care and unemployment compensation for laid-off workers and their families was ballooning at a time when the state's tax revenues had collapsed. Walker and the Republican senators had been elected to start fixing all of that at once.

When the tidal wave at the polls receded, they found that they held nineteen of the thirty-three seats in the Senate—a comfortable majority—and had a full sixty seats in the ninety-nine-member Assembly—a margin giving them complete mastery. By comparison, the Democrats controlling the Legislature the previous session had eighteen seats in the Senate and fifty-two in the Assembly. This boon at the ballot box was to some expert eyes a curse for governing. The Republicans' margins were so great and their new lawmakers so conservative that it was more than simply a Legislature that would allow Walker to pass his policies. Especially in the Assembly, the caucus of GOP lawmakers was liable to balk at bills that were out of line with any conservative principle. Yet the state and voters who had elected these officials were not as conservative as their new leaders, just as Wisconsin was not as Democratic as its bright-blue 2008 election results might have suggested. Wisconsin was and is a battleground state in American politics, one that closely follows the national mood. It is at best for Republicans a moderate state, a so-called purple state, which could range from red to blue in any given election. More often than not, however, Wisconsin had leaned slightly Democratic in recent contests. Republicans had lost every presidential race in Wisconsin since 1984, though George W. Bush had lost by only the smallest of margins in 2000 and 2004.

That fundamental disconnect that faced Walker and the senators—governing alone as conservatives over a centrist state with deep challenges—might have daunted many. But Walker told his audience that he was glad Republicans had the full responsibility and power to deal with the problems arrayed against the state. Walker had campaigned with fervor for slicing spending, cutting taxes, and shrinking the role of government. Those who closely watched him govern as the Milwaukee County executive and then run for the state's highest office had no doubt that in this new role he would seek to follow through on every one of those promises. Walker had one piece of advice for the senators, and one implicit rebuke for anyone who had ever imagined that he might forget his pledge and somehow slip into the comfortable channel of business-as-usual in Madison. "You'll appreciate this, Senator Ellis," Walker said to the incoming Senate president. "It's put up or shut up time. Somebody told me recently, kind of cynically, they said, 'Wouldn't it have been nicer if . . . at least one of the two chambers wasn't in your same party?' I said, 'No, this is our time. This is our moment. We face incredible challenges but great challenges bring great opportunities and for us there's a time, I think it's probably the first in a generation, for us to put this state government in the direction it probably needed to be headed for years.'"

Walker then laid out his two priorities for the new Legislature: fixing the state budget, and calling a special legislative session on bills that would address unemployment and meet his ambitious campaign goal of creating 250,000 jobs over the next four years. At no point in his pep talk to the senators did he mention the words that would consume the lives of everyone in the statehouse for most of the coming year: "union," "collective bargaining," and "labor contract." There was, at that moment, no warning that a still unmentioned piece of Walker's special session legislation would make a blaze of the state's political passions. Over the next three months, the governor-elect and other conservatives racked up a whole series of what were then hailed as victories. The day Walker met with the senators, Jim Doyle, the outgoing Democratic governor, suspended work on a proposed passenger rail line between

Milwaukee and Madison. Even though this $810 million project would have been federally funded, Walker considered it a boondoggle. In one of the signs of the rightward tilt that the state and the country were facing, Walker joined Republican governors in Ohio, New Jersey, and Florida in turning down major infrastructure projects in their states, which would have created jobs in the short term at an immediate cost mostly to federal taxpayers. Next, in a dramatic showdown on the Wisconsin Senate floor, Walker and his allies succeeded in blocking new state union contracts, which for half a year would have tied the hands of his administration and prevented significant cuts to employees' pay and benefits. Before even taking office, Walker was making a major mark on the state. After he was inaugurated, he wasted no time in passing a series of bills that he said would spark economic growth.

As the political spotlight nationwide turned to conservatives, Wisconsin's other rising GOP leaders were grabbing an outsized share of it. Reince Priebus, the state party chairman who six years earlier had unsuccessfully sought a seat in the state Senate, was chosen as the head of the Republican National Committee after promising to "work like a dog" to raise money and right the dismal finances left behind by his predecessor and former ally, Michael Steele. Congressman Paul Ryan, a telegenic fiscal hawk from the blue-collar city of Janesville, was already the clear heir to the chairmanship of the influential House Budget Committee—a role that would soon make him a leading figure in the House of Representatives. In 2011 *Time* magazine named Ryan as a runner-up for the Person of the Year, and in August 2012 Ryan won an even bigger prize—selection by GOP presidential nominee Mitt Romney as his running mate. In the weeks after the November 2010 election and throughout the following two years, the state seemed almost the center of American politics. Adding to the sense of high times, the University of Wisconsin Badgers would go on to the Rose Bowl, and the Green Bay Packers would win the Super Bowl. The optimism lingered among some of the Republicans in the meeting with Walker, even the ones in potentially difficult seats for re-election.

Not everyone, however, thrilled to the sight of conservatives' ascent in Wisconsin. Jenni Dye, a twenty-nine-year-old lawyer who lived in the Madison suburb of Fitchburg and commuted to a law firm in Janesville, watched in horror the victory of Republican Ron Johnson, an accountant and manufacturer who spent $9 million of his own money to unseat U.S. Senator Russ Feingold, a favorite of liberals around the country. The feisty Democrat and Janesville native was a hometown hero to Dye, who had also grown up in the city. Dye wasn't new to politics. A graduate of the University of Wisconsin Law School with an undergraduate degree in political science, she had interned as an undergraduate for the Democratic state senator then representing Janesville and eventually snagged a paid internship in the lawmaker's office. But since then, she hadn't been as active in politics, limiting her involvement to following the news and doing some occasional volunteering for Democrats like Walker's opponent, Tom Barrett.

The election losses jolted her. Shortly after the November 2010 election, she organized meetings to talk politics with fellow Democrats who were disheartened by the big GOP victory and were looking for ways to respond. Dye didn't seem to be much of a power broker, but she had something that would in the coming year make elected leaders and tyrants around the world take notice: a Twitter account. Social media were as much a part of her routine as eating and sleeping, and over the next year they became even more important at times than rest and nourishment. When *Time* named "The Protester" as its 2011 Person of the Year over Ryan, the magazine didn't name Dye but had people like her in mind. Twitter gave her something in common with Walker, who used two BlackBerry cell phones to tweet official and campaign messages. Social media would play a role on both sides in the Madison demonstrations that Dye would soon participate in and that would gain attention around the world.

The protests in Wisconsin would join the Arab Spring uprisings as precursors of the Occupy Wall Street movement that would gather force in 2011 throughout the United States; Dye and some of the other most committed demonstrators in Madison even traveled to participate in the Occupy events on the East Coast. Among more epic demonstrations around the world against autocracy and economic austerity measures, *Time* made note of the crowds in Madison. Like thousands of others in her home state, Dye wanted to make an impact, and within months of Walker's election, an opportunity arose.

On February 10, 2011, the date of another meeting between the Walker administration and the caucus of Republican senators, the governor's aides privately detailed for those lawmakers Walker's plan for a so-called budget-repair bill. Such bills, all too common in Wisconsin, were introduced to fix the state's budget when a dip in expected tax collections or a rise in spending put those finances out of balance for a few months. Since such bills could cut spending or raise taxes, they were usually the subject of controversy.

Nonetheless, they typically didn't bring about the intense battles reserved for the most crucial legislation, such as a full two-year budget.

The Republican senators all attended the private meeting over the budget-repair bill, knowing that things could be different this time. Rumors had ricocheted through the Capitol's stone hallways for weeks, and for once the actual news about the bill was more explosive than the gossip. The plan, later known as 2011 Act 10, was a combustible mix of cuts to public workers' benefits and their union bargaining power. The proposal would affect all state and local workers except local police officers, firefighters, and State Patrol troopers. Under it, workers would see more of their take-home pay siphoned off to cover the cost of their health insurance and pension benefits. The average state worker in Wisconsin, who made roughly $50,000 a year, would see his or her take-home pay drop by $4,228, or 8.5 percent, according to the Legislature's budget office. That drop would be cushioned somewhat for workers by not renewing unpaid furloughs, put in place by Doyle, that had also eaten away at workers' income. But the benefit cuts were the lesser of the two main thrusts of the bill.

Most state and local public workers in Wisconsin—likely more than 200,000 people—would lose the ability to negotiate as a group with their employers over nearly everything that they had bargained over for decades. They would no longer be able to negotiate for their health care, their pensions, or the rules or safety of their workplaces. Employees in unionized offices who chose not to belong to the union would no longer have to pay union dues or "fair share" payments meant to ensure that they didn't benefit from the bargaining by unions without covering that cost. Now they could simply skip those payments and keep that part of their salary, cutting off funding for a key group of Democratic supporters. Public employee unions in the state would also face a host of new restrictions that would make it a struggle for them to collect dues and remain officially recognized by the state. Those unions that did manage to retain their official status could bargain only over salaries. Even in those cases, the unions effectively would have any salary increases limited to at most the rate of inflation. In addition, in the event of an impasse in bargaining with unions over salaries, employers were free to impose their last best offer. If workers did see any cost-of-living raise, it might be effectively canceled by higher health and pension contributions, which their employer could increase at will. No real bargaining power would remain for public-sector unions. The proposed limits on them would be the tightest since they were first authorized in Wisconsin decades earlier.

Senate leaders like Fitzgerald and Ellis had already seen the plan, and others had heard about parts of it, but for those senators who hadn't, the details were a shock. The dynamite packed in the proposal, and the political danger to those around it, was clear to some of the senators immediately. The law-makers knew that the battle ahead would draw the eyes of the state. What they didn't realize was that it would also attract the focus of the nation, even the world. Walker was proposing a major change of course in a state that had long been a national leader on labor issues. As a bastion of the turn-of-the-century Progressive movement, the state had been home to liberal leaders like the famous "Fighting Bob" La Follette, who became a symbol of that era of reform. Wisconsin had been the first to provide injured worker compen-sation and unemployment insurance, and the state's example and its leading academics helped inspire and shape the Social Security program and the New Deal. In later decades, Wisconsin was the first state to allow widespread bargaining by public workers. It was also the birthplace of the American Fed-eration of State, County, and Municipal Employees (AFSCME), the public employee union that had grown into a powerful national force in politics. For years, private-sector unions had waned in the United States. Walker's legis-lation was a strong sign that public-sector unions might soon see the same decline. If passed, Walker's bill would send an unmistakable signal to other states that public employees and their unions were now fair game for legis-lation to weaken them.

Wisconsin didn't just lead on liberal causes, however. The Badger State was in the nation's political center, and it had large numbers of rural, working-class whites, who were prone to swing between political parties. The state's culture had produced politicians on both sides who bucked their parties. For Democrats, that included La Follette, known for his battles with party bosses; U.S. Senator William Proxmire and his famous "Golden Fleece" awards skewering government waste; and Russ Feingold, the only member of the U.S. Senate to vote against the Patriot Act in the wake of the terrorist attacks on September 11, 2001. On the Republican side, the populist strain ran from Senator Joe McCarthy's bile and Red-baiting to the innovations of Governor Tommy Thompson, who built prisons and expanded health care for the poor even as he worked to end traditional welfare programs and in 1989 approved the nation's first school voucher program for low-income students.

With sizable blocs of both strong liberals and conservatives in Wisconsin, half of the state's partisans were always unhappy and out of power. Walker had gotten his start as a lawmaker representing Milwaukee's western suburbs, which are affluent and strongly Republican in their voting patterns and in their candidates. Voters in those districts reward politicians for taking conservative stands and showing distrust of government. Its elected officials include U.S. Representative Jim Sensenbrenner, the sponsor of the Patriot Act and one of the lead managers of the impeachment of President Bill Clinton. But as Walker pursued his policies, he would do it in Madison—a political environment the exact opposite of those GOP-dominated Milwaukee suburbs.

The state's liberal capital city is sometimes called the "Berkeley of the Midwest," and it lives up to its billing. The Vietnam War years were marked by such events on the UW–Madison campus as the Dow Chemical confrontation, in which police beat and tear-gassed protesters of the company, and the bombing by antiwar radicals of the Army Mathematics Research Center in Sterling Hall, an attack that ended up killing an innocent postdoctoral researcher. Elements of the old-school liberal activism remain, such as the fact that UW–Madison has produced more Peace Corps volunteers than any other college in the nation except, of course, the University of California in Berkeley. Former Wisconsin Governor Lee Sherman Dreyfus, a Republican, famously declared that "Madison is thirty square miles surrounded by reality." The city's residents wear this insult as a badge of honor.

A city of schoolteachers, bureaucrats, and professors, Madison has remained relatively prosperous in recent years, in part because of the stability that traditionally comes with government jobs and the growth from high-tech businesses spun off from university research. The city has long shown up in lists around the country as an ideal place to live and work, helping to make its residents more confident—their detractors would say more arrogant— about their liberal views than their counterparts in most of the Midwest. City residents not only favor Democrats but have also flirted with more liberal candidates, for a time boosting the independent party Progressive Dane as a strong alternative in local races. Tammy Baldwin, the Democrat who represented the region in the House of Representatives, was among the most liberal members of that body as ranked by academics studying its voting patterns.

The coming months soon became an epic struggle between those two sides of the state—conservative and liberal—for the soul of its body politic. Before the eyes of the public, the fight changed the course of Wisconsin's government, if not its economy, and played a role in the 2012 presidential campaign, a fact made clear by Ryan's place on the unsuccessful ticket with Mitt Romney. Behind the scenes, in details not revealed until now, the fight brought high-stakes disagreements between Walker aides and police on handling the crowds, a confidential meeting between President Obama's top campaign aides and recall organizers, and a secret Illinois rendezvous between Senate Democrats and the incoming head of the nation's largest union. The upcoming fight was unlike anything that the senators Walker addressed had ever seen, bitterly dividing politicians in Madison, the electorate, and even families around the state. In the weeks ahead, one unprecedented spectacle followed another in a stream that flowed through days and nights: outrageous I a.m. parliamentary maneuvers, a camel slipping on icy Madison streets, and demonstrations so massive they filled the Capitol square, clogged the marble halls of the statehouse, and made its rotunda ring. Walker's law was held up when Democrats fled the state, passed three weeks later amid tumult, blocked within days by a judge, and then restored by a state Supreme Court so bitterly divided that two of its members had a physical altercation over the case. When all that was over, a federal judge and a state judge separately struck down major parts of the law, and the appeals process began all over again.

The Senate was at the heart of that fight, seeing its majority party flip not once but twice over the next two years. Act 10 cost three lawmakers their place in the Legislature through recalls and triggered only the third recall election against a governor in the nation's history and the first in which the incumbent won. If that weren't enough, a secret criminal investigation into the governor's former aides from Milwaukee County quietly threatened Walker's administration the entire time. Stories about the state at critical times led the *New York Times* front pages and beat out its coverage of the budding democracy movement in the Middle East. The stories broke all records for readership on the *Milwaukee Journal Sentinel*'s website, registering millions of clicks to the site in a single day and surpassing in interest the still fresh coverage of the Packers win in the Super Bowl. Walker had identified himself more than anyone else with attempts to cut the compensation and curtail the influence of public employees. When Walker compared his confrontation with the state's unions to that of President Ronald Reagan against the air traffic controllers union in 1981, some hostile union leaders and seasoned labor historians agreed with the young governor about the significance of his legislation.

The budget battle and the protests brought out much that was worthy of praise. The citizens of Wisconsin and indeed the country as a whole, sometimes derided as apathetic and out of touch, showed that they were eager to engage on both sides, to defend the rights of workers, and to safeguard the state's financial future. They marched, they sent hundreds of thousands of e-mails and tweets, and they overwhelmingly held themselves to a peaceful,

democratic purpose, which asserted itself even in the face of the many exceptions to that general rule. Likewise, the police and authorities also managed to
handle the protests without serious injury or loss of life on either side. When
it came time to vote, citizens set turnout records. But the leaders of the state
from both parties found that they weren't entirely prepared for the national
stage, intense pressure, and, above all, the dumbfounding fact that the institutions of the state—from the Legislature to the Wisconsin Supreme Court—
at times seized up and ceased to work as they had for years. In that sense, it
was clear how thin a line could separate a vibrant, respected democracy from
illegitimacy and chaos. One insight also became clear in Wisconsin even as it
revealed itself at the national level during the debt ceiling crisis later that year:
at a time when the state and nation faced their greatest financial challenges
in decades, Republicans and Democrats were less likely than at any time in
generations to work with members of the other party. At no point during the
entire crisis did those who favored a bipartisan compromise come close to
getting the backing they needed to move forward with a plan. Compromise
had become, as one dissenting GOP lawmaker later put it, a "dirty word."

When the February meeting of Republican senators on Walker's plan
adjourned, the lawmakers had to run a small gauntlet to return to the Senate
floor. The first details of the plan had leaked to a few reporters just ahead of
the end of the meeting, and they were waiting when the senators exited, with
some of the legislators looking very different than they had at their post-
election meeting in November. Some of the senators in safely conservative
districts favored the plan or wanted it to go even farther. But the GOP senators who had swing seats, who had prisons and universities in their districts
and union workers among their supporters, walked briskly by without taking many questions. "Ashen" was how one Republican later described those
deeply worried faces.

Senator Luther Olsen of Ripon, one of the few Republicans willing to give
their initial impressions of the bill, said he supported making workers pay
more for their benefits but had reservations about taking away their powers
to engage in union negotiations. Olsen took no position for or against the bill
but made his hesitation clear. The legislation, he said, was "pretty radical."
Senator Randy Hopper of Fond du Lac had a more typical reaction to the
reporters: "I can't talk about it," he said as he quickstepped past. Within
months, Hopper and Olsen would be in a fight for their political lives, a struggle in which only one of them would prevail and which would presage the
recall campaign later to face Walker. The battle had begun.

2

A Preacher's Son

Scott Walker's rise to governor was set up by a fall. It started with the young star of his party delivering a message of disappointment to boosters at a suburban Milwaukee hotel in March 2006. Walker dropped out of the GOP primary for governor, but by deferring his ambition that day he created a far better opportunity for himself later. His gracefully executed departure helped carry him to victory in the gubernatorial election four years later. At the time, however, in early 2006, the only thing that seemed certain was that Walker was running for a dream he couldn't quite catch. The elected executive of Wisconsin's most populous county, Walker was just thirty-eight at the time and was already a legitimate contender to be the GOP nominee for governor. He had announced his candidacy in January 2005 and had already been running on his anti-tax message for more than a year, gaining enough support to snag $1.5 million in donations and large numbers of volunteers. Walker was up against Congressman Mark Green of Green Bay, a former colleague from the Wisconsin Assembly who was seven years older and the favorite of their party's establishment. With his seven years in Congress, Green had gained more than experience. He had a sizable federal campaign fund that he had transferred into his state account, giving him $2.1 million in campaign funds at the end of 2005—nearly four times more money than Walker. At that moment, the GOP primary for governor in Wisconsin was a prize to covet. Democratic Governor Jim Doyle was looking vulnerable, with less than stellar poll numbers and a federal prosecutor looking into the awarding of a state travel contract—a case that Republicans claimed would lead to damaging revelations about his administration. It seemed that the right opponent could beat him.

Walker had hoped to be that candidate, but with the party's primary six months away, he could see he wasn't making enough progress. One big problem was money. A tireless worker, Doyle was effectively raising money. He had $4.2 million in cash left at the end of the year—twice as much money as Green, his nearest challenger. By early 2006 Walker had a difficult choice. He could continue against Green and, if he was willing to attack his opponent, possibly win. But even if he won the primary, Walker might be setting up a victory for Doyle by exhausting his party's resources and leaving its nominee with little defense against a well-funded incumbent. Walker didn't bow out entirely without a scuffle. He criticized Green in radio ads aired statewide in early March. The attacks were short lived, though, with Walker giving up on them after less than a month. In a surprise Friday evening announcement, Walker told supporters at a GOP gathering at the Country Springs Hotel in Waukesha that he was pulling out of the race to make sure that Republicans didn't squander their opportunity to defeat Doyle. "A campaign that does not focus on Doyle before the primary will almost certainly ensure his re-election," he said. "To me, that outcome is unacceptable. With this in mind, I regret to inform you that I am withdrawing from the race for governor." Party activists from southeastern Wisconsin gave Walker three standing ovations as he announced his decision, hugged Green and friends, and then waved goodbye. Walker made no public mention that night of future political plans, but there was a sense among insiders, even on that evening of defeat, that Walker's time would come.

Walker's decision turned out to be the best move he could have made. Doyle, the seemingly weak governor, had more muscle and more allies than Republicans had expected. As Green emerged as the default Republican nominee, union-backed liberal groups like the Greater Wisconsin Committee quickly pounded him in television ads as too extreme a conservative for the state. The investigation of the travel contract in Doyle's administration had little effect on the electorate; it led to one conviction that was later overturned on appeal when a federal judge said the evidence was "beyond thin." As for Doyle and his lagging poll numbers, he had come from an influential political family and had won three races for state attorney general as well as his first campaign for governor. Green never gained momentum against him. Even the money from his congressional campaign account, one of Green's seemingly big advantages, evaporated when Doyle allies on the Elections Board prevented him from using it. Most important, over the course of 2006 the national mood had shifted sharply against the Iraq War, President

George W. Bush, and Republicans in general. Doyle won 53 percent of the vote, served out his term, and left office without ever having lost an election.

When Walker, a minister's son, dropped out of the 2006 race, he pointed to a divine design. "I believe that it was God's will for me to run," he said. "After a great deal of prayer during the last week, it is clear that it is God's will for me to step out of the race." It took less than a year for Providence to return to fomenting a Walker candidacy for governor. Walker began work on his 2010 campaign shortly after Green lost, determined not to start from behind again. Walker visited every corner of the state to meet with hardcore Republicans and get to know local officials. By the time he was elected in November 2010, he had been campaigning for governor for nearly six years with only one short break. During all that time, Walker held an elected position managing a large and troubled county.

Those two qualities, industry and religion, were with Walker and his family from the start. Walker's father, Llewellyn Walker, was a Baptist minister whose work took him from Colorado to Iowa to Wisconsin. A fiscal conservative, the elder Walker seasoned their dinner conversations with talk of politics and served on the municipal council in Plainfield, Iowa, during the family's time there. His father's life in the public eye meant that Walker was already accustomed to living in what he later described as a "fishbowl" long before he entered politics. "Friends of mine, when they would swear in front of me, would apologize," Walker told the *Milwaukee Journal Sentinel* in the fall of 2010.

At age seven, Walker founded a "Jesus USA" club to do good deeds, and at eight he went door to door with a mayonnaise jar, collecting money to buy a flag for the local village hall. A year later, the family moved to the Wisconsin community of Delavan, thirty-five miles southwest of Milwaukee. Walker helped out in his dad's churches, and during the summer as a teenager he sometimes took to the pulpit to fill in for vacationing Baptist ministers, gaining skills as a public speaker. Outside of church, Walker achieved the rank of Eagle Scout in the Boy Scouts. He was learning to be at ease around other people, even those with whom he sharply disagreed.

Along the way, Walker followed politics and adopted the Republican Party from his parents. As a high school student in 1985, Walker attended the political leadership camp Badger Boys State and was selected to go on to Boys Nation in Washington. He went to Marquette University, attending the private Jesuit institution in Milwaukee from 1986 to 1990, long enough to enter his senior year. A lackluster student, Walker has never released his academic transcripts from Marquette, saying only that he had a 2.59 grade point average. At Marquette, though, Walker got a taste of campaigning—and a whiff of political scandal—when he ran for student president. Walker ended up losing that race, in which his campaign supporters were accused of minor infractions such as disposing of copies of a newspaper endorsing his opponent. In a later interview he said the defeat was "probably the best thing for me." "I had gotten a little bit too caught up in the office and not in the reason why you run," he said. "So it was a great, humbling moment for me."

Walker ultimately left Marquette without graduating and in 1990 ran unsuccessfully for the Wisconsin Assembly. He later said he left school to take a good job with the American Red Cross. During his 2010 campaign, Walker was dogged by rumors that there had been some less-than-savory reason for his departure from Marquette, but those spreading the rumors never produced compelling evidence. When voters chose Walker as governor, he was the first Wisconsinite in sixty-four years to be elected to the office without a college degree. Nationally, he joined just three governors already in office without degrees.

During his 1990 run for the Assembly against incumbent Milwaukee Democrat Gwen Moore, Walker said he wore out three pairs of shoes while campaigning fruitlessly against the future congresswoman. But three years later, after moving to Wauwatosa, Walker took advantage of the first of several lucky openings in his political career, winning a special election for an Assembly seat in a deeply conservative district. In that same year, he married Tonette Schleker, a widow twelve years his senior. They met at a karaoke night and on the first date Walker told Tonette's roommate that he had found his future wife. "He told me in the beginning that he was getting ready to run for the state Assembly," Tonette Walker told the *Journal Sentinel* years later. "Did I have reservations? My parents were Democrats and they were union workers." Tonette, however, was taken by the younger man's maturity and stability. "He was a good guy, then and now," she said.

Walker started his political career and his family. He served for nearly a decade in the Assembly representing one of that body's most Republican districts. In the Assembly, Walker had a solid conservative record; he supported GOP budget proposals, tougher sentences for criminals, and taxpayer support for private schools in Milwaukee. He courted the media, taking the time to return phone calls, driving to television studios, and putting his name and views before the public. Walker became a darling of local talk radio and Sunday television shows. Charlie Sykes, a conservative radio host and

Sunday host for Milwaukee's WTMJ-TV, said in 2002 he regularly called
Walker because he was articulate, prepared, and—perhaps most important—
"week in and week out, he was available."

Then in 2002 Walker got another big break, one that not every Republican
politician could have seen. Milwaukee County Executive F. Thomas Ament
and the county board had rewritten pension rules to make them far more
generous for county workers. The move got little attention initially, but recall
fever swept the county once the media and voters realized that a string of
employees was retiring with one-time payments worth hundreds of thousands of dollars while still collecting at times $60,000 a year in annuities.
Ament and supervisors were targets of recalls as a grassroots group sprang
up and volunteers spread across neighborhoods with clipboards in hand to
gather signatures. Ament resigned before a recall election was ordered, triggering a special election that gave candidates just weeks to assemble campaigns. The beneficiary of a recall process that he would later criticize, Walker
ended up among those seeking to lead one of the most Democratic counties
in Wisconsin.

The short special election gave an advantage to candidates like Walker who
had already built up some campaign cash and public exposure. In addition,
county executives in Wisconsin are elected on a nonpartisan ballot. That
meant that voters who considered themselves Democrats didn't need to dwell
on the fact that Walker wasn't one of them. On the other hand, the lawmaker
was just thirty-four years old and was seeking to lead a county with nearly
a million residents, 7,100 employees, and an annual budget of $1 billion.
But here, Walker turned his flaws into assets, billing himself as an outsider
and his opponent as part of the status quo. With simple proposals like cutting
his own salary by $60,000 and freezing property taxes for one year, Walker
carried the county with 55 percent of the vote.

The property tax freeze became the central goal of Walker's eight-year
tenure as county executive. Each year he introduced budgets that held to the
previous year's property tax levy. The county board, still controlled by liberals,
routinely added in more spending increases that the supervisors said were
needed to provide vital services. Walker vetoed the increases but saw some
of them reinstated when the board voted to override his vetoes. Walker in
turn would then build those into his next year's budget. The net result in
2010 was a property tax levy that was nearly $44 million greater than it was
in 2003, for an average annual increase of 2.6 percent. Still, the number of
county employees during Walker's tenure fell by more than 1,600, or nearly

23 percent. Walker did it through attrition—not replacing workers who quit or retired—as well as layoffs and transferring some work to private-sector firms. To Walker and his supporters, this was proof that he had managed to get spending in line in a county controlled by Democrats, a once unthinkable task for conservatives and one that proved popular at the ballot box. His critics questioned whether the county board was effectively allowing Walker to remain "pure" in his opposition to tax and spending hikes without facing the full consequences of the cuts to programs that his hard-line approach would have entailed. There was, however, little question that Walker believed in the cuts that he advocated. In 2009 he even called for dismantling the county government he led, saying that the county's functions could be parceled out to the state, cities, and municipalities.

Walker's agenda quickly brought him and the county's public employee unions into conflict. In negotiations, he struggled to get concessions and agreements that would produce the kinds of savings for taxpayers that he had built into his budgets. Union officials countered that Walker was budgeting in bad faith, plugging numbers into his budget plans that he knew unions would successfully oppose at the bargaining table. Over time the disputes between the county executive and his union workforce piled up, from unpaid furloughs imposed to meet budgets to privatization of county services. Walker also struggled to resolve all of the problems in the pension fund that first propelled him into office. Under his tenure, the county negotiated away the controversial lump-sum retirement benefits for new employees, but attorneys advised him that existing employees' benefits were already their property and couldn't be touched. Because of the generous benefits and poor investment returns amid the recent declines in the stock market, taxpayers' required contribution to Milwaukee County's pension fund skyrocketed. It rose from $900,000 in 2000 to nearly $41 million in 2008, an increase of more than 4,400 percent, according to the Public Policy Forum of Milwaukee. Health insurance costs also rose, boosted by factors such as difficult-to-undo guarantees to pay the health insurance premiums for certain retirees, their spouses, and their dependents. The share of the county tax levy going to health care and pension benefits rose from one-third in 2000 to more than two-thirds in 2008. In other ways the county was being quite austere with its workforce, actually reducing its payroll modestly during that period. But the growth in benefits was unsustainable.

Elsewhere in Wisconsin, public employees were almost always covered by the much better funded state pension system. At the time Walker became governor, the state system had enough assets to cover all the obligations that the state and local governments had made to their workers and retirees. In 2010 Wisconsin was the only state in the country that could boast of that, according to a study by the Pew Center on the States. As a share of its overall spending, the state's contributions to its pension system in 2009 were also less than the national average and compared favorably with those of its neighboring states. Some local governments in Wisconsin, such as school districts, did have significant unfunded obligations to provide health care to retirees, but unlike many other states Wisconsin's state government didn't have even those liabilities to worry about. Yet Walker dealt not with the state pension system but with that of Milwaukee County. As a result, his experience with public employee unions and their negotiated benefits had more conflict and problems than was the case in most other parts of Wisconsin.

Walker didn't have the ability as county executive to impose his own solutions to those problems with the local unions. As governor, though, he would have that power, not just in troubled Milwaukee County but in the state as a whole. This wouldn't reduce his conflicts with unions. On the contrary, it would make them far worse.

3

"Open for Business"

SCOTT WALKER TALKED FRUGALITY as he dropped a ham-and-cheese sandwich into a paper bag, explaining that he brought his lunch to work every day to help him afford Wisconsin's taxes. He was starring in one of his first ads of the campaign, and his message was clear: I pack my lunch to save money, so why can't state government do the equivalent? The ad and others like it mingled his biography with his philosophy. In another early spot, he told voters while seated on his living room couch about his decision to take a $60,000 pay cut as Milwaukee County executive to keep government spending down. "My wife was like, 'We're doing what?'" Walker said into the camera. In still another ad, he talked from behind the wheel about how he'd saved money by hanging onto his 1998 Saturn with more than 100,000 miles on it. In ads and campaign speeches, he urged voters to join a "brown-bag movement" for frugality in government, creating a website with that name and passing out paper lunch sacks at campaign stops.

Democrats dismissed the ads as lightweights and no real answer to a state facing the worst economic times since the Great Depression. They noted that while Walker gave up part of his county executive pay during his first term, he allowed it to rise later by $50,000 a year. He may have had sack lunches and an old car, but he still had a nice suburban house and the same dinners that other statewide candidates had with wealthy donors at high-end restaurants. Democrats also pointed out that the brown-bag theme was recycled from the 1998 U.S. Senate run of George Voinovich of Ohio, who had the same campaign consultant. But just as he had in his county executive race, Walker found a simple message and stuck with it.

Walker wasn't just preaching frugality for himself. He talked openly during the campaign about how he believed that state workers should pay more for their benefits, and Wisconsin Republicans hadn't always taken that approach. During the booming 1990s, GOP Governor Tommy Thompson preferred to keep unions close rather than push them away, at one stage fattening their pensions along with his own. After forcing out Walker during the 2006 governor's race, Mark Green also avoided taking on the unions, which had a bloc of ready voters and, more important, campaign cash. Green even attempted unsuccessfully to keep AFSCME neutral in the 2006 election. By contrast, Walker made the issue a hallmark of his campaign. In a conference call with reporters exactly one year before election day, Walker pledged to reverse the tax increases approved by Democrats that year—a promise that he, as governor, turned away from in part so he could pursue other tax cuts that he considered more important. He also pledged to use cuts to employee wages and benefits to help offset the lost revenue. As the campaign progressed, Walker described public workers as "haves" siphoning money from average taxpayers who were "have nots." "Public-sector employees have been the untouchables," he said during one debate.

Nonetheless, Walker never mentioned the notion of wiping away nearly all collective bargaining for public workers. He was more candid than most candidates about wanting to slim down government, but he withheld many of the specifics of how he would make his campaign rhetoric a reality. If the state's bargaining laws remained largely in place—and Walker never suggested they wouldn't—he would have to extract concessions from employees through negotiations. Many expected tough talks, with employees resisting cuts and Walker reprising his county executive tactics of threatening to outsource thousands of jobs and impose long furloughs if he couldn't get the concessions. No one—not the media, not Walker's opponents, not even the unions themselves—seemed to guess that he might seek to eliminate collective bargaining. Had Walker put forward his labor proposal during the campaign itself, his path would have been more difficult because unions and their members would have been even more active in spending money, volunteering, and voting against him. As it was, his campaign succeeded in getting him elected, but it failed to fully prepare state residents for his agenda.

Because the public never saw how far Walker was willing to go, his talk of massive savings seemed questionable. If Walker secured the concessions he sought from state workers, he could save perhaps $300 million over a two-year budget. Those would be significant dollars, but the deficit was ten times that size. The $3 billion budget shortfall projected over the two years was substantial but still better than that faced by some states. It was in another sense not as bad as it seemed because it was figured using agency budget requests for more money, and those are never fully granted. Cutting the benefits of teachers and local government workers might give the state leeway to cut its aid to schools and municipalities, but at the time of Walker's campaign, employee compensation was in the hands of local officials and their unions alone, and no one talked publicly about the fact that this system could change. At that time, the union contracts between local governments and workers seemed enough to prevent the state from ever imposing cuts to benefits. Walker himself gave only a few signs of how he would intervene as governor, never making the connection for the public. During the campaign, he talked primarily of workers' benefits, not collective bargaining, and focused on state workers, not local ones. He did often cite what he considered public employees' excessive insurance and retirement benefits as a place to cut government and bring it in line with the private sector, where workers were being squeezed by large premiums, ever-increasing deductibles, and dwindling retirement contributions. Public employees responded by pointing to a study by the liberal Economic Policy Institute showing that their pay in Wisconsin lagged behind that of comparable private-sector workers by 4.8 percent, with the largest difference affecting white-collar workers with graduate degrees. Even with their generous benefits, their total compensation could still fall behind that of their peers in the private sector, they said. Walker ignored that argument and kept his focus on benefits rather than overall compensation.

Twice Walker's campaign talked about changing unions' ability to bargain specific issues. The first time was his campaign proposal to save millions of dollars for taxpayers by having schools switch their health coverage away from the WEA Trust, an insurer affiliated with the state's largest teachers union, the Wisconsin Education Association Council (WEAC). Local union affiliates in many cases insisted that costly but comprehensive WEA Trust coverage be included in their labor contracts. While Walker didn't dwell on his plan's details, one of his advisors acknowledged that the candidate planned to change state law and eliminate that aspect of bargaining. The second time was in June 2010, when Walker promised to voluntarily pay 5 percent of his salary toward his pension, or half of the overall retirement contribution, saying that he believed all state workers should do so. The state for years had paid essentially all of its employees' pension contributions as part of their overall compensation. Walker argued that workers should shoulder half of that cost, essentially accepting a decrease in their take-home pay, and he promised to pay his own half immediately if elected. As it happened, Walker wouldn't follow through on that promise when he took office; instead he would wait until he and all other state workers were required to make payments starting in August 2011 under Act 10. On pensions, Walker gave the biggest hint that he would consider encroaching on the state's collective bargaining laws, stating that he would seek to make employees pay more for their pensions any way he could, including through union negotiations or by changing state law. During the campaign, however, he focused his comments on making those changes through negotiations, saying that unions would go along with them rather than face furloughs or layoffs. In September 2010 a Dane County sheriff's deputy e-mailed Walker's campaign policy adviser asking whether the deputy or his wife, a teacher, would be affected by Walker's proposal to require state employees to make higher pension contributions. Ryan Murray, the campaign policy adviser and later an aide in the governor's office, replied that Walker would not require teachers and municipal employees to pay higher pension contributions, just state workers. "Scott's plan will apply to active state employees only, not to all participants in the Wisconsin Retirement System such as teachers and local government employees," Murray wrote to the deputy. In October 2010 Walker met with the editorial board of the *Oshkosh Northwestern* and was asked how he would get state employee unions to pay more for their pension and health plans. "You still have to negotiate it. I did that at the county as well," Walker said. No one fully saw what Walker intended, including the unions. The longtime executive director of the Wisconsin State Employees Union, Marty Beil, viewed Walker's pension pledge through the lens of labor relations as they had been conducted for decades. "He cannot expect in the give-and-take of bargaining to wave a magic wand and get everything he wants," Beil said of Walker in a statement issued at the time.

Before Walker could have his reckoning with unions, though, he would need to win the election. To do that, he expected that he would have to beat Jim Doyle, and he had been running against the Democratic governor since shortly after Doyle was re-elected in 2006. In a move that caught some of Doyle's own top aides by surprise, the governor in August 2009 decided not to seek a third term. No Democrat had laid the groundwork for a 2010 gubernatorial campaign, assuming that Doyle, who had been raising sizable sums, would seek another term. That gave the state its first wide-open governor's race— one with no incumbent—since 1982.

A brutal attack on the Democrats' instant frontrunner for the nomination left the field in further disarray. On the night that news leaked of Doyle's plans, Milwaukee Mayor Tom Barrett left the Wisconsin State Fair in suburban Milwaukee with his two daughters, his sister, and her daughter. A woman holding her one-year-old granddaughter screamed, "Call 911! Call 911!" The woman was in the midst of a dispute with the child's father, Anthony Peters, but as Barrett came upon them he knew only that the woman was asking for help. The mayor took out his phone, but Peters charged toward him, slapped it from his hand, and stomped on it. "Now I'm going to have to shoot all of you," Peters said. Barrett told his sister to take the girls away. "No, no, no. Everybody stays here," Peters said. Barrett looked at his sister, pleading with his eyes for her to get the girls to safety, and she slipped away with them. "I was only trying to help," Barrett told Peters.

At six foot four, Barrett was a big man. But he was also fifty-five, unarmed, and up against a twenty-year-old with a weapon. The mayor could see a flash of metal under Peters's shirt but couldn't tell what it was, only that it was large enough to be a sawed-off shotgun or pipe. Peters told Barrett to lie face down on the sidewalk. Barrett, sensing that doing so would be his death sentence, instead punched Peters, who responded by smashing the mayor's head with a tire iron hidden under his clothes. Barrett wrapped his right hand over his head to protect himself. The blows crushed Barrett's hand, split his skull, and knocked out three of his teeth. Peters was caught the next day and eventually pleaded guilty to first-degree reckless injury, disorderly conduct, and bail jumping. In the months ahead, Barrett underwent three surgeries and dozens of physical therapy sessions. His right hand was useless in the weeks after the attack, but Barrett tried to make light of it by telling his brother that he would never again play the piano—an instrument he had never played in the first place. Later, he taught himself to write with his left hand, joking that he had the penmanship of a third-grader.

The attack boosted Barrett's profile around the state and country as Milwaukee's "hero mayor." Both President Barack Obama and Vice President Joe Biden called Barrett during his hospital stay, and the White House later supported his run for governor. But the mayor's recovery slowed his entry into the race and added to Walker's already lengthy head start. Barrett finally announced his bid for governor in November 2009, but by that time even Barrett's allies worried that the mayor didn't have the burning passion to be governor that Walker did, and the attack clearly hadn't made campaigning any easier.

Barrett had been first elected to the Legislature from Milwaukee's north-west side in 1984 and by 1992 had won his first of five terms in Congress. When Wisconsin lost a congressional seat because the state's population growth hadn't kept pace with the rest of the country, Barrett decided not to seek re-election and instead ran for governor. He came in second to Doyle in the 2002 Democratic primary but ahead of a third candidate, Dane County Executive Kathleen Falk. He briefly returned to practicing law before being elected mayor in 2004. The earlier contest between Barrett and Doyle had left a chilly relationship between the two men, but Walker saw them as close enough. He and his supporters began portraying Barrett as an ally of the unpopular incumbent Democrat—Doyle's approval ratings were well below his disapproval ratings in polls during that time—and said Barrett's election would be a de facto third term for Doyle.

The one positive for Democrats in late 2009 and early 2010 was that no one from their party ultimately mounted a major challenge to Barrett, allowing him to hoard his cash for November 2010 rather than burning it up in the state's September primary. Walker, in contrast, had to contend with a well-financed challenger in the GOP primary. Walker formally announced his candidacy on April 21, 2009, and within days former GOP Congressman Mark Neumann put out word that he too would run. Neumann had a profile that under normal circumstances should have appealed to conservative voters, even though he was a decade out of the political spotlight. In 1998 he'd taken on and only narrowly lost to Russ Feingold, the U.S. senator and liberal favorite. Neumann had made a fortune as a developer and homebuilder, and had the wealth to fund much of his own campaign. He was also co-chairman of three Lutheran schools in Milwaukee that participated in the state's twenty-year-old voucher program that allowed low-income children from the city to attend private schools at taxpayer expense.

The Republican establishment and Neumann mistrusted each other, though. He felt spurned by them in his first two unsuccessful runs for Congress in the early 1990s. Republican officials found it galling that Neumann wouldn't bow out of the primary to clear the way for Walker, as Walker had for Green in 2006. Still, they were confident that Walker could beat Neumann. At the May 2009 state Republican Party convention in La Crosse, Walker won 93 percent of the vote in a straw poll by the website WisPolitics, and he won the endorsement of forty-six state lawmakers—a large chunk of the Republicans in the Legislature at the time—and a majority of the state's county party chairmen. Six months later, Jim Klauser, Neumann's most prominent GOP backer and a former top aide to Governor Tommy Thompson, abandoned the former congressman to join Walker's team. Yet in spite of Walker's advantages, his supporters worried that Neumann would drain their candidate's finances by forcing him to spend heavily in a primary while Democrats socked away money for the general election.

Their fears were valid. Neumann started advertising early and spent $6.6 million during the race, most of it his own money. He ran a scattershot campaign, sometimes presenting himself as a candidate for the middle and other times appealing to the most conservative wing of the party, and Walker had to tack to the right to avoid being outflanked by Neumann. Even though Neumann found a couple of cases where he could stake out a position more conservative than Walker's, he could not gain enough traction with a base that was so completely committed to his opponent. Walker's years of relentless campaigning at conservative events and his support from talk radio made him the rare Republican who had the firm support of the GOP establishment and the Tea Party groups that were then gaining strength. At the state Republican Party convention in Milwaukee in May 2010, Walker won the party's endorsement in an overwhelming vote.

Walker locked up the endorsement even though the convention came during a difficult time for him. On May 11, 2010, a judge authorized Milwaukee County District Attorney John Chisholm's office to open a "John Doe" investigation into the finances of a county event that honored veterans. A John Doe probe is similar to a federal grand jury inquiry except that it proceeds before a judge rather than a panel of citizens. John Doe investigations are secret, and witnesses can be compelled to testify and forbidden from publicly discussing the questioning. Investigators first met with Walker's chief of staff, Tom Nardelli, in 2009, when he alerted them that he believed $11,000 in privately raised money had gone missing in 2007. Prosecutors eventually used the John Doe investigation to look into the matter because Walker's office was "unwilling or unable" to provide records, possibly because the situation was politically embarrassing, as an assistant district attorney wrote to a judge in his request for opening the Doe.

The investigation soon grew other tentacles. Within days, the John Doe judge expanded the investigation so prosecutors could look into donations to Walker from railroad executive William Gardner. On May 19, 2010, Walker's campaign announced it would return almost $44,000 in donations after learning that Gardner had used company funds to reimburse employees for donations they'd made to Walker. This amounted to donating corporate money to a candidate, which is illegal in Wisconsin. Also that month, *Milwaukee Journal Sentinel* columnist Daniel Bice ran a piece about Darlene Wink, Walker's constituent services coordinator in his county office. The column detailed how Wink had posted online political comments favoring Walker during the hours that she was being paid by taxpayers to do public work. Wink was asked by the Walker administration to resign, and she did so two hours after Bice asked for her payroll records. When the Wink story broke, Walker's deputy chief of staff, Kelly Rindfleisch, quickly dismantled a private Internet router set up in her office, which was twenty-five feet away from Walker's. During her few months on the job, she had been using the secret router and a laptop—both separate from the regular county system—to trade electronic messages with Walker's campaign staff and raise money for state Representative Brett Davis, a GOP candidate for lieutenant governor. With attention suddenly on Wink, who had also used the router, Rindfleisch stuffed the device into a credenza in her office. "I took the wireless down," she wrote in an e-mail to Tim Russell, who had served as Walker's deputy chief of staff before Rindfleisch. Russell, then working as Walker's housing director, had initially set up the router for Wink and Rindfleisch to use, prosecutors alleged.

Walker e-mailed Russell that night, telling him he had talked to Wink and felt bad about what had happened. "We cannot afford another story like this one," Walker wrote to Russell. "No one can give them any reason to do another story. That means no laptops, no websites, no time away during the work day, etc." Walker would later point to that e-mail as evidence that he did not tolerate improprieties in his office, but the e-mail also seemed to show that he was aware of the unusual computer systems. Hiding the router provided little cover from Chisholm and the John Doe investigation. On August 9, 2010, investigators raided Wink's house; on August 20 they seized Russell's work computer.

In November 2012 a prosecutor presented in court detailed records showing Walker's campaign and county office routinely collaborated in 2010 to ensure the county was being run in a way that lined up with Walker's political image. His campaign manager, Keith Gilkes, and his campaign spokeswoman, Jill Bader, held daily conference calls with Rindfleisch; Walker's county chief of staff, Tom Nardelli; and Walker's county spokeswoman, Fran McLaughlin. Rindfleisch did research on issues in the race for the Walker campaign and traded nearly 3,500 e-mails with campaign officials between January and October of 2010, with more than 2,200 sent during regular business hours, according to the Milwaukee County district attorney's office. Without saying that it was illegal, the prosecutor said that Walker's campaign staff influenced and even reviewed and directed the actions and public statements of county officials. "You guys are in the driver's seat," Rindfleisch wrote in one message to Gilkes. When a fifteen-year-old youth was killed by a concrete panel that fell from a county parking garage in June 2010, Gilkes emailed Rindfleisch to "make sure there is not a piece of paper anywhere that details any problem at all." When media attention focused on sexual assaults of patients at the county's mental health facility, Gilkes e-mailed county staff to tell the county's top attorney that "we're getting the crap kicked out of us. I would like him to stop being a lawyer and think political."

Over the next year and a half, the investigators also concluded that Russell, a longtime aide and personal friend of Walker, had a hand in more than just the alleged illegal campaigning on public time, according to criminal charges later filed against Russell that were eventually proved in court. He had a long history in Milwaukee politics and for a time had run Governor Thompson's office in the city. But an alert employer—and politician—could have found reasons to be wary of Russell. In 1993 he was fired from the Wisconsin Housing and Economic Development Authority because he improperly billed more than $1,100 in hotel stays to that quasi-public agency. In time, Russell would be accused of far worse. Luckily for Walker, at the time of the campaign few details surfaced about the confidential John Doe probe into Russell and the other aides. The ones that did, almost entirely in Bice's columns, didn't draw much attention from the public at first. Voters were more concerned about the struggling economy, and Walker seized on that worry early in the campaign with a simple pledge. He promised to create a quarter of a million jobs during his first four years in office, about the same number that were created in the first four years of Thompson's time as governor, from 1987 through 1991. The promise posed an obvious risk—it would be difficult and perhaps impossible to fulfill in an economy that no longer created new jobs as easily as it had a generation earlier. Walker embraced that risk, repeating the pledge as a kind of mantra. Barrett initially said Walker was coming up with an arbitrary figure, but by March the mayor was saying he wanted to make up within three years the 180,000 jobs that Wisconsin had lost during the recession. Neumann initially criticized the other candidates for plucking numbers out of the air, but he later announced his own plan to generate 300,000 jobs by 2020.

Walker provided few concrete details on how he would carry out his pledge, focusing instead on overarching themes such as reducing the size of government, loosening regulations, and cutting taxes for businesses. He promised to convene a special session of the Legislature to pass bills making it harder to sue businesses, giving tax breaks to small businesses, and turning the state's Department of Commerce into a partly private entity. He generally steered away from specific questions like which types of regulations or lawsuits should be pared back and how he would balance an already battered budget after reducing state revenues with tax cuts. Barrett, for his part, promised not to raise taxes in his first budget, which would cover his first two years in office. He wouldn't go beyond that, however, and he warned that the Republicans' plans to lower existing taxes would mean deeper cuts for schools and local governments given the looming shortfall in the state budget.

Another resonant issue in the campaign was passenger rail. Doyle had secured a federal economic stimulus grant for $810 million to fund building a train line from Madison to Milwaukee in order to connect with an existing line to Chicago. Doyle had said it would create construction jobs in the short term and economic development in the long term, and would be a first step toward running up to 110-mile-per-hour passenger trains between Chicago and the Twin Cities. Critics like Walker and Neumann called the line a boondoggle that didn't justify the $7 million or more a year needed to operate it, and both stated that they would reject the rail line and with it the massive federal investment. Barrett, like Doyle, praised the proposed line as a once-in-a-generation opportunity for Wisconsin. But for the moment the critics of the train and President Barack Obama's economic stimulus plan showed much more passion than the rail line's supporters.

Walker easily won the September 14 primary against Neumann by 59 percent to 39 percent. He racked up huge margins in his home base of southeastern Wisconsin, where he was well known. Neumann won much of the rest of the state but not by big enough percentages to offset his losses in suburban Milwaukee. Meanwhile, Barrett still had some hope. Walker, facing a campaign funding gap, had just seven weeks before the November general election to catch up. Barrett had $2.6 million on hand as of August 30, to Walker's $1.2 million. Walker tapped into a network of both large- and small-dollar donors and soon caught up, collecting more than twice as much as Barrett through the end of the campaign. With the primary behind him, Walker stayed focused on his theme of creating jobs and continued to take every opportunity to tie Barrett to the unpopular Doyle. In the general election, Walker benefited from the support of the unions representing state troopers and Milwaukee cops and firefighters. The mayor found support from a much larger number of other unions, including police and firefighters outside of Milwaukee, but their support was often tepid. Highlighting that point, the biggest teachers union—usually an active Democratic ally—didn't run any ads for Barrett. The union was less than thrilled with the mayor as a candidate, in part because Barrett had backed a plan by Doyle to give the mayor control over Milwaukee's troubled school system.

In the final stretch of the campaign, Barrett emphasized that he was a candidate who embraced compromise and serious ideas. He prided himself on having laid out the most specific plans of any candidate, detailing ways to cut government spending and providing a sixty-seven-page economic development proposal with ideas for tax credits and revolving loan funds. His plans were more comprehensive than Walker's calls for trimming government, though even Jim Doyle's administration questioned whether some of them were feasible. Barrett also tried to distance himself from Walker on social issues like abortion and embryonic stem cell research, which had been pioneered on the UW–Madison campus. Barrett also had a plan that would have required local governments to insure their workers through a state pool—thus diminishing their collective bargaining rights as well, though to a much lesser extent than Walker did.

The contrasts were not enough. Barrett was not just facing a challenging and talented opponent; he was up against a national Republican wave. With the country mired in recession, the popularity of the president and Democrats controlling Congress sank. Republicans hammered on the federal stimulus plan and health care reform as examples of overreach by liberals and, with the help of the Tea Party, took control of the U.S. House and gained seats in the U.S. Senate. On election night, November 2, 2010, Republicans gained eleven state legislatures from Democrats' hands, winning Alabama and North Carolina for the first time since Reconstruction. Before the election, Republicans had complete control of only nine states, but afterward they held both the Legislature and governorship in Wisconsin and nineteen other states.

In Wisconsin, Republicans also won their first U.S. Senate election since 1986. It was a blow to Jenni Dye, the young lawyer living in a Madison suburb. On election night she and her roommate went to the Marriott West hotel in the Madison suburb of Middleton, where Senator Russ Feingold was holding his election night party. Dye knew that Feingold's event might not be a celebration, but she was a longtime supporter, and if this was going to be the end for the liberal senator, Dye wanted to be there to see it. At the hotel, however, it was hard to get returns. The Internet connection there was poor, and there were only a few televisions, but it soon became clear that Feingold would not be winning another term. He took the stage to concede and said he respected the voters' decision. "Being your senator has been the greatest honor of my life," Feingold told the crowd.

After Dye cried and went home, she began to look for a way to help reverse what she saw as a bad turn for the state. She started a discussion group for other like-minded Democrats who were depressed by the outcome of the elections and were looking for a way to respond. As a young professional, Dye didn't have the time she had had as a college student to volunteer on campaigns or other political projects. And she didn't have enough money yet to make large political contributions to candidates or causes. But she knew that she had both something to contribute and the duty to find it.

In contrast, conservatives were exultant. After big losses in the 2006 and 2008 elections, Wisconsin Republicans made a dramatic turnaround. In the governor's race, Walker beat Barrett 52 percent to 47 percent, once again winning big in the suburban counties around Milwaukee. Barrett found support in Dane County and beat Walker in the candidates' shared home base of Milwaukee County. Republicans also took back both houses of the Legislature from the Democrats, flipping the complete control of state government from one party to another. They gained one seat in the U.S. Senate and two in Congress, and ousted the state Senate majority leader, the speaker of the Assembly, and the longest-serving member of the Assembly in the state's history. As the extent of the victories sank in, Walker took the stage at the Country Springs Hotel in Waukesha, the same venue where he announced that he was dropping out of the governor's race four years earlier. Now triumphant, the crowd whooped and held aloft their campaign placards and camera phones. Grinning, the governor-elect waved and high-fived the crowd. He'd turned forty-three that same day, and the crowd welcomed him by singing "Happy Birthday" as he stationed himself behind the lectern. Walker turned to his wife, then told the crowd, "I think this topped the year she got me a Harley." The body heat from the crowd made the temperature in the room soar, but Walker kept his dark suit coat on, his face shining with sweat. He said the three most important days of his life were when he met Tonette and when his two sons were born. "Though I gotta tell you, today's pretty close to those three," he added. He thanked his parents, his in-laws, his running mate Rebecca Kleefisch, and his top campaign advisers. He thanked his volunteers and average voters. "You have given us a mandate for true reform and I appreciate that," he said. "I will not let you down."

Mounted on the lectern and hanging from a banner behind him was his new campaign-like slogan for governing: "Wisconsin is open for business." Walker incorporated it into his speech, repeating it three times and urging the crowd to join him in reciting it. It was his new brand for the state. Later, he hung a plaque with that phrase on the door leading to his personal office in the Capitol and had similar ones mounted on signs along the state's borders welcoming visitors to Wisconsin. Businesses and workers could be confident that his administration would reignite the state's economy, he told the crowd.

Unions got no mention. Walker and his aides viewed the scope of the Republican victory as marching orders from the public. Acting on that belief, Walker and lawmakers rewrote the state's laws and budget in the coming months in ways that now seem likely to transform government in Wisconsin for a generation. But with respect to collective bargaining, arguably the biggest part of his agenda, Walker had no claim to a mandate because his campaign had never explicitly sought one. The campaign also left the governor-elect with another hidden problem. On the eve of the election, John Chisholm's office had quietly served subpoenas on Walker's campaign for e-mails and also sought materials from his county office. For assistance, the campaign had quickly hired Steven Biskupic, a former U.S. attorney for eastern Wisconsin. The John Doe investigation was ongoing and would have to be added to the long list of challenges facing the administration. But at least it was out of the public eye for the moment.

Walker wrapped up his twelve-minute speech. "It is time for we the people of Wisconsin to stand up and put the government firmly on the side of the people again," he said. "It is time for us to send a clear message here across this state and across this great country that Wisconsin's best days are yet to come. God bless you, thank you, and let's get the job done."

He winked, then waved to the crowd.

4

"The First Step"

NAMED FOR THE ROMAN GOD OF WINE AND EXCESS, the Bacchus restaurant had dark wood trim and shining hardwood floors, making it a fine place for the powerful and influential to celebrate. Six days after winning the governorship, Scott Walker dined at the downtown Milwaukee establishment with some of the people who had helped him get where he was and who would be among his staunchest allies going forward—the board and senior staff of the Lynde and Harry Bradley Foundation. This conservative heavyweight had a low profile among the general public, receiving much less attention than some others on the right, like the billionaire industrialists David and Charles Koch; the newspaper publisher and tycoon Richard Mellon Scaife; and the American Legislative Exchange Council, a corporate-backed group promoting conservative legislation. But the Bradley Foundation, as it was commonly known, was very much in their league. From 2001 to 2009 the foundation had paid out nearly as much money as the Koch and Scaife family foundations combined, a 2011 *Milwaukee Journal Sentinel* review of the organization found. Bradley's charitable giving from 2001 to 2010 to arts organizations and conservative groups of various stripes amounted to $350 million. It gave millions of dollars to groups like the Milwaukee Symphony Orchestra, the Milwaukee Public Museum, and Marquette University. But that was just a slice of the donations made by the foundation, which seeks to promote limited government, unfettered markets, and national defense. Its projects range from supporting private voucher schools in Milwaukee to deregulating campaign spending and promoting "right-to-work" laws that would limit the power of private-sector unions.

The group had a massive endowment honoring the namesake brothers of the foundation, high-school dropouts who helped found an industrial giant, the Allen-Bradley Company. With that money, the foundation helped sustain such well-known conservative institutions as the Heritage Foundation and the Federalist Society, the libertarian magazine *Reason*, and other major conservative publications. The foundation donated to Hollywood film companies to further conservative ideas and sponsored the Bradley Prizes to honor pundits. Bradley also provided major funding to lesser-known right-wing groups inside and outside the state, such as the Wisconsin Policy Research Institute, a local think tank; and the David Horowitz Freedom Center, creator of the Jihad Watch website. One Bradley-supported group created a website called Teachers Union Exposed. Another relatively new think tank, the John K. MacIver Institute for Public Policy, served to advance free markets and other conservative ideas in Wisconsin.

It was no mere chance that brought Walker together with the Bradley Foundation. They had in common Michael W. Grebe, a prominent seventy-one-year-old Republican lawyer who was both the president and chief executive of the foundation and the chairman of Walker's successful gubernatorial campaign. Grebe was also serving as the chairman of Walker's transition team and would go on to interview candidates for some cabinet posts in the new administration. In short, the Vietnam veteran and former top executive at the law firm Foley & Lardner was a key backer of Walker and his projects for governing. Grebe later said there was nothing conspiratorial or secretive about the Bradley Foundation or his work. In an interview with the *Journal Sentinel*, Grebe, a former high school quarterback, likened the foundation to the 1960s Green Bay Packers and their seemingly simple but effective ground game: "We're going to run off tackle, right over there, and we're telling you we're going to run there and we're going to knock you on your butt and carry the ball down the field," Grebe said. "There are no surprises."

Nevertheless, the foundation had at least a financial link to what would soon be a great surprise in Wisconsin politics. On November 24, 2010, just a few weeks after the meal at Bacchus, the MacIver Institute posted on its website an editorial by its communications director, a Republican operative named Brian Fraley. Bradley was a primary funder of the relatively small MacIver outfit, giving it $360,000 in its first three years of operation. Founded in 2009, at a time when Republicans were out of power in Wisconsin, MacIver had advocated for less government spending and, in its many reports, often focused on what it saw as problems associated with unions, such as higher health insurance costs for school employees. A scrappy outfit, the Madison-based group had slowly ramped up its operations. Fraley's article urged Walker and the Legislature's new Republican majorities to reduce public spending and get businesses hiring again by curtailing the influence of unions over the government. "This growth [in spending] is fueled by the influence of public employee unions, who gain their power through taxpayer paid union dues, which in turn are used to leverage policies that lead to the increase in the size, scope, and cost of government, which means more public employee union members, which means more union dues and the cycle continues," Fraley wrote.

In later interviews, Fraley and MacIver's president, Brett Healy, said they never spoke directly to members of the Walker administration about the plan. After it was released, Fraley did a few radio interviews on his column, not really expecting elements of it to become the law of the state. But in hindsight he said he believed his group did have an impact. "While it's flattering to hear we helped in this wave, I think it's accurate too," stated Fraley.

MacIver was a member of the State Policy Network, a Bradley-supported enterprise that linked free-market think tanks in all fifty states. Other member groups in the network in states like Michigan and Ohio also pushed in the coming year for overhauls of collective bargaining by public employees. These groups also benefited from Bradley funding. For example, the Mackinac Center, a group in Midland, Michigan, which helped promote legislation similar to Act 10, has received hundreds of thousands of dollars from Bradley since 2001. MacIver would not release the funding proposals that it made to the Bradley Foundation but said it didn't discuss legislation such as Act 10. For his part, Grebe denied to the *Journal Sentinel* that he or the Bradley Foundation were at all responsible for Walker's collective bargaining legislation, though Grebe clearly supported reining in public-sector unions. He said there was still some place for unions in American life, "just not as prominent as it used to be." Grebe also noted that he was careful to keep his Bradley work separate from his campaigning for Walker, which included one fund-raising letter asking supporters to help the governor fight "the Democrats and Big Government Union Bosses." Walker also denied the involvement of any outside group. He later said that his work as county executive had been the real impetus for Act 10. "There's no other group. There's no other involvement. It literally came from eight years of being the Milwaukee County executive," he stated in a spring 2012 interview.

The fledgling Walker administration was slow to announce cabinet appointments but not to act on the union question. In private, the administration was already drafting legislation to limit public employee unions. To help meet the rapidly approaching deadline for drafting a state budget bill, incoming governors were granted the courtesy of using analysts and experts within the State Budget Office in the Department of Administration, which for another month was still under the nominal control of outgoing Governor Jim Doyle. On December 3, 2010, a budget analyst requested a bill draft on behalf of the governor-elect that would mandate higher health care contributions for state employees and eliminate all union bargaining over health care for state and local employees in Wisconsin. By then the incoming Walker administration was also looking at changing state law on public employees' pension contributions as well. Around that time, the budget office also asked for a labor attorney to help in its work for the incoming governor. But Walker's aides never formally requested the attorney, and the Doyle appointees never provided one. By January, the private drafting requests from the Walker administration to the Legislative Reference Bureau had expanded to include the repeal of all collective bargaining by most state employees. A month earlier, on December 7, Walker appeared at a luncheon of the Milwaukee Press Club and said he was mulling over abolishing public-sector unions. Asked what options he was considering, Walker said, "Anything from decertify all the way through modifications of the current laws in place. The bottom line is that we are going to look at every legal means we have to try to put that balance more on the side of taxpayers and the people who care about services."

Walker made clear that if necessary he would impose the savings that he wanted on workers' health and pension benefits. His comments got the attention of both his political allies and enemies. Scott Fitzgerald, the Republican leader who would soon be struggling to push Walker's union legislation through the Senate, said later that he hadn't considered repealing laws governing union bargaining until Walker raised the possibility at the Press Club. "That was the first time I was like, 'Hmm, decertify the unions; how does that work?'" Fitzgerald said.

Unions and many public employees were alarmed and angered by Walker's comments at the luncheon. That included AFSCME Council 48, which represented more than four thousand Milwaukee County workers who had been battling Walker for years. "His union-busting attitude shouldn't surprise anybody," Rich Abelson, executive director of Council 48, said then. "This is very much in keeping with his conservative philosophy. In Scott Walker's world, CEO's never make enough money, and there isn't a working person who deserves what he earns."

After Walker put forward his plan for ending collective bargaining two months later, there was a great deal of speculation about how or where he got it. One possibility commonly mentioned by liberal critics was that Walker had taken it from the American Legislative Exchange Council (ALEC), the group that drew on corporate funding to advance conservative bills in state legislatures. Mary Bottari of the liberal Center for Media and Democracy in Madison has argued that ALEC influenced Walker, a former member of the group, with its past bills dealing with union issues. Those bills included legislation to end government's automatic payroll deductions for employees for union dues and to end requirements that public employees make fair share payments to unions if they weren't members. Bottari pointed to Scott Fitzgerald's acknowledgement at a luncheon sponsored by the website WisPolitics that he attended an ALEC meeting in Washington, D.C., held from December 1 to December 3, 2010, in which there was talk about pushing right-to-work legislation. This would prevent unions, including those in the private sector, from reaching contracts with employers that would force all workers to pay union dues.

ALEC's leaders, however, denied having been the source of Walker's legislation, and in fact there was little evidence that ALEC was directly involved. In addition, ALEC is known for providing model legislation to advance conservative goals—bills that are ready to be introduced in state legislatures with relatively few changes. ALEC model legislation on other subjects was introduced that session in the state Legislature, but the staff at Wisconsin's Legislative Reference Bureau wasn't handed such a finished bill in the case of the governor's union legislation. Cathlene Hanaman, the deputy chief of the Reference Bureau, said that her agency got the drafting requests from long-time state budget analysts and never talked with Walker aides. The requests always came in plain English, not in the legalese of ALEC-style model legislation. "There was no prefab language," Hanaman said later.

Representative Robin Vos of Rochester, a powerful Republican lawmaker, was both a state co-chairman for ALEC and a supporter of right-to-work legislation. He readily acknowledged that ALEC promoted such bills and that he had met years ago with members of the National Right to Work Committee at an ALEC conference. But he also said he was convinced ALEC played no role in what became Act 10. "It was happenstance that made everything happen because of the complete [Republican] takeover of state government. It wasn't any one group," Vos said.

Still, the changes in Wisconsin clearly didn't happen in a vacuum. Too many other states were taking up similar changes for it to be a coincidence.

Ideas for diminishing unions' influence were in circulation. The *New York Times*, for instance, reported that the conservative group Americans for Prosperity helped push for measures to rein in unions in states like Wisconsin, Indiana, Ohio, and Pennsylvania. The group was created by and drew funding from the billionaire brothers Charles and David Koch, whose Koch Industries owned two paper mills in Green Bay, making it a major employer in Wisconsin. Americans for Prosperity had helped organize substantial rallies at the Wisconsin Capitol for the past two years, as it had around the country. Koch Industries' political action committee donated $43,000 to Walker's campaign, and David Koch indirectly supported Walker by giving $1 million to the Republican Governors Association, which ran ads for Walker and other Republicans. In the same month that Walker introduced his union plan, Americans for Prosperity spent hundreds of thousands of dollars on television and radio ads promoting it, and the group helped organize a rally at the Capitol as well. Americans for Prosperity continued to back Walker over the next year and a half.

The Bradley Foundation had given $600,000 to the Americans for Prosperity Foundation between 2004 and 2010. In late 2011, when the recall effort against Walker gathered steam, the MacIver Institute and Americans for Prosperity teamed up to spend more than $1 million to defend the governor's policies. Small wonder—Walker had done what those groups had urged him to do. The Bradley Foundation was much closer to Walker than Americans for Prosperity or ALEC but never got as much attention. Another in-state group wielding influence was Wisconsin Manufacturers & Commerce (WMC), the state's largest business lobby. WMC had traditionally been the biggest foil to organized labor, one of the most influential groups in the state Capitol, and one of the Republicans' biggest backers. WMC also strongly supported Walker's union legislation after it was introduced.

One final inspiration—this one much better known—for governors like Walker who pursued legislation to weaken unions was a person, not an institution. In Mitch Daniels's second day in office in 2005, the Indiana governor rescinded collective bargaining for public employees in his state. Daniels could act unilaterally in Indiana because the power for public unions to bargain with that state government had been granted in 1989 through an executive order by Democratic Governor Evan Bayh. The repeal of collective bargaining did not spark the same massive protests in Indiana that it would in Wisconsin. Because Daniels did not need approval from legislators, the Republican governor could unveil the change as a fait accompli. In addition, Indiana is a more conservative state than Wisconsin, and collective bargaining had been in place there for less time.

After issuing his executive order, Daniels used his new power to cut government by outsourcing food and medical services in the prison system, scrapping government print shops through contracting, and centralizing information technology and human resources. Meanwhile, public unions in Indiana withered without the power to bargain for wages or compel members to pay dues. In 2005 there were 16,408 employees who paid union dues. By the spring of 2010 there were only 1,490. Walker knew and admired Daniels, and was in touch with him while Act 10 was being finalized. On January 25, 2010, Walker's calendar shows a fifteen-minute phone call scheduled with Daniels. On February 5 Walker was also scheduled to attend a reception by Daniels and the Indiana Economic Development Corporation at the Super Bowl. In an interview in March 2011 Walker said that "Mitch, as much as anyone, has the clearest road map for the two big issues I ran on, fixing the economy—jobs—and fixing the budget—spending." Scott Fitzgerald put it even more plainly: "It's not like we dreamed this up. It was Mitch Daniels. It came from Mitch Daniels." Daniels also turned out to have had one other Wisconsin connection: he was a former board member of the Bradley Foundation.

The Bradley Foundation was determined that other states should learn from Indiana's experience in dealing with their budget challenges. In October 2010, right before the elections, the Bradley Working Group on State Finances brought leaders from largely right-wing groups like the Mackinac Center and ALEC together in Indianapolis to do just that. A later write-up of the takeaways from the event mentioned Indiana's savings through outsourcing and the need to overhaul state pension systems. For states like Wisconsin, there would be just one glitch: the public employee unions still in place would be in a position to potentially block those changes.

Walker made his Milwaukee Press Club comments about decertifying unions while Democrats and unions were seeking to pass labor contracts before Walker took office. For seventeen months, unions and Governor Doyle had not been able to find an agreement on contracts. But after Walker's November 2010 victory, the unions quickly reached deals with the outgoing administration. Because of the drawn-out negotiations, the state's union employees had been working without a deal for the better part of the two-year contract period set to expire in June 2011. If approved, the contracts would cover the past seventeen months as well as the seven months ahead. Getting the lame-duck Democratic Legislature to approve the contracts before Walker was sworn in would mean that union workers would be protected for at least the first six months of Walker's term. Once the Doyle administration and the unions reached the deals, Democrats in the Legislature moved to approve them. Using his bully pulpit as governor-elect, Walker made it his priority to try to defeat the contracts and require unions to deal only with him.

The governor-elect also tried backdoor communications. In early December a Republican with ties to labor unions contacted Marty Beil, the executive director of the AFSCME council known as the Wisconsin State Employees Union. Beil was a blunt, old-school labor leader who had started working for the state in 1969 as a parole officer, helped organize his area in the early 1970s, and soon moved on to work full-time for the union. The Republican told Beil he was contacting him on behalf of the governor-elect to deliver a message: Walker wanted labor unions to call off the approval of the contracts so he could work with them on his own deals. The proposed contracts included $103 million in concessions for workers over two years, such as furloughs that were the equivalent of 3 percent pay cuts. But the contracts would also prevent Walker from immediately making any deeper cuts to union workers' compensation or bargaining power. Beil told the Republican, who like Walker aides would not discuss the call, that the contracts would move forward and the governor-elect could negotiate new deals starting in July 2011. In spite of Walker's threat to decertify the labor unions, Beil knew that would take legislative action and didn't believe Walker would try it.

"My frame of mind at the time was, given the context of the standing law, 'How can you decertify us?' I thought, 'Boy, he's just blowing off here,'" Beil remembered later. "Never did we think that he would change the law to actually do that." But there were signs of trouble ahead for unions, and AFSCME lobbyist Susan McMurray saw one of them. In meetings during that period with Scott and Jeff Fitzgerald and their aides, McMurray was told by both brothers that unions would face problems if they tried to push through the contracts before Republicans took control. "There will be consequences," the Fitzgeralds told her. Scott Fitzgerald said later he had thought the consequences would be something like additional furloughs for state workers rather than the dramatic scaling back of collective bargaining that would soon take place.

Walker had already won one big victory as governor-elect on the issue of passenger rail. Two days after the Milwaukee Press Club luncheon, the federal government dropped the planned line between Madison and Milwaukee that the Doyle administration had felt forced to suspend. At a July 2010 stop in the state, the U.S. transportation secretary, Ray LaHood, had declared, "High-speed rail is coming to Wisconsin. There's no stopping it." Yet it was LaHood himself who canceled Wisconsin's grant on December 9, 2010, because of the stance of Walker and the Republicans who would be taking over the Legislature. Walker wasn't the only GOP governor to shut down such a project. The day LaHood announced he was taking away Wisconsin's money, he did the same thing in Ohio, where Republican John Kasich had just won election as governor. In New Jersey, GOP Governor Chris Christie halted work on a train tunnel to New York, one of the most expensive public works projects in the country. The rail money from Wisconsin and Ohio was redirected to California, Florida, Illinois, and other states where there was more support for passenger trains.

The rail issue proved a sign of things to come. First, it established Wisconsin as a new national leader in conservative causes. Second, it showed that some of the Democrats who slept during the recent elections were beginning to wake up. When work on the Madison-to-Milwaukee line was halted, there was a flurry of criticism on Facebook and Twitter from train supporters. Many seemed surprised that Walker was shutting the line down, even though it had been a campaign promise and even part of one of his ads. The governor-elect's union bargaining changes, which were not part of his campaign, would generate far greater dismay.

The other threat to Walker, the John Doe probe, continued in secret. The investigation had widened since the summer of 2010, and District Attorney John Chisholm needed help to complete it. Chisholm reached out to state Attorney General J.B. Van Hollen. Even though Chisholm was a Democrat and Van Hollen a Republican, the pair had collaborated in the past on voter fraud cases and at least one other John Doe investigation. The Department of Justice (DOJ) could offer Chisholm expertise important to the investigation such as the sophisticated review of computer files. Van Hollen's involvement would have also lent a bipartisan cast to Chisholm's potentially explosive case.

On November 15, 2010, Chisholm and his top deputy came to DOJ headquarters in Madison to meet with Van Hollen; his top deputy; and Ed Wall, head of the DOJ's Division of Criminal Investigation. But DOJ officials weren't eager to help investigate the aides of a newly elected governor from their boss's own party. "This is one to try and stay away from. I can't see any good coming from it," Wall wrote in an e-mail to a subordinate just hours before the meeting. The DOJ was already involved in vetting potential appointees to

Walker's incoming administration, and the list included some of the same people that Chisholm was investigating. Van Hollen subsequently turned down the request for help, but the investigation didn't stop. On December 7 the authorities raided the Milwaukee home and West Milwaukee business office of Tim Russell, Walker's former deputy chief of staff in Milwaukee County. On December 21 Rose Ann Dieck, a retired teacher and Milwaukee County Republican Party activist, received immunity for her testimony. On January 20, 2011, investigators seized a checking account connected to other alleged crimes by Russell.

Walker, however, was still winning victories in the public eye. Ten days before Christmas 2010 the Capitol had its showdown on the labor contracts when Democrats called a lame-duck session—the first in Wisconsin since 1974—to vote on them. The Assembly approved all of the contracts, with sixteen of the seventeen deals passing by a vote of forty-eight to forty-seven. The deciding vote came from Representative Jeff Wood, a Chippewa Falls independent and former Republican who had been arrested three times in less than a year for driving under the influence of drugs or alcohol. At the time, Wood was serving a jail sentence that included work release, and he outraged Republicans by getting permission from jail officials to go to Madison to vote.

The drama then shifted to the Senate, which took up the contracts at 7:30 p.m. on December 15. The nagging bell that called the senators to the chamber chimed through the south wing of the Capitol as the lawmakers straggled in. The Assembly had seemed the greater hurdle for the contracts, and many expected them to easily pass the Senate. When the floor debate began, Scott Fitzgerald explained that for a decade and a half he had voted for every labor contract that had come before the Legislature. But this year was different, he said, because Democrats were trying to push them through ahead of a change in party control.

The debate continued for the next forty-five minutes, until Senate Majority Leader Russ Decker of Wausau asked to speak. A former bricklayer and union negotiator, the sphinx-like Democratic leader sometimes hid his plans from the members of his own party. Decker had risen to his leadership position through a 2007 coup of a fellow Democratic leader, but he would soon lose it—along with his seat in the Senate—because of his recent surprise defeat at the polls. During his two decades in the Senate, Decker had been a staunch supporter of unions, but he also felt labor groups had failed to do enough to help him in the recent elections, and that heightened the drama over what he would do now. He stood straight but kept his eyes on the prepared remarks on his desktop. "These contracts would not be in front of us at this time except for the election results of November 2," Decker noted. "Some people lost in that election, including myself. Like it or not, state employees are going to have to negotiate four years of contracts with the new governor. Before I came to the Senate, I negotiated contracts for bricklayers and one of the worst things you could do was poke a stick in the eye of a new employer."

Like other Democrats, Decker assumed even then that the Walker administration would be seeking concessions from workers at the bargaining table. The Democratic leader occasionally peered up from the text of his speech to gauge his colleagues' reaction. He saved his intentions for last. "Now that the election has been held and the voters have spoken, I do not feel comfortable casting a vote in favor of these contracts," he said.

One GOP senator was absent and the vote came in at sixteen to sixteen— one vote shy of what was needed to approve the contracts. Members of both parties were stunned by Decker's vote. Even some of his own staff didn't know how he would vote until he spoke on the Senate floor. After the vote, Democrats broke to go behind closed doors to take the symbolic action of stripping Decker of his leadership position for his final three weeks in office.

"In twenty-eight years I've never seen a leader stick it to his members like this," Senator Bob Jauch, a Democrat from Poplar, said after the vote. "Psychologists probably write books about this type of behavior. It's a disorder that's probably now being named." Marty Beil, the labor leader, was even blunter. "Decker's a whore," he told reporters. "He'll never ever hold a seat as a Democrat [again]."

In fact, Decker didn't receive anything for his vote except the disdain of his colleagues. To date, he hasn't gotten a job with Walker's administration, as some speculated he would. Senator Jeff Plale of South Milwaukee, a second lame-duck Democrat who voted against the contracts after being defeated in a September primary by a liberal candidate with backing from labor, did snag a Walker appointment. But the governor-elect won the biggest prize. By killing the contracts, Walker had shown that Republicans could stand up to unions and win. With the relationship between him and the unions deteriorating, he also ensured that immediately upon taking office he could push to repeal their collective bargaining power—a blessing that would turn out to be decidedly mixed for the governor.

By January 18, 2011, Walker had his plan for dealing with public employee unions, and he was beginning to share it with people in the inner circle of Republican politics. He showed up early that morning at the Beloit headquarters of ABC Supply Company, a roofing wholesaler and siding distributor founded by Diane Hendricks and her late husband, Ken. Hendricks, whose net worth *Forbes* estimates to be $2.8 billion, has a history of bankrolling conservative causes and candidates. Along with Ken, Hendricks since 1997 had contributed some $500,000 to political candidates and committees in races ranging from the Wisconsin Assembly to the presidency, with the overwhelming majority going to Republicans. Walker had so far garnered $9,100 of those donations. Hendricks was also the co-chairwoman of the economic development group Rock County 5.0, which Walker planned to visit that day. The group was seeking to revitalize the southern Wisconsin county in the wake of a shutdown of its anchor General Motors plant that had proved disastrous for the local economy.

Hendricks and her co-chairwoman, Mary Willmer-Sheedy, left the meeting to greet Walker when he arrived. Accompanying the two women was Brad Lichtenstein, a filmmaker with connections to the Public Broadcasting Service, who for months had been working with Rock County 5.0 and others to record a documentary about the community's efforts to revive its economy. As Walker and Hendricks hugged, Lichtenstein recorded their frank conversation. The governor and Hendricks discussed right-to-work legislation, which Hendricks strongly supported, even though none of her companies were unionized. In 1993 Walker had co-sponsored right-to-work legislation as a freshman in the Assembly, but it had failed and had not been introduced again in the eighteen years since. Now, a few conservative lawmakers had drafted such legislation, but they had not and would not introduce it because of a lack of support, particularly once the furor over Walker's public union legislation erupted.

"Can we talk just for two seconds before we get up there?" Hendricks asked Walker on Lichtenstein's video.

"Yeah, yeah, that's fine," Walker said.

"Some issues we're just going to avoid a little bit [at the meeting]. And by the way, this is Brad and he is part of Rock County 5.0 and he has been filming everything," Hendricks said.

"I've been doing a documentary—" Lichtenstein started to say.

"Oh, cool," Walker said, cutting off Lichtenstein before the filmmaker could explain what his documentary was about.

"So what we're going to do and talk about right now is just concerns that Mary and I have that we probably—are a little controversial to bring up upstairs. Okay? I don't want to—because there's press up there," Hendricks said.

"Okay, sure," Walker said.

"Just so you know, nothing I do is going to see the light of day for over another year," Lichtenstein said.

"Okay, that's fine," the governor answered.

"So we'll just take five minutes," Hendricks said. " . . . Any chance we'll ever get to be a completely red state and work on these unions—"

"Oh, yeah," Walker broke in.

"—and become a right-to-work [state]?" Hendricks asked. "What can we do to help you?"

"Well, we're going to start in a couple weeks with our budget-adjustment bill," the governor replied. "The first step is, we're going to deal with collective bargaining for all public employee unions, because you use divide and conquer. So for us the base we've got for that is the fact that we've got—budgetarily we can't afford not to. If we have collective bargaining agreements in place, there's no way not only the state but local governments can balance things out. So you think city of Beloit, city of Janesville, any of the school districts, that opens the door once we do that. That's your bigger problem right there."

The conversation moved on to talk of cutting regulations and liability lawsuits on businesses. Walker had stopped short of saying explicitly that he would pursue a right-to-work law. But his "divide and conquer" comment to Hendricks had gone well beyond what he would say publicly in the weeks and months ahead when he talked about unions. A month later, for instance, once the uproar exploded over his bill on public unions, he said he had no intention of touching private unions. "If we were ultimately about attacking the unions, we'd be doing something to the private unions," Walker stated. "I don't have any interest in doing anything to private unions. I think the private unions are a key part to getting this state's economy going." The governor, however, repeatedly refused to say over the next year whether he would veto a right-to-work bill if it came to his desk. In the meantime, Lichtenstein, a Democrat who prided himself on capturing a range of views in his documentaries, held on to the video until the documentary was nearly finished more than a year later, as he had told Walker he would. The public at the time knew nothing of the governor's comments. For her part, Hendricks appeared delighted with Walker's plans, and the group went upstairs to the meeting. Two weeks later, on February 1, 2011, Hendricks gave Walker a $10,000 donation—the maximum at that time for a four-year election cycle. On February 16 her ABC Supply Company gave $25,000 to the Republican Governors Association, which had run ads in support of Walker. But the biggest show of Hendricks's support for Walker—and the outcry over the video itself—was more than a year away.

5

"Dropping the Bomb"

A BLIZZARD WAS BEARING DOWN ON MADISON on February 1, 2011, and a political storm was gathering inside the Capitol. Out of the clutches of the cold, Senate President Mike Ellis was tucked away in his elegant office just off the Senate floor, where the pictures on the walls told of his lifetime in politics and past encounters with giants like presidents Ronald Reagan and Bill Clinton. Ellis still had no clue about the approach of this political storm, which was to rage long after the snows of the first had melted. But he was about to find out. Senate Majority Leader Scott Fitzgerald marched into Ellis's office to tell him what he had learned from the governor's office about Walker's plan on collective bargaining. "You better sit down; you're not going to believe what I'm going to tell you," Fitzgerald said. "He's going to do away with all [public-sector] unions."

"What?" the Senate president replied. "Holy shit! I can't believe this."

Fitzgerald, too, had been taken aback when he learned of the plan, even though he had known something big was likely. During the transition, Walker adviser and campaign manager Keith Gilkes—a former aide to Fitzgerald—had told the Senate Republican leader that there would be a budget-repair bill and that it could be contentious, but that Republicans could mitigate the controversy by passing it quickly. Fitzgerald didn't know details, but he knew polls were being conducted to gauge voter perceptions of public-sector unions. As it turned out, the governor was planning to eliminate all public-worker unions in the state except those for police and firefighters. Private-sector unions would not be affected, but the unions of school, municipal, county, and state employees would lose their official standing. When Fitzgerald found out to his surprise what the package would include, he took the matter to Ellis. He saw gaining Ellis's support as crucial to getting the measure passed because he knew Ellis was a master at burying a bill if he opposed it. Walker's office also understood Ellis's ability to undermine their agenda and approved of Fitzgerald talking to him early. "He's not a great friend, but he can be a fantastic enemy," Gilkes said of Ellis more than a year later.

Ellis felt strongly that bold moves were needed to rescue the state's budget, which was a long-standing crusade of his. At the same time, he knew from experience which subjects at the Capitol were firecrackers and which were dynamite. A former teacher and a political survivor, Ellis led Senate Republicans through much of the 1990s, a time when control of that house ping-ponged between the two political parties and the art of political compromise was still practiced and appreciated. The idea of blowing up the state's unions seemed to him ill-advised and, more to the point, impossible to pass in the Senate. Though more conservative than Ellis, Fitzgerald also opposed eliminating public-sector unions altogether because he thought it would be viewed as an attempt to destroy the Democrats politically. Ultimately, Democrats did come to exactly this conclusion, even after the proposal was loosened a small amount. After hearing about the plan from Fitzgerald, Ellis went further than Fitzgerald by arguing for keeping in place fair share payments that would allow the unions to require nonmembers to pay fees equivalent to dues. That would have let unions keep more of their financial resources and the power that they conferred.

Ellis and Fitzgerald had a series of meetings on their own to decide what to do and then sat down with the governor for a face-to-face meeting. Walker argued that his plan was a bold but necessary stroke that was essential to setting Wisconsin on solid financial footing for the future. In his blunt style, Ellis dissented. "My God, this is going to cause a firestorm," he said.

Ellis argued for leaving the unions in place and instead concentrating on money-saving moves such as the benefit concessions included in the bill. Rather than negotiating with unions for such givebacks as state officials had for decades, the governor's bill would simply impose the concessions on employees. The move could be immediately invoked since the Senate in December had rejected the labor contracts that would have locked the state into a deal with its unions until June 2011. Like everything else in the bill, the change was also possible because unions for state and local government employees were governed by the state laws that had created them. In that respect, they were different from unions at private companies, which were largely controlled by federal law. Walker was proposing simply wiping away the state laws creating the public-sector unions. The groups could continue to exist—their members still had the fundamental freedom as citizens to associate with one another—but government officials would now be prohibited from bargaining with them or giving them any other consideration. The workers would have no more leverage than they could scrape together through their value in the labor market, work actions like pickets, and appeals to public opinion.

Public-safety workers such as police officers and firefighters would be exempted from Walker's plan. A few of those groups, such as those representing Milwaukee cops, Milwaukee firefighters, and state highway troopers, had supported the governor's campaign, later prompting questions of whether Walker's treatment of them amounted to political payback. Walker denied the allegation and said the groups were exempted to make sure they would not illegally strike, since that would invite serious consequences, both for the people of the state and his own career. No one could replace those public-safety workers overnight, so Walker's proposal protected them. But every other public union—including those for police officers who kept the peace at state universities and the Capitol—was no longer needed or wanted, he argued. Besides any talks on benefits, the plan would eliminate bargaining on workplace safety, on seniority in the event of layoffs, and a host of other work rules that for decades had dictated how governments across Wisconsin had dealt with their employees.

Ellis asked Walker, "If you can't identify fiscal savings from a collective-bargaining item, why not leave it alone?" There was also the question of whether striking at public-sector unions—the last real bastion of organized labor—wouldn't also prove a blow to the state's unions at private companies. Ellis figured the private-sector unions would recognize the stakes and join with their publicly employed brothers to fight Republicans, a notion the governor dismissed. Walker also talked about the plans that his administration had in place to handle strikes or other job actions by state workers. Long after the struggle, the governor acknowledged that it was "absolutely correct" that he and his aides had focused their planning on ways to keep the state's prisons, bureaucracy, and other functions running if state employees refused to show up for work—a challenge that never materialized. But the governor's new administration hadn't planned for the problem that did arise: a lengthy political standoff in which unions demonstrated significant support both within the state and outside it.

The senators later met with a larger group to negotiate and refine the details of the plan. The meeting included Ellis and Scott Fitzgerald; Assembly Speaker Jeff Fitzgerald; Administration Secretary Mike Huebsch; and the governor's deputy chief of staff, Eric Schutt, who as a legislative aide had served in past budget negotiations. The group met down the hall from Ellis's office, in a conference room just off the Senate floor. Republicans used the room for meetings, and in it Ellis kept a pair of blackboards, of the sort he had once used as a teacher, that he filled with numbers charting the financial woes of the state.

In the short term, the budget problems were modest, but in the long term they were grave. The state was halfway through a fiscal year that ended on June 30, 2011, and the best predictions of impartial budget experts at that time put the state's budget more than $100 million short. Some Democrats and union supporters would soon be claiming that the state didn't have a budget crisis, pointing to a report by the Legislative Fiscal Bureau, the budget office serving lawmakers of both parties. This report showed that under what was then current law, the state would end the year with a surplus. But the claim of Walker's opponents was misleading. It was true that the state would end the year with a surplus *if no changes were made* to the budget then laid out in state law. But it was also true that a number of unbudgeted costs had arisen for the state in areas like health care for the poor, prisons, and a tax deal with the state of Minnesota. Failing to address the added costs for health care and prisons could have endangered or disrupted nursing home care for the elderly, doctor's visits for children, and the imperative to keep prisoners behind bars.

Walker's opponents said that that shortfall added up to only about twenty-four dollars for each man, woman, and child in Wisconsin, a relatively minor sum to pay in added taxes or fees to right the state's financial ship. This was true as far as it went—each family of four in the state would have to contribute only a single hundred-dollar bill to tide the state over until the next budget started. But here, however, things got worse. For the two-year budget starting July 1, 2011, estimates at the time put the state on track to spend more than $3 billion more than it was expected to take in from taxes and other revenues, assuming that the agencies would get all of their budget requests fulfilled, something that didn't normally happen. To cover *that* total, each family of four would have had to come up with an average of roughly $1,230 for each of the two years in added taxes and fees to close the gap. This showed the difficulty of solving the deficit with new taxes alone. On the other hand, using only spending cuts appeared daunting as well. For instance, shutting down all of the state's public universities and half of its prison system would not have produced enough savings in spending of state tax dollars to close that two-year gap.

As Ellis knew all too well, the challenges for the state's budget were far from new. The fundamental imbalance went back at least fifteen years, through both Republican and Democratic governors and legislative houses controlled by both parties. For years, leaders had made it a point to govern as if there would never be any financial crisis in the future. The state's rainy-day fund had long been a joke. Many other states routinely deposited large sums in their reserve accounts during good times because, unlike the federal government, states can't borrow money in bad times to fund their day-to-day operations. But when the recession hit in 2001, Wisconsin's rainy-day fund had just forty-nine dollars in it, barely enough to buy a dinner and drinks for two. When the next recession came in late 2007, the state had $57 million dollars in its reserve fund, enough to run state government for only one and a half days. The money was used to help balance a shortfall in the state budget before the worst of the recession even arrived.

Perhaps part of the problem in Wisconsin was its near-perfect status as one of the most evenly balanced political states in the country. Because control of state government was often split between Democrats and Republicans, both parties struggled to impose their ideas and policies on the state, and could move forward with only the most popular elements of their agendas. Democrats often had enough clout to preserve or expand spending programs, and Republicans often had enough leverage to hold down taxes or cut them. But in many cases, neither side had the political muscle to push through the tax increases or real spending cuts that would be needed to pay for the favored items on their agendas. In the 1990s, Governor Tommy Thompson and the GOP-controlled Legislature followed through on a state commitment to pay two-thirds of the costs of Wisconsin's public schools—a huge initial cost of $1.2 billion for the state that would grow year by year—without pairing it with the same amount of sustainable spending cuts or new taxes or fees. The lower property taxes the state had bought through this deal were a plus for voters, as were decisions to provide an income tax cut starting in 1999 and a one-time sales tax refund in 2000.

As long as the state's tax revenues grew strongly year after year, this budget imbalance could be managed without any great pain. But, of course, nothing grows forever. For Wisconsin, as for other states, the first reckoning came in the wake of the recession following the bursting of the dot-com bubble. The state had no cushion, either in financial reserves or conservative budgeting, to meet the fiscal challenge that arose when the twin brakes of the recession and tax cuts were applied. So to make it through the downturn, first Republican Governor Scott McCallum in 2001 and 2002 and then Democratic Governor Jim Doyle from 2003 on, largely with the blessing of lawmakers, turned to different forms of borrowing. McCallum borrowed against the future payments the state was set to receive from a settlement of a lawsuit against tobacco companies. Doyle raided money from the state's road fund, largely replacing the cash that was taken out of the fund with borrowing. Both of these strategies were necessary to make an end run around the state's constitutional prohibition on borrowing to fund its ongoing operations. The state is only allowed to issue bonds to cover long-term investments such as roads and buildings, but these strategies allowed the state to have cash up front and to pay for it later.

The state didn't do enough to shore up its finances in the years that followed, and then a deep recession, much worse than the last, hit in late 2007 and worsened over the next year. After stumbling through the 2000s, the state hit disaster—a $6 billion potential shortfall over the two years from July 2009 to June 2011. The state had one of the worst budgets in the country by several measures, such as its deficit according to the standard rules known as Generally Accepted Accounting Principles, which are more rigorous than the state's usual method of accounting. Doyle and the Democrats who then controlled the Legislature made some difficult choices such as cutting state aid to schools and raising a number of taxes, which helped to lessen some of the state's long-term budget imbalances. But the Democrats also relied in part on a massive injection of one-time aid to the state from the federal economic stimulus plan, which meant that much of the state's financial troubles were pushed off into 2011 and beyond. The state had a smaller but still formidable potential shortfall in the next budget, the one for which Republicans now had responsibility. Over the last decade, Mike Ellis had watched these budget practices with increasing disgust. He would pigeonhole reporters, aides, other lawmakers, and anyone he could compel to listen to him, and rail about the state's profligacy and the need to reform it. Now Walker and his aides were telling the senator that the way to do that was to end collective bargaining.

Ellis wasn't satisfied, however. In the meeting in his conference room, Ellis and the other lawmakers pressed Walker's aides for changes to his proposal. They weren't looking for something that would make it palatable to

Democrats—that would be impossible—just acceptable for moderate Republicans. In two small respects, the legislators made headway. They insisted that unions continue to be recognized under state law and also be allowed to bargain over their salaries within an effective limit tied to the rate of inflation. The salary proposal came from an offhand remark by one of Ellis's aides, Mike Boerger, who didn't think much of his own suggestion at the time and was surprised when it became part of the bill. That proposal essentially guaranteed that through bargaining, the wages of union workers would stay flat or erode over time—not rise. "We came over here, and over the course of the next week we started talking about what we could live with. And what we could live with was, you can't do away with the unions, you've got to leave them there. So we went from getting rid of them to leaving them," Ellis said later.

For their part, Walker's aides tried to reassure the senators that the governor's plan amounted to both good policy and good politics, and that there would be "air cover" in the form of expensive television ads defending the proposal. Ellis's office soon got back a sheet of paper with the terms of what the senators had supposedly agreed to in the meeting: they would eliminate all collective bargaining for most public employees except for a limited amount over wages. But it also called for requiring unions to have annual elections in which at least 51 percent of their members and other eligible employees in a given workplace would have to vote that their union should keep its official status. If they didn't reach that threshold each year, the labor group would lose its standing before the state and with it the limited ability to bargain over wages. This meant that if only half of the members showed up to vote, the union would then be decertified even if all the ballots were in favor of retaining it. Ellis said that he and Fitzgerald later met again over the memo. "We said, 'Well, we didn't agree to this,'" Ellis said.

At around the same time the Fitzgerald brothers were deciding how to handle the governor's stunning proposal, their father, Stephen Fitzgerald, was being given a choice job in the Walker administration. To get the $105,700-a-year political appointment as the head of the State Patrol, the elder Fitzgerald interviewed with the governor and beat out five other top officials already in the agency, including the acting superintendent. Fitzgerald, sixty-eight, had four decades of law enforcement experience, including service as the Dodge County sheriff and the U.S. marshal in the Western District of Wisconsin under President George W. Bush. But he now was in need of a job after having run for his old sheriff's post and lost to his successor in the job by a two-to-one margin in the GOP primary. Stephen Fitzgerald said he learned he would receive the job around February 4, the same time that jockeying was going on privately in the Senate around Walker's bill. The Fitzgerald brothers and Walker's office flatly denied that politics played any role in the choice. "We knew the optics of it were going to be bad," Scott Fitzgerald said later, adding that he was comfortable with the decision because of his father's law enforcement credentials.

Walker also had other longstanding ties to the Fitzgeralds that he could draw on to influence them. Jeff Fitzgerald had served with Walker in the Assembly for a little over a year before Walker had left to become Milwaukee County executive. Though Walker is actually a year younger than Fitzgerald, he had served as a kind of mentor to Jeff by virtue of Walker's seniority. "I remember we sat in caucus together in the corner and I remember meeting him and thinking, 'Wow, this guy knows his stuff,'" Fitzgerald recalled more than a decade later. "I was new to the Legislature, we were in the budget debate, and I asked him a lot of questions on what he thought of the budget. I knew he was a conservative. We had the same kind of beliefs. He really helped me out as a freshman to learn the ropes."

Besides their own conservative beliefs, the Fitzgeralds also faced pressure from incoming lawmakers in both of their caucuses who were often very conservative. "Actually my caucus wanted to go further. I had people . . . wondering if we were going to do right-to-work [legislation] in this state," Jeff Fitzgerald said later. "So to tell you the truth, the collective bargaining [bill on public employees] to me was more of a middle ground, if you can believe that."

Meanwhile, Walker's plan was moving closer to becoming public. The governor met with his cabinet to discuss the bill on February 7, one day after the Green Bay Packers' victory in Super Bowl XLV. Still feeling a boost from the Packers' win, the group had dinner at the spacious lakeside mansion that Wisconsin governors have called home since 1949. Holding up a photo of Ronald Reagan, Walker reminded his cabinet that the day before marked what would have been the former president's one hundredth birthday and compared his legislation with Reagan's stand against a group of striking air traffic controllers. There were differences between Reagan's views and his own: Reagan had his showdown with the air traffic controllers union because its members were involved in an illegal strike; by contrast, the unions in Wisconsin hadn't broken any laws. As a former president of the Screen Actors Guild, Reagan supported the right of federal workers to collectively bargain, just not to strike. Later, in what Walker thought was a private conversation, he recalled what he told his cabinet that evening. "You know, this may sound a little melodramatic, but thirty years ago Ronald Reagan . . . had one of the most defining moments of his political career, not just his presidency, when he fired the air traffic controllers," he said. "To me, that moment was more important than just for labor relations or even the federal budget. That was the first crack in the Berlin Wall and the fall of communism because from that point forward the Soviets and the communists knew that Ronald Reagan wasn't a pushover. . . . This may not have as broad of world implications but in Wisconsin's history . . . this is our moment, this is our time to change the course of history."

Walker still hadn't talked to the public about what he saw as a historic change. After the crisis was over, Walker looked back on the year in a December 2011 interview and acknowledged that he should have talked with voters about the issue before dropping his proposal on them. "I would have spent more time, if I could do it over again, in January and February [2011] making the case," Walker said. "Because what I hear is even people who kind of appreciate what's been done still occasionally will say, 'Yeah, but you should have told us more about why you were going to do [that],' and I can see that. . . . The mistake was I should have done more of that. I should have laid it out."

On Thursday, February 10, 2011, Walker and his aides met with the full caucus of Republican senators to brief them on his bill. The meeting was held in the same room where the senators had greeted the triumphant governor-elect three months before. When the plan and its cuts to union bargaining were explained, there was concern from the more moderate senators over how much opposition the proposal could generate. Several people in the room confirmed the deep unease of those senators, which they expressed after Walker had left. For instance, when conservative Senator Glenn Grothman argued that the controversy over the proposal would quickly dissipate, Senator Dale Schultz insisted that the conflict would be more bitter and costly than they imagined. "Come on, people kill each other's dogs over this shit," Schultz told his colleagues. Growing up not in his rural district but on the near west side of Madison, Schultz had seen the worst of social strife. His family lived near the UW–Madison campus, the site of Vietnam era demonstrations and the August 1970 bombing of Sterling Hall by antiwar radicals that killed postdoctoral researcher Robert Fassnacht. Schultz had delivered newspapers to the Fassnacht home, and Schultz's mother, an attorney, had done some legal work for the widow and children. Schultz remembered the

divisive Hortonville teachers strike of 1974 and had also heard from his wife
and her family about the bitter labor struggles in the 1930s in Kohler near
their home. The senator feared the governor's new plan might lead to some
other ugly outcome for the state.

Elements of the plan had been widely expected, and some were popular
with the general public. These included the requirements to make most public employees pick up at least 12.6 percent of the cost of their health care
premiums and pay half the required contribution to the workers' pensions—
an amount that equaled 5.8 percent of the workers' salaries in 2011. These
cuts were not easy to swallow for rank-and-file workers, particularly for those
with lower incomes. A worker making $50,000 a year would end up losing
about 8.5 percent of his or her take-home pay, according to an analysis by
the Legislature's budget office. A worker making $25,000 a year—on the very
low end of government workers—would end up losing a larger share of his
or her take-home pay, about 11.3 percent.

The governor also met with the Assembly Republican caucus to present
the budget-repair bill. Nearly half the caucus had been first elected just three
months earlier in the Tea Party wave, and the group largely backed Walker's
plan. As Jeff Fitzgerald pointed out later, some lawmakers had wanted to go
even further than the governor. But a few were wary, if not outright opposed.
Among them were Representatives Dick Spanbauer of Oshkosh and Dean
Kaufert of Neenah, who sat together during the presentation. Both represented
areas with a strong union presence. A number of Spanbauer's constituents
worked at three nearby prisons, and he knew some of them personally because he had spent seventeen years as a volunteer assistant to a prison chaplain. The son of a factory worker, Spanbauer had always viewed unions as a
way of giving people a voice in their workplaces. As Walker spoke, Spanbauer
felt a physical reaction—an actual pain in his chest. The governor and Assembly leaders warned those present to be braced for nasty e-mails and pickets,
but told them it would last only two or three weeks. Spanbauer knew they
were in for a much longer fight. "I looked at Dean and said, 'That man does
not understand what he has done,'" Spanbauer recalled later.

The union provisions weren't the end of Walker's bill, however. There
were also other controversial details that were completely new to the lawmakers, like a provision authorizing the no-bid sale of state power plants.
That provision later drew the attention of the public as well, raising questions
about whether corporate interests might be seeking to force a bad bargain on
state taxpayers. On the one hand, the state's power plants were decades old—

outdated, mostly coal-burning plants that had attracted criticism for belching pollution into their predominantly urban surroundings. Given the expensive upgrades they needed, the plants were not so much assets as liabilities, something the taxpayers would be happy to sell at almost any price. On the other hand, if the state sold its power plants, the buyer presumably would be in a position to push future price increases on the state for its heating and cooling needs. That could turn a short-term advantage into a long-term loss for the state.

The bill also swept into a range of other critical areas, such as Medicaid health programs that covered more than a million needy state residents. These programs, jointly administered and paid for by the state and federal government, were big contributors to Wisconsin's budget troubles. Medicaid, at nearly $7 billion in state and federal money a year, had grown more quickly in Wisconsin between December 2000 and December 2009 than in any other state in the nation except Arizona, driven by high unemployment and decisions made by governors and lawmakers of both parties to expand eligibility. Because of the skyrocketing costs and the end of extra federal money provided through the economic stimulus law, the program faced a roughly $1.7 billion shortfall over the coming two and a half years. Walker had a simple solution: giving his administration the ability to reshape the state's programs providing medical care for the poor, prescription drug plans for seniors, nursing home care for the elderly, and long-term care for the elderly and disabled outside of nursing homes. The move had some precedents. Two years earlier, Doyle's administration had been authorized by Democratic lawmakers to find hundreds of millions of dollars of savings, though not the power to drop participants. Even if state lawmakers approved Walker's proposal, President Barack Obama's administration would still need to sign off on most changes to the program. But that was small comfort to Democrats and advocates for the poor.

For decades, Wisconsin governors of both parties had used bills dealing with the budget as vehicles to further their power, and Walker didn't shrink from his opportunity. For instance, the bill would make political appointments out of some three dozen civil-service positions. The positions—chief legal counsel, public information officer, and legislative liaison—helped the agencies develop, lobby for, and defend the administration's positions. Those workers also had the charge of making state government transparent, handling many of the records requests from the public, and answering questions from reporters and lawmakers. Many, if not most, of these posts had been stacked over time with Democrats loyal to Doyle. Turning the positions into appointments would allow Walker to move his own people into those jobs at once—and quickly dump them if they displeased him. Finally, the bill would also refinance state bonds to push principal payments on that debt into the future. That would free up cash that could be used to help pay the $59 million owed to Minnesota following the breakdown of an income tax agreement covering citizens who work across state lines.

When Walker's meeting with the senators ended, the sobered Republicans headed back downstairs to the Senate floor. Along the way they tried and mostly succeeded in evading questions from the reporters clustered outside the Senate chamber, but a few stopped to give their reactions. Glenn Grothman, one of those who favored right-to-work legislation, said he would have liked to see an even bolder plan. "It's about time," he said. "It's not as far I'd go, but it's about time."

Luther Olsen wasn't so sure. The Republican from Ripon said he could support the changes on pensions and health care but had reservations about taking away other bargaining rights. "It affects a lot of good working people," Olsen said.

Moderate Republican senators like Olsen had the ability to block Walker's union-bargaining provisions, but they could no longer negotiate without publicly disagreeing with a governor who was extremely popular within their party. Now that the bill was being introduced to the public, they had lost their best chance to change it.

6

Laboratory of Democracy

T HE NEXT MORNING, A PAIR OF DEMOCRATIC LAWMAKERS strode
through the first floor of the Capitol's east wing. It was 9:30 a.m. on
Friday, February 11, and Assembly Minority Leader Peter Barca, Senate Minority Leader Mark Miller, and their chiefs of staff were headed to see
the governor. They had been hearing rumors that week that Walker's budget-
repair bill would hit unions hard. The day before, Barca had run into some
union officials in the statehouse and found them deeply depressed. This
meeting with Walker was the second scheduled for that week—another sign
something was up. The previous evening, news had broken about Walker's
plans, and the two Democrats had been stunned by the details. The minority
leaders were going to get an early briefing about the plan from Walker himself before the bill was made public later that morning.

The Democratic leaders had been thrown together by the crisis. Barca said
later that it was as if the two men had gone to bed the night of the November
2010 election as cousins and awakened as brothers. Barca, the younger of
the two at fifty-five, nevertheless had had a longer career in politics. With a
short stature and a giant plastic cup of diet soda or water with him at all
times, the Kenosha County native at the time looked and acted more like an
actuary than the firebrand he would soon prove to be in debates. He had
served in the Assembly once before, from 1985 to 1993, when he was elected
to Congress in a special election. When he lost his re-election two years later,
President Bill Clinton appointed Barca to the U.S. Small Business Administration, where he served as the administrator of the Midwest region and the
national ombudsman. He returned to elected office by winning a seat back in

the Assembly in 2008 and emerged as minority leader for the Democrats after the disastrous election of 2010.

Born in Boston but raised almost entirely in the Madison area, Miller had just turned sixty-eight and had silver hair and a grandfather's demeanor. Miller, who now lived in the Madison suburb of Monona, was a former fighter pilot in the Wisconsin Air National Guard. He retired after three decades of service in planes like the F-102 fighter interceptor and the A-10 Thunderbolt, but he had a self-effacing manner and none of a pilot's supposed swagger. In civilian life, Miller had been an executive in a property management company who had been responsible for as many as ninety people. It had been a surprise to some that the soft-spoken senator had been chosen by his colleagues as the minority leader after the 2010 elections, but Miller did have a political pedigree. He had served on the Dane County Board for four years before being elected to the Assembly and then the Senate. He benefited from having a stepmother who had been a giant in liberal politics in Madison, the former state representative and antiwar activist Midge Miller. Mark Miller's diffident, straight-arrow persona didn't lend itself to tough negotiations, but it did help him come across as less Machiavellian than his predecessor, Russ Decker, whose political maneuvering was legendary.

Miller and Barca walked past the police guard and intern outside Walker's office and into the large main room in the governor's suite. To either side were leather couches and chairs, and beyond that secretaries, schedulers, and young aides at fine, wooden desks. The walls were adorned with filigrees and wooden wainscoting, and two massive square columns clad in wood bore up the ceiling. To the right, an elegant staircase descended to the lieutenant governor's office. On the other side of the large room was the door leading to the governor's private office. It too was richly appointed, with a beautiful wooden armoire, lights in wall sconces, a small desk, a great wooden table, and a plaque declaring "Wisconsin is open for business." The governor greeted them, and they sat down at the table. Walker first apologized for the lawmakers learning about the bill from the media before he could tell them. Explaining the plan, he touted the cost savings to be gained for taxpayers by curtailing collective bargaining, saying aggressive action was needed to close the state's budget deficits. During the conversation, he sought to reassure the lawmakers that he was prepared for every contingency, telling them he had consulted with the National Guard for a couple of months about ensuring that government would keep running smoothly in the event of problems, presumably work stoppages in prisons and other state institutions. That did little to calm the

Democrats. When Barca countered that Walker had not mentioned a word of such a radical proposal during his campaign, the governor took exception, saying he had talked on the campaign trail about being bold and cutting employees' benefits. But Barca, who grew up just outside a city with a strong union presence, was unmoved. "You're making a huge mistake, and this is going to be met with massive resistance," the Democrat said.

Miller was likewise aghast. As a former supervisor in both the National Guard and the real estate firm, he believed employees should have input in their jobs. As a senator, he believed the state should be an exemplary employer and saw this as an unacceptable move away from that. He also expected a fight. "You're going to blow up the state," Miller told the governor. Walker acknowledged the move would be controversial but said it was needed. "It's tough times," Walker told the Democrats. "The public expects this." The three men said later that they were prepared for a battle, but all of them were still taken by surprise by the furor that soon erupted.

Barca told Walker that he had thought the governor shared his value of protecting the middle class. He said he understood the cuts to workers' pension and health benefits but questioned why the governor felt it necessary to abolish their bargaining power. Walker pointed to his experience serving as the Milwaukee County executive and the positions taken by the unions of county workers, giving examples of the times he'd been blocked at the negotiating table. Demands over workplace conditions and other bargaining issues add up to money for taxpayers, he told the Democrats. The meeting lasted perhaps twenty or thirty minutes.

Though they didn't predict the overwhelming demonstrations at the Capitol, Barca and Miller had good reason to expect a fight. Miller grew up in the heart of Dane County with family members who were public workers. Barca grew up the son of an Italian immigrant in the shadow of Kenosha's American Motors plant. Many members of his blue-collar family had union jobs there, and Barca knew how important unions had been for generations in their manufacturing-dependent state. The Democrats were also aware of Wisconsin's long history of labor organizing and of legislation focused on workers. The state was home to Progressive Republican leaders like Robert La Follette Sr., a liberal lion who served first as governor and later as one of the most influential U.S. senators in the nation's history. With his mane of hair combed back from his forehead and his fist in the air, La Follette earned the nickname "Fighting Bob" during tireless campaigning across the state and nation for progressive causes. An uncompromising opponent of political bosses, World War I, and powerful interests like railroads, La Follette practiced a populist brand of politics that shifted power to voters. He helped institute open primaries to elevate popular candidates and helped lay the groundwork for recall elections to unseat unpopular politicians. For him, unions served as one more check on the power of large corporations. La Follette failed in many of his grand designs, such as running for president in 1924 as a candidate for the Progressive Party calling for government ownership of railroads. It was also worth remembering, as his nickname suggested, that La Follette generated more than his share of controversy, but he made a lasting mark on the state and nation.

With the help of labor groups and La Follette Progressives, the Wisconsin Legislature in 1911 passed the nation's first workers' compensation law to aid those injured at their jobs. Theodore Roosevelt said that Wisconsin had become "literally a laboratory for wise experimental legislation to secure the social and political betterment of the people as a whole." Twenty-one years later in the midst of the Great Depression, unions also led the way in getting the state to pass the nation's first unemployment insurance legislation. Several months later, in that same year of 1932, a group formed in Madison with the clunky name of the Wisconsin State Association of Administrative, Clerical, Fiscal, and Technical Employees. When the evolving union changed its charter and name in 1936 to the American Federation of State, County, and Municipal Employees, the new moniker sounded almost snappy by comparison. At first, the union existed to protect the state's civil service system, according to a book about the state's labor movement by UW–Madison economist Robert W. Ozanne. The union received much of its early support from state personnel workers such as Arnold Zander, the state's senior personnel examiner. The union got strong backing from a Progressive Republican governor, Fighting Bob's son Philip La Follette, and faced its first challenge opposing a power grab by Democrats.

A landslide election in 1932 turned Philip La Follette out of office and put Democrats in charge of the state for the first time in almost forty years. When Democrats sought to roll back the state's 1905 civil service system and open the way for more political patronage, Zander and the public workers' union led a successful effort to save the law. After that, Ozanne writes, the union grew quickly, becoming a national force with Zander at its head until 1966. For more than two decades, it also kept its national headquarters in Madison before moving the main office to Washington, D.C., in 1957, and by 1958 it had 185,000 members. By the 1940s the union was already working with economists and graduate students from UW–Madison to achieve political victories like a state retirement system and automatic increases in state wages. As the law professor Joseph Slater notes, the union shifted from a focus on the civil service to one on gaining formal recognition and bargaining powers. Wisconsin had already been at the forefront of progressive changes in the country, such as providing academic leaders who helped craft the federal Social Security system. Now it became a pioneer in public employee unions.

When AFSCME came into being, it was still a novel idea that state and local government employees, from teachers to police officers and garbage workers, could have the same rights to bargain with their employers as private-sector welders and construction workers. No less a Democrat than President Franklin D. Roosevelt had expressed concerns about public employee unions in 1937, a year after AFSCME took its present name—a fact Walker seized on in the coming weeks of the Madison protests. Roosevelt said that such unions couldn't take the same approach or militancy given that their "employer is the whole people, who speak by means of laws enacted by their representatives in Congress." The federal Wagner Act of 1935, the landmark National Labor Relations Act that helped pave the way for private-sector unions to expand, didn't apply to public-sector unions. It took state and local employees decades before they achieved the same recognition in Wisconsin, and when they did they would lead the nation.

Around the country, private-sector unions flourished and grew in the 1930s, '40s, and '50s. Gradually, government employee unions began to sprout up as well, formed by teachers in various cities and by the employees of New York City, who won certain bargaining rights in 1958. In 1951 labor leaders helped introduce in the Wisconsin Legislature a bill that would have protected public employees seeking to join a union. Labor historians like Slater found that the attorney and labor leader John Lawton had written the legislation, which academics saw as part of a process of unions gaining support for making their status official. It's worth noting, given how much Walker's critics in the labor movement later questioned whether his bill had been written by a special interest group outside of state government. The Lawton measure passed but was vetoed by Republican Governor Walter Kohler Jr., who came from an influential family of industrialists whose company had clashed with labor groups over the years. The next time such a bill was passed, in 1959, Democratic Governor Gaylord Nelson—a former lawyer for AFSCME and former partner to Lawton—readily signed it. The rise of public unions in Wisconsin mirrored that of the Democratic Party in the state and the ascent of its leaders such as Nelson, who went on to become a U.S. Senator and the founder of Earth Day. As Slater noted, public unions tended to be politically active. After all, their members worked in government and were directly affected by decisions made about it.

Other states had pockets of public employees who had won the ability to bargain collectively for their wages and working conditions. But the legislation made Wisconsin the first state where all municipal employees had such an opportunity. The law protected municipal workers who chose to join a union from being fired or treated unfairly, though it stopped short of requiring local governments to bargain with them. That requirement came two years later, and in 1965 lawmakers gave state workers some bargaining power as well. In 1972 public employees got the ability to reach fair share agreements requiring employees to pay dues to a union even if they chose not to belong to it. In the early 1970s harsh conflicts, like a teachers strike in Hortonville, led the state to ban strikes and create binding arbitration to resolve impasses between labor groups and public employers.

Over this period, public-sector unions swelled in numbers. By 1972 the Wisconsin Education Association Council and AFSCME had become some of the state's largest unions, rivaling the biggest of their private-sector brethren. Public employee unions loomed even larger in the succeeding decades, in which factories and private unions declined in Wisconsin and nationwide. The overall share of workers in the country who belonged to unions declined from 20.1 percent in 1983 to 11.8 percent in 2011, according to federal statistics. By 2009 the number of private-sector employees in unions nationwide had fallen below that of public-sector union workers. In 2011 in Wisconsin, 13.3 percent of employees overall belonged to a union, higher than the national average but not leading the country. This worked out to about 339,000 workers, a sizable minority in a state of 5.7 million people but one that was steadily shrinking. Public employees had been the last ones to arrive at the party for organized labor, but in this state as elsewhere they were becoming some of the few remaining guests. During the 2011 budget battle, the story of Wisconsin as a labor leader gained great prominence in the national media, the labor movement, and political groups on both sides. If Walker could defeat public employees in their birthplace, the argument went, that would spell further decline for labor throughout the nation.

Still, there was another side to the Badger State than simply a nursery for organized labor. Wisconsin was a swing state and a state of political insurgents, a place where some Republicans once called themselves Progressives, and where this group competed in elections against more conservative candidates from both the Democratic and Republican parties. This made the state a place of setbacks as well as victories for organized labor. After a big election win in 1936 the short-lived Progressive Party took control of state government and set to overcoming immense opposition to push through a "Little Wagner Act." Often referred to by the name of its sponsor, U.S. Senator Robert Wagner of New York, the 1935 National Labor Relations Act and its Wisconsin counterpart gave unions greater protections for their organizing efforts. Prompted in part by a popular backlash, the next Wisconsin election, in 1938, became a kind of precursor to Walker's triumph generations later. A conservative businessman from Milwaukee, Julius Heil, took back the governorship and a working Republican majority in the Legislature. As Ozanne relates in his book, the Little Wagner Act and other labor laws were rolled back, and a new piece of legislation, the Wisconsin Employment Peace Act, was put in place to sharply restrict unions. That law was a forerunner to the federal Taft-Hartley Act of a decade later, which like the Wisconsin law prohibited certain kinds of strikes and a range of other "unfair labor practices." As Ozanne puts it, "Thus Wisconsin, noted for its progressive and pro-labor legislation, became for a time a national leader in anti-labor legislation." In the 1950s Republicans passed the Catlin Act, a law that prohibited unions from making political contributions using membership dues. In 1959 Democrats regained enough power to repeal the law.

The biggest symbol of the conservative, even at times reactionary, strain in Wisconsin politics was U.S. Senator Joseph McCarthy. A former Marine, McCarthy won his way into the Senate by waging a nasty but effective fight against Fighting Bob's namesake son, Robert La Follette Jr., in the 1946 Republican primary. McCarthy attacked "Young Bob" for not having volunteered for World War II, even though La Follette was forty-six when Pearl Harbor was bombed. After several uneventful years in the Senate, McCarthy made headlines for himself by attacking Americans for alleged communist ties. McCarthy went too far, was censured by his fellow senators, and died a broken man at forty-eight. His career served as a reminder that in the politics of Wisconsin and Washington, D.C., leaders could rocket skyward and there, at their zenith, explode.

As Barca, Miller, and Walker met in the statehouse where leaders like Philip La Follette had worked, they all knew at some level that they were at a pivotal point for Wisconsin. None of the trio spoke of it at the time, but all three knew public employees and unions were among the most critical backers of Democrats in both money and volunteers. Nearly one out of every five dollars raised by Democratic senators in the 2008 and 2010 election cycles came from public employees and their unions, a *Milwaukee Journal Sentinel* analysis of campaign records found. And of the nearly $7 million labor unions had contributed to state candidates in Wisconsin over the last six election cycles, ninety-three cents of every dollar had gone to a Democrat, a separate *Wisconsin State Journal* review found. For public employees, it was seventy-three cents. More significantly, they bankrolled independent ads to help Democratic campaigns, either by producing them themselves or by donating funds to liberal groups like the Greater Wisconsin Committee. Unions also helped groups such as One Wisconsin Now, which sought to dig up unpleasant facts on Republican leaders and policies while advancing its own left-wing agenda. Labor groups likewise paid for other activities important to Democrats, such as lawsuits over maps of legislative districts and other political issues. This phenomenon had intensified over time as the agendas of labor unions and Republicans grew ever farther apart. And that made unions the Democrats' most reliable allies—and by extension the GOP's most consistent enemies. "It's very simple," said Richard Abelson, executive director of AFSCME District Council 48. "We have interests, and because of that, we attempt to support candidates who support our interests. It's pretty hard to find Republicans who support our interests these days."

As soon as Walker unveiled his proposal on February 11, 2011, Democrats charged that the governor was seeking to crush not only unions but their party. Up until that time, the flow of donations had been smooth. Public-worker unions, once organized, were able to secure contracts with employers requiring workers in their units to pay dues. Employees in a unionized work unit could choose not to join the union, but they would still have to make fair share payments that amounted to almost as much as normal dues. By shutting off that spigot of dues, and thus donations, Republicans were doing more than simply changing the way that government worked—they were also helping themselves politically. Later on in the conflict over the bill, the Senate majority leader, Scott Fitzgerald, helped bolster this Democratic charge when he said that President Obama would have a "much more difficult time" getting elected in Wisconsin without union money. Other Republicans responded that they weren't pursuing the bill for political reasons. Walker repeatedly said he wanted to give public employees a choice about union dues and a chance to recover some of the additional money being taken out of their paychecks for benefits.

Vulnerable as the unions were, no one would have mistaken them for being defenseless. They had at their disposal protests, pickets, sickouts, strikes, television ads, letters to the editor, marches, and, above all, the ballot box. The unions were cornered, and any Capitol veteran knew that they would fight for survival, which was the reason that Walker tried to reassure Barca and Miller by telling them he was working with the National Guard. The worst potential danger was a strike by correctional officers at a prison. The possibility seemed so real in those weeks leading up to Walker's unveiling of the bill that a few former high-level state officials had taken to speculating that the Waupun Correctional Institution was the prison most likely to see a strike. As one of them put it, Waupun was "straight out of central casting," a Gothic Revival–style maximum-security prison that housed murderers and had been in operation since before the Civil War. Conveniently, the prison was relatively close to Madison, Milwaukee, and the Fox Valley, which would make it easier for television news crews from the state's largest media markets to broadcast any crisis to voters. Union members insisted they never contemplated such a drastic step as a strike at the prison, and they certainly never took such an action, but Walker wasn't taking that for granted. The budget-repair legislation itself had provisions in it to deal with such unrest. The legislation provided that if the governor declared a state of emergency, the state could fire any employee who participated in a strike, work stoppage, or other action designed to disrupt the operations of government, or fire any employee who failed to report to work as scheduled for three days without an excuse. In February 2011 National Guard members in plainclothes toured at least one state prison.

The provisions of the budget-repair bill, however, revealed a crucial assumption in Walker's plan—that Republicans would be able to pass the legislation by the time any work actions hit and then use the provisions of the new law to deal with it. Two days before Walker met with Barca and Miller, an aide to the governor e-mailed GOP colleagues a timeline showing that Walker's office wanted to pass the bill within a week of publicly announcing it. Passing a budget-repair bill in just days was blindingly fast for the Legislature, although it had happened before for repair bills, such as the one that Democrats passed two years before. The timeline called for Walker to unveil the bill on Friday, February 11. It would then be formally introduced in the Legislature on Monday, February 14, have a budget committee hearing the next day, be voted out of the committee on Wednesday, and then pass both the Senate and Assembly by Friday, February 18. For most of the next week, Walker and GOP lawmakers kept to this ambitious timeline, trusting it to help control the controversy over the plan. But what would happen if Republicans couldn't pass the measure quickly? The question was more than academic, for Miller and Barca would soon discuss a plan that would blow up Walker's timetable.

7

First Protests

CLUSTERED IN TWOS, THREES, AND FOURS, university students marched up State Street over the noon hour. Spray-painted on a banner that led their parade was "This Is What Democracy Looks Like"— a phrase that became an anthem in the weeks and months ahead. That bright, clear February 14 they gave their demonstration a Valentine's Day theme by chanting, "Spread the love! Stop the hate! Don't let Walker legislate!" Most wore coats and hats, but some found it warm enough—it was unusually nice weather, in the low forties—to march in nothing heavier than a sweatshirt. "Hey, hey, ho, ho, union busting's got to go," they called as they made their way up the mile-long pedestrian street that connects the UW–Madison campus to the Capitol. One marcher waved a large union flag bearing the logo of the Teaching Assistants' Association, while others carried homemade signs. When they arrived, they were greeted on the Capitol steps by Peter Rickman, an unshaven law student from Neenah and a leader of the assistants union who wore a red-and-black-checked hunting jacket. "Let's show Governor Walker that we will stand up for our university and the people that make it work," he told the crowd and led them, chanting, inside the Capitol.

Security had been strengthened there, and officers refused to allow placards on sticks inside for safety reasons. The protesters planted their signs in snowbanks beside the entrances. "Worker Rights Are Human Rights!" was scrawled in marker on one of the signs. Others were professionally printed with phrases like "Solidarity" and "Care About Educators Like They Care About Your Child." The chants of the demonstrators reached a crescendo as they entered the rotunda. Their cheers and claps reverberated off the marble walls, driving one protester to wedge her fingers into her ears. Another held a sign drawn in marker that showed the university's mascot, Bucky Badger, holding a placard that read "Kill This Bill." A red helium balloon bobbed above the crowd as one protester held aloft a giant cardboard heart that read "I ♥ UW." Many shed their coats to reveal Badger red sweatshirts and T-shirts. "Kill this bill, kill this bill," they chanted—another phrase that would echo through the Capitol for weeks to come.

The rally had been planned even before Walker unveiled his proposal on collective bargaining and had been originally meant to oppose expected budget cuts to the university. Rickman and other organizers refocused their aims after news of Walker's plans broke, and their efforts bolstered the crowd to about a thousand people. The students filled the floor of the rotunda, with others on upper floors jamming up against the marble railings that overlooked the ground level. Shoulder to shoulder, they filled the broad hallway in the east wing that leads to the governor's office and demanded to speak with Walker. The governor's press secretary, Cullen Werwie, told Rickman that appointments with the governor—who had spent the morning discussing his bill with conservative radio talk show hosts around Wisconsin—had to be arranged in advance. Using his megaphone, Rickman then told the crowd Walker wouldn't meet with them and asked them to pass forward the overflowing boxes of valentines they had brought. Rickman and others spread the valentines across the top of the security desk outside the governor's office. "I ♥ UW. Governor Walker, Don't Break My ♥," many read. They piled them so high they slid off the desk as the crowd whooped. Rickman pulled out a red heart-shaped plastic bowl full of candy hearts and gave it to Werwie, who popped a couple of them into his mouth. "Kill the bill," the crowd chanted.

The gathering at the Capitol wasn't the only demonstration that day. Protesters also gathered on the UW–Milwaukee campus, at a state office building in Milwaukee, and near the Racine home of Van Wanggaard, a newly elected GOP senator. From the beginning, unions organized feverishly to stop Walker's bill. Stephanie Bloomingdale, secretary-treasurer of the Wisconsin AFL-CIO, found out about the legislation when it leaked on Thursday, February 10. She got the news on her BlackBerry in Michigan City, Indiana, where she was speaking to "Women of Steel," a conference of female members of the United Steelworkers union. Bloomingdale stayed up most of the night making plans and calling other union leaders. "We immediately began to organize that very minute," she said. "We resolved to fight back each and every way possible."

More than a thousand Wisconsin Education Association Council volunteers called teachers around the state that weekend, making sure that calls were made to every member of the union. Labor groups pushed members to contact lawmakers and provided phone numbers and e-mail addresses. The Wisconsin AFL-CIO did its own mobilizing of members by e-mail and automated phone calls to let them know about the bill as well as rallies that would be held in Madison starting Tuesday of the following week, when the Joint Finance Committee would hold its public hearing on the measure. On Saturday, another labor official asked Bloomingdale what the legislative strategy was to stop the bill. She answered that she wasn't sure and decided to pull together all the available labor lawyers to figure it out. Union officials called around, and the next day, Sunday, February 13, a score of attorneys gathered at the AFL-CIO's Milwaukee office. They hashed out strategies for blocking the bill in the Legislature and suing to strike it down if it made it through to Walker for his signature. Also on Sunday, the AFL-CIO launched radio and television ads accusing Republicans of attacking workers' rights. By Monday, February 14, many legislators had full voice-mail boxes and more e-mails than their staffs could handle. Senator Jon Erpenbach, a Dane County Democrat with many state workers in his district, received about 1,400 e-mails and more than 120 voice messages over that weekend. Also on Monday, labor leaders held a press conference near the Capitol in which two dozen officials from both private- and public-sector unions voiced their united opposition to the bill. "It was the most powerful speaking out that I've ever been a part of," Bloomingdale said.

It wasn't by accident that the private-sector unions had been able to organize so quickly. The AFL-CIO had started holding meetings with labor leaders weeks earlier in anticipation that Walker would move against them. That made it easier to respond quickly once the governor unveiled his plans, said Marty Beil, executive director of the Wisconsin State Employees Union. The unions representing electrical workers, laborers, steelworkers, and others made clear right away they were standing with the public-sector unions, according to Beil. "The private-sector guys said, 'This is a prelude to right-to-work. It's right-to-work for the public sector,'" Beil said. Within days, a broad spectrum of Wisconsin unions formed a "labor table" that met twice daily in a room at the Concourse Hotel across the street from the Capitol to develop plans and exchange information. Soon, national union officials were in town to assist with polling and messaging as well as to speak at rallies. Polls were conducted every two or three days, Beil said.

Walker hadn't been idle either. After the meeting with Barca and Miller on Friday, February 11, Walker unveiled his proposal at a crowded news conference and then promoted it every way he could that day. He visited the editorial boards of the *Wisconsin State Journal* and the *Appleton Post-Crescent*, appeared at a Wisconsin Builders Association event, and spoke by phone with the *New York Times*, the *Milwaukee Journal Sentinel* editorial board, state senators, and Republican Congressman Jim Sensenbrenner of Menomonee Falls. "Our boss is a machine," one staffer on the trip gushed to other Walker aides in an e-mail that evening. Over the weekend, the governor made more calls to state lawmakers to shore up support for the bill; then on Monday Walker countered the college students' protest and union news conference by addressing reporters in the governor's conference room. An ornate chamber of rich, dark wood panels adorned with epic paintings, it would be packed with journalists many times over the coming weeks. Walker took his place before the cameras in front of two American flags, two Wisconsin flags, and one of the room's huge murals. The usual Capitol press corps was in attendance but not the pack of national reporters who would soon travel to Wisconsin. The governor said the benefit cuts for public workers were essential to balancing the state budget in the short and long term. He stressed that his proposal would prevent thousands of layoffs and argued that the general public supported such changes. The other collective bargaining changes—such as making dues voluntary and requiring annual certification votes—would let workers choose whether to be in a union, he said. "That's free choice," Walker said. "That's the American way. It's true democracy."

On Tuesday, February 15, the Legislature's Joint Finance Committee was to hold what was expected to be a daylong hearing on the bill, and the members of the budget panel were to vote at the conclusion of it. With it now clear that the committee hearing room could not hold all the people who would want to attend, state workers installed 42-inch flat screen televisions along the second-floor railings overlooking the rotunda so visitors could watch them from the floors below. Braced for potential work stoppages or other job actions, managers at state agencies also began reporting their absence rates to the Department of Administration; but the state unions never called on their members to leave work, and the state never suffered from staffing shortages. They had little time, but labor leaders believed they could stop or at least rewrite the bill in committee, and they turned their attention to eight Republicans— Mike Ellis, Dale Schultz, Rob Cowles, Dan Kapanke, Luther Olsen, Sheila Harsdorf, Randy Hopper, and Van Wanggaard.

Buses organized by AFSCME unloaded workers from around the state at the Capitol. Over the course of the morning, the crowd grew until it was at least 13,000 strong. They circled the building and crowded its hallways, chanting, drumming, and yelling. Using blue painter's tape, they attached hundreds of handmade posters to the walls of the statehouse urging legislators to stop Walker's plan. "Never did we think those first two lobby days we'd see that many people," Beil said more than a year later. By 11 a.m., the crowd filled the Capitol grounds all the way out to State Street. Workers, many of them in green AFSCME shirts, marched around the partially snow-covered grounds while others with drums pounded away. Homemade signs poked up from the crowd. Some mocked Walker for not having a college degree; others urged people to "Stop the Imperial Walker," riffing on the elephantine robots from *The Empire Strikes Back*. Many placards drew parallels to the uprisings in Egypt and other Arab countries: "Hosni Walker, Wisconsin Dictator, Must Go," said one. From a table near the Capitol, volunteers handed out signs to people who hadn't brought their own. A semitrailer with "Teamsters" emblazoned on its side roared down Mifflin Street in front of the Capitol, honking its horn to cheers from the crowd. A public address system blasted Twisted Sister's "We're Not Gonna Take It" and Credence Clearwater Revival's "Fortunate Son." The crowd sang along, pumping fists in the air. One group in the crowd also yelled "Recall!" while another group immediately responded "Walker!"

"We know what this is all about," AFSCME International's president, Gerald McEntee, told the crowd on the Capitol lawn. "It's about breaking the back of the middle class. It's about making sure the only people who have a say in American politics are the well heeled and the politically connected."

The protests would go on for a month without major incidents. Law enforcement and Democrats repeatedly praised the crowds for remaining overwhelmingly peaceful in spite of their heated emotions. Republicans, however, saw the huge gatherings differently, viewing the demonstrators as hostile and often sensing at least the possibility of violence. "When I've got to have five cops get me out of the building, that ain't peaceful," Ellis said more than a year after the Capitol occupation. On the first day of major protests, J.B. Van Hollen, the Republican attorney general who would later be responsible for defending the collective bargaining changes in court, had parked his car at the Capitol. When he went to his vehicle, the crowd berated him and spat on him. It took a dozen officers to part the crowd so he could pull away as demonstrators screamed at him and beat on his car. From then on, Van Hollen relied on an underground tunnel to get into the Capitol.

The unions' attempts to get Republicans weren't limited to public rallies—they also happened in private meetings. One of AFSCME's lobbyists, Tim Hoven, was a Republican who spent eight years in the Assembly. As the protests ramped up, he and other AFSCME representatives met with Scott Fitzgerald to urge the Legislature to keep collective bargaining intact. They were willing to accept the higher pension and health care payments, but they asked that collective bargaining otherwise be left alone. Fitzgerald felt the unions could have agreed to a deal like that in the past rather than trying as they had in December to push through contracts with fewer concessions before the changeover in party control of the Legislature. "It's too late," he told them. "You had your chance."

In the Capitol that Tuesday, groups milled about, chatted, and watched the large televisions mounted above as the clerk called the roll for the Joint Finance Committee. Soon the crowd filled every available spot on the ground floor of the Capitol, as well as the areas of the two floors above it that overlooked the rotunda, as police patrolled around them.

The governor continued to travel the state, making the case for his bill at stops in Green Bay, Wausau, Eau Claire, and La Crosse. Protesters greeted him wherever he went, including some in La Crosse who surrounded his SUV and pounded on it. That night, hundreds gathered outside Walker's suburban Milwaukee home to protest. In the meantime, more law enforcement arrived to help the Capitol Police, including state troopers, UW–Madison police officers, and Department of Natural Resources wardens. They guarded stairwells, roped off some corridors, and stood outside the office of Scott Fitzgerald, where staff had posted a sign saying visitors now needed an appointment "due to threats of personal violence against certain legislators."

As the Joint Finance Committee held its public hearing, there were indications that the protests were failing. Mike Ellis, the Senate president who had sought to tone down the proposal behind the scenes, told the Associated Press that Republicans had the seventeen votes needed in the Senate to pass the bill. Democrats simply didn't have enough votes to stop the bill in the Assembly, so if the proposal passed in the Senate it would almost certainly become law. "They've got the votes to pass it," Ellis said from the hallway outside his Capitol office. "We're broke and we don't want to lay off almost twenty thousand people." In a blow to opponents, Ellis stated that he would vote for the bill, even though he would have preferred an alternative. "We didn't set this menu," Ellis said. "The governor did."

The large, open room where the budget committee met was inelegant compared to most parts of the Capitol, looking like a hotel conference room. There were about a hundred simple chairs for the public, normally more than enough. The lawmakers sat in a semicircle before them on a dais, with the committee co-chairs, Representative Robin Vos and Senator Alberta Darling, in the middle. A crowd rapidly filled the hearing room, and a long, orderly line formed outside. Some people held up signs and others chatted or scanned their smartphones for news and Twitter updates. They filled out slips of paper stating that they wished to testify, creating a list of hundreds of people who would wait for hours to speak for a couple of minutes to the twelve Republicans and four Democrats on the committee. The crowd included state workers, cops, firefighters, laborers from the building trades, university students, and, once school let out, a surge of teachers. Committee testimony started with Mike Huebsch, Walker's administration secretary. "We have nothing to give" employees, he said. "The state's broke."

Also testifying early on was Sanna Huebschmann of Chilton, who with her husband ran Sunny Hill Enterprises, which made rifle accessories. The couple had stopped taking a salary in the midst of the recession so they could pay their employees. "Significant cuts have to be made," she said. "I feel this is a wonderful start and the best way to avoid [layoffs]." But after that, almost all the testimony came from opponents of the bill. Public employees said they knew the state was in a bind and were willing to sacrifice some of their benefits, but stressed that they had difficult jobs and deserved to keep their bargaining rights. Some warned lawmakers they would face recalls if they went through with Walker's plan. Some in the labor community worried about that early chatter about recalls, fearing it could undermine their lobbying effort to scale back the bill. More than seven hours into the hearing, at 5:20 p.m., Jamie Domini slid behind the table where the public was giving its testimony. She wore a dark blue T-shirt with the iconic labor image of a large fish being chased by a school of small fish swimming together to form a giant fish. Domini told the panel she was a civics teacher at a Madison school and the daughter of AFSCME's state political director. "I would like to thank Governor Walker for this opportunity for unions to rally together and be as one. . . . You have united the unions in this state and I don't think you've even come close to seeing what is going to happen as a result of this action," she said. Domini told the committee she was glad her students could witness democracy firsthand and connect with it in their daily lives, rather than just reading about what was happening halfway around the world in Egypt. "I came here at ten o'clock in the morning and I'm just testifying now, so any of you listening, you've got a long wait," she said. "But stay here because this is a citizens' filibuster. As long as we stay here and testify, this bill can't get rammed down our throat, which is what is happening. So I'm going to make sure— and I'm sorry—and I'm going to make sure you're here as long as humanly possible because this bill stinks."

Testimony continued, with a stream of public workers from all parts of the state and all sectors of government. Teachers, highway workers, lab technicians: they all came to tell the committee that passing the bill would upend their lives. Around 9 p.m., legislative staff stationed at the doors told the crowd outside that they could no longer sign up to testify, although people who had already signed up could still address the committee. The crowd erupted in chants of "Let us speak, let us speak." Their cries, however, could barely be heard through the double sets of heavy wooden doors that separated them from the hearing room.

"Mr. Co-chair, Mr. Co-chair," Democratic Senator Lena Taylor called out to Vos.

"I will call on you in a second," Vos replied, telling Taylor he wanted to announce the names of the next people to testify. Taylor talked over him. "People are chanting outside, 'Let us speak,' because they have been told they will not be able to speak in this hearing," Taylor boomed. "I am wondering why the rules keep changing in this hearing and that the people of Wisconsin are being denied a right to speak, a right to be heard." The crowd applauded, some of them standing, as Taylor kept trying to speak over the chairman. Vos told Taylor that he was waiting for her to finish her filibuster. Taylor exploded: "It's not a filibuster and you know it. That's BS."

As the argument went back and forth, Darling said that allowing everyone to speak who had signed up so far would take another ten or so hours. The crowd yelled back, saying people deserved to be heard. "It's our whole lives," someone cried. Now Vos told lawmakers and the audience that two years earlier when Democrats were in charge they hadn't held a public hearing on a fast-moving budget-repair bill that included tax increases opposed by Republicans. He said he was trying to let everyone have a say but with three hundred people still on the list of speakers, he was troubled by the notion of opponents simply stalling the process. "Just trying to do a citizen filibuster doesn't necessarily serve your purposes, it doesn't necessarily serve to persuade, and it certainly does not serve to educate the public," he said.

Downstairs, the protests increasingly took on the feel of a rock festival. Friends chatted, students typed on laptops, and others slept. More members of the Teaching Assistants' Association joined the demonstration, and dozens of them rolled out sleeping bags in the rotunda and hallways of the Capitol. Some said they would stage a sit-in if they weren't allowed to testify. At 2:15 a.m., Senator Glenn Grothman hit a button at his desk to indicate he wanted to speak. The prematurely white-haired senator was one of the most conservative and free-thinking members of the Republican caucus, known for his incendiary statements, gruff but affable demeanor, and the "TAXCUTR" vanity plates on his Pontiac Vibe. He delighted in provoking liberals and didn't shrink from bucking his own party, usually—though not always—when he wanted to push his colleagues farther to the right.

"Thanks for calling on me," he said to Vos. "I just wanted to let the folks know I'm going to be leaving now. I have a lot of people who want to talk to me from my district. I appreciate how well spoken everyone was tonight, but I think, you know, between now and the vote I'd rather spend time sleeping now so tomorrow morning I can talk to the dozens of people who wanted to talk to me from my own district." Grothman told the crowd that if anyone submitted written testimony he and his staff would review it the next day. Vos thanked him and said he would adjourn the meeting within the hour. He noted later that the people who were coming up to testify had signed up around 6:15 p.m.—more than eight hours after the meeting had started. "At three o'clock we are going to adjourn the public hearing and we are going to come back tomorrow to vote on the amendments," Vos announced.

When the testimony was cut off at the promised hour, the Democratic lawmakers invited the remaining members of the public to join them downstairs for an impromptu news conference. A hundred or so protesters surrounded them in a loose semicircle. Radio and television reporters aimed their microphones at them. Veteran Democratic Senator Bob Jauch of Poplar, rotund and bleary-eyed, struck a hopeful note. "At three o'clock in the morning, after a daylong hearing, this is the rebirth of the Progressive movement!" he declared to the cheering crowd. "This morning I felt depressed. . . . I told the committee members that I had been to happier funerals. Everybody was really down because they recognized the depth of the moment. At three o'clock in the morning, I feel exhilaration because of your presence. I don't know what the outcome will be in the next two days but we're going to do our very best to make sure the voices surely influence that outcome. But you cannot deny that you have made a difference in all of us."

From there, it was on to a new hearing room, where opponents of the bill spoke through the wee hours about how the bill would affect them. The Capitol normally closes at 6 p.m. but remains open to the public when the Legislature or any of its committees are in session. Because the Democrats informally continued the hearing, police decided on the spot to treat it as an official meeting and kept the doors to the building unlocked, allowing protesters to spend the first of many nights in the building. Buoyed by fresh Democratic lawmakers to replace the exhausted committee members, the informal hearing continued into the next week. From then on, the Walker administration and the police lost some control of the Capitol and didn't fully regain it until the building was cleared through a judge's order two weeks later.

As the next work day started—Wednesday, February 16—the crowds swelled. Many of those flocking to the Capitol were Madison teachers. The district's superintendent had canceled classes after nearly 40 percent of the district's 2,600 teachers had called in sick so they could show up to demonstrate at the statehouse. Some parents were displeased, but others were public employees themselves or supported them, and they didn't mount any great outcry. In fact, some of the parents who had to stay home from their jobs with their children ended up coming to the protests.

Some demonstrators set up a makeshift area where parents could care for children, while others created an information center to tell visitors where the ad hoc hearing was and how to find a particular lawmaker's office or the restrooms. Some affixed signs to the wall reminding people to keep "our house"—the Capitol—clean and others hung posters with slogans opposing Walker with every imaginable argument. Protesters brought food, sometimes to share with strangers. Others poured into nearby restaurants, providing an unexpected jolt to their late winter business. Many munched on pizzas randomly delivered, several boxes at a time, by Ian's Pizza, a restaurant a half block from the Capitol that turned its mission into feeding the masses. Delivery staff marched up State Street to drop off hundreds of pies to the hungry crowds. At the restaurant, the staff handed out free slices to whoever walked in the door regardless of political affiliation. Their operation went viral, and people from every state in the nation and dozens of other countries donated money online to pay for the pizzas. Whenever a donation came in from a new country, workers recorded it on a chalkboard behind the counter, and they let the crowd know when a celebrity had donated. One famous contributor, the actress Susan Sarandon, even dropped by the restaurant later on. Downtown

Madison hotels, restaurants, and bars saw double-digit increases in their business as protesters looked for places to eat, drink, and sleep when they weren't demonstrating.

One insistent chant rose above the others. "This is what democracy looks like!" Its words were shouted out by the demonstrators. Its rhythm was thumped out by ragtag bands with snare drums and overturned buckets and even honked out by the cars circling the Capitol square: "Beep beep BEEP bee-beep bee-beep BEEP BEEP." The call-and-response wound its way into the heads of those who protested or worked in the statehouse—Democrat or Republican—so that it played there in a continuous loop, whether they were at their desks or at home in their beds. "Show me what democracy looks like!" "This is what democracy looks like!" The chants were so catchy that Vos, the GOP budget committee co-chairman, jokingly sang them as he walked into Assembly Speaker Jeff Fitzgerald's office at one point. The cacophony in the Capitol—whether it was from drums, bagpipes, horn, chatter, or chants—echoed off the marbled walls through the days and long into the nights. Often it was as loud as a rock concert or athletic contest, with the noise sometimes hitting 105 decibels.

Into this chaotic scene came Susan Riseling, the longtime chief of the campus police for UW–Madison. An unimposing figure at five foot five with short, dark graying hair, the fifty-year-old officer had for the moment no official role in the crisis though she did have some of her officers on the scene helping out. However, she immediately had ideas about what needed to be done in the building. Riseling was concerned about the overcrowding in the statehouse and surprised that no one else in authority seemed to share her urgency. "The building was way, way, way overcrowded. That to me was dangerous. You could hardly move," Riseling said later.

Riseling was well qualified to assess such a scene. At UW–Madison, she and her officers routinely handled demonstrations by students—like those who were part of the group protesting at the Capitol—as well as rowdy crowds of football fans who often reached more than 80,000 in nearby Camp Randall stadium, with tens of thousands of more outside. Tragedy had taught Riseling the need to handle such crowds with care. Following an October 30, 1993, win over the Michigan Wolverines, celebrating UW–Madison students had sought to storm the field. The first students were blocked by a guardrail and crushed and trampled as their unwitting peers in the stands above them kept pushing. Scores of students were injured, a few critically, as a much younger

Chief Riseling looked down on the scene from her post. The UW–Madison police and private security took criticism for initially trying to hold back the students at the guardrail and not opening a gate to let them through.

Insulated as she was within her regular campus job, Riseling was also more independent of the Walker administration than the Capitol Police, a fact that some close to the governor saw as arrogance or sympathy for the demonstrators. That surprised Riseling, who liked working with some Walker aides and felt it was her job to leave lawmaking to elected officials. Police work, though, she ceded to no one. She believed in upholding public safety and the constitution, a copy of which she carried in her pocket throughout the crisis. She supported collective bargaining overall and, in spite of some problems, believed it helped relations with her own officers. In one more difference between her and the Walker administration, her estimate for the number of the people in the building was far higher than the one put out that day by the administration. Soon, she would have a major role in controlling that crowd and keeping it safe.

For now, however, the statehouse was controlled by Capitol Police Chief Charles Tubbs and his deputy chief, Dan Blackdeer, who had less experience than Riseling in dealing with such massive crowds. Tubbs was the public face of the police in the Capitol, shuttling between high officials and protest leaders, most of them tense and indignant with the other side. Blackdeer attended the daily meetings with other law enforcement and for now had the charge of running the statehouse interior using officers from a jumble of state and local agencies. Of those three top officers inside the Capitol—Tubbs, Blackdeer, and Riseling—all three had assumed their jobs long before Walker's election and none of them necessarily had a strong affinity for the new Republican administration. Riseling considered herself a political independent and had given thousands of dollars in total to mostly Democratic candidates for office over the previous decade, including Walker's 2010 opponent, Milwaukee Mayor Tom Barrett. Tubbs had given $2,750 to Walker's old nemesis, Governor Jim Doyle, while serving under him. A little over a year after the protests, in June 2012, Tubbs would take a pay cut to leave the Capitol to work for a Dane County executive who was a former Democratic state representative.

Outside the Capitol, the Walker administration was working with a Democratic Dane County sheriff, Dave Mahoney, and the police force for the city of Madison under Chief Noble Wray and Mayor Dave Cieslewicz, a Democrat and vocal opponent of the governor's proposal. Mahoney was a former president of the state police officers union who had also served as a regional vice president of the National Association of Police Organizations. He personally opposed the governor's bill and he told his deputies—who weren't directly affected by the measure—that they were free to protest at the Capitol when they weren't on duty. But he said later he also sought to protect the free speech rights of all the demonstrators at the Capitol, including Tea Party groups favoring Walker. Madison police concentrated on policing the adjoining city streets rather than state property, and Wray made clear his policies. "I gave a standing order to my officers that if there was a request to remove people from the Capitol for what appears to be a political reason, if there wasn't an emergency, a disturbance, destruction of property, an injury, then that would have to come through me," Wray said later. The city of Madison racked up significant police overtime and other costs for handling the demonstrations, afterward billing the state more than $700,000. Still, city police later faced an accusation that they hadn't helped the Capitol Police at an hour of urgent need.

Walker had just appointed Stephen Fitzgerald as State Patrol superintendent, but otherwise the governor and his aides were working with law enforcement leaders whom they largely would not have picked and didn't necessarily know well. Because the governor's aides hadn't planned for such massive demonstrations and opposition to Walker's bill, they also hadn't considered the awkward question of how they would work with the police officers responsible for protecting both them and the demonstrators. The troopers and local police brought into the statehouse from around Wisconsin kept their union bargaining power under Walker's bill, but all the other state officers—Capitol Police, university police, wardens, and Department of Justice agents—lost most of it. In spite of that, the officers all worked together to protect those seeking to pass the law and those seeking to stop it. "I was very proud quite frankly of all those agencies," Riseling said later. "There was this irony and uncomfortableness and a sense of unfairness but all of the law enforcement banded together."

The afternoon of February 16, 2011, the crowd packed up against the Capitol steps to hear a series of speakers discuss how being in a union affected them. David J. Olson, a Madison social studies teacher, reminded the crowd that his district had to close its schools because of the strength of his union local. Olson waved his finger and stabbed the lectern to punctuate his points. "Inside these walls"—he pointed behind him at the Capitol—"they will try to bust our spirit," he said. "They will try to bust our wallets. But they will never bust our unions." Though it was anger that brought the crowd to the Capitol, a festive air dominated. The crowd bobbed up and down to House of Pain's "Jump Around," the hip-hop tune that had been adopted as a UW Badgers theme song. People in costumes increasingly showed up. Two were dressed up as the tycoon from the game Monopoly, wearing oversize, rounded cartoon masks, long-tailed coats, and top hats. They held ironic signs that read "Thanks, Scott." A woman holding a baby on the fringes of the crowd wore the consummate Wisconsin headwear—the foam cheddar hat so often seen at Packers games. She'd slapped a handmade sign on the side of hers that read "Cheeseheads against Walker." Firefighters—some in helmets, others in their black coats with neon yellow stripes around the cuffs—marched up the sidewalk in what would become a daily ritual. They were led by a firefighter playing a bagpipe and another playing a snare drum, but their music was all but drowned out by cheers, yelps, and applause.

The protests were growing, and organizers wanted them to get bigger. In a speech that day to the massive crowd, Mary Bell, president of the Wisconsin Education Association Council, stopped short of telling public workers to go on strike, which was illegal under state law. But she said that "on Thursday and Friday, we are asking Wisconsinites to come to Madison." A leader of local government workers around the state, Rick Badger of AFSCME Council 40, said, "This is not about a strike," but he also urged more demonstrations. Around the time they spoke to the crowd, officials from local teachers unions e-mailed, texted, and called their members with the same message. The next day, schools shut down in Milwaukee, Madison, Racine, Beaver Dam, Watertown, and elsewhere. That move drew outrage from conservatives, including talk radio host Rush Limbaugh, who said on February 17 on his national program that "union thugs" and "freeloaders" had turned Wisconsin into a scene of protest and incivility. Limbaugh's language was echoed by some conservatives in the following weeks, though typically not by elected officials. Demonstrators in turn embraced the epithet conservatives hurled at them, and in the days to come many middle-aged women and others could be seen wearing buttons or carrying signs that read "union thug."

To answer his opponents, Walker called a news conference. Reporters had difficulty getting through the crowd gathered outside his office, and Walker's aides had to let some of them in through a door normally used only by staff so the journalists could get in. Walker, standing in his conference room before the state and national flags, downplayed the significance of the crowds. "The bottom line is that's a fraction of the three hundred or so thousand state and local government employees, the good professionals we have that work at the state and local level," he said. "And obviously that's a much smaller fraction than the five-and-a-half million people who live and work here in the state of Wisconsin, both in and out of government." He went on to state that those others also deserved to have their voices heard. Ignoring for the moment the La Crosse protesters who had pounded on his vehicle the day before, the governor said that almost everyone he talked to during his tour of the state had told him his proposal was modest. He said he was undeterred by the protests. "We're going to make sure we're not going to be intimidated into thinking that they're the only voices out there," he said.

Behind the scenes, Walker and his aides had been pushing to get his bill out of the Joint Finance Committee. Dale Schultz, the veteran GOP senator from southwestern Wisconsin, had been working on an amendment that would have seriously weakened the governor's proposal. Van Wanggaard, the freshman Republican senator from Racine, had been helping. Late the week before, Wanggaard and an aide had told other Republican senators and Walker's aides that he wouldn't vote for the bill as written. A former cop who served on his union bargaining committee and provided security in schools, Wanggaard worried the bill left public employees with no recourse against unfair discipline or even a politically motivated firing. He said later that the weekend after Walker introduced his bill, he spoke with the governor multiple times by phone for a total of about three hours, telling Walker, "Hey, I'm not there." Wanggaard felt he had made progress addressing his concerns with the governor, who promised to take up the issue on Monday, February 14, either personally or through his deputy chief of staff, Eric Schutt.

No one from the governor's office called on Monday, and for the next two days Wanggaard privately worked with Dale Schultz on an alternate plan, with the two men leaving the Capitol at one point to put it together. That day, word of the effort leaked to the press, showing that Schultz appeared to have one of the two other GOP senators he needed to scale back the bill. On Wednesday, the day of the Joint Finance Committee vote, Schultz and Wanggaard presented their alternate plan privately to their fellow Republican senators. At that point, Walker's office re-engaged with Wanggaard. "Van just told me that you said you would call him on Monday and that he still hasn't heard from you," Schutt e-mailed Walker over the lunch hour, asking for him to get in touch with Wanggaard. Working quickly, Walker's aides reached an agreement with Wanggaard to provide a few more nominal protections to workers. Under that amendment, local governments and schools would be required to create grievance systems similar to the one under the state's civil service code. It would allow workers to go to an impartial arbitrator if they had been fired, disciplined, or had workplace safety concerns. Unions saw problems with the proposal once it was made public. For instance, the agreement left the final decision on whether to uphold a worker's dismissal up to school boards and city councils—the same bodies that oversaw the worker's supervisors. The proposal appeared to be largely an afterthought; after it became law no one with the state systematically checked to see if local governments were implementing it. But the changes convinced Wanggaard to take a vote for which he would later pay a high political price. Before he would give his final approval, however, Wanggaard insisted on seeing the language of the bill. Late in the day, the governor's staff showed it to him in Scott Fitzgerald's office. Wanggaard left the office to discuss it for a few minutes with his chief of staff and then came back. "This is exactly what I wanted. This is perfect," Wanggaard told the governor's aides.

That put the bill back on track. Besides Wanggaard, other Republicans in moderate districts—such as Luther Olsen and Dan Kapanke—pointed to the changes as helping them support Walker's proposal. Kapanke, of La Crosse, represented a Democratic-leaning district along the Mississippi River with a university and thousands of public employees in it. If Kapanke voted for the bill, he appeared almost certain to lose his seat in a recall. A former seed salesman and local official, Kapanke had been elected to the Senate in 2004. Representing an increasingly Democratic district, he was nevertheless re-elected in the liberal landslide of 2008 and ran unsuccessfully for Congress in 2010. At one stage later on in the crisis, Kapanke had a troubling thought—that his vote on Walker's union legislation could affect more than his political career. Kapanke owned the La Crosse Loggers, a baseball team made up of unpaid college players similar to a professional minor league team. The team he started in 2002 employed his wife and grown children, as well as others. Kapanke realized that a vote against public employee unions could cost the baseball team business.

That morning Kapanke called together a family meeting, which he later remembered as difficult and emotional. The senator and his family reconciled themselves to his decision, and he drove to Madison. Along the way, he got a telephone call asking him to meet privately with Walker before he went to the floor. At the Capitol, Kapanke went to the governor's office, walked inside, and hugged Walker. "I'm with you, governor," Kapanke said. The governor and Kapanke read from a spiritual devotional together and talked about leadership before the senator left. "I knew what I had to do," Kapanke said later.

But to help cement the support of other moderate Republican senators, the Joint Finance Committee would have to act. To take that vote, Vos and Darling planned to bring the panel together on the afternoon of Wednesday, February 16. But the meeting was pushed back while Wanggaard's concerns were sorted out. At 7:45 p.m., Vos and Darling called the meeting to order, and the room was again packed. Staff for the nonpartisan Legislative Fiscal Bureau described to the committee the proposed changes to the bill. Besides Wanggaard's addition, Republicans also changed how the bill would affect limited-term employees. Such employees receive fewer benefits and are meant to be temporary, but they sometimes work for the state for years. Walker's version of the bill would have taken away all health care and retirement benefits for those 1,500 workers. The amendment kept those benefits in place. Nonetheless, the amendment still included the repeal of most collective bargaining, and the crowd in the rotunda thundered with "boos" when they heard the report. Vos, Darling, and the other Republican legislative leaders insisted no further changes would be made to the bill, even as Schultz was pushing to modify it. On his own now, Schultz was still working on his alternative, which would have suspended collective bargaining for two years and then brought it back. But he would have to seek to make the changes on the floor; Wanggaard and the Republicans on the Joint Finance Committee were moving on without him. Scott Fitzgerald, the majority leader, knew he might lose Schultz but was comforted by the solidifying support among the others in the caucus. "I never worried about the Dale thing too much because I knew everyone else was rock solid," he said later.

While the budget committee debated, Jenni Dye was stuck in a Capitol stairwell and wondering—mostly jokingly—whether she would ever get out. Using her iPhone, she pecked out her predicament in a tweet a little before 9 p.m. "I am trapped in a stairwell," she wrote, adding another tweet a couple of minutes later. "This is the loudest stairwell I've ever been stuck in."

She had come to the protests for the third straight night after work and met up with a group of friends. Walking into the Capitol, she thought to herself that she was witnessing something that she probably wouldn't see again in her life. Dressed in red sneakers and a Nike zip-up hoodie, she was now crammed in the stairwell with hundreds of the demonstrators who were in the long line of people trying to get into the packed committee room. Dye never made it farther than the top of the stairs, but she still got the sense that something uncanny and overwhelming was happening around her. What was most remarkable about Dye's dedication to the demonstrations that day and in the coming weeks was how many other people shared it and brought to the protests the same fire that she did.

Earlier that week, on Sunday, February 13—the date Dye later called "day zero"—she had only a vague notion of Walker's bill. That day she saw a few dozen demonstrators with signs—a common and unimpressive sight in the liberal city. Dye thought, "Another Madison protest. It's another week and another group is demonstrating at the Capitol." But then she noticed among the protesters an old colleague from her days as an intern at the statehouse. As she read the signs about unions and worker rights, she became more interested. Dye wasn't a union member and never had been, but her father was a math teacher and union member at Janesville Parker High School, where he also coached football and boys track. Dye's mother, though not a union member, was a preschool teacher at a site that also had a publicly funded kindergarten. Dye saw unions and collective bargaining as something that had helped her family, and she believed in them. She read up on Walker's bill, and she didn't like what she found. Having done little to oppose Walker in the recent election, Dye felt motivated to seize this opportunity.

An avid user of Twitter, Dye had signed up for the social media service in 2006, joining early enough to snag the admittedly clichéd handle of @legaleagle. She later described herself on her Twitter profile—borrowing some language from what others said about her—as a "Public school graduate. Ninja for democracy. Lover of all things Wisconsin, especially cheese." But going into the demonstrations, Dye's Twitter account was protected so that only her relatively small circle of friends and other followers could read her tweets. That Wednesday, Dye opened her Twitter account so that anyone could read her messages, a decision that would change her involvement in the protests and help lead her to run for local office. Like other Twitter users among the demonstrators, Dye marked her tweets with a #wiunion hashtag that allowed them to be grouped with other posts about the protests and found easily by people engrossed in the budget crisis.

In the coming days, Dye sent out so many tweets some days—at a pace of one thousand or more in twenty-four hours—that Twitter sometimes froze her account. She had to wait at least an hour or two before she could send new messages. By her number of updates, she ranked as one of the most prolific tweeters of the thousands who participated in the protests, and that was no small feat. One Southern Illinois University in Carbondale study found that more than 775,000 tweets were posted using the single hashtag #wiunion over the next twenty-four days. Making that number more impressive was the fact that this hashtag was just one of a number employed by Twitter users discussing Walker's legislation and the response. Others included #WeAreWI, #NotMyWI, #killthebill, and, on the Republican side, #standwithwalker. Under the #wiunion hashtag alone, 90,000 Twitter users contributed some bit of commentary, news, or reaction. Many of those, of course, were simply re-tweeting the messages that had already been sent out by a group of diehard tweeters. Still, even that core group was stunning, with several dozen users sending more than a thousand tweets during that three-and-a-half-week period. Over those days, the #wiunion stream averaged tens of thousands of tweets a day and hit a peak of some 60,000—enough material from one day to fill perhaps a dozen books. Ranked by the number of tweets sent, Dye came in at eleventh out of the people using the #wiunion stream. Some of the more prolific Twitter accounts belonged to groups like the state teachers union that likely had more than one person sending out messages. The Twitter updates drew not only attention but also attendance to the demonstrations from people around the state and country. They also helped inform the thousands of protesters at the Capitol about the complicated events going on around them. The tweets weren't always correct, but they were fast and available to anyone with the right kind of cell phone.

Stuck outside the budget committee's hearing room, Dye joined the people around her as they shouted the Latin American protest chant, "The people united will never be defeated!" She was amazed at how the fourth floor of the statehouse, usually quiet and often nearly deserted, was full of people that night. Powerful forces, not least of all social media, were already at work drawing people there. In a sign of how unusual the protest was, Dye got an unexpected text message from her father, who had decided to come to the Capitol that night. The two met up. "Wisconsin, you brought tears to my eyes today. Thanks for caring and sticking with us," she tweeted just after 9:30 p.m.

While Dye tweeted and shouted, the worn-out members of the Joint Finance Committee spent three hours going over the details of the changes and debating the bill. Democrats described it in stark terms, repeating the criticisms they and the protesters had hammered on around the clock for days, but they knew they couldn't block the bill in the committee. At about 11:30 p.m., Representative Tamara Grigsby, a fiery lawmaker from Milwaukee, acknowledged the "sad, somber moment" of the looming vote but struck an uplifting note as she saluted the efforts of ordinary demonstrators and asked them to return to the Capitol in the coming days. As she spoke, some of the bill's opponents in the audience wept openly. "To those fighting for their rights today, I want you to know that you are patriots. You are patriots," Grigsby said. "And we thank you for fighting for the rights of working families and for Wisconsin values that everyday people cherish. We hear you."

The debate appeared set to end on an unexpectedly quiet note. Then Senator Glenn Grothman leaned into his microphone. "Okay, I'll just make a little comment here," he said. "One of the things that's a little bit frustrating is the state's facing a difficult time. And I think it's important for people—important for so-called community leaders—not to inflame passions. Instead, one of the disappointing things we've had tonight is we've told people who—I mean, nobody's dying because of this budget." He swept his hand to the side dismissively. "Nobody's getting sick. Nobody's even getting laid off, okay? In the real world if I go to work and my boss tells me, 'We had a bad year; we're taking away your 401(k) match,' or 'You've got a new health insurance plan; you've got to kick in another fifty or a hundred bucks a year in health insurance,' you get over it in about thirty seconds." His hand kept moving, back and forth. "When Scott Walker was sitting at that desk in closed caucus about a week ago and told me my pension was going down, which I wasn't expecting, I got over it in about ten seconds, okay? We're living in the greatest state in the greatest country in the world and y'all got a job, okay? . . . We all love ya, nobody's against ya, but . . . much worse things have gone on to other employees all over this state the last three years and you still got a great life. Thanks."

The demonstrators in the audience now gazed angrily at Grothman, and the Democratic lawmakers suddenly were eager to debate again. "We had a woman yesterday testify she lives in a house that's 575 square feet. And she's a nursing assistant. You know what? She's not going to be thinking about this for ten seconds," said Representative Jennifer Shilling of La Crosse.

As Grothman made his comments, Dye was downstairs watching him. When it became clear that she and her friends were never going to make it into the packed committee room, she had gone to the rotunda to watch the debate on the monitors. To Dye, it was as if Grothman didn't understand the impact the bill was going to have or how the state's citizens would react. She looked at the crowd around her and thought his comments could backfire. "Sen Glenn Grothman just used phrase so-called community leaders. I hope some of those leaders organize our communities against him," she tweeted. Already, Dye had stumbled into a role she would play for the coming weeks of reporting and commenting on the events. She knew enough from her time working in the Capitol to give online updates on the committee action to her followers, and quote from and comment on the debate.

As the committee vote approached, the Democratic minority leaders were having a desperate private meeting. Representative Peter Barca and Senator Mark Miller huddled for their third talk of the night, this time in Miller's office. They were brainstorming on how they could stop the bill or at least slow it down. They had few options, none good. Normally, state lawmakers wanting to slow down a bill did so by bringing up dozens of amendments on the floor and making long speeches. It was a kind of filibuster, but one that unlike the filibuster in the U.S. Senate could eventually be stopped by the majority party. There was one tactic that Democrats could take that could actually halt the bill's progress. It had been tried elsewhere in American politics but not in Wisconsin, at least not on this scale. Miller and Barca made no decision, but they agreed on the need to move quickly.

Back in the committee room, other Republicans were striking a less combative and more conciliatory tone than Grothman had taken. One of them was Representative Pat Strachota, who like Grothman was from West Bend, a conservative haven northwest of Milwaukee. Wrapping up for the Republicans, she told the crowd that her parents and one of her daughters were teachers and that she respected public workers. State officials, however, had no options left for fixing the state's budget, she said. "We're not assaulting the public-sector employees in this bill. That's not what this is about. You've made it into that, but that's not what this is about," she said. "What this is about is that the state of Wisconsin is facing a fiscal crisis. We owe $3.6 billion. Is it your fault? No. Is it our fault? No. Is it collectively the people in Wisconsin's fault? Yes, because for years and years and years . . . they've been spending more than what we had the ability to pay.

"The day of reckoning has come."

When Strachota finished just before midnight, the lawmakers voted. Dye sent out an urgent alert and followed it moments later with the results: "12–4 on party lines, the budget repair bill is sent to the Legislature. And with that, it's back to protesting." Upstairs, demonstrators weren't the only ones who were emotional. GOP Senator Luther Olsen, a former school board president whose wife worked in public education, had just voted for the measure, and he was crying. He had been one hope for unions looking to stop the bill, but Olsen had instead voted with his party and now faced a likely recall effort against him. Another blow to union hopes came a minute later as Senator

Wanggaard sent out a statement announcing that he too backed Walker's bill. "No compromise is perfect, but I am thankful that the bill has been substantially modified to add additional worker protection," the statement read. "I will be voting 'Yes' on the amended budget repair bill."

Like the other GOP senators, Wanggaard thought he would be voting on the bill within twelve hours, but it turned out that he was off by almost three weeks. He had locked himself in just as the Democrats were about to spring a surprise. Downstairs, Dye signed off of Twitter, saying she was going to get some rest. She hadn't planned to stay out so late; she wouldn't get home until after 1 a.m. and would get only a few hours of sleep before she had to wake up and drive to her job in Janesville. Outside the statehouse, the night was quiet, a stark contrast to the reverberating shouts inside. In spite of the poor odds, Dye was still hopeful the bill could be stopped. She had no idea it would soon take over her life, as well as many others'.

8

The Interstate to Illinois

On the cold Madison morning of February 17, Senator Mark Miller walked down King Street toward a meeting that might decide the fate of Walker's bill. The Senate was scheduled to convene at 11 a.m. for the sole purpose of considering the measure, and already crowds were gathering outside the statehouse. Miller wasn't headed to his office as he normally would be—he was going in the opposite direction. A half block from the Capitol square, he slipped through an unobtrusive door between a coffeehouse and a restaurant and climbed the stairs to the office of the state Democratic Party, where he had told his colleagues to meet him supplied not with amendments or speeches but with a toothbrush and change of clothes. He had told the other Democrats that he had a bold plan to slow down, perhaps even block, Walker's swiftly moving bill.

"Pack your suitcase and come to Democratic headquarters," he told one senator in a 6:30 a.m. wakeup call. "We are going to have a conversation and talk about leaving the state."

When the senators arrived, no one knew if they all would back the plan as they had to for it to succeed. Newly elected Senator Chris Larson of Milwaukee was so desperate to stop the bill that he had had his staff research filibusters only to find there was no permanent block in Wisconsin. And Larson was skeptical his colleagues would agree to leave the state. "We're Democrats," he said. "You get fourteen in a room and you've got twenty-two different opinions."

The meeting got started with chit-chat, not drama, but it also moved quickly. Miller laid out the idea: By departing the state, Democrats would leave Senate

Republicans powerless to vote on the bill. Ordinary bills needed only a simple majority of senators—seventeen of thirty-three—to be present to hold a vote. But under Section 8 of Article 8 of the state constitution, bills that imposed taxes, borrowed money, or spent money required three-fifths of either house of the Legislature to be present for a vote. In the Senate, that worked out to twenty senators, or one more than the nineteen that Republicans had. Given that the bill included spending provisions like additional money for state prisons, there was no way it could pass the Senate if all Democrats boycotted the vote. Miller told his colleagues, "It only works if all fourteen of us go."

Miller's plan came out of his office and had been privately discussed for weeks among a small group before Walker actually announced his union measure. The senator and his aides had talked about what they would do if Walker followed through on the idea he floated in December of seeking to decertify unions. In the brainstorming sessions, they discussed whether the Democratic senators could leave the state as legislators in Texas had in 2003 to block a controversial bill to redraw congressional districts. As it turned out, in certain cases they could. Jamie Kuhn, Miller's chief of staff, had the idea of denying Republicans a quorum, and the senator and his staff worked together to explore it. When Walker had unveiled the legislation on Friday, February 11, another Miller aide reached out within hours to an attorney at the non-partisan Legislative Council to see whether Walker's bill would trip the constitutional requirement for a larger quorum. By Tuesday, February 15, the Legislative Council had delivered a memo to Miller confirming that the three-fifths quorum would be needed for that bill. Heading someplace safe—like Illinois—would block a vote. "It was clear we controlled the progress of the bill once we did that," Miller said later.

That week, Miller quietly discussed the idea with a few other Democratic lawmakers. Many didn't take the idea seriously, believing that the entire caucus would never agree on it. Miller and his staff have adamantly denied ever discussing the plan with unions until after they put it into motion. In spite of the preparation, there was little more to the plan that Miller presented to his colleagues the morning of the vote than simply crossing the state line. The plan, Miller told the senators, was to slow down the bill's progress and allow time for voters to get more details about it. The senators said later that they believed they were leaving the state for a few days or perhaps a week and had only vague ideas of what might come next. "I thought we'd be gone for a couple of hours, honestly," said Senator Jon Erpenbach, who ended up as one of the most vocal supporters of remaining in Illinois in the coming weeks. Once Miller explained the idea, the Democrats quickly agreed to it. Senator Julie

Lassa, who as caucus chairwoman ran the meeting, noted later that at that stage Democrats had little choice: if they went to the floor it was just a question of time before Republicans would pass the bill. They decided to drive to the Clock Tower Resort, a Best Western hotel just beyond the border in Rockford, Illinois. True to the hotel's name, it sported a prominent tower, which could be seen from Interstate 39/90. The momentous decision to leave the state had taken just thirty minutes. There was one catch, though—two of the fourteen Democratic senators had been absent. One of them, Bob Jauch of Poplar, had arrived late because he was catching up on sleep after the long Joint Finance Committee meeting the night before. The sixty-five-year-old senator straggled into the meeting at 7:50 a.m. and found his colleagues already getting ready to leave. They asked if Jauch would go with them. "I don't think that we have any choice," Jauch said.

That left just one more Democrat, Tim Cullen of Janesville. Cullen had just been elected, but the gaunt, sixty-seven-year-old senator wasn't a newcomer to politics. He had previously served as a senator for twelve years, rising to majority leader before serving in 1987 and 1988 as state health secretary under Tommy Thompson. After that, he prospered for years as a health insurance executive before returning to public office in the final years of his career.

Miller had called Cullen the night before to tell him about the caucus meeting, but Cullen told him he wouldn't attend because it was so early. Miller gave no hint of the explosive idea that would be discussed. The next morning, Cullen got a call telling him that his close friend, former senator and former Supreme Court Justice Bill Bablitch, had died. Cullen and Bablitch's family had known for weeks his death was imminent, and Cullen had earlier agreed to handle alerting the Capitol press corps. Then, Miller called. "We're going to Illinois," Miller said. "What?" a surprised Cullen responded. When Miller had explained, Cullen agreed to go with them, but he told Miller that he needed to first go to the Capitol to fill reporters in on Bablitch's death. Miller urged him not to do that because he could get caught, but Cullen told him he wasn't worried. To make sure he was not detained in the Capitol, Cullen called Senate President Mike Ellis, who had served with Bablitch. "He said, 'I'll make sure you don't get caught here,'" Cullen later recalled of Ellis. "Mike said, 'Can you be gone by 10:45?'"

A vestige of the old collegiality of the Senate still survived. Ellis cautioned Cullen he would institute a "call of the house" shortly after the Senate started at 11 a.m. to try to compel the fourteen senators back to the chamber. Cullen went to his office, told reporters about Bablitch's death, and confirmed for them the Democrats were leaving the state. He left his office to find a mass of demonstrators, and he was unsure if he could get through them. An aide shouted that he was a Democratic senator trying to leave and the crowd moved aside. "It was like the parting of the Red Sea," Cullen said. He headed south toward Illinois, and within fifteen minutes Ellis called him. "Did you get out?" Ellis asked. "Yeah," Cullen replied, giving Ellis the okay to go ahead. Not much later, Miller called Cullen to make sure he was on his way. He told him not to use Interstate 39/90 because the police might stop him. Cullen thought that was unlikely and continued on.

The Democrats' move took even some family members by surprise. Miller hadn't given his wife of forty-three years, Josephine Oyama-Miller, any hint that he might be leaving the state. The couple had been scheduled to attend a family reunion in California, and on the morning of the scheduled Senate vote Miller's wife left without him. At O'Hare International Airport in Chicago, Oyama-Miller was getting on a plane when she saw on television that the fourteen Democrats had left the state. She then had to board her flight and go without news until she landed. When she was able to talk with Miller, she told him that she had left a dinner cooking for him in a Crock-Pot on the kitchen table. A neighbor was called to turn it off.

Up until the Democrats left, Republicans had been on track with the schedule put together by Walker's office the week before to pass the bill within days of its introduction. But by leaving the state, the Democrats had thrown out that timeline and with it the Republicans' chance to avoid a long and costly political battle. That morning, the crowd at the statehouse built steadily. Shortly after 8 a.m., several hundred people were already in the Capitol rotunda, holding signs, talking, and, in short bursts, chanting their opposition to the bill. A small but growing group was gathering in front of the Senate chamber in anticipation of the vote to come. "Recall this Bill," one small group began to chant for a minute or so. The handmade signs held by the protesters included: "Proud to Teach," "Middle Class Closed for Business," and, in a reference to the state animal, "Walker is not a badger, he's a weasel." Many of the protesters had stayed the night again, and they filled small alcoves throughout the building. For the second day, Madison schools and some surrounding districts were closed because of teachers calling in sick to join the ranks of those protesting the bill.

As the crowd grew, the scene was part angry protest and part carnival. There were placards, valentine balloons, banjos, air horns, and a huge American flag, which at one point was briefly draped across the rotunda floor. From a second-floor alcove, someone had hung a bed-sheet-sized sign, which remained throughout the protests: "W(isconsin) needs 3 cou-(R)-ageous senators"—a reference to the three Republican "no" votes that would be needed to stop the bill. By 10 a.m., the crowd had swelled into the thousands. Trying to move through some hallways, especially on the second floor where the Senate chamber is, was like working through a crowd at a concert. The building of densely packed people now smelled like a gymnasium. The noise from the chants and drums was overwhelming, something that was felt as much as heard. Police in the building wore earplugs to help them make it through their long shifts.

Estimating the crowd size was difficult at best. The Walker administration said in a statement that the Capitol Police put it at five thousand inside the building and twenty thousand outside it. The real situation in the Capitol, however, was probably much more overcrowded than the official report suggested. Susan Riseling, the chief of the UW–Madison police, estimated the crowd inside the statehouse at midafternoon at nearly twenty-five thousand, or five times the official count released that day by the Walker administration. She made the calculation based on the crowd's density and the amount of floor space it covered. The numbers released by the Walker administration, she said later, came from a command post located at a Madison Fire Department station. "There is no way the command post could know the count in the building accurately. Whoever the officer was who reported the information—well—I can't imagine how they got their numbers. Way, way, low. Now, crowds did ebb and flow. My kindest interpretation would be these numbers come from a real ebb." Madison Police Chief Noble Wray was also skeptical of the figures coming from Walker's Department of Administration. "It's not an exact science but it was always kind of strange because when we would give a crowd estimate the DOA was consistently lower than what we were giving," he said later. Soon Riseling would put in place a count to keep track of those entering the building but hadn't started yet. So sorting out the total number of daily visitors to the Capitol was all but impossible even for experienced hands like her because the crowds gathered not just for an hour or two but often for entire days. That meant that on any given day, many more people had come and gone than had been present at any one point. The debate on the crowd's size was in one sense academic. Everyone involved agreed that it was a stunning show of political force.

Law enforcement also had an impressive presence that day. But the crowd was so large that there was little police would have been able to do if an emergency had caused people to stampede for the exits. Plus, the crowd had grown so quickly that week that the police had still not taken steps that later became routine, such as roping off the area in front of the Senate chamber so people couldn't press up against its main doors. The masses of people remained overwhelmingly peaceful and generally respectful, and that wasn't accidental or simply spontaneous. Unions assigned people to self-police their protests and try to intervene before problems developed. When the Senate convened, urgent messages on Twitter called on demonstrators to remain calm and respectful to law enforcement, emphasizing how damaging any act of disrespect or violence would be for their cause. Inside the statehouse, police and demonstrators often spoke to one another with an almost exaggerated respect and friendliness, seemingly aware that this was no time for a careless word or gesture.

This didn't mean that the crowd wasn't loud and assertive. The demonstrators that day had some of the rowdiest moments of the budget standoff, and at times they unnerved the Republicans. The protesters who had stationed themselves in front of the main doors to the Senate chamber purposely blocked the entrance and chanted fiercely. Republicans avoided them by using a side entrance accessed by a stairwell that law enforcement managed to keep clear. At times during the day, the Senate staff and reporters could reach that entrance only by going to a different floor of the building where there were fewer protesters and then walking up or down the stairs to the second-floor entrance. At least nine people were arrested that day, mostly for disorderly conduct, though no one was taken to jail. Dane County Sheriff Dave Mahoney said officers from roughly a dozen law enforcement agencies were in the Capitol and saw a strong part of their role as protecting demonstrators' constitutional rights to both free speech and assembly. "We are exercising extreme measures of tolerance," Mahoney said.

Riseling was scrambling to ensure they worked. At a little after 2 p.m. she arrived at the Capitol with her assistant police chief at UW–Madison, Brian Bridges. They walked into the Capitol through the State Street entrance and, just inside the door, found that they were stuck in a press of people and unable to move in any direction. It was a clear danger in the event of an emergency or panic.

"This isn't good," Riseling said to Bridges.

"No, this is trouble," he answered.

"We've got to get out of here and get up high so we can see," she said.

They jostled their way to a reserved staff elevator and ascended to the third floor, where they looked out at the throng from a balcony. Riseling thought again of the tragedy at Camp Randall two decades earlier—she was resolved to prevent that from repeating itself here.

"I've had enough of this," Riseling said.

The pair headed up to a room in the northeast part of the fourth floor, where police had relocated the Capitol command post from its usual spot in the basement. There, Riseling laid out her concerns to Dan Blackdeer, the deputy chief of the Capitol Police, who was ready to give her a chance to take over. At 3 p.m. that afternoon, she took charge of the interior of the state-house and immediately set to planning how to reduce the crowd in the build-ing to its capacity as set by the city fire marshal, only to find that the Capitol had no such maximum level set because state officials had exempted the statehouse from this regulation. But Riseling happened to have studied at the National Fire Academy and knew something about how to figure a building's maximum occupancy. She sat down and calculated a rough figure for the Capitol, taking into account factors such as the number of exits and the pub-licly available space in the building. She came up with a maximum capacity of nine thousand people—far fewer than the number that she calculated was actually crammed into the building. Now she and the other officers would have to work out how to safely reduce the number. But the next day, Riseling would find herself opposing a hasty order from Walker's office to do just that, out of fears that it would prove even more dangerous than doing nothing.

That morning, Senator Dale Schultz found protesters outside his Richland Center home, just as several other Republican senators did. That gathering, however, was nothing like the one he witnessed hours later when he drove through the busy streets of downtown Madison. Staff from the sergeant at arms' office put out a warning that Schultz not even try to park in his regu-lar space on the Capitol square. Instead, he had to go to the Risser Justice Center, a building across the street from the Capitol that includes the state Department of Justice, where he would be escorted through a tunnel leading to the basement of the statehouse.

Inside the Capitol, Schultz's chief of staff, Todd Allbaugh, was panicking. Schultz was supposed to meet with the governor before the session began, and its 11 a.m. start time was fast approaching. So many calls were pouring into Schultz's office and home that Schultz and Allbaugh had difficulty co-ordinating their plans. Allbaugh knew if Schultz met with Walker the senator might miss the first part of the floor session, when he would have a chance

to offer the compromise amendment that he had worked on with Senator
Van Wanggaard. Allbaugh was inside Schultz's office, which, as befitted a
hunter, farmer, and centrist Republican, was decorated with a black bear
pelt and a portrait of Theodore Roosevelt. Allbaugh couldn't easily leave
the office, though, and get to the floor because the crowd in the corridor outside was packed so tight. Schultz would have the same problem negotiating
the crowded hallways and getting to the Senate on time. Allbaugh tried calling Schultz on his cell phone. "Hello," Schultz answered. "We're going
through the tunnel." "Dale! Dale!" Allbaugh said, trying to warn his boss to
skip or postpone the meeting with the governor. But Schultz had already
stepped into the tunnel, where cell reception was patchy. The connection
went dead.

A little over half an hour later, at 11:27 a.m., the repeated sound of an electronic bell beckoned the senators to the chamber. The senators' overstuffed
leather chairs were mostly empty. A dull winter light filtered through the
stained-glass ceiling of the chamber, just as the sound of thousands of chanting protesters inside the nearby rotunda forced its way through the thick
walls. In the small media area, television cameras pointed toward the floor
like a firing squad, with print reporters squeezed into seats in front of them.
In the viewing galleries above sat protesters, many in Badger red shirts.
Republican senators came onto the floor, but no Democrats were to be seen.
Minutes before the bell sounded, Scott Fitzgerald walked into Miller's office
suite just off the Senate floor. A couple of Miller's aides were sitting in the
outer room of the office; the door to the inner room was closed. Noting that
it was time to start the session, Fitzgerald asked, "Where's Senator Miller?"

The aides looked uncomfortable, as if Fitzgerald were asking them if they
knew who had eaten the last office pastry. They said they didn't know where
Miller was. That had been part of the plan—to keep as many Democratic
aides as possible from knowing where the senators had gone so they could
say truthfully that they didn't know where the senators were.

"Well, have him call me," Fitzgerald said and went back to the floor.

By then, Democrats had confirmed for reporters that they had fled, and the
news was zipping out through websites, tweets, and the old-fashioned grape-
vine. The ringing chime signaled it was time for senators to take their seats
on the floor. Senate President Mike Ellis took his place at the podium and
said, "Senators, please return to the chambers so we can begin. Would the
sergeant at arms staff please notify Senator Miller, the minority leader, that
the Senate is about to convene and we are about to begin the process?"

Then, putting on his aviator-style glasses, Ellis read, "The January special session of the Senate will come to order. The first order of business: the clerk will call the roll."

Senate Chief Clerk Rob Marchant read off the names in alphabetical order in his clipped, professional voice. "Senator Carpenter . . . Coggs . . . Cowles . . . Cullen . . . Darling . . . Ellis . . . Erpenbach . . . Fitzgerald. . . ."

Only Republicans hollered, "Here!"

They had only seventeen senators on hand, the minimum number needed to conduct any Senate business. Schultz and another Republican were both absent along with the Democrats.

"There are seventeen members present. A quorum is present. The clerk will keep the roll open for Senator Miller and the other senators who are not here yet," Ellis said.

After a prayer and the Pledge of Allegiance, Ellis ordered Marchant to read the title of Walker's bill, the first step in moving it toward a vote. Back in the rotunda, some members of the crowd could see the Senate action on the big-screen televisions that had been set up earlier in the week for the Joint Finance Committee action. The shouting outside rose—protesters were beating on the ornate metal tracery that protected the windows looking in toward the Senate. Republicans moved to adopt the amendment the Joint Finance Committee had recommended the night before. It was 11:32 a.m.

"Freedom! Democracy! Unions! Freedom! Democracy! Unions!" the crowd in the galleries above the senators chanted. And the refrain was repeated as Republicans took a voice vote to adopt the amendment.

"The amendment is adopted," said Ellis. "Go ahead and order it to a third reading."

It hadn't taken even five minutes. With few of the usual formalities and delays, the Senate had rolled up to the third reading of the bill, the stage at which a piece of legislation could no longer be amended, only approved on an up-or-down vote. Allbaugh by then had worked his way through the crowd to let Fitzgerald's staff know that Schultz would be a few minutes late because of his meeting with Walker. But the Senate wasn't slowing down. The bill was seconds away from being locked into its current form, and Schultz and his amendment weren't in sight.

Schultz was one floor down in the governor's office, where Walker and his administration secretary, Mike Huebsch, were seeking the senator's support for the budget-repair bill. A moderate who believed in bipartisanship, Schultz sometimes received eye rolls from the fellow Republicans whom he had once led in the Senate. Ellis, for instance, had nicknamed him the "pope of pomposity," a title Schultz laughed off in stride. But Schultz could stand firm when he felt he was right. Walker and Huebsch mostly listened to Schultz explain why he couldn't vote for the bill as written. Schultz and the governor were sitting; Huebsch was standing. After perhaps twenty-five minutes, as Schultz recalled later, he learned that the Senate was moving the bill to third reading. In a flash, the senator saw he'd made a costly error in missing the action. He jumped up and started to leave the governor's office, grabbing the handle of the door. But as he did he realized he was too late to make it through the crowds and reach the floor in time. He sat back down.

"If I ever find out that either one of you had anything to do with this, I'll be very disappointed," Schultz said he told the governor and Huebsch.

Walker's spokesman Cullen Werwie strongly denied later that there was any intent to lure Schultz into missing a vote in the Senate. Werwie said that during the meeting, aides to the governor had relayed to Schultz a message from the frantic Allbaugh that he might miss the vote. The senator replied that if the vote was important, the Senate would wait for him, Werwie said.

For his part, Fitzgerald said he recalled hearing that day that Schultz was in Walker's office, but said he wasn't trying to keep him from voting. He said that if Schultz had asked for a chance later to offer his amendment and have it inevitably voted down by all or most other Republicans, "we would have been in caucus within two minutes" talking about whether to reverse the Senate's earlier action and allow a vote on the amendment. "The idea that I would pull a quick one on one of my members, that's ridiculous," Fitzgerald said. "It doesn't work that way. It wouldn't work that way. It couldn't work that way."

Back in the Senate, Ellis pounded his gavel and looked up at the shouting protesters in the galleries. The other absent Republican senator had arrived, and the Senate ordered the bill to a third reading. But without Schultz and at least one Democrat, they could take no further action on the bill.

Fitzgerald rose. "Mr. President, I would ask that five senators stand to acknowledge a call of the house," he said. His colleagues stood to initiate the process of forcing all the senators to come to the floor. "All right, the Senate is now under a call of the house and we will try to find the members who decided not to show up for work today," Ellis said. "We will stand informal pending the call of the house."

The senators left the floor while above them the chanting continued. Fitzgerald saw the Democrats' move as a stunt but figured they would be back by the end of the day. By putting in place a call of the house, the Republicans had triggered an action that they said would allow the Republicans to compel the attendance of the absent Democrats. They argued they could get the police to bring the Democrats back if they found them in Wisconsin, and that legal question got intense debate in the coming days. Lawyers from both sides, however, agreed that there was no authority for Wisconsin police to go into Illinois or for police there to round up the Democrats when they hadn't committed a crime. About ten minutes later, Ellis came back to the floor. In the meantime, the galleries had quieted. "Under the Senate rules, we cannot move to passage of a [fiscal] bill unless we have twenty people. We need three-fifths. We do not have the three-fifths," he said, acknowledging that they could take no action that day.

The galleries erupted in a cheer.

At her law firm in Janesville, Jenni Dye had skipped lunch—and most of her work—as she tried to follow the action in the statehouse. Dye tweeted a little before noon, "Once again, have failed to actually eat on my lunch break. Too absorbed."

She had spent her morning tweeting about the budget battle. Some posts questioned whether most lawmakers had actually read the bill as it moved quickly through the Legislature. Others offered demonstrators advice on places to park and bus lines to take to get downtown. She trolled news sites, but since even a delay of a few minutes was too much for her, she spent much of her time on the lightning-quick Twitter site. She was among the first people to tweet about the senators' absence, though at that point she was only repeating an online rumor.

"Sen. Dems. absence apparent effort to prevent quorum, block vote," she tweeted at around 11:14 a.m. and then, a few minutes later, "To be clear, no personal knowledge re. absence of Dems. Just reporting what we're hearing."

At first, all Dye felt was confusion—she wasn't sure what Democrats were trying to accomplish with their move. She quickly found the Senate rules online, trying to see which one the Democrats were relying on to hold up Walker's bill in their absence. Like many on Twitter in the early moments, Dye missed the distinction between the quorum needed in the Senate to pass regular bills and the larger quorum needed for fiscal bills. Dye was offering her readers what she herself wanted—immediate updates even if at times they were inaccurate. As Dye gradually realized what the Democratic senators had done, her confusion gave way to relief and elation. In politics, she saw Democrats as too willing to heed Republicans' demands, but here was a group of Democrats taking one of the boldest steps imaginable, and for her it was inspiring.

As soon as she could get off work, Dye hurried to the Capitol. Arriving at 6:45 p.m., she tweeted that she could hear the chanting from blocks away. "Back downtown. My red sneakers are on the ground, in solidarity with our teachers & public employees!" she tweeted. She did her best to post about the exuberant protests. With thousands of people around her often using their own phones, it was at times impossible to get enough bandwidth to make calls with her iPhone or get her Twitter app to load. Already, Dye had figured out that she needed to have the charger for her beleaguered phone with her at all times. A little before midnight she informed her audience that she was heading to a restroom to "get my charge on." Sometime that day she decided she would try to reply to everyone who put a question or request to her using Twitter. It was a bigger commitment than she realized at first. That Thursday night, February 17, Dye was already tweeting frequently on the events, and she was contacted by someone at a Madison restaurant a mile away from the Capitol who knew about her posts and wanted to give the demonstrators hot soup, chips, guacamole, salad, and, most important to Dye, cheese. "Hungry protesters find support & sustenance from the folks at Weary Traveler. THANK YOU," she tweeted at 1 a.m.

She didn't leave to go home until around 2:30 a.m. Friday, once again giving herself just a few hours of sleep before she had to wake up for the long drive to her law office. She would spend most of her free moments at the Capitol in the coming days, working full days at her job and long nights at the demonstrations. To keep up in the first two weeks, she had to take some vacation time. Her commitment and her thousands of tweets earned her a loyal band of followers. At one point early in the protests, she went to a bar near the Capitol with friends to have a drink and checked her phone. It had twenty-five new messages—all notifications from Twitter that a new person was following her updates. She refreshed her phone and found she had twenty-five more. Dumbfounded, she refreshed it again and again, and each time found that she had another twenty-five notifications that new people were following her. Dye shot up to some three thousand followers on Twitter and began getting requests and questions from readers as far away as Norway and Japan.

On Friday, she could visit the Capitol only briefly because she had to take a short trip to Milwaukee for her job. She spent most of the visit responding to requests on Twitter and coordinating donations. The unions were quickly organizing and moving toward handling more of the basic needs at the demonstrations, but in that first week Dye and other individuals played a crucial role. She sent tweets to her followers requesting necessities like water, food, and phone chargers. Meanwhile, a website was set up where people could offer to donate goods and then have those donations connected to people who needed them. "That became almost the only thing I could do," Dye said later.

While Dye was fanning the protests on Twitter, Michael Brown was taking on a much bigger task to oppose Walker. The effort involved would make it, as Brown said later, "by far the best and worst year of my life." He was a thirty-two-year-old single father living in Appleton and the owner of a small marketing company that focused on online business. Brown had grown up in the strongly Republican community of Brookfield, a suburb of Milwaukee, and had never been a member of a union. However, the mother of Brown's kindergartener son was a teacher, and Brown's father had risen from a blue-collar factory job to become a technical college instructor and union member. All of this gave him a soft spot for teachers. Deeply interested in politics, Brown tended to vote for Democrats. But he admired centrist leaders like Republican U.S. Senator Olympia Snowe of Maine and Democratic Senator Claire McCaskill of Missouri, and he had voted for Republican Tommy Thompson while he served as Wisconsin's governor. He believed politicians should govern from the middle and had become disillusioned with the country's ever more polarized politics.

In 2010 Brown briefly ran for the Assembly as an independent, challenging a Democratic incumbent. But Brown dropped his campaign without doing much more than knocking on some doors and paying for a web domain name in February 2010—www.unitedwisconsin.com—that reflected his belief that politics should bring citizens together. The state Democratic Party complained to state elections officials that the website didn't list who was paying for it, as required by law—an omission that Brown fixed. He reported to the state that his campaign had raised just $57.45, all from a single donation he'd made to it. Later, Brown would laugh at his effort. But he'd had some ambitious ideas such as using his website to create a platform where his future constituents could tell him how to vote. When he talked to voters, Brown told them that his views were less important than theirs; he wanted to vote according to their wishes. "People thought I was full of crap," he recalled.

Brown had previously held a marketing job at a Milwaukee radio station and had spoken with Walker while the latter served as Milwaukee County executive. Brown hadn't liked Walker's politics then, and he had been furious when as governor-elect Walker had blocked the creation of the Milwaukee-to-Madison passenger rail line, which Brown had hoped to see eventually extended to his area. But learning about Walker's budget-repair bill—and watching the governor refuse to change it in the face of strong opposition—had sent Brown into action. He was upset that Walker hadn't campaigned on the repeal of union bargaining, and he was also unhappy with Walker's pro-posed cuts to health programs for the poor and other parts of the bill that he saw as bad policy or outright shady, like the possibility of the governor selling the state's power plants. "He wasn't honest with us; that's what this is about," Brown said later.

Working with his laptop at home or sitting with a cup of tea in a downtown Appleton coffee shop, Brown refashioned the website he'd meant to use for his aborted Assembly campaign. His idea was simple but audacious—use it as a vehicle to advance the first recall of a governor in Wisconsin history. Brown wanted the website to target Walker as well as Lieutenant Governor Rebecca Kleefisch, whom he saw as inept and as unfit for office as Walker. But he didn't include any Republican state senators as recall targets because he believed that would have amounted to a partisan witch hunt. He connected the website to a database that could store the names, addresses, and contact information of people who signed its online pledge to back a recall of Walker and Kleefisch. The power of the Internet was telling here. It gave a single tech-savvy man of modest means the ability to help launch a movement with no more start-up cost than his own time. That morning, just hours before Brown learned about the Democratic senators heading to Illinois, he launched his website from the living room of his Appleton duplex. Like the web mar-keter he was, he began to promote it on social media sites such as Face-book, waiting to see if it would catch fire. That day, about one hundred people signed up. For the next three days—Friday, Saturday, and Sunday—Brown went to Madison to demonstrate against the bill. On Saturday he took his five-year-old son, who held a sign celebrating his grandfather and mother for being public employees. "My poppa is a teacher and my mother is a teacher," it read. Caught up in the protests, Brown realized that their energy had to be harnessed before it dissipated fruitlessly—a problem that he later saw with the Occupy Wall Street movement. Brown described himself later as a dreamer, someone with an unusual faith in his own ability to leave a lasting mark on his world. But even he didn't imagine how his idea would grow or how it would take hold of his life.

Dye and Brown weren't the only ones using the web. At about 1 p.m. Thursday, Democratic Senator Lena Taylor of Milwaukee posted three teasing letters to her Facebook page—"brb," slang for "be right back." By the time she had posted, the Democratic senators had already crossed the state line and arrived in Rockford. The senators waited in the lobby at the Clock Tower but realized that people would probably be looking for them. They rented a business suite and ordered food. About the time Ellis adjourned the Senate, an e-mailed statement from Miller on behalf of the group landed in reporters' inboxes. It read: "Democrats believe it is wrong to strip people of their right to have a say in the conditions of their employment and to use state law to bust unions. Over the last several days tens of thousands of citizens, young and old, union and non-union, labor and management, from every corner of the state, have travelled to the Capitol to peacefully and respectfully exercise their right to speak to their elected officials. These people deserve to be heard and their rights ought to be respected."

After their meal, the Democrats talked about their next steps and began to reach out to Walker's office and other Republicans. Senator Bob Jauch said later, "Most of us were at the Clock Tower and had some lunch. And then we had a discussion of where to go next. It wasn't, 'Let's keep running.' It was, 'What do you say? How do you make it useful? How do you find an end to it?' We had those conversations from the very first day."

To the surprise of Miller and the others, their Illinois boycott hit the national media like a bomb. By the end of that afternoon, the story had shot to the top on Google News and was the number two story on the *New York Times* website, with cable news and the Huffington Post heavily hyping it as well. Ed Schultz, the liberal host of MSNBC's *The Ed Show* and a critic of Walker's union legislation, came to Madison to broadcast his talk show that night. The interest was at peak levels inside Wisconsin too. By 11 a.m., the website of the *Milwaukee Journal Sentinel* had passed one million page views and was averaging two hundred thousand views an hour—and that was before the paper reported that the senators had left. Reporters quickly moved to follow the Democrats to their new location at the Clock Tower. The Rockford media were the first to show up, taking pictures of senators and interviewing them. But once word of their location spread, it was CNN and then, seemingly, everyone else. Milwaukee's WTMJ-TV had a helicopter hovering over the tower, as if in hopes of catching the Democrats fleeing in their cars like O.J. Simpson. The mailboxes for the senators' cell phones clogged with messages from reporters and associates.

From afar, the biggest figures in national politics also jumped into the debate. President Barack Obama had already scheduled an interview on the federal budget with a Milwaukee reporter, Charles Benson of WTMJ, for the day the Democrats left the state. Benson flew out to D.C. for the interview and used it to ask about the sudden conflict in Madison. The president acknowledged the need for teachers, police officers, and social workers to sacrifice along with the rest of the country and "make some adjustment to new fiscal realities." But Obama criticized the proposed cuts to workers' bargaining power. "Some of what I've heard coming out of Wisconsin, where they're just making it harder for public employees to collectively bargain generally, seems like more of an assault on unions," the president told Benson. "I think everybody's got to make some adjustments, but I think it's also important to recognize that public employees make enormous contributions to our states and our citizens. . . . I think it's important not to vilify them or to suggest that somehow all these budget problems are due to public employees."

The next day, the *Washington Post* reported that the White House had done more than just an interview. Citing a party official, the report said that Obama's political operation, Organizing for America, had gotten involved in Wisconsin on February 14 after Democratic National Committee Chairman Timothy Kaine, a former Virginia governor, spoke to union leaders there. "The group made phone calls, distributed messages via Twitter and Facebook, and sent e-mails to state and national lists to try to build crowds for rallies" on February 16 and 17, the newspaper reported. It's worth noting, however, that such efforts can't create the kind of motivation needed to get tens of thousands to show up for a normally boring attraction—a piece of state legislation. Just like the organizers of Tea Party rallies, national groups can invite thousands of people to a rally and help coordinate efforts to transport them from distant cities. But only a rare sort of enthusiasm can move a Teamster or a Tea Partier to travel for hours to attend a rally about a bill in their own state, let alone a bill in another state. In the face of the president's comments, national Republican leaders were quick to defend Walker. House Speaker John Boehner chastised Obama and called on him to drop the criticism of the governor. "This is not the way you begin an 'adult conversation' in America about solutions to the fiscal challenges that are destroying jobs in our country," Boehner said in a statement, alluding to the president's recent call for civility in federal budget talks. "Rather than shouting down those in office who speak honestly about the challenges we face, the president and his advisers should lead."

Reince Priebus, the Republican National Committee chairman and Wisconsin native, also criticized Obama's efforts and vowed that his committee would mobilize on the other side for Walker. "Our party's all in. We're going to be all in," he said. "We're going to do whatever we have to do to help [Wisconsin Republicans] be successful. The rest of the country is watching. The Democrats are not winning this battle of public perception from folks outside of Wisconsin looking in."

In the end, neither side gained an effective national spokesman from outside Wisconsin, perhaps because the controversy around the issue was so toxic. After briefly speaking out on the matter, Obama left it to his aides to address and never re-engaged on the issue. The lost opportunity was a great one for Democrats, who instead were left with national figures like the Reverend Jesse Jackson, who had nothing like the president's broad appeal. Lacking the presidency or even a decided nominee to face the president in 2012, Republicans also had no dominant leader in Washington, D.C., to turn to in the fight. But for them, it was less important because they had Walker, an effective speaker who by the end of the conflict had become a national figure in his own right who could handle everything from network news interviews to East Coast fund-raisers. Throughout the conflict and into the recall elections beyond, Democrats lacked a figure—either inside Wisconsin or outside it—who could speak as their primary voice opposing the governor on the airwaves or at the ballot box.

That didn't stop Democrats from seeking and finding significant support from outside Wisconsin. A day after leaving the state, the Senate Democrats launched a fund-raising appeal through their umbrella committee, calling for donations to "raise the resources they need to continue the fight standing up for workers' rights and working families in Wisconsin and across the nation." The cash quickly flowed in through ActBlue, a website that helps funnel money from contributors to Democratic candidates. Just one day after the senators left Wisconsin, the site had already recorded thousands of dollars in donations for the State Senate Democratic Committee, and it shot upward from there. By February 21, four days after the Democrats left the state, about twelve thousand donors had given more than $300,000 to the committee. To put that into perspective, those four days brought in almost as much as the $320,000 that the committee had raised in all of the previous year and made the Senate Democrats the hottest issue on ActBlue's running tally of donations to various left-wing causes. For any Democratic senator who was nervous about remaining in Illinois, the influx of money provided at least some reassurance.

Republicans weren't missing their chance to pull in money either. On that day, the Republican Party of Wisconsin gave visitors to its website the chance to "stand with Walker" by giving money to its campaign fund. The Virginia-based Republican State Leadership Committee, which aims to elect GOP politicians to state offices around the country, did its own fund-raising by pointing out how the battle in Wisconsin was playing out in other states as well. Priebus of the RNC made a similar appeal to supporters to back Walker: "Today the fight is in Wisconsin, but soon it will be nationwide."

But for the moment at the Clock Tower, the Democrats began to feel exposed, and they decided at about 4 p.m. to find another place to stay. As news broke about the Democrats' exodus from Wisconsin, Tea Partiers headed to the Clock Tower with video cameras in hand. One of them confronted Senators Jim Holperin and Bob Jauch as they left the Clock Tower.

"Excuse me, sir, why aren't you doing your job in Wisconsin today?" the Tea Partier asked as Holperin stood in front of his open car door.

"I'm leaving right now to do my job in Wisconsin," Holperin responded.

"Why didn't you do it earlier today, sir?"

"I believe we did do our job in Wisconsin," Holperin said.

The Tea Partier kept the camera trained on Holperin. The cameraman disputed Holperin's claim, saying he had a duty to appear on the Senate floor and vote on the budget-repair bill.

"I'm not so sure that's my job today," Holperin said. "My job today is to delay a vote on a piece of legislation that the people of the state have said we have not had time to consider the consequences of."

The senators headed to the Country Inn and Suites in Freeport, just a short jaunt to the west of Rockford. There, most of the senators got their own rooms and spent the night. Senator Kathleen Vinehout stayed with her sister and brother-in-law in Woodstock, which was on the opposite side of Rockford. The next morning, the other senators decided to go there as well, continuing to improvise their course almost hour by hour. They stuck to their story that they had formed the plan to leave without union involvement. "This was entirely initiated on our own. We did not coordinate it in advance with any interest group whatsoever," Miller said later.

Marty Beil, executive director of the Wisconsin State Employees Union, and some other union officials heard about the possibility the Democrats might leave the night before they did so. "We knew they were thinking of something. We weren't quite sure until it actually happened. . . . This had happened [with lawmakers] in Ohio and Texas with some success so we figured *hmm*," Beil remembered later. "We got it from some fairly reliable sources."

But the actual departure still galvanized the union leaders. Within an hour of the senators leaving Madison, Susan McMurray, a lobbyist for Beil's council and other Wisconsin AFSCME units, had confirmed that the Democrats were bound for Illinois. She broke the news to Beil in a conversation outside the Capitol on the State Street side, where Beil was resting his hefty frame on a stone bench. McMurray hadn't known about the Democrats' plans until that morning, and when she told Beil he appeared to her to almost fall off the bench in surprise. Because of his reaction, McMurray assumed that like her Beil had also known nothing about the plans. "Much to their credit it was like herding cats for a little bit there and they herded them up and got them out of here so it was like, 'Oh, wow,'" Beil remembered later.

McMurray then called Rich Abelson, executive director of AFSCME Council 48, which represents city and county workers in the Milwaukee area. Abelson was with other union leaders in their "war room" at the nearby Concourse Hotel planning a statement to respond to the bill when it passed the Senate. They were all depressed. "Then we found out they left," Abelson said. "I was elated. . . . Any day we live is a good day."

Once in Illinois, the senators worked closely with union officials from both Wisconsin and Washington, D.C. Late that evening, Miller's spokesman received an e-mail to his personal account from Blaine Rummel, a spokesman from the national AFSCME office who had been helping coordinate the union's opposition to Walker's bill. Marked "TPs," for talking points, the e-mail included statements that were phrased as if one of the Democratic senators were saying them. One read, "We're on the job. The fact is, Wisconsin legislators are sworn to protect people's rights, not take them away. And we are fulfilling our oath."

The sudden stalemate arose from more than just unions and budgets. It was part of a national trend away from bipartisanship. In Wisconsin, the number of moderate lawmakers had dwindled, leaving almost no Republicans who would ever vote for tax hikes, unions, or abortion rights and few Democrats who opposed abortion or favored strongly conservative social values. As the parties grew purer and further apart ideologically, opposing legislators had become less likely to even have a meal or a drink together. Signs of dysfunction had grown, from more late-night sessions to delayed budgets when the control of the Legislature was split. Congress had been suffering from the same problems, and it had become acceptable for one party to pursue an agenda wholly on its own and for the other side to obstruct it by any means available. More than acceptable, it had become admirable—at least to the partisans on both sides.

At noon back in Madison, unions rallied their now fired-up supporters on the King Street steps of the Capitol. As the Beatles' "Revolution" blared over the sound system, demonstrators marched around the Capitol, and scores of students crowded the building steps. One man held up a sign that read "John Lennon Would Love This." But it wasn't just union supporters who got a jolt of energy from the Democrats' departure. Inside the Capitol and around the country, Republicans were reacting to the move with fury. The usually amiable Walker revealed a note of that anger shortly before 5 p.m., when he stepped to a lectern in his conference room in the east wing of the statehouse. He was wearing a dark suit and red tie and stood alone in the glare of the television cameras; cable news networks were broadcasting his remarks live. The roar of the still massive crowd bled through the walls as he spoke: "I'll be here all day working and I'll be here tonight working at the job I'm paid to do on behalf of the people of the great state of Wisconsin," he said. "I continue to work and I'm calling on the members of the state Senate to show up and do the job that they are paid to do as well."

Walker said the cuts to employees' compensation through their health and pension benefits would help avoid the layoffs of ten thousand to twelve thousand state and local workers. The governor was careful not to mention the repeal of most collective bargaining for public workers, the part of his bill that had most angered the shouting protesters outside. Other states such as New York would make cuts in areas like education without giving schools the ability to avoid layoffs, Walker stated. Wisconsin would also make sizable cuts in state aid to schools and municipalities but would provide local governments help with their costs to blunt the impact on core services. "While in the last couple of days we heard a lot from government workers who are protesting a very modest change in terms of their pension and health contributions, of the eight thousand e-mails we got today, the majority are telling us to stay firm, stay strong, to stand with the taxpayers," he said. "And, again, while the protesters have every right to be heard, I'm going to make sure the taxpayers of the state are heard and their voices are not drowned out by those circling the Capitol."

Reporters repeatedly asked Walker whether he would talk with the Democratic senators in Illinois, whether he would negotiate with unions rather than imposing cuts, and whether he would allow some aspects of collective bargaining, such as workplace safety rules, to remain in place if they had no obvious cost to taxpayers. Walker didn't pull back an inch on any of his positions, calling the Democrats' move a "stunt" and the unions' offers of negotiations "pretty disingenuous." "They tried to ram through a bill [on labor contracts] after the election, when they were hoping the people weren't paying attention. . . . They had no interest in negotiating with us then," he said. "I think it's a red herring."

Within ten minutes, Walker had left the conference room. He had said almost nothing new, showing only the same quality he'd displayed as Milwaukee County executive—what his friends saw as firmness and his enemies saw as recalcitrance. But there were two takeaways from what Walker had said. One was obvious: By leaving the state, Senate Democrats had shifted the power dynamic within the Capitol. For the last week, Walker and GOP lawmakers hadn't engaged Democrats. The Republicans had simply moved forward quickly with their plans to pass the bill. But suddenly Walker and GOP lawmakers were no longer fully in control. For the first time in his short tenure as governor, Walker needed something from a Democrat. The other takeaway from Walker's comments had to do with the e-mails. When the Associated Press sued, along with the Madison alternative weekly *Isthmus*, to get the e-mails and then analyze them, the international news service found that the messages in the governor's account were running strongly against him from the time he unveiled his legislation to the day the Democrats left the state. During this time, Walker said nothing about these e-mails publicly. But when the senators headed to Illinois, the tide turned dramatically.

The Democrats' departure sparked more than just celebration and renewed enthusiasm for the fight from their already energized allies. It also triggered an avalanche of anger from conservatives who saw the Democrats as seeking to undo the election victory that Republicans had won in November. E-mails supporting Walker and his proposal—including many from out of state— poured into the governor's inbox and by the end of the day had reversed the balance to one of support. The e-mails in no way represented a scientific survey of public opinion. But they showed an important trend. The Democrats' unprecedented tactic had helped ensure that both sides were angry and energized. Suddenly, it wasn't just Democrats talking about mounting recall elections against Republicans for supporting Walker's bill. Some of the Senate Democrats in Illinois would be targeted for recall as well, and in every election over the next sixteen months, Republicans would be at least as energized as Democrats. A political grudge match was on.

9

First Assembly Vote

THE NEXT DAY WOULD END IN AN UPROAR and recriminations in the other house of the Legislature. In the morning, the massive crowds returned and grew by the hour. By the end of that Friday, February 18, the throng of tens of thousands of people had grown even larger, with their shouts and drumming once again producing a deafening din inside the Capitol rotunda. The unreal stalemate of the day before was now looking all too real and substantial. The Senate Democrats were still somewhere in Illinois—Republicans weren't sure exactly where—and neither side knew when they would return. Before the day ended, the disorder in the upper house would arrive in the Assembly and have it, too, teetering on the edge of chaos. In the meantime, both sides tried to take their case to the media. So far, Walker had kept much of the coverage and debate in the national media focused on the increased benefit payments that he wanted to require from public workers to help balance the budget. The provisions that the unions and Democrats hated most, the ones that largely repealed collective bargaining in Wisconsin, didn't always get top attention from the national television networks and press. That made it more difficult for average viewers outside the state to understand the uproar in Madison. In an interview that morning with the national show *Fox and Friends*, the host didn't ask Walker about the repeal of most union bargaining. Instead, he shifted his questions to the Democrats, emphasizing how they had left the state to block a vote in their house. "Did you have any idea something this cockamamie was going to happen?" host Steve Doocy asked. Walker chuckled. "Not at all."

Some Senate Democrats believed they now had both momentum and time on their side. That morning, Senator Jon Erpenbach sat down to a breakfast of pancakes with his aunt and uncle at a Chicago hotel. Erpenbach had left his colleagues in northern Illinois the night before for a CNN interview, and he was settling into the Windy City, where he had family. His location gave him more opportunities for media interviews, and he happily took advantage of them by appearing on *Good Morning America* and *The Rachel Maddow Show*. He represented thousands of public employees in his suburban Madison district and had already become one of the primary spokesmen for the Democrats in their self-imposed exile. The televisions around Erpenbach played the CNN interview with him while he ate, but none of the diners around him seemed to notice. Erpenbach texted and talked with his fellow Democrats by cell phone, took a call from MSNBC, and then booked his hotel room for another night, revealing that the chances of an immediate breakthrough were dim. "We certainly think we're winning the public debate on this," Erpenbach told the *Wisconsin State Journal*. "People understand this isn't about money, it's about stripping collective bargaining rights, and that's unsettling to them."

Most of the other Democratic senators had spent the night 115 miles northwest of Chicago in Freeport, and they were doing interviews of their own. Senator Jim Holperin, from a Republican-leaning northern district, told the *Milwaukee Journal Sentinel* that he and his colleagues would return in time to debate and vote on Walker's budget-repair bill. "We will be back eventually. We won't obstruct the vote forever," he said.

The problem for Democrats, however, was the same one as for Walker: how could they force an ending without giving up on their demands? Their leader, Mark Miller, issued a statement that day. "We continue to call on the governor and Republicans to allow us to get serious about addressing fiscal issues and creating jobs and drop the unrelated items that do nothing to help us balance our budget," it said. But what if the governor wouldn't bend?

Enraged Republican senators were struggling to respond to the unprecedented departure. At 9:30 that morning, all but one of the GOP legislators gathered in the Senate chamber and called for all senators to come to the floor. For the second straight day, the chief clerk went through the empty exercise of taking the roll, getting only silence after the names of the Democrats. When that was done, Scott Fitzgerald moved for a call of the house. "We have . . . eighteen members present, not sufficient to move forward. The call will continue to be on. The Senate will stand informal pending the call of the chair," Senate President Mike Ellis said and banged his gavel.

In less than four minutes, Republicans had exhausted their limited plans to get their colleagues back. Later, amid a scrum of reporters, Fitzgerald blasted the Democrats, saying he had barely had any contact with them since they left. Fitzgerald kept his composure as he answered questions, but he didn't try to conceal his fury over the impasse. The GOP leader sent state troopers to Miller's house in Monona to see if he was there, but it was just more political theater. First, the Democrats were beyond Wisconsin's border and outside the jurisdiction of every elected official at the Capitol. Second, they had done nothing more than cross into a neighboring state, something that tens of thousands of Wisconsin residents did every day. However distasteful Republicans found the Democrats' action, there was nothing illegal about it. Fitzgerald confronted the uncomfortable reality that the rules and traditions of the state's democratic institutions could not always be relied on when relationships between its leaders utterly broke down. The Republican admitted that, even if by some miracle the troopers found Miller at his house, they would not be able to force him to come to the Senate. "It's never going to happen, that's the point," Fitzgerald said. "I don't know what the practical ability [is] to force a senator to sit in their chair and vote. They shut down government is what they've done and that's not acceptable."

The visit that day to Miller's suburban Madison home highlighted the futility of Republicans' efforts. Ted Blazel, the Senate sergeant at arms who had served under both Democratic and Republican leaders, got out of his car and walked to Miller's home not far from the eastern shore of Lake Monona. Blazel knocked and, visibly uncomfortable, waited with a trooper on the stoop. A protester called out repeatedly from the street, "This is not what democracy looks like. This is not what democracy looks like." No one came to the door. After a short wait, Blazel walked down the driveway of the house to check if anyone was in the backyard and then returned. "What's your next move?" a reporter asked him. "Going back to the Capitol," Blazel said, heading toward his car.

The stalemate in the Senate posed a number of practical problems for Walker and the Republicans deciding what to do next. They were dealing with three intense issues at once: passing a repair bill for the current budget that also overturned decades of labor law; managing the massive, raucous demonstrations; and preparing a larger bill for the two-year budget that started in July. Something had to give. The most obvious place to start was the speech Walker had scheduled for Tuesday, February 22, in which he was supposed to unveil his first two-year budget bill. The new governor had intended to break with tradition for that budget address and deliver it to lawmakers at a Madison company, Vita Plus, which made supplements for livestock feed. The change from the longtime practice of giving the speech in the Capitol

was meant to put a spotlight on private business and the governor's plans for
overcoming the recession. But it was now clear that Republicans would never
make the original timetable laid out by Walker's office of passing the bill
through the Legislature by the weekend. State law also complicated the question because it required the governor to deliver the budget message to the full
Legislature, which except for emergencies is required to meet at the Capitol.
Bowing to circumstance, Walker postponed his budget address by one week,
to March 1, and moved its location from Vita Plus to the usual place, the
Assembly chamber. At 1:22 that afternoon, the GOP senators returned to the
floor, quickly approved a resolution changing the date of the budget address,
and broke for the day.

With their plans stalled in the Senate, Republicans turned their attention
to passing the bill in the Assembly. That morning in the Capitol rotunda,
hundreds of protesters cheered as Assembly Democrats walked through on
their way to the floor session. Peter Barca, the Democratic leader, met with
spectators, shaking hands and offering his thanks for the large turnout. "This
was unprecedented, unparalleled," Barca said as he prepared to go to the
floor. "And still the Republicans ignore it. They hear it but don't listen."

Just after 9 a.m., Assembly Chief Clerk Patrick Fuller barked out the roll
like the former military man he was. "August, Ballweg, Barca, Berceau . . . ,"
he called. Republicans and Democrats milled about. The Democrats had
pulled over their collared shirts and dresses Halloween-orange T-shirts that
declared "Assembly Democrats Fighting for Working Families!" Representative Bill Kramer, who as speaker pro tem was responsible for presiding over
the session and enforcing Assembly rules, took his place on the highest part
of the dais at the head of the chamber. He was new to the role, having taken
it after Republicans gained the majority two months earlier. He sometimes
still made miscues and leaned on his staff to keep the business on track. But
he also had a sharp sense of humor, which he used to leaven the long debates
and to try to keep lawmakers, often Democrats, in line. "Members, please take
your seats; members, please take your seats," Kramer said. "We are on the
eleventh order of business on the special session calendar. . . . The clerk will
read the title of the bill."

In his authoritative baritone, Fuller gave the summary of an identical
companion bill to the one that had been blocked in the Senate. In the traditional way of the body, Kramer moved forward with the session by asking for
amendments on the bill. But first, Democrats asked to do a few introductions
and break for a private caucus meeting. "Fair enough," Kramer answered.

A long line of Democrats stood, one after the other, to welcome and thank some of the constituents who had come to Madison to protest the bill. The public galleries high above them were packed with union supporters, and the shouts of the much greater crowd in the rotunda could be heard. The Democrats had solicited notes with the names of demonstrators who had arrived from Republican districts and handed those out to GOP lawmakers. Not all of them were read from the floor, but in all there were 854 entries of visitors that day in the official Assembly Journal, often with more than one name per entry.

The length of the introductions gave a sense of the coming day. Democrats took their time with them; they were in no hurry to move on toward a vote on the bill that they would certainly lose. Even though three Republicans had left the Assembly to take appointments in the Walker administration, the majority party still had fifty-seven members, easily outnumbering the thirty-eight Democrats. The lone independent lawmaker, Bob Ziegelbauer of Manitowoc, typically voted with Republicans, meaning that the majority could afford to lose nine of its members and still pass the bill. In practical terms, the most that Democrats could do was slow the bill down and perhaps amend it in some small way. Republicans knew that all they needed was the patience to outlast the Democrats, so they mostly sat silent. Finally, Speaker Jeff Fitzgerald stood. "First, thank you guys, Assembly Democrats, for showing up to work. That is one thing we're very bipartisan on—we work harder than the Senate," Fitzgerald said, getting the first cheers of the day for a Republican. "I would ask for a recess for the purpose of a Republican caucus."

Less than an hour after they began, the representatives headed to the caucus meetings, a tradition that could last hours even when they debated routine business. Both sides spent the rest of the day behind closed doors, although the Assembly Democrats did emerge for one errand. In a made-for-television moment, they tramped down a flight of stairs and a couple of Capitol hallways from their caucus room to Walker's office to ask for a meeting and deliver a letter. Walker's spokesman, Cullen Werwie, emerged to say that the governor wasn't available and that he would accept the letter on Walker's behalf. In the letter, the Democrats called on Walker to drop a range of provisions that had been found by the Legislature's nonpartisan budget office to be policy items without a clear financial impact. "As governor, you are the leader of this state. Now is the time for you to show some leadership and end this chaos," the letter stated.

The Democratic lawmakers weren't the only ones making an offer. Later that day, the leaders of the biggest public-sector unions in the state said they would accept Walker's proposed cuts to their benefits if he dropped his repeal of collective bargaining. Union members had been making this point since right after Walker unveiled his plans, but Friday's announcement marked their most formal statement on the matter, and it came from their top leaders. Marty Beil, executive director of the Wisconsin State Employees Union, had excoriated Walker in recent months, but he adopted a somewhat more conciliatory tone in a news release that day. Beil's union represented 23,000 mostly blue-collar workers, but he was speaking for all of AFSCME's 68,000 members in Wisconsin, which included everyone from correctional officers to county highway workers. He said that his members would agree to pay more of their pension contributions and health insurance benefits as Walker demanded but would never agree to give up decades-old bargaining rights. "We are prepared to implement the financial concessions proposed to help bring our state's budget into balance, but we will not be denied our God-given right to join a real union. . . . We will not—I repeat we will not—be denied our rights to collectively bargain," Beil's statement said. Mary Bell, the president of WEAC, the state's largest teachers union, quickly made a similar offer in a conference call with reporters. "This is not about money," she said. "We understand the need to sacrifice."

The offer of concessions—made by unions as well as Democratic lawmakers—marked a potential turning point in the struggle. First, the flat acceptance of the benefits and compensation cuts by the unions had an effect on the news coverage of the crisis, particularly the stories in the national media. The offer of concessions made clear that the fight in Wisconsin was about more than just getting the state through a two-year budget crisis; it was also about the long-term relationship between the government and its employees. The concessions created an opportunity for Walker as well. The unions hadn't previously offered that level of givebacks—as recently as December they had pushed for lawmakers to approve a contract through June 30, 2011, with much smaller concessions. Walker could have taken that offer and perhaps sought even more, saying that he had gotten it only because he had been willing to stand up to the unions on behalf of taxpayers. That victory would have made up for part or even all of the sting of being forced to give in on the collective bargaining repeal. Nor did Walker have to trust the unions when they said they would give the concessions. His legislation already had provisions specifically requiring the benefit cuts that the unions were now accepting. He could simply agree to remove the other provisions and move the legislation forward. If the unions objected, they might have been accused of operating in bad faith.

Walker had one more reason to consider the bargain. A poll released that Friday underscored that there were political dangers for him as well as the Democrats in the continued standoff. The poll was conducted and paid for by We Ask America, part of a subsidiary of the Illinois Manufacturers' Association, hardly a liberal group. The poll, conducted hours after the Senate Democrats left Wisconsin, found 43.1 percent approved of Walker's plans, 51.9 percent disapproved, and 5.1 percent were uncertain. But the survey also had bad news for union supporters. On whether the Democratic senators should return to Madison, 56 percent said yes, 36.4 percent said no, and 7.6 percent were not sure. There was a fleeting hope on that Friday afternoon that a bargain could be made.

In his east wing office, Walker sat unimpressed and uninterested. That afternoon, he brought in a series of journalists for private interviews. During his interview with the *Milwaukee Journal Sentinel*, the thick walls of Walker's orderly office muted the thunderous shouts of the demonstrators a short distance away. The governor looked a bit tired—he said he was getting little sleep—but he looked unruffled and resolved. In his usual affable manner, he acknowledged that his wife and teenage sons were "stressed out" but didn't talk about the threats against him. As for the protesters, Walker conceded that they had "passion and it's legitimate" and had a right to be heard. But he went no further. When asked whether he would take Beil, Bell, and their unions up on their offer, Walker left himself no wiggle room. "It's not going to work and the reason is, having been a local official, we've got 72 counties, 424 school districts, and over a thousand municipalities. And like every other state, or nearly every other state in the country, our budget is going to have cuts in aids to local [governments]," he said. "In fact, New York and California, which I've talked about before, have cut billions of dollars out of the schools, the university system, and local governments and not given them any tools. My goal all along has been to give all these folks—and [as a local official] I asked for it in the past—the tools to control their own budgets; you've got to give them some flexibility. . . . I can't guarantee if Marty Beil says we've got the state workers and AFSCME—there's other bargaining units out there—that there's any guarantee that every other school district, town, county, village, or town board is going to get those same sorts of agreements."

In the interview, Walker pointed out how the unions had aggressively sought contracts in December with much smaller concessions. All that was reason not to trust the labor groups, he said. But the governor ducked the question of why not simply require the cuts in benefits by law, which would prevent the savings from getting hung up in bargaining. He presented the choice as nearly eliminating union bargaining or leaving it alone, with no middle ground. "Let's not kid ourselves. The reality is, it's about the money," Walker said. "For the national union leaders that are here, it's about the money as well. And they want to be able to continue to mandate without say that union dues are taken out of the pay of these workers. . . . The bottom line is, if the argument is about democracy, which you've heard all week, it's letting people choose whether or not they want to be in the union."

Walker finished his private interviews and moved on to a larger news conference. As he did, tensions exploded in the Assembly. All day, the Democrats had been holed up in their caucus room just outside the chamber, studying the bill and putting together an arsenal of amendments to it. Even for regular business, the Assembly moved at a glacial pace. Caucus breaks lasted hours, as did the floor debates that were often dysfunctional, if not downright chaotic. The Assembly regularly voted on bills after midnight, and action on a real controversy often happened closer to sunup than sundown. With ninety-nine members, there were ample opportunities for the body's debate to be hijacked by individual members of either party who were quirky, angry, drunk with power, or just plain drunk. The freewheeling deliberations camouflaged the fact that the actual votes on the floor were almost always choreographed. Neither side influenced the other much, and bills were rarely modified in unexpected ways on the floor.

For this session, the lawmakers were set to reconvene at 5 p.m. Republicans knew they had an epic session of arguments and insomnia ahead of them, and they saw a way to avoid some of that by quickly advancing Walker's bill to a stage where amendments could not be considered. So between 4:54 and 4:55 p.m., Fuller, the chief clerk, quickly began taking the roll. Kramer determined that a quorum was present and called for the vote on the first amendment to the bill—a GOP change that was quickly adopted on a voice vote. It was 4:58, two minutes before the scheduled start time, and Democrats had yet to catch on and show up on the floor. With no lawmaker from the minority objecting, Republicans were about to move the bill to a third reading, the stage in which Democrats would no longer be able to offer the more than one hundred amendments they were drafting. "The question is shall January 2011 Special Session Assembly Bill 11 be engrossed and read a third time?" Kramer said.

At that moment, Gordon Hintz, a Democrat from Oshkosh, jogged into the chamber. He had been standing in the Assembly's vestibule talking to a staffer when he realized the Republicans were doing more than just taking the roll. He ran down the center aisle to his seat, past the Republican lawmakers and the empty desks of his Democratic colleagues. "Rule 61, point of personal privilege, Mr. Speaker," Hintz shouted, referring to a rule that allowed lawmakers to interrupt a session to make a point.

Kramer didn't recognize Hintz to let him speak, and Hintz started waving his hand, as if he thought Kramer had simply not seen or heard him. Barca and some other Democrats poured onto the floor now, and Barca pointed at Hintz and shouted for the speaker pro tem to give him the floor. "Mr. Speaker, recognize him! Recognize him!" Barca yelled.

"The question before the body is shall January 2011 Special Session Assembly Bill 11 be ordered engrossed and read a third time?" Kramer continued. "All in favor—"

"Mr. Speaker, I demand the floor under a point of Assembly privilege," Barca shouted over him.

More Democrats flooded into the chamber and screamed, "No! No!" along with Barca and Hintz. Aides to Republicans near the podium motioned to Kramer and the other leaders and urged them to "keep going, keep going." "The ayes have it. The bill is engrossed," Kramer said.

The bill was now at a stage in which it could no longer be amended. Another Republican leader called for taking the next step toward a final vote on the bill, but Barca interrupted again. "You said five o'clock. It's 4:59! Mr. Speaker, I have a point of personal privilege under Rule 61!" Barca bellowed. "I don't know if you're deaf or what the problem is, but I demand you recognize me!"

Kramer at last recognized him. Barca didn't skip a second. "What you have just witnessed here once again is unprecedented, and we'll have a number of members speak to that," he said. "Now I know that many of you are new and many of you are not aware of the traditions of this body that your leaders are so willing to trample on. But it's no surprise. Obviously, in six days you want to trample on the values of this state, and I cannot tell you how vigorously we object to that.

"But it is unbelievable to me, absolutely *un-be-liev-a-ble*, that you would first of all be here before five o'clock and take an illegal vote before even the time that the proceedings are supposed to start. Unbelievable! Unprecedented! Un-American! Not in keeping with the values of the state! You should be ashamed of yourselves," Barca screamed, pointing his outstretched index finger at the seated Republicans.

"Now, a lot of you—I know there's twenty-five of you didn't—but a lot of you served last session. Look me in the eye and tell me we ever did this to you. Didn't happen! For those of you that served twenty years, look me in the eye and say it happened. Never happened!" Barca said, gradually working himself up toward making a motion.

"There's a stench in this body," he said. "It is a stain on the history of this state what you have done. It is outrageous, absolutely outrageous. I would like to ask unanimous consent to strike the last vote."

"Objection," called back one of the Republicans who didn't want to back down. "Then I would like to make a motion to strike the last vote," Barca said. Now the floor was quiet, with only the chatter of voices speaking in undertones.

Kramer, Fuller, and one of the top Republican aides conferred for a few moments. It was just eleven minutes into the proceeding, and just five minutes after it had been scheduled to begin. Barca raised a question. "Mr. Speaker, I was told by the chief clerk that you took a voice vote on amendment one. What time did this body take that action?" he asked.

There was another long pause as lawmakers walked back and forth, but no answer. This was that rarest of moments on the floor of the Legislature, when the action was fluid and the outcome in doubt, even for those in charge.

"Mr. Speaker and members, it is even more outrageous," Barca said. "I didn't think it could possibly be any more outrageous but in fact amendments 2 and 3, which were before the body, were never addressed. Now I don't think there's a legislative body in the country, maybe the world, that ignores amendments that are before you.

"You may think because you were elected to the Legislature you can do whatever you damn well please. But you can't! We have rules!" Barca shouted, holding up a copy of the Assembly rulebook. "And whether you like it or not, you've got to follow the rules. Amendment 2, amendment 3, you've got to take those amendments up and you've got to vote 'em down. You can't just say we're not going to take them up. What is wrong with you? Honest to God! This is worse than a kangaroo court.

"I renew my request," Barca continued. "Mr. Speaker, I rise to ask for unanimous consent that the previous action on this bill be stricken from the record."

A Republican again objected.

"Mr. Speaker, I move that the previous action on this bill be stricken from the record and let me speak to that for a minute," Barca said, the room still quiet. "Now, if any of you have a shred of decency in you, a shred of decency, you will not allow these people up here to ignore these rules," he said, sitting down at last.

Hintz then rose and gave the Republicans a tongue-lashing of his own. Then several more Democrats spoke, the last of them a young representative from Madison. "This is the United States of America," Kelda Helen Roys said, nearly in tears. "We will disagree passionately. We will raise our voices. We will protest. We will be peaceful. But, by God, by God, we will give each other a basic level of respect and human dignity when we disagree. You can win on this, but do not win this way. Do not win this way."

During the public debate, another one had been happening privately in Speaker Fitzgerald's office just off the Assembly floor. Fitzgerald said later that he had received a call from an aide to Walker telling him that the Capitol Police wanted to talk with him. In the speaker's office, Capitol Police Chief Charles Tubbs had then arrived to tell Fitzgerald that with the large crowds and controversial vote, he no longer felt the police could guarantee the safety of the lawmakers. In a brief conversation twenty months later, Tubbs said he didn't remember the conversation recounted by Fitzgerald but allowed that it could have happened. But Susan Riseling, the chief of the UW–Madison police who was in charge of the statehouse interior, later expressed surprise over the situation, saying she never felt during the protests that she couldn't protect lawmakers. In any case, there was certainly tension in the Capitol, and Fitzgerald had experienced it firsthand. The day before, he had ridden an elevator that turned out to be carrying correctional officers who gave the speaker an earful on Walker's legislation. "Talk about awkward," Fitzgerald joked later.

The Assembly's GOP leaders had a choice—they could press ahead with the bill, not knowing what would happen in the night, or they could adjourn until the following week, not knowing whether their members might catch so much criticism in their districts over the weekend that they would return to Madison and drop their support for the bill.

"I didn't want to go home," Fitzgerald said. "If the legislators saw the same opposition in their own districts as they had at the Capitol, then it was 'game over.' I'd have never kept those votes. . . . I didn't know if it was 'Hey, did you go too far?' you know? I didn't know what the normal person out there would think. It's always tough to get outside this bubble here. I didn't know what would happen that weekend, what the average Joe that they ran into at the diner, what they'd be thinking."

Fitzgerald felt that he couldn't risk going forward. After conferring with others, the speaker made the final decision and went back out on the floor to announce it. "It's been a long week and a long couple of days and, obviously, we have a job to do. You have a job to do," Fitzgerald told the Democrats. "You guys caucused all day yesterday and caucused all day today. I talked to your leader [Peter Barca]. Had a conversation with him and said, 'Peter, I have got to go to the floor and get this bill moving. Let's debate the bill.' You're right, I put out a thing at five o'clock. Honestly, I didn't think you guys were showing up. . . . I checked with the chief clerk, there were two amendments in there. You know what? You guys are right. You're right. We're going to go back to the amendable stage of this bill, that's what we're going to do. Because you're right.

"So we have a job to do. You have a job to do. Your job in the minority is to delay. I honestly didn't think you were going to show up. Because your leader started out with, and I said, 'What time do you think you'll be out of caucus?' And he said, 'How's Monday, Fitz?' That was unacceptable to me, Sunday or Monday. So I would ask unanimous consent to go back to the amendable stage of the bill."

This time there was no objection. And like that, amendments could again be considered.

"It's been a long week," Fitzgerald repeated. "We would like to adjourn until Tuesday at 10 a.m. Everybody go home, get rested. We'll have a good healthy debate next week."

"All in favor of adjournment until Tuesday—" Kramer said.

The crowd in the galleries roared its approval and drowned out the rest of his words. Barca rose and thanked Fitzgerald. He pointed out that Republicans, in their haste to put the ugly episode behind them, were about to adjourn without passing the resolution from the Senate that would allow Walker to move back his budget address for a week. The lawmakers quickly passed that measure, and barely thirty minutes after they had reconvened they adjourned until the morning of the following Tuesday, February 22. That meant the unprecedented pressure would stay on Republicans—and the absent Democrats—for at least several days to come.

Afterward, Fitzgerald defended his party's actions, said that the events were not a defeat, and affirmed that he still had the votes to approve the bill. "I wanted to see if they were going to come to the floor. I had to force the issue, but obviously they did come," he said. "Democracy isn't pretty all the time."

The session adjourned just after 5:30 p.m.—almost exactly at sunset—and state troopers and Capitol Police officers hustled the Republican lawmakers past the crowds and out into the winter evening. Meanwhile, another drama was playing out two floors up from the Assembly. In the police command post, Chief Tubbs was delivering an order from the governor's office to Chief Riseling. Tubbs told her that all the demonstrators in the Capitol—the group that had now been there day and night for most of the week—needed to be removed from the building by the Capitol's normal closing time of 6 p.m. That was less than a half hour away.

Riseling knew from the second she heard the order that she would not comply with it. At that moment, she estimated there were some twenty thousand people in the Capitol. From her training and previous experience, she believed that police should communicate with large crowds and not surprise them. The closing time was the normal hour, and yet it would still come as a surprise for those who had been camping out in the rotunda for most of the week. Getting them to leave would have meant a potentially ugly confrontation. Rather than say no to Tubbs directly, Riseling said she instead asked him a series of questions.

"There's so many people in the building that the PA [public address] system can't be heard. How do you expect to tell the people that they need to leave?" Riseling asked in one of those questions.

Tubbs got the point—the building couldn't be cleared so quickly. He went back down to the governor's office on the second floor to talk with Walker's chief of staff, Keith Gilkes. After getting a little more information on the crowd size, Riseling went down to the governor's office herself and waited there for Tubbs to finish speaking with Gilkes. "Keith gets it that it's not going to happen now," Tubbs told Riseling when he came out.

The plan of clearing the building that night was dropped. Two possible confrontations, one on the Assembly floor and one among the demonstrators and police, had been averted within minutes of one another. Jubilant over the one and ignorant of the other, the crowds demonstrated late into the night.

10

A State Divided

O N T H E M I S E R A B L E , S L U S H Y D A Y of February 21, as Jack Craver
later described it, the Madison blogger was walking near Wisconsin
Avenue and the Capitol square on his way to the gym when he heard
a worker at a bratwurst stand say, "Is that a fucking camel?" Craver assumed
the blue-collar type was talking about some kind of machinery. But when he
looked, Craver found that, yes, there was indeed a camel on the city's icy
streets. The one-humped camel had what appeared to be a saddle on its back,
and a handler had the animal by a bridle. They were standing beside a horse
trailer and behind a series of metal barricades similar to those used to direct
crowds. Craver began to shoot a video with a flip camcorder he'd had with
him and ask questions of someone standing outside the shot. "You know
why there's a camel here?" he asked.

"Isn't it pretty obvious?" the man replied, as if it should be clear to the
bundled-up bystanders how a camel came to be there. "It's for a bit we're
shooting for *The Daily Show*."

The camel flicked its tail and defecated.

"For *The Daily Show*? Oh, I recognize you guys. Wow," Craver said.

The man nearby was John Oliver, the British comic and "correspondent"
for the satirical comedy show featuring Jon Stewart. The camel's handler led
the animal in a circle around the metal fencing as Craver looked on, amazed.
At that moment, the handler tried to lead the animal by a tight spot between
the fencing and the trailer. That maneuver turned out to be a mistake—just
like bringing a camel to a chaotic Wisconsin street in the middle of winter in
an attempt to compare the Madison protests with the Arab Spring uprisings.

Within seconds, the animal got its leg caught between the bars of the fencing and fell into the slush. The handler and two men struggled to free it, with
one of them slipping onto his butt like the camel, as the frightened animal
made deep guttural sounds.

Oliver later joked about the mishap with the "typical Illinois camel" and the
numbness in his toes that supposedly lasted for weeks after leaving frozen
Madison. But at that moment he wasn't laughing. Oliver held his hand in
front of Craver's camera and told him to "put that down." Craver ignored him
and kept shooting the video, which he posted afterward on his blog, The
Sconz. (The blog's name played off the slang term 'Sconnie, for Wisconsinite.)
Soon, a few protesting firemen showed up to help, though as Craver later
pointed out, camel crises had probably not been part of their training. As the
cheers of a rally carried over from the nearby square, the group tugged and
eventually raised the camel to its feet. The fencing fell off, and the crowd that
had gathered to watch cheered as the camel took a few steps, showing no sign
of any grave injury.

The scene summed up Walker's legislation and the action of recent days:
the sense that things both unprecedented and unbelievable were afoot in the
city. Many on both sides of the debate found the demonstrations exhilarating.
The incredible outpouring in the streets convinced union supporters that
they were sweeping Republicans before them on their way to victory. But for
Walker and his allies, the protests helped confirm they were close to achieving something of great moment that was worthy of the national attention
they were receiving. Day by day, the events got even stranger. Like the camel,
the crisis was outlandish and at times funny, but unlike *The Daily Show* gag
it was no joke. The fight seemed to be doing harm to the state and to the ties
between its citizens, maybe just temporary damage, maybe something more
crippling. It showed up in media reports from around the state. A veteran bar-
tender at the Whiskey on Water tavern in Princeton in central Wisconsin for
the first time in decades cut her patrons off from talking about politics. On the
Internet, the decline in civility was even worse. David Coyle, a history teacher
in the Milwaukee Public Schools, said his wife, Jessica, a school psychologist,
was left in tears after reading a cousin's Facebook post calling public employees "whores and a bunch of other nasty things." "What made matters worse
was that her godmother 'liked' the comment," David Coyle told the *Milwaukee
Journal Sentinel*. "My wife sent a message [to the cousin] to say, 'Hey, remember me, your family member, I am a public employee and I am not a whore.'
Her intention was for the cousin to say, 'Oops, sorry, I forgot,' or something

along those lines. He didn't. He only said, 'That is how I feel, you can defriend me if you want.' We thought that blood was thicker than water. Guess not."

The newspaper found several examples of people who had dropped friends or at least lowered their opinion of them because of the disagreement in Madison. When the fourteen Democratic senators left the state, Daryle Wooley of Elkhorn posted on Facebook that the lawmakers needed to come back or lose their jobs. "Democracy is twenty-four/seven; not just when it's something you're in favor of," he wrote. He was flooded with critical responses from friends on Facebook, some of them very close, and couldn't believe the tone. Wooley told his critics that he had had to cash in his retirement account and take out a second mortgage on his house to keep from losing his cast limestone manufacturing business. "This is the real world," he said. "You don't understand pain. If my wife wouldn't have gotten a new job, my health insurance would have gone away. I'm down from thirty-three employees to three." Wooley had several private e-mail conversations with the friends that helped to lower the tensions, but he was still struck by them. "Three weeks ago, we were all one happy family with the Packers," Wooley said, referring to the team's Super Bowl victory. "And now we're all at each other's throats. This is ripping us apart. It's sad."

More than a year later, a Marquette University Law School poll would find that one in three Wisconsinites had stopped talking about politics with someone they knew because of disagreements over the recall elections or Walker. Richard Ginkowski, an assistant district attorney in Kenosha County, said he defriended some Facebook acquaintances because of what they wrote about public workers like himself. "The discussion by one friend was that we're all parasites, leeches on society, overpaid and incompetent," said Ginkowski, a thirty-year prosecutor whose wife is a schoolteacher. "You listen to that for a few days, and you just delete them," he said. "There are going to be some strained relationships. I can't sit in a room and look at some of these people without biting my tongue very hard."

Many managed to phrase the arguments on both sides in civil fashion. Faith leaders such as Jerome Listecki, the Roman Catholic archbishop for Milwaukee, and Linda Lee, bishop of the Wisconsin Conference of the United Methodist Church, offered measured statements of support for unions. But Walker and other state officials of both parties received death threats. The state's cost for providing security for Walker and Lieutenant Governor Rebecca Kleefisch doubled the costs for their predecessors, a fact that reflected the increased threats as well as the need to guard Walker's second home in

Wauwatosa and his teenage sons still living there. In the face of the protests, the Walkers decided against an earlier plan to move their sons to Madison. "It was really something that we started out talking to the boys about and I was looking for schools and as soon as everything broke out in Madison we just knew that the schools in Madison were not going to be the right place for our boys," Tonette Walker said later.

The camel in the winter street also signified the way the events in Madison had leapt into the psyche of the nation and even the world. In bringing the camel, *The Daily Show* was teasing about a comparison being made between the Madison protests and those then going on in Egypt. For days, the peaceful unrest in Wisconsin and the revolutionary demonstrations in Cairo had so dominated the news that some people had begun to connect them in their minds, referring to Walker on protest badges as the "Mubarak of the Middle West." Meanwhile, Wisconsin Congressman Paul Ryan, Republican chairman of the House Budget Committee and soon to be Republican vice-presidential candidate, said on February 17 on MSNBC's *Morning Joe* program that Walker's "getting riots. It's like Cairo has moved to Madison these days."

That was a laugh. The protests on the two continents were both arresting displays of democracy, but beyond that, they didn't have much in common. Those in Egypt were carried out against a tyrannical regime that sought to suppress them violently and that in turn saw itself essentially overthrown by crowds in the streets. The Wisconsin protests were carried out largely peacefully with few arrests. They targeted a democratically elected governor and lawmakers who ignored the demands of demonstrators but who also worked with law enforcement to avoid a violent crackdown on the crowds. Ryan later acknowledged to the *Journal Sentinel* that his comments were an "inaccurate comparison."

Even in Madison, a city of prosperity, education, and midwestern manners, the coming days and weeks would test both sides' commitment to fair play. More demonstrators poured onto the Capitol square and more of them began spending nights in the statehouse, moving their protest into the building. As they did, the Walker administration gradually tightened access to the Capitol, starting in subtle ways that grew more noticeable in the following days. On February 18 Republicans took the unusual step of limiting access to the Senate chamber while senators were in recess. Normally, members of the public on tours could walk onto the floor during a recess and plop onto

a senator's leather chair. The change limited access to the vestibule outside
of the Senate chamber to senators and staff, although journalists were still
allowed in the media gallery during sessions. On February 19 the outer doors
in the east and west wings of the Capitol were also closed, but the doors in the
north and south wings remained open. Republicans said the changes were
needed to restore order.

Susan Riseling, the UW–Madison police chief, took other steps, roping off
more areas in front of the Senate and Assembly chambers so that protesters
could no longer come up to their very doors but had to stand a short distance
away. She'd acquired a profound respect for the demonstrators, who in turn
constantly thanked her for the efforts of the officers. Still, Riseling wasn't taking anything for granted. She wrote evacuation plans for the lawmakers so
they could be taken safely out of the building in the event of a threat. She
instituted a count of protesters at the doors of the Capitol so police knew
how many people were inside and could keep that number at a safe level. For
instance, the state was able to report in a court filing more than a year after
the demonstrations were over that nearly 40,000 people passed through the
Capitol on February 22, though the impressive figure wasn't publicized at
the time.

Riseling was a take-charge person, saying later she is "genetically pro-
grammed to take over" in a vacuum of leadership. Keith Gilkes, Walker's chief
of staff, viewed it differently, seeing Riseling as knowledgeable but arrogant.
In a way, Gilkes was filling his own vacuum because Mike Huebsch, the administration secretary who was rushing to help the governor pass his union
measure and to finish Walker's two-year budget proposal, still wasn't aware
it was his job to oversee the Capitol and the state's other buildings. Gilkes
answered questions and made decisions as Riseling and Tubbs came to him
and soon found himself heading daily security meetings in the offices of the
Senate chief clerk. Eventually, Gilkes handed the duties over to Huebsch, and
when that happened Riseling began to get more questions answered. "All of
a sudden it's like there's Secretary Huebsch and for me things got better once
I was engaged with the secretary," she said later. "One of the highlights for
me was working with him."

As it got harder to enter the statehouse, more people were tuning in to what
was happening inside. Journalists poured into Madison, from the *New York
Times* and the major broadcast networks to wire services like Reuters and
Bloomberg, photo services like Getty Images, and magazines like *Harper's*
and *Time*. Outlets that were regularly on hand at the Capitol—the *Milwaukee*

Journal Sentinel, the Associated Press, and the *Wisconsin State Journal*—beefed up their teams. Normally, the Capitol had fewer than a dozen journalists on hand and on days with truly big news perhaps two or even three dozen. But at the height of the crisis, scores of journalists—including some from Japan, Mexico, Germany, France, and Russia—tromped through the snow to the statehouse to get even the tiniest developments in the stalemate. There were overflow rooms, but the small pressroom on the second floor of the Capitol was continually packed with as many as forty journalists—only a portion of those in the building—who filled every seat and most spots on the floor. Their presence reminded the leaders in the Capitol that their actions were playing out on a far greater stage than most of them could have ever imagined. With his usual appetite for media coverage, Scott Walker chomped through the national talk shows like candy, starting some days before sunrise with his first interview and doing his last in the evening. He wasn't the only one. Senators who normally worked to get their names in Wisconsin newspapers suddenly found themselves repeatedly in front of national broadcast audiences. The coverage varied from the support for the Democrats and the protesters from Ed Schultz of MSNBC—who traveled to Madison for his show several times during the more than year-long fight—to the skepticism of Fox News personalities. On February 28 the Fox show *The O'Reilly Factor* ran a segment in which conservative host Bill O'Reilly interviewed a correspondent about the protests in Madison. The segment included background video of a scuffle at a labor protest in Sacramento that showed palm trees in the background. The piece drew outrage from labor supporters who said Fox was essentially mixing out-of-state turmoil—and tropical plants—into its coverage of the protests in frigid Wisconsin. In mockery, some protesters brought inflatable palm trees to the Capitol in the following days.

A plethora of niche and alternative media outlets also showed up, from liberal groups such as the Center for Media and Democracy and the Waging Nonviolence blog to documentary filmmakers and ordinary citizens with social media accounts. One man showed up in the Capitol pressroom seeking media credentials to shoot video of the action for his blog. When asked for the name of his blog, he admitted that he didn't actually have one, just the sudden idea of launching one. He didn't get the credentials. But there were lone photographers and videographers who did connect with the public. Matthew Wisniewski, a Madison professional, took a series of still photos and videos of the protests that got wide circulation—one video showing crowds of impassioned protesters and set to the music of the band Arcade Fire had received

247,000 total views on Wisniewski's Vimeo page and on YouTube as of May 2012. Wisniewski received hundreds of e-mails from around the country from admiring viewers. This group of citizen web posters had an impact because social media gave them a ready-made audience. These outlets fed the public genuine news, but also rumors. One whopper that spread through social media was that a private security firm called DCI had been hired by Walker to guard the Capitol during the protests. There were indeed agents watching the building in uniforms reminiscent of those worn by private security guards. But those familiar with state law enforcement knew that they were part of the Division of Criminal Investigation, or DCI, at the state Department of Justice.

A string of celebrities visited Madison, including the liberal filmmaker and provocateur Michael Moore. At a March 5 rally, Moore cheered the crowds and the fourteen Democratic senators for their efforts and was lauded in turn. Moore hit a theme, already heavily present in the demonstrations, that average citizens were being shortchanged in favor of the wealthy. He argued that neither Wisconsin nor the rest of the country was broke and that there was more than enough money to pay public employees—if the wealthy paid their fair share. "Right now, this afternoon, just four hundred Americans— four hundred—have more wealth than half of all Americans combined," he told the protesters.

The crisis was also fodder for musicians and writers, from the silly to the serious. Most of them were critical of the governor. Madison's Broom Street Theater did a run of Doug Reed's *The Lamentable Tragedie of Scott Walker*, a Shakespeare-inspired retelling of Walker's story with, as one reviewer noted, "iambic pentameter, soliloquies, swordfights, and, of course, codpieces." A few creators were sympathetic to Walker. One country rock song by Walker supporter Glen Shulfer with a style reminiscent of Lee Greenwood swore that citizens would "stand with Governor Walker / 'Cause he does what he says; not just a big, fancy talker." Another, younger wag, noting the similar sound- ing "Skywalker" and "Scott Walker," put out a *Star Wars*–themed YouTube rap video called "My Governor's a Jedi" in which he mugged for the camera, dressed up like Princess Leia, and danced around the Capitol with a plastic light saber. "My governor's a Jedi / I know without a doubt / He's got a saber in his pocket / Don't make him whip it out!" he rapped.

Tom Morello, the Grammy-winning former guitarist for the band Rage Against the Machine, flew in to Chicago and then drove up to Madison through a sleet storm to perform outdoors on February 21. He played his own songs and Woody Guthrie's "This Land Is Your Land" with fingers so cold he dropped his guitar pick and didn't even realize it. Months later he told one interviewer, "I've played hundreds and hundreds of demonstrations but I've never been in the middle of anything like this." He later wrote his own song about the protests, "Union Town," singing, "Some say the union's down / But I asked around / And everybody said / This is a union town." At one of his Madison performances, Morello read a letter he said he'd received from Egypt. Though surprising, such international letters were not uncommon—the Wisconsin AFL-CIO, for instance, received hundreds of e-mails of solidarity from supporters around the world. Morello's letter came from Amor Eletrebi, a participant in the demonstrations in Tahrir Square in Cairo:

> To our friends in Madison, Wisconsin: We wish you could see firsthand the change we have made here. Justice is beautiful, but justice is never free. The beauty in Tahrir Square you can have everywhere, on any corner, in your city, or in your heart. So hold on tightly and don't let go, and breathe deep Wisconsin! Our good fortune is on the breeze, in the Midwest and in the Middle East. Breathe deep, Wisconsin . . . because justice is in the air! And may the spirit of Tahrir Square be in every beating heart in Madison today.

The crisis was also fodder for humorists besides those on *The Daily Show.* On March 2, *Late Night with Jimmy Fallon* spoofed the standoff in his "Slow Jam the News" segment, which plugs news stories into funk music by the show's band, The Roots. Playing off the idea that Walker was stripping union rights, host Jimmy Fallon said in his best bedroom voice, "The governor wants to do some stripping. He says it's the only way he knows to make ends meet. The other Republican governors ain't mad at Madison. They're getting a thrill from this budgetary peep show. Looks like they want to take it all off too."

The bit got a few things right. In Ohio, Indiana, Tennessee, Arizona, and Minnesota, Republican leaders were following Wisconsin's lead in seeking new limits on unions. The two states that prompted the closest comparisons were Ohio and Indiana. The Ohio legislation had similar goals to the Wisconsin bill, though it was structured somewhat differently. Unlike in Wisconsin, the Ohio measure applied to *all* state and local workers, including police and firefighters. In its final form, it had a number of measures to limit and weaken unions and reduce spending on public employees, from prohibiting strikes to forcing state and local governments to cut workers' health and pension benefits. Those last provisions especially bore a strong resemblance to the Wisconsin legislation in the way they mandated benefit cuts at a statewide level. But there were also different provisions from the Wisconsin measure, for instance, allowing unions in Ohio to retain the power to bargain over certain safety issues.

The similarities between the Ohio and Wisconsin bills were too striking to be the result of mere coincidence or even similar responses to the same fiscal challenges. Some of that could be explained perhaps by the fact that Walker and Ohio's new GOP governor, John Kasich, spoke regularly. The national conservative groups also played a role, directly or indirectly, as did the past example of Governor Mitch Daniels in Indiana. At the same time, the many differences between the separate bills showed that Republicans in each state weren't simply mindlessly passing some piece of legislation as written by a national group. In Columbus and Madison, Republicans pursued their goal of cutting government spending and weakening unions by tailoring their legislation to the politics, history, and, most important, the existing labor laws of their respective states.

The Ohio measure was ultimately repealed by voters in a referendum in November 2011, but cutbacks for union workers were advanced around the country. In Indiana, one piece of legislation to limit unions would have eliminated collective bargaining for teachers. Another, a so-called right-to-work bill, prohibited union membership and fees from being a condition of employment in private businesses. Backers of the measure in Indiana said it would spur business expansions, but critics like Indiana Democratic Party Chairman Dan Parker called the bill "an assault on working people." The right-to-work bill was blocked that year by Democrats but ultimately passed in February 2012, making Indiana the first state in the Rust Belt to have such a law. In spite of calls from some conservative groups, Walker did not propose similar legislation affecting private employee unions in Wisconsin and said he didn't intend to pursue it—though Governor Daniels had said the same thing in Indiana only to reverse himself and later sign the bill.

In Washington, D.C., the presence of President Obama and the Democratic-controlled Senate made federal legislation a nonstarter. But later the GOP presidential front-runner, Mitt Romney, talked during the primary about his support for right-to-work legislation and curbing unions' influence over free-trade deals. Other states also had their own proposals. In Tennessee, for example, Republicans pushed a bill to restrict bargaining rights for teachers. In Massachusetts, Democratic Governor Deval Patrick signed legislation putting comparatively modest limits on local employee unions' ability to bargain for their health insurance. In New York, another Democratic governor, Andrew

Cuomo, sought to trim union workers' pension benefits. In Arizona, law-makers considered legislation to ban all bargaining between unions and local governments and schools. And in a bit of symbolism in Maine, Republican Governor Paul LePage decided to remove a thirty-six-foot mural depicting the state's labor history from the lobby of that state's Department of Labor head-quarters because it was deemed too one-sided.

Still, the biggest fires burned in Madison, Indianapolis, and Columbus. Just as in Wisconsin, big crowds showed up to rallies in the other two states against the union restrictions. On February 17 thousands of public employ-ees and their supporters jammed statehouse hallways in Columbus to protest the bill even as Tea Party groups demonstrated in favor of it. As in Wisconsin, labor opponents there put intense pressure on Republicans. For instance, in the Ohio Senate, the limits on collective bargaining passed that house by the bare margin of seventeen to sixteen, with six Republicans voting against it. But as much attention as Ohio and Indiana got, Wisconsin and its dynamic governor received even more.

"What if Ohio had gone a week earlier? What if Florida had gone two weeks earlier? They might be the center of attention. But Wisconsin is now," Grover Norquist, president of the conservative group Americans for Tax Reform, said at the time.

Norquist was right that Wisconsin was in the vanguard, but ultimately Madison would have likely headlined the story anyway. The city's residents are uniquely positioned among residents of the Midwest to distrust Republi-cans and support unions; Walker had to push his plan in what was for him the worst possible place. Public employee unions had sunk deeper roots in the city and the rest of the state than perhaps anywhere else in the Midwest. In Ohio, collective bargaining for public workers went back to 1983, not nearly as far as the half century it went back in Wisconsin. Elected leaders and the public in places like Ohio and Indiana could remember when things were done at least somewhat differently. But that wasn't the case in Wisconsin and especially in Madison. There, the rank-and-file protesters saw the fight not just as one of dollars and cents but as one of long-standing fundamental rights. This perspective kindled in them a righteous anger akin to that of the Tea Party and a zeal reminiscent of the antiwar protesters from the 1960s.

On February 21 the South Central Federation of Labor met over what to do if Walker's bill passed. A group of ninety-seven unions in a six-county region in southern Wisconsin, the federation had more than 45,000 workers as members. The sixty delegates to the federation voted unanimously to hold a general strike nationwide if the governor signed his bill into law. "Everyone in that room was thinking the same thing—we're going down if we don't repel this," Tony Schaeve, a federation delegate from Plumbers Local 75, later told the Wisconsin State Journal. "It's not about us anymore, it's about the nation, and we're at ground zero." The nation, however, didn't respond to the idea of a general strike and neither did the local unions. The focus stayed on electoral responses to Walker's legislation, and no general strike—or individual union strike—was ever held.

Opponents found other ways to fight the legislation. In March, a group began meeting at noon every weekday to hold a Solidarity Sing Along in the Capitol rotunda or the square outside to belt out folk songs and, above all, civil rights anthems like "Keep Your Eyes on the Prize," often with rewritten lyrics opposing Walker. The group never missed a weekday in more than a year and a half and turned to revamped Christmas carols in December. The Wisconsin writer and actor Callen Harty showed up around 4:30 each afternoon to sing a somber version of "We Shall Overcome," almost like a Gregorian chant, even though he claimed to be afraid of singing in public.

Like Tea Party activists, the union supporters believed that what previous generations had fought and sacrificed for was being taken away by politicians for the wrong reasons. That gave them an urgency and vehemence rarely seen in recent Wisconsin politics. The protests in Madison fit into a worldwide wave of demonstrations in 2011 and prefigured the Occupy Wall Street protests that would soon erupt across the country. At the same time, Wisconsin also had strong numbers of Republicans who didn't see union bargaining as a fundamental right like freedom of speech. That difference in perspective made it almost impossible for the two sides to find a compromise or even have a meaningful dialogue. It ensured big protests and a big fight.

On their own, the national unions could not have willed those mass protests in Madison into existence, but they could and did harness them. They quickly grasped that Wisconsin represented their best chance to turn back legislation that would weaken them, even perhaps mortally wound them, there and around the country. Organizers and leaders began showing up, taking up rooms at the Madison Concourse Hotel just a few yards from where the camel had appeared. They began to take up the slack of organizing and supplying the demonstrations away from the early wave of volunteers like Jenni Dye. At the hotel, members of the Wisconsin AFL-CIO handed out food and drinks to protesters, with the organization bringing 33,000 brats to be grilled by members of building trades unions. In addition to the food, the state AFL-CIO ran radio and television ads, rented buses to bring in labor supporters from out of town, and urged its members to oppose Walker's bill. Other groups organized volunteer marshals to make sure the demonstrations stayed peaceful. Union officials didn't always provide specific details, but their efforts in Madison were hard to miss, ranging from the buses unloading pro- testers downtown to the Teamsters' semitruck parked on the Capitol square.

Stephanie Bloomingdale, the secretary-treasurer of the state AFL-CIO, said afterward that she wasn't sure how many people she had been expecting at the demonstrations, but she remembered that only two months earlier her union and other community groups had been holding rallies to protest the cancellation of the Madison-to-Milwaukee train project and been pleased to see several hundred people show up. Like some other labor leaders, Blooming- dale sometimes slept at the Capitol, starting with the night the Joint Finance Committee hearing was shut down, and at times her children and husband, a union member, joined her and also spent the night there. "A lot of it did [happen organically] but there was a lot of hard, hard work that went into it," she said. "It was the ultimate in very quick problem solving. . . . It was like every union staff person, every union activist, everyone stepped in and helped."

While union officials saw to lobbying and logistical matters, some chal- lenges were resolved by ordinary people and chance encounters. During that second week of protests, Sarah Briganti, an aide to Senator Fred Risser of Madison, found a woman breastfeeding her baby in a bathroom. Briganti had worked on a law barring discrimination against women breastfeeding in pub- lic and she felt strongly that no one should have to feed a child in a bathroom. Risser was in Illinois with the other Democrats, so Briganti invited the woman to Risser's two-room suite, set her up in the senator's personal office, and shut the door. Word soon got out that Risser's office was a safe haven, and every day after that one or two members of a rotating cast of women stopped by to nurse their infants or pump milk in the relative calm of Risser's office.

Top union leaders from around the country converged on Madison, in- cluding Richard Trumka of the AFL-CIO, Dennis Van Roekel of the National Education Association, and Harold Schaitberger of the International Associ- ation of Firefighters. The union leaders weren't the only national figures at the protests. On February 18 the Reverend Jesse Jackson showed up at the Capi- tol, leading protesters in civil rights–era chants. He wound his way through the statehouse hallways with hundreds crowding in his wake and then went on to speak at a union news conference and a twilight rally. "This is a Martin Luther King moment, this is a Gandhi moment," Jackson said, as he linked the week's demonstrations to past nonviolent protests and the civil rights movement. "When we fight, we win. We fight in Montgomery, we win. We fight in Selma, we win. . . . We march in Madison, Wisconsin, we win." He returned often throughout the coming weeks.

No effort or expense was spared by either side in the fight. More than eighty groups registered with the state to lobby on the bill. They ranged from the top forces for the political left and the right in the Capitol, to the teachers union and the state business lobby, to the American Cancer Society and U.S. Cellular. Most but not all of the lobbyists were focused on the collective bargaining issue, though many were also interested in the bill's health care provisions. Lobbyists and their organizations spent 22,300 hours working on the legislation, or nearly thirteen times as much as was spent on the next-most-lobbied bill that spring. Unions reported spending more than any other groups on lobbying in the first half of 2011, with the state AFL-CIO, the teachers union, and two AFSCME affiliates together spending a total of $6.3 million.

Crowds continued to grow, once again hitting tens of thousands. The size of the demonstrations stunned even longtime politicos from both parties. Paul Soglin, an iconic liberal who had done two stints as Madison mayor and was about to be elected to a third, was a student leader during the anti–Vietnam War protests. Not even the legendary crowds of his youth could top what he saw on the streets now. "I've never seen anything like this," Soglin said. "It's fascinating the dynamic of what's going on here."

Soglin, who had participated in the protests all week, said he was impressed with the conduct of both the crowds and the law enforcement agencies keeping watch over them. He compared the mood of the demonstrations to those he saw during the civil rights movement. There was anger, he said, but also "elements of joy and enthusiasm." The antiwar movement was "all energized and angry—because it was focused on stopping a war. It could not have the almost spiritual nature of what's going on in Madison today."

On Saturday, February 19, a confrontation was looming that might crack the sense of relative order. Up until then, the union supporters had had the Capitol square almost entirely to themselves. Now, thousands of Tea Party supporters were headed to the Capitol to show their support for Walker. Big crowds belonging to the two most passionate groups in American politics were meeting in the same spot for the biggest day yet of demonstrations. If there was a moment in which provocation could triumph over peace, this would be it. Like the union demonstrations, the Tea Party event had come together quickly. Dave Westlake, a small businessman and former long-shot

GOP candidate for U.S. Senate, came up with the idea for the rally on February 17, the day the Democrats left the state. The event got a big boost when
the Koch-backed group Americans for Prosperity kicked in its support. "For
a long time we were on the defense; now we're on the offense," AFP's president, Tim Phillips, said in an interview in the run-up to the rally. "We can
stand with the governor who is courageous."

Like so many events that winter, the Tea Party demonstration seemed to
happen organically. But as with the union demonstrations, it wasn't that simple. Americans for Prosperity was helping harness the raw enthusiasm of supporters for Walker's proposal. The free-market group and its backers in the
business community had helped elect Walker and other Republicans around
the country three months earlier and urged them to take steps to limit union
bargaining. Now that Walker was trying to deliver on that, the group rallied
around him. Americans for Prosperity launched a website, www.StandWith
Walker.com, where citizens could sign online petitions to support the governor's bill. The conservative group also pitched in to provide buses for out-
of-town activists to attend the rally and ran radio spots to urge support for
Walker's measure.

The competing Saturday rallies resulted in few problems or controversy.
One big and curious exception involved—of all people—doctors. At the demonstration, physicians from several hospitals and clinics set up a station near
the Capitol to provide notes covering public employees' absences. Lou Sanner,
a fifty-nine year-old family physician from Madison, helped organize the group
calling itself "Badger Doctors." He later told his employer he had given out
just eighteen absence notes. But on the day of the protest the Associated Press
quoted him as saying that hundreds of notes had been written for people who
were braving the cold but who seemed to Sanner to be suffering from stress
from the "threat of loss of income, loss of job, loss of health insurance."

It didn't take long for the backlash. Officials from the Madison and Milwaukee school districts and the UW School of Medicine and Public Health—
the employer of Sanner and some of the other doctors—said they would consider disciplinary action against the physicians issuing the notes and the school
workers who received them. They said the doctors appeared to be acting dis-
honestly and weren't keeping good records or necessarily providing adequate
care. The state Medical Examining Board later sanctioned twenty doctors who
wrote absence notes with reprimands and extra classes or administrative
warnings. Separately, the UW medical school disciplined nine residents and
thirteen faculty members, fining the faculty members up to $4,001 in the

case of Sanner, and suspending him and other supervisors from management positions for four months. Sanner unsuccessfully appealed his discipline, arguing he had done nothing wrong and had followed his usual practices. But UW administrators pointed to a sheet given to doctors participating in the event saying that they would "attempt to keep minimal records for this contact in case employers inquire about the validity of work excuses provided."

The controversy over the doctors, though, was the exception on that sunny winter day. In general, the behavior of the demonstrators on both sides was impressive, even astonishing. Madison police estimated the size of the overall crowd at 68,000. Estimating the overall crowd was as tricky and open to political fudging as always, as was guessing what share of the people was made up of the Tea Party supporters. Their leaders put their crowd at somewhere between 8,000 and 10,000, union demonstrators put it at 2,500 to 3,000, and police gave no breakdown. Whatever the number, it was clear that the Tea Party group that day was big by any normal standard at the Capitol but still dwarfed by the throng of union supporters.

For the event, the police had a force of up to five hundred officers from forty law enforcement agencies, with some driving well over two hours to get there. Orange plastic barriers were set up to separate the two groups of demonstrations, and lines of officers were formed to ensure that they stayed apart. But that didn't keep verbal confrontations from breaking out between the two sides during the nearly ninety-minute Tea Party rally. The two groups, the one with thousands, the other with tens of thousands, met on the south side of the Capitol square. "Tea Parties Are for Little Girls. Grow Up!" read one union supporter's hand-lettered sign and "Corp. Fascism Bad for YOUR business" read another. On the other side, a pair of signs read "Thank You GOD for Scott" and "We Protest on SATURDAYS. Too Busy Working M–F Paying for Union Greed."

Across the police line the shouting intensified. A Walker supporter and Marine Corps veteran, Jory Mikkonen, did his part to keep it going. The Milwaukee man, at six foot eight, stood above the crowd and shouted loudly at the pro-union sympathizers, "Unions go home!"

"Get a degree!" another protester yelled in response.

"Bring your legislators back, so we can pass the bill," Mikkonen said.

That set off another protester, who yelled, "You're ignorant."

"Maybe you should have voted on election day," Mikkonen shot back.

Mikkonen said he lost two jobs in manufacturing and now held three jobs, including one as a waiter and another as a pizza deliverer. "Jobs are hard to come by, but I found something in less than a month," he said. "And these guys want more benefits at our expense."

But not all exchanges were so heated. Another Walker supporter, John Poehling, debated intensely, but amiably, with a public employee for ten minutes. They shook hands and walked away. "We had a dialogue, but we didn't change each other's mind," Poehling said with a smile.

Toward the end of the event, Madison police spokesman Joel DeSpain gave a stunning report: There had been no arrests and no major incidents. Any number of factors probably helped, from the massive police presence to the fact that there wasn't a lot of alcohol available. But much of the credit had to go to the restraint on both sides. "If the eyes of the nation and the world are truly upon us, then I think we've been able to show that democracy can work well, even if those who have passionate views on different sides come together," DeSpain said.

Westlake, the rally organizer, delivered an impassioned speech and afterward reflected on the scene. "It's a great show of what can happen in America," he said. "People can vehemently disagree on a topic, co-locate, and not have any terrible things break out. This is exercising our freedom of speech."

Protesters packed themselves so tightly into the Capitol on February 17, 2011, that moving through the crowd was often a struggle. (*Milwaukee Journal Sentinel*, photo by Tom Lynn, © 2012 Journal Sentinel Inc., reproduced with permission)

Demonstrators bang on the metal bars over the doors of the state Senate chamber on February 17, 2011—the same day plans to vote on the collective bargaining limits were abandoned when Senate Democrats fled to Illinois. (*Milwaukee Journal Sentinel*, photo by Mark Hoffman, © 2012 Journal Sentinel Inc., reproduced with permission)

Demonstrator Jenni Dye (center) stands with her friend Shayla Dvorak on the second floor of the statehouse overlooking the rotunda during the protests on the afternoon of February 20, 2011. Dye, a social media addict, holds a sign with a slogan and a Twitter hashtag. (Photo by Ed Knutson, reproduced with permission)

Governor Scott Walker discusses his legislation to repeal collective bargaining for most public employees with reporters on February 21, 2011, four days after Senate Democrats' departure from Wisconsin. (*Milwaukee Journal Sentinel*, photo by Rick Wood, © 2012 Journal Sentinel Inc., reproduced with permission)

During the February 26, 2011, rally, Governor Scott Walker's opponents decked out the *Forward* statute on the Capitol lawn with a blindfold and "For Sale" sign. (*Milwaukee Journal Sentinel*, photo by Tom Lynn, © 2012 Journal Sentinel Inc., reproduced with permission)

Assembly Minority Leader Peter Barca, standing, unsuccessfully urges Senate Majority Leader Scott Fitzgerald that a hastily convened conference committee violates the state's open meetings law. Barca is holding a copy of a memo on the open meetings law at the meeting on March 9, 2011, in the Senate parlor. (*Wisconsin State Journal*, photo by Michael P. King, © 2012 *Wisconsin State Journal*, reproduced with permission)

Capitol Police Chief Charles Tubbs urges protesters to leave the state Capitol after the building closes on March 10, 2011, the day the Assembly sent what would become known as Act 10 to Governor Scott Walker for his signature. (*Milwaukee Journal Sentinel*, photo by Kristyna Wentz-Graff, © 2012 Journal Sentinel Inc., reproduced with permission)

Protesters swarm the Capitol on March 12, 2011, a day after Governor Scott Walker signed the collective bargaining limits into law. That rally saw the return of the fourteen Democratic senators after they left the state for three weeks in a failed effort to block the bill. (*Milwaukee Journal Sentinel*, photo by Michael Sears, © 2012 Journal Sentinel Inc., reproduced with permission)

Dane County Circuit Judge Maryann Sumi makes a point as she listens to arguments on March 18, 2011, on whether Republican lawmakers violated the state's open meetings law in passing Act 10. Later that day Sumi issued her first restraining order in the case, putting the union bargaining law on hold for months. (*Milwaukee Journal Sentinel*, photo by Mark Hoffman, © 2012 Journal Sentinel Inc., reproduced with permission)

Milwaukee Mayor Tom Barrett celebrates winning the May 8, 2012, Democratic primary for governor, giving him the chance to take on Scott Walker in the state's first recall election for governor. Barrett had lost to Walker in the 2010 race for governor, and he would do so again on June 5, 2012. (*Milwaukee Journal Sentinel*, photo by Gary Porter, © 2012 Journal Sentinel Inc., reproduced with permission)

An exultant Scott Walker greets his backers at the Waukesha Expo Center on June 5, 2012, the night he became the first governor in the nation's history to survive a recall election. (*Milwaukee Journal Sentinel*, photo by Rick Wood, © 2012 Journal Sentinel Inc., reproduced with permission)

The Beast from Buffalo

T HE PHONE CALL WAS A LONG SHOT, but Ian Murphy wasn't
afraid of those. The blogger and self-described art school dropout telephoned Governor Scott Walker's office on February 22 and said he
was David Koch, billionaire businessman, donor to conservative causes, and
arch-bogeyman of the left. As throughout the crisis, the most outlandish of
all possible scenarios occurred—the hoax worked and the call produced damaging, though not ultimately deadly, revelations about the governor. No one
was more surprised than Murphy, who as the editor of the satirical website
The Beast specialized in outrageous articles and stunts. In a piece published
on the one-year anniversary of his phone call to Walker, Murphy recalled
that he conceived of the idea after waking at midnight on Tuesday, February
22, and sitting up the rest of the night drinking coffee and smoking a joint.
Murphy may not be an entirely reliable storyteller—after his prank broke he
told journalists that he was thirty-three years old when he was apparently
only thirty-two. "I'd plain forgotten how old I was," he wrote later. But according to his account, Murphy originally had planned to impersonate the ousted
Egyptian leader Hosni Mubarak and call to offer Walker his support, but realized in time that was not much of a plan, especially for someone who didn't
know how to fake an Egyptian accent.

So Murphy settled instead on Koch (pronounced "Coke"). The blogger
had read comments by Senator Tim Carpenter, a Milwaukee Democrat who
said the governor would not return calls from the absent senators in Illinois.
Maybe, Murphy thought, the governor would talk to David Koch. He knew
that the political action committee for the company owned by Koch and his

brother Charles was also one of the biggest donors to Walker's 2010 campaign. Even before the prank call, the Kochs' company and its owners had drawn sharp criticism from demonstrators at the Capitol for their support of the Tea Party and Americans for Prosperity. Unsubstantiated rumors swirled that Koch Industries wanted to buy the state power plants that Walker was seeking to sell through his budget-repair bill. Protesters' signs derided Walker and the Fitzgerald brothers as "Koch whores" addicted to corporate campaign cash.

Murphy first spoke with an executive assistant in the governor's office and, after a second call, was transferred to Keith Gilkes, Walker's thirty-three-year-old chief of staff and former campaign manager. Gilkes assumed someone on the staff had already vetted the caller and told Murphy he could arrange a talk with the governor, asking for a number for Walker to call. Murphy said he was calling using the Internet-based service Skype and didn't have a way for the governor to call him. "My goddamn maid, Maria, put my phone in the washer," Murphy later said he told Gilkes. "I'd have her deported, but she works for next to nothing."

A source close to the governor said later that this story had been given to someone else in Walker's office, not Gilkes, but in any case the chief of staff told Murphy to call back at 2 p.m. that same afternoon. At that moment, Walker's green aides were contending with pandemonium at the Capitol and the total breakdown of their plan to pass his union legislation, so checking on the governor's callers wasn't as high a priority as it should have been. Plus, Wisconsin was for the moment a center of the national and international news; famous figures were showing up in Madison and weighing in on the events on a daily basis. Why not David Koch?

Murphy, of course, was no ordinary journalist and The Beast was no typical news outlet. Founded as an alternative weekly in Buffalo, New York, in 2002 by later Rolling Stone contributing editor Matt Taibbi and two others, it became an online-only publication in 2009. Defiantly liberal, the site injected its reporting with strong doses of attitude and satire, and it embraced controversy. As editor, Murphy had established himself as a troublemaker in the spirit of Taibbi, writing a 2008 editorial headlined "Fuck the Troops" that began: "So, 4,000 rubes are dead. Cry me the Tigris. Another 30,000 have been seriously wounded. Boo fucking hoo. They got what they asked for—and cool robotic limbs, too." In his call to Walker, Murphy was engaging in a kind of journalistic entrapment that he hoped would disgrace the governor. His tactics drew an immediate reproach from the Society of Professional

Journalists, which called his methods "underhanded and unethical." But the backstory of the prank and its instigator got little attention compared to the details in the conversation itself. It brought Murphy notoriety and a certain cachet from some on the Left, which he parlayed weeks later into a mocking special election run for Congress as a Green Party candidate.

By midafternoon, the gonzo blogger was astounded to find himself talking to Walker. He hadn't expected to get through and said later he was "wildly unprepared" for the call. Murphy didn't know how well Walker and Koch might know each other. In fact—and this was key for the prank to work—the two had never talked, though they later would as Walker became a national force in conservative politics. On Murphy's recording of the conversation, Walker greeted his caller with an upbeat, "Hey, David." Murphy adopted a terse, gruff voice for his prank, a kind of clichéd CEO persona. Throughout the call, he asked mostly generic questions and let the governor take the lead. When Murphy did speak, he often made bizarre asides that might have been expected to raise the governor's suspicions. But Walker spoke to him at length with little prompting and seemingly no alarm. He told Murphy he was committed to his cause and that the "small group" of protesters at the Capitol was mostly from out of state, even though that was clearly not the case. He updated Murphy on where the bill stood in the legislative process and explained that Republicans were doing whatever they could to pressure the absent Democrats to return. The Senate was taking up bills important to Democrats, thus preventing them from having a chance to debate them. Later that day, Walker said, Republicans would publicly announce that pay for the Democrats would no longer be deposited in their bank accounts and would have to be picked up on the floor. "Each day we're going to ratchet it up a little bit," Walker said.

"Now you're not talking to any of these Democrat bastards, are you?" Murphy asked, goading Walker as he would throughout the conversation.

The governor gave no reaction to that and told Murphy that he had talked over the weekend for forty-five minutes with Senator Tim Cullen of Janesville. He called the moderate Democrat "about the only reasonable one there."

"All right, I'll have to give that man a call," Murphy said.

"Well, actually, in his case I wouldn't call him and I'll tell you why: He's pretty reasonable, but he's not one of us. . . . He's not a conservative. He's just a pragmatist," Walker said.

Continuing to share more private details of his plans, Walker said that in two days he would announce potential layoffs for as many as 6,000 state workers. He said he was putting out the word that he wouldn't give in. "If they think I'm caving, they've been asleep for the last eight years because I've taken on every major battle in Milwaukee County and won even in a county where I'm overwhelmingly overpowered politically, and it's because we don't budge," Walker said.

"Goddamn right," Murphy said.

"If you're doing the right thing, you stay firm. In this case, we'll wait it out. If they want to start sacrificing thousands of public workers who will be laid off, sooner or later there's going to be pressure on these senators to come back."

"Beautiful," Murphy replied.

Walker said he planned to announce the next day that he would be willing to sit down with the Fitzgeralds and the Democratic minority leaders, but only if all fourteen Senate Democrats agreed to return to the Capitol. The plan, devised by Gilkes, was actually a ruse. "Legally, we believe once they've gone into session, they don't physically have to be there," Walker explained. "If they're actually in session for that day and they take a recess, the nineteen Senate Republicans could then go into action and they'd have a quorum because they started out that way. . . . If you heard I was going to talk to them, that would be the only reason why. . . . But I'm not negotiating."

"Bring a baseball bat," Murphy said in his gruff voice.

"I have one in my office; you'd be happy with that," Walker said with a chuckle. "I've got a [Louisville] Slugger with my name on it."

Walker never advanced his plan to fool the Democrats into returning to Wisconsin—Murphy exposed it for what it was when he released the prank phone call on Wednesday, February 23. The governor told Murphy he talked to the Fitzgeralds every night and asked for "a list of the people I need to call at home, to shore 'em up." The governor said there were about a dozen of these wavering lawmakers that he worried about. Walker went on to tell Murphy about his recent television appearances on *Good Morning America*, *The Sean Hannity Show*, *Morning Joe*, and *On the Record with Greta Van Susteren*. He said that Nevada's governor, Brian Sandoval, had joked with him that he didn't want Walker to visit his state because he might beat him.

"I talk to [Ohio Governor John] Kasich every day," Walker volunteered. "John's got to stand strong in Ohio. I think we can do the same thing with Rick Scott in Florida. I think [Rick] Snyder if he got a little more support could probably do that in Michigan. You start going down the list, you know, there's a lot of us new governors who got elected to do something big."

"You're the first domino."

"Yep," Walker replied. "This is our moment."

"Now what else could we do for you down there?" Murphy asked.

The governor said the first thing that he needed was more people calling GOP lawmakers with their support to combat the message that the tens of thousands of protesters were sending each day. "The other is more long term and that is after this, you know, in the coming days and weeks and months ahead, particularly in some of these more swing areas, a lot of these guys are going to need—they don't necessarily need ads out for them, but they're going to need a message out about reinforcing why this was a good thing to do for the economy, a good thing to do for the state," Walker said. "So the extent that message is out over and over again, that's obviously a good thing."

Walker was talking about two activities that Koch's Americans for Prosperity specialized in. The first was finding motivated conservatives to demonstrate and volunteer, and the second was shelling out large sums of money for television and radio ads. In the months following the call between Walker and Murphy, Americans for Prosperity spent $530,000 on ads to help the governor and Republicans in the first round of Senate recall campaigns. More came months later when Walker himself faced recall. After the Murphy call was released, Democrats said that Walker was violating the law by trying to coordinate with an independent group on a political campaign. Complaints to ethics investigators on this point were rejected because Walker's generic advice to the fake Koch wasn't a response to a real offer.

"Right, right. We'll back you any way we can," Murphy said. "But what we were thinking about the crowd was, uh, was planting some troublemakers."

Walker let three seconds pass before he responded.

"You know, the—well, the only problem with, because we thought about that," the governor stammered. "The problem with, or my only gut reaction to that, would be right now the lawmakers I have talked to have just completely had it with them. The public is not really fond of this. The teacher's union did some polling and focus groups, I think, and found out that the public turned on them the minute they closed the school down for a couple days. . . . My only fear would be is if there was a ruckus caused, is that that would scare the public into thinking maybe the governor's got to settle to avoid all these problems. Whereas I'm saying, 'Hey, we can handle this; people can protest; this is Madison, you know, full of the Sixties liberals; let them protest; it's not going to affect us.'"

Walker's admission that he had considered planting outside agitators in the crowds of peaceful protesters drew blistering criticism from Democrats. The day after the recording of the call was released, Madison's police chief, Noble Wray, said Walker should explain what he meant and how much his cabinet discussed it. "I find it very unsettling and troubling that anyone would consider creating safety risks for our citizens and law enforcement officers," he said in a statement. Walker defended his comments by saying he had rejected the idea but never said who had brought it up.

During the call, Walker went on to tell Murphy that the media would lose interest in the protests if the demonstrators were left largely alone.

"Not the liberal bastards on MSNBC," Murphy said.

"Oh, yeah, but, who watches that?" Walker responded.

"You've got to like that Mika Brzezinski," Murphy said, referring to a host of the MSNBC program *Morning Joe*.

"Oh, yeah," Walker agreed readily.

"She's a real piece of ass," Murphy said.

Walker didn't react but said that during a recent visit to Washington, D.C., he ran into Brzezinski with President Obama's adviser David Axelrod.

"That son of a bitch," Murphy said.

"Yeah, no kidding, huh?" Walker said. "I introduced myself and said, 'I figured you probably knew who I was since your boss was campaigning against me.' It's always good to let them know you know what's going on."

Walker said it was an exciting time and told Murphy about the dinner he had at the governor's mansion right after the Super Bowl when he discussed the plan with his cabinet. "We had already built plans up but it was kind of the last hurrah before we dropped the bomb and I stood up and I pulled out a picture of Ronald Reagan and said, 'You know, this may sound a little melodramatic, but thirty years ago Ronald Reagan'—whose hundredth birthday we had just celebrated the day before—'had one of the most defining moments of his political career, not just his presidency, when he fired the air traffic controllers. . . .' I said, 'This may not have as broad of world implications, but in Wisconsin's history'—little did I know how big it would be nationally—'in Wisconsin's history,' I said, 'this is our moment, this is our time to change the course of history.'"

Walker continued, "I had a cabinet meeting this morning and I reminded them of that. I said, 'For those who thought I was being melodramatic, you now know it was purely putting it in the right context.'"

For two weeks, Walker had been telling the public his plan was a modest request. By describing its unveiling as "dropp[ing] the bomb," he revealed that he knew all along that it was explosive and transformative. Comparing it to the air traffic controllers' illegal strike a generation earlier also showed how seriously he took the effort. That 1981 strike led to Reagan firing more than 11,000 air traffic controllers, and within weeks federal authorities decertified the Professional Air Traffic Controllers Organization. It proved a devastating blow to labor.

Murphy laughed. "Well, I tell you what, Scott, once you crush these bastards, I'll fly you out to Cali and really show you a good time," Murphy said.

"All right," Walker responded. "That would be outstanding. Thanks for all the support and helping us move the cause forward. . . . The bottom line is we're going to get the world moving here because it's the right thing to do."

"All right."

"Thanks a million!" Walker told the fake Koch as the conversation wrapped up.

"Bye-bye," Murphy said.

Walker's opponents later questioned whether Walker was agreeing to take an illegal gift. The governor said he was actually simply trying to wrap up a call that had lasted twenty minutes and didn't know that Murphy was talking about California. "I didn't even know where Cali is," he said during later congressional testimony, pronouncing it "KAW-lee." Regulators found that Walker did not violate the state's ethics laws because, again, no actual offer was made.

In spite of the bizarre nature of the call, the governor hung up without suspicions, aides said later. The exchange had been undeniably bad for Walker. He had revealed that he preferred to talk to out-of-state billionaires over elected Democrats, was willing to resort to trickery and layoff notices to lure Democratic senators back to Wisconsin, and had understood his plan was a major shift rather than a modest tweak in the way state government operated. He had even acknowledged considering using potentially dangerous outside agitators. But the call could have been worse. After speaking unguardedly at length, Walker had still avoided many of the traps set by Murphy.

For his part, Murphy couldn't believe his luck. He frantically checked his recording to make sure it was good and then, still in a frenzy, called his website's publisher. He spent the rest of the day and much of the night preparing a post for The Beast along with a transcript and audio of the call.

"I posted the call, got into my bathrobe, smoked a joint, and started with the scotch. A pretty decent single malt. It was something like 2 a.m. [on Wednesday, February 23]. I'd already been awake for twenty-six hours, but I was way too excited to sleep, and I wanted to watch the thing grow legs," Murphy wrote later.

The day of the prank call, February 22, Republicans kept the pressure on the Democratic senators to return to the Capitol. Mary Lazich, a GOP senator from New Berlin, sought to do that early that afternoon as she gaveled to order the Committee on Transportation and Elections. The committee met not in one of its usual locations but in the Senate parlor, a long, narrow room behind the Senate chamber normally reserved for leadership meetings, receptions, small weddings, and news conferences. This was no ordinary committee hearing. Lazich's committee was meeting to consider a bill that Republicans had been pushing for almost a decade that would require voters to show photo identification at the polls. Democrats had blocked the measure in the past, saying it would keep minorities, the elderly, and college students from voting. But Republicans finally had the control of state government they needed to pass the bill, which they said would boost confidence in the state's election system. The bill—soon to hit the Senate floor—served as bait to draw the Democrats back so they could make their arguments against it.

A clutch of citizens viewed the proceedings, along with reporters, camera crews, and legislative staff. State troopers were positioned along the wood-paneled walls, while drums and chants from the rotunda echoed in the room. Two of Lazich's fellow Republicans joined her at the dark wooden table while Democratic Senator Jon Erpenbach was patched into the meeting by speakerphone from Illinois. Committees for years have allowed senators to participate by telephone, but Lazich wasn't pleased about it that day.

"Will you be here in a fashionable time?" she asked, her voice on edge. "If you are in Illinois, you can be here in two hours. I can wait."

"Mary! I'm here now," Erpenbach said. "I'm ready to vote."

Lazich told Erpenbach he could comment on the bill but not offer amendments or vote on it because she didn't consider the reason for his absence valid. "I won't extend courtesies for unethical behavior," she said.

"Do you want the headline to be, 'Republicans won't let Democrats vote,' even though we've allowed that many, many times?" Erpenbach responded.

"We are under a call of the house," Lazich told Erpenbach. "If you refuse to grace us with your presence and continue to participate in unethical behavior, we refuse to extend our courtesy to you."

The demonstrators in the committee room snickered as Lazich and Erpenbach sparred, but otherwise didn't disrupt the proceeding. When the committee finished debating and it came time to vote, the committee clerk called the roll for the three Republicans, but not for Erpenbach. Undeterred, the Democrat repeatedly yelled, "No!" over the speaker as Lazich tried to wrap up the meeting.

"Okay," Lazich said. "The members present—"

"I vote no!" Erpenbach interjected. "Erpenbach votes no! I vote no!"

"—have voted for the bill. The bill is approved. Seeing no other business—"

"No!"

"—before the committee, we are adjourned."

Lazich slammed her gavel onto the table.

Republicans tried other ways to make the Democrats' lives uncomfortable. That morning on the floor, GOP senators approved a resolution honoring the Super Bowl champion Green Bay Packers, authored by the Democratic senator from that area, as well as another bill to help the state's dairy industry. The Packers and cheese have about the same value for Wisconsinites as holy relics did for medieval pilgrims, but Democrats had to clench their teeth and let themselves be recorded as absent. For the session, state troopers were stationed outside the chamber, and the side door leading into the chamber was locked. A page unlocked it for senators, reporters, and legislative aides with identification badges, and then locked it again behind them—unprecedented security for the Wisconsin Capitol.

That day the Senate Organization Committee—the panel of top lawmakers that sets Senate policy—voted to withhold pay for absent senators. Scott Fitzgerald and the other two Republicans outvoted the two Democrats on the committee, who sent in their ballots by fax. As Walker had explained to the fake David Koch, the Senate rules were changed to say that those who missed two consecutive floor days could no longer have their paychecks automatically deposited into their bank accounts. Instead, they would have to pick up their checks in person from Fitzgerald on the floor. The measure was aimed at senators of modest means like Erpenbach, who worked a second job driving a hotel shuttle. To get around the measure, Erpenbach later gave his chief of staff power of attorney and sent him and another aide to Fitzgerald's office to pick up the check. The two aides waited more than an hour outside Fitzgerald's office until the GOP leader emerged, walked away, and eventually returned, telling them, "I put the fucking check in the mail."

Pressure—on both sides—also came from outside the Capitol. The conservative Wisconsin Club for Growth ran ads urging people to call Walker to support him as he kept his pledge to trim state government. "Even though the special interests don't like it, he's keeping his promise, making them pay their fair share," a narrator said over images of the Capitol protests. Also on the air that day was Americans for Prosperity. The spot said public employees "walked off their jobs, abandoning our children." The AFL-CIO countered with a pro-union ad featuring a Racine firefighter who said the unions had agreed to financial concessions and were asking only that their rights not be taken away.

Walker also sought to keep up the pressure. As he had discussed on the fake Koch call, he warned that he could send out layoff notices as soon as the following week if lawmakers didn't pass his bill. He repeated that message later that night, February 22, in a televised speech aimed at the citizens of the state. Walker billed the speech as a "fireside chat," deliberately invoking President Franklin Delano Roosevelt's reassuring radio addresses that gave comfort to the country during the Great Depression. Roosevelt was generally a champion of labor rights and legislation to expand them, but the Democratic president had spoken out against the unionization of federal workers—a fact that Walker and other conservatives mentioned frequently during the stalemate. Walker gave the speech sitting in front of a marble fireplace, but there was no fire in it because all the Capitol chimneys had been stopped up years earlier for safety reasons. He told the national audience that Wisconsin was having a "passionate but civil" debate and that he hoped it would remain that way as "people pour into our state from across America." "The bill I put forward isn't aimed at state workers," he continued. "And it certainly isn't a battle with unions. If it was, we would have eliminated collective bargaining entirely or we would have gone after the private-sector unions. But we did not, because they are our partners in helping economic development. The budget I put forward is about one thing—it's about balancing our budget now and in the future."

The protesters openly mocked the idea that Walker wasn't engaged in a battle with the unions. They watched the speech from the rotunda's television screens as they chanted "Kill the bill!" Walker also mentioned a laid-off Janesville factory worker, "a union guy from a union town who asks simply why everyone else has to sacrifice except those in government." He was referring to former auto-worker Richard Hahn, who was featured in the lead of a

New York Times story the day before. The February 21 story referred to Hahn with a similar phrase as it described the disconnect between suffering private-sector workers in that city and public-sector workers. The story noted the names of well-known Wisconsin companies that had sought concessions from private-sector workers and their unions—manufacturers like Harley-Davidson, Kohler, and Mercury Marine. But days later, the *Times* ran a correction on the story, telling readers that Hahn had worked at General Motors but the UAW had no record of him belonging to the union.

Once Walker finished speaking, television newscasts flipped over to Mark Miller, who gave an unpolished response speech from a bland room, which was a sharp contrast to the elegant setting of Walker's address. "This was a railroad," Miller said. "The only action available to us to slow this down, to allow democracy to work, was to take ourselves out of the Capitol, to use a constitutional procedure that allows us to do that and allow people to have their voice."

Miller's speech angered Republicans just as Walker's had upset the Democrats. The senator's claim that they had used a "constitutional procedure" to slow the bill down particularly frustrated Republicans because they said it implied Democrats were drawing on a process spelled out in the state constitution. In fact, the constitution didn't mention such a move; it just left open the possibility. Miller said Walker should cut a deal with public workers who were willing to make the financial concessions the governor wanted if they could retain their union bargaining ability. "In a democracy, you get a little bit of what you want or a lot of what you want, but you don't get everything of what you want," Miller said.

The strongest rejoinder to Walker's fireside chat was his own soon-to-emerge chat with the fake Koch. The first inkling that Walker had been tricked came on February 23, when Murphy posted the conversation online. The Beast's website, www.buffalobeast.com, crashed for much of the day because of the volume of traffic, but audio from the call soon appeared elsewhere on the Internet, making it widely available. Walker's aides quickly acknowledged that the governor had been on the call and insisted that it showed Walker said the same things privately that he said publicly.

The call provided a jolt of righteous anger and needed energy for Democrats, from the thousands of protesters to lawmakers on both sides of the state line. In the Assembly, where Democrats were engaged in a marathon debate over the budget-repair bill, it motivated them to push on. It also hardened the resolve of the absent Democrats in Illinois. "This tape would make Richard

Nixon blush," Tim Carpenter, the Democratic senator who had inspired Murphy to make the call, wrote to Walker in a letter. The call also left some Democrats overconfident, expecting that the recording would prove politically fatal to Walker or at least force him to seek a hasty compromise with them. But the governor and his bill survived the prank, in part because other Republicans stuck by them both. "The bill is non-negotiable," Scott Fitzgerald said that day.

Walker hustled to contain the damage. Few politicians would have been willing to wade into a room of reporters the day that a snafu like the Koch call surfaced, but Walker had long thrived on media attention. He had also gotten the benefit that day of expert counsel when he met with pollster and messaging guru Frank Luntz, who is credited with recasting the "estate tax" into the "death tax" and "drilling for oil" into "exploring for energy." Luntz never commented on the meeting, and Walker's office said the pollster had already been in the area and that the meeting wasn't held to discuss the Koch call. Nonetheless, it certainly didn't hurt the governor to meet with him amid a public relations setback.

At 2:30 p.m., Walker went before the media. The roar of the Capitol crowd and the steady beat of drums were muffled by the conference room's heavy doors, but they were still loud enough for Walker to joke that the protesters gave him a good rhythm for the news conference. He told reporters he'd received 100,000 e-mails for and against his plan since he'd introduced it—a seemingly fantastic number that turned out to be true. As he did daily, he chastened Senate Democrats for not showing up to work as he had and made the threat of layoffs that he had shared with the fake Koch. In responding to questions, Walker downplayed the significance of taking a call from someone whom he'd never met but believed to be a major source of political support. "First, I want to say, I take phone calls all the time," he said. He noted he'd talked to Tim Cullen, the Democratic senator, over the weekend. "The bottom line is the things I've said are things I've said publicly all along," he said.

Asked about the plan to plant troublemakers among the protesters, Walker said he got suggestions from staff, lawmakers, and citizens but didn't say who had suggested the idea. He said his greatest fear over the weekend was that the protests could lead to some kind of disturbance. "As you've heard on the tape, we dismissed that and said that wasn't a good idea," Walker said. "Now I'm not going to allow one prank phone call to be a distraction from the reality that we have a job to do here and the job we have is to debate this bill."

That day, Walker wouldn't own up to how foolish he looked, but in a spring 2012 interview he admitted he was embarrassed by the incident. "It was idiotic that we took the call in the first place. . . . It made me look stupid," he said.

Cutting off the questions, the governor slipped out of the conference room and back into his office. A moment later, Representative Brett Hulsey elbowed his way through the reporters, photographers, and videographers. Over his dress shirt, the Madison Democrat and environmentalist wore his Assembly caucus's standard-issue orange labor T-shirt. Hulsey, who has salt and pepper hair and a sizable gap between his front two teeth, had been elected to his post for the first time in November after working as a Sierra Club lobbyist and Dane County supervisor. He stepped over a reporter and got behind the lectern. "What you just heard was unadulterated, complete nonsense," he told the reporters.

Someone opened the doors to the room, and the chants and drumming from the rotunda flooded into the conference room, nearly drowning out Hulsey. Against the backdrop of Walker's relatively staid news conference, the bizarre nature of the legislative crisis reasserted itself. The Democrat argued that the state's budget problems were not so dire and blamed Walker aides for trying to prevent journalists and the public from hearing the other side of the story. But it was the demonstrators who were drowning Hulsey out for the moment. "Those are my people," he said. "I wish they'd be quiet."

"As you heard on the tape, the guy's a megalomaniac," Hulsey continued. "I mean, he's comparing this to the PATCO strike that Ronald Reagan used to break the backs of the national union movement. That's what he wants to do."

Hulsey had a wild look in his eyes. The Assembly was a day and a half into what would be a three-day debate on collective bargaining, and Hulsey had caught just a half hour of sleep. Hulsey predicted the debate would go on much longer. "I have my sleeping bag and I have about three days of food right now," he said. "But, you know, we can order more."

12

Lost Sleep and "Hallucinazations"

I T WAS NO ORDINARY DEBATE that had so exhausted Representative
Brett Hulsey. After the last Assembly session, when Democrats had reacted angrily to Republican efforts to shut down discussion on Walker's
proposal, Speaker Jeff Fitzgerald said Republicans would cut off debate to
make sure Democrats didn't drag it out to unreasonable lengths. It turned out
he was speaking in relative terms—the Assembly was about to embark on a
debate of historic length. On Tuesday, February 22, lawmakers had returned
to the Capitol after a long weekend of demonstrations and hardening positions, which had followed the early vote taken by Republicans in the Assembly without Democrats present on the previous Friday, February 18. The
rotunda on Tuesday roiled with drumming and chanting protesters, including a couple of hundred correctional officers who marched into the rotunda.
The public was able to enter through doors in the east and north wings of the
Capitol, though most of the building's doors were locked. For the debate in
the Assembly and the separate action by Republican senators that day, there
was unparalleled security in the statehouse. A squad of state troopers was
stationed on the second floor, both inside and outside the Assembly chamber.
Metal detectors had been set up, and officers were screening visitors before
they could enter the Assembly viewing galleries. The rest of the crowd could
still watch the debate on the television screens set up on the second floor of
the rotunda, but they often couldn't hear anything because of the noise.

The Assembly was to start at 11 a.m., but lawmakers, as usual, were late.
In the meantime, Assembly Republicans held a news conference to reinforce
their commitment to passing the collective bargaining changes. Fitzgerald

told reporters that he and his GOP colleagues had visited their districts over the weekend and found that their constituents wanted them to move forward with Walker's legislation. The speaker's gamble in letting his members go home for the weekend without voting didn't seem to have hurt the proposal's chances. "They want us to hang in there and pass the bill," Jeff Fitzgerald said.

At 11:51 a.m., the roll was taken. This time, both Republicans and Democrats were at their desks in the great hall. The lawmakers sat in their leather chairs facing the great two-tiered wooden rostrum at the head of the chamber. The podium was flanked with the flags of the state and nation and surveyed by a stuffed bald eagle nicknamed Old Abe. The high marble walls rose above the representatives to four massive arches ornamented with gold leaf and four paintings of eagles. Still higher, a great disc of stained glass was set into the ceiling. Brass-edged scoreboards to show voting results hung on the wall to either side of the platform at the head of the room. Looking down from the three viewing galleries were the demonstrators, some of whom had placed tape over their mouths to protest what they saw as the silencing of their voices. On the floor, Assembly Democrats once again wore their orange union T-shirts over their collared shirts and dresses. On the podium, GOP Representative Joan Ballweg of Markesan offered the customary prayer at the beginning of the session and asked the Almighty for patience, wisdom, and "civil discourse."

During a brief moment of bipartisanship, lawmakers unanimously adopted a resolution commending law enforcement for their work in handling the protests so far. But quickly the rancor of Friday evening returned. Peter Barca, the Democratic leader, recapped the action taken by Republicans before 5 p.m. the week before, calling it an illegal meeting and illegal vote. He said that if any other rules were violated, he would seek to remove Speaker Pro Tem Bill Kramer, the presiding officer. Barca also called for revoking the floor privileges of some Republican aides because they had encouraged representatives on Friday to hold the vote despite the Democrats' calls to halt it. Republicans, of course, would never have allowed Kramer to be removed from his post. But as Barca talked, the normally outspoken Kramer quietly thumbed through a rule book. When Barca was finished, Jeff Fitzgerald accused him of engaging in stall tactics and said that it was the Senate Democrats who had made the real affront to democracy by "not showing up to work."

Democrat after Democrat rose along with a few Republicans to hash out the action of the week before. It wasn't until 1:44 p.m., nearly two hours after the Assembly had started, that the lawmakers shifted to the debate on the bill itself and the proposed changes to it. At the time the session started that Tuesday, Democrats had offered about fifteen amendments, but more were streaming in as quickly as the Legislature's nonpartisan lawyers could draft them on the lawmakers' behalf. By the time it wrapped up, the Democrats would offer 128 amendments. Representative Cory Mason, a Racine Democrat and former labor organizer, rose to debate one of the first amendments from his party. His proposed change to the bill would remove several sentences giving the Walker administration sweeping power to head off strikes and other work stoppages by its employees. That section of the bill would allow the governor and his appointees, if he had declared a state of emergency, to fire workers who participated in a strike or similar action or who failed to show up for work for any three days without approval. Republicans moved to table, or essentially kill, Mason's amendment, and the Democrat stood up to argue against that.

"You have two minutes on tabling," Kramer said.

Mason replied that public employees had given up their ability to strike in exchange for laws and protections that were now being eliminated. "Labor peace. Labor peace. . . . A lot of the laws that we're talking about taking away this week, when they were passed it was called labor peace," he said. "For a long time in this country, working people working together found strikes were the only way they could get recognition from their employer and from the law."

Kramer eventually interrupted, "Gentleman, your two minutes are up." But now Mason asked for permission to speak longer. "Any objection? You have two more minutes," Kramer said when he heard none.

Mason finished and, in a sign of what was to come, a line of Democrats rose to echo his arguments. Some spoke quickly but others asked for more than their two minutes. And not all of them used Mason's high-minded rhetoric.

"If we take this right away, if I work at UW–Madison, my boss can say I can't go to the bathroom. That means I can't go pee," said Milwaukee Democrat Leon Young, a former policeman. "And it sounds ridiculous, but they're taking this basic right away to have a lunch break. Give me thirty minutes for lunch."

"Gentleman, your two minutes are up," Kramer interrupted. When the Democrat asked for more time, a Republican objected. "The Assembly will stand informal," Kramer said, giving lawmakers a short break.

The leaders of both sides talked it over. When they started again, the Republican withdrew his objection. When the vote on tabling came, Republicans easily won it without even bothering to explain their arguments for why the amendment was a bad idea. But it still took the majority close to half an hour to dispense with it. The question of time would be a delicate one over the coming days. The tradition of the Assembly dictated giving the minority party time to make its case on bills even when it was stalling. Nonetheless, the Republican majority ultimately had the final say over how much time was fair. As the debate continued, Democrats tried a new tactic, referring the bill to a labor committee where it could receive more study and possible changes. Democrats debated that motion until just after 10 p.m. When the motion failed, Democrats asked for an hour to meet privately in caucus. It had been almost twelve hours since the Assembly had started, and so far only two amendments had been discussed. There were dozens more already lined up and dozens more coming, hinting at how long the debate could go.

Republicans met privately as well. The GOP Assembly caucus held its meetings in a large fourth-floor room in the Capitol that could comfortably accommodate its fifty-seven members. A police escort had accompanied the lawmakers to the meeting, and through the walls came the sound of drumming and chants. Michelle Litjens, a newly elected representative from the town of Vinland near Oshkosh, had come into the meeting expecting high emotions and conflict. Instead, she found the caucus mostly unified against the opposition outside the room. The Republican lawmakers talked about what their vote might mean for their constituents and careers.

The Republicans' landslide in November 2010 had given their party some seats in Democratic areas that they would have difficulty holding in the future. One Republican who had worked in the Assembly referred to those seats as the ones that his party was "renting." For the lawmakers in those districts, Walker's bill could spell a certain end to their budding legislative careers. Early on in the meeting, one of those lawmakers stood up to speak. Joe Knilans, a former worker and supervisor at the unionized General Motors plant in his labor-friendly hometown of Janesville, had already drawn the attention of Walker's staff. On the morning of February 16 the governor's legislative director had sent Walker a message about Knilans saying that "word is that Rep. Joe Nylans (Ny-lens) needs a call from you to keep him on board" for the bill, adding the correct way to pronounce a potentially unfamiliar name. A half hour later, Walker sent back a message saying he had left Knilans a voice message on his cell phone. Knilans ultimately stuck with the governor but understood the risks. "I just want to say that taking this vote today will probably cost me my job," Knilans told the Republican caucus at the meeting. "But that's why I came to Madison—to take votes like this. I never wanted to be a career politician—it's about doing the right thing." Knilans wasn't lying about his prospects for re-election. He would lose his 2012 race by a nearly two-to-one margin to the Democrat in his heavily union district. But his speech made a deep impression on other lawmakers like Litjens and set the tone for the rest of the meeting. "You didn't know what to say after he said that," she recalled.

Dick Spanbauer, the Oshkosh lawmaker who had predicted the huge fight over the legislation, stood up to say that he could not support it. He was the only one to say that explicitly. Perhaps a dozen lawmakers spoke. While they talked, the longest-serving member of the Assembly Republican caucus made up his mind to speak at the end. Al Ott had been in the Assembly since 1987, and though he was certain that Walker's bill was the right thing for the state's budget challenges, he considered it far and away the most difficult vote of his career. Ott was a devout United Methodist, and he suggested his colleagues pray together. They gathered in a great circle, joined hands, and he recited two biblical passages from memory, the first from the book of Isaiah 9:6.

For unto us a Child is born,
Unto us a Son is given;
And the government will be upon His shoulder.
And His name will be called
"Wonderful Counselor, Mighty God,
Everlasting Father, Prince of Peace."

The second verse came from the book of Romans 13:1.

Let every soul be subject to the governing authorities. For there is no authority except from God, and the authorities that exist are appointed by God. Therefore whoever resists the authority resists the ordinance of God, and those who resist will bring judgment on themselves.

Ott prayed for wisdom and guidance and then began to recite the Lord's Prayer. When the lawmakers finished praying, they left the meeting confident that the bill would pass. "That was one of those crucial moments when I knew we had the votes," Robin Vos, the co-chairman of the Joint Finance Committee, said later.

By the time Democrats and Republicans had finished their closed-door caucus meetings and gotten back on the floor, it was 11:35 p.m. First up in the next long slog was an amendment that would have added the prosecutors in local district attorneys' offices to the group of police, firefighters, and public-safety employees who were allowed under the bill to keep their union bargaining powers. Just before 1 a.m., the Republicans set this third amendment aside, keeping the debate on a dauntingly slow pace. Lawmakers took a break at 3:20 a.m. and came back just before 5 a.m. to take up more amendments. Democrats were looking for any way they could to kill the bill or at least scale it back slightly. They lacked the votes to do either and so they aimed for the next best thing—talking for hours to stall the proposal in the hopes that the force of public opinion would accomplish what they couldn't. Democrats stuck to discussing the merits of their amendments, never resorting to reading from phone books or dictionaries, but the power of their filibuster was limited. In the U.S. Senate, the majority party often doesn't have enough votes to shut down debate, but Republicans in the Wisconsin Assembly had the ability to force votes and were prepared to do that if necessary at some point.

By Wednesday, February 23, nerves were frayed and attendance on the Assembly floor was thin. Lawmakers from both sides were drifting back to their offices or across the street to the Inn on the Park hotel to catch some sleep or just relieve the boredom. Those who were left on the floor looked haggard. As the Democrats' energy waned, they got a jolt from the release of Ian Murphy's prank call to Walker. After the news had broken, the Assembly took a break at 10:45 a.m., giving lawmakers a chance to listen to the recording of the call. After a few hours to rest up, Democrats came back to the floor with renewed vigor just before 2 p.m., making the fake Koch call a central part of many of their speeches. At one point that Wednesday, Jeff Fitzgerald told reporters he thought the Assembly could approve the bill soon. "We hope to finish later tonight," he said.

He wasn't even close. The returning lawmakers waded into other amendments contesting most aspects of the bill. Among other goals, the changes sought to restore collective bargaining for public workers; treat public safety workers and regular workers the same; and limit the Walker administration's ability to impose cuts on state health programs for the poor and to sell aging state power plants without taking bids. "The amendment is tabled," Kramer said over and over.

A little after 6:30 p.m. that Wednesday, the Assembly broke for three hours and then returned. The parade of amendments continued, with Democrats putting forward one to prohibit furloughs of public workers until the start of 2014. Walker had said that the elimination of union bargaining and the higher health and pension contributions were allowing the state to end furloughs for state workers. The amendment tried to lock in that promise.

The Assembly rolled into the wee hours of Thursday, February 24, and took a break at about 3:15 a.m. The lawmakers returned just after 6 a.m., with another GOP lawmaker spelling Kramer in the speaker's chair. Republicans were now making progress in dispatching the Democrats' amendments, but after nearly two days of debate they had only handled about half of them. Not a single one had even come close to surviving. Now there was hope of an exit strategy for the exhausted lawmakers. Assembly leaders announced what they described as an agreement under which Democrats would keep any remaining debate to thirty-eight amendments with no more than ten minutes of discussion on each. That would limit the debate to six and a half hours more—though ultimately that constraint didn't hold. For their part, Democrats said later that the deal amounted to an ultimatum from GOP leaders.

Republicans, meanwhile, rolled their bloodshot eyes. The Assembly kept going through the morning, hitting the forty-eight-hour mark in the debate. By then, it was clear that something unprecedented was happening. The length of the debate now showed on the lawmakers' faces, from the stubble darkening the cheeks and jawlines of the assemblymen to the darkening circles under the eyes of men and women alike. For an afternoon, night, day, night, and a morning, the ninety-six lawmakers had been engaged in a sleep-starved debate, with Democrats holding the floor at almost all times and Republicans reluctant to offer any rebuttal that would further drag out the process.

Veteran statehouse figures said the debate was the longest in their decades of memory. Dick Wheeler, the dean of the Capitol press corps who had covered the Legislature since 1972, said he had never before seen a continuous forty-eight-hour debate. Wheeler ran a news service for political insiders and paid careful attention to floor votes in both houses, making him one of the most knowledgeable people about the Legislature in the state. Three longtime legislators of both parties—Dean Kaufert, Bob Turner, and Fred Kessler—agreed. Kaufert, one of the few Republicans who had expressed concerns about the bill, said he had had forty minutes of sleep in the last fifty-two hours. He called the debate a "once-in-a-lifetime" event. "I've never seen anything this intense with the volume of e-mails, calls, passion, threats that this has generated on both sides," he said.

Kaufert and Turner, a Democrat, had been in the Assembly since 1991, and they said a budget debate in the Assembly in the early 1990s went for several days, but in that case lawmakers took breaks in the evening to return to their homes or hotel rooms to sleep. That wasn't happening in the debate over Walker's bill. Kessler, a Democrat who had served during most of the 1960s and then returned after the 2004 election, said the debate also recalled the 1969 takeover of the Assembly floor by demonstrators led by Father James Groppi while the body was addressing welfare legislation. In that case, the National Guard was called in. There were no state records that could speak to whether there had ever been a longer legislative debate in the history of Wisconsin, but by the time these speeches were done, they seemed certain to be at or near a record.

Just before 1 p.m. on Thursday, February 24, the Assembly broke for a little over two hours. Assembly Democratic leaders headed downstairs again to the east wing of the Capitol to try for a second time to meet with Walker. They brought with them a plan that called for achieving the savings in state and local worker benefits being sought by the governor without repealing the unions' ability to bargain. Walker's administration secretary, Mike Huebsch, himself a former speaker of the Assembly, met with Democratic lawmakers, but no progress was made. By just after 3 p.m., lawmakers were back on the floor; a little after 6 p.m., they came to what would be the final amendment that Republicans allowed in the debate. It was a proposal by Barca and several other Democrats requiring that Walker's bill be approved by voters in a referendum before it could take effect. Republicans had sometimes asked for similar referenda to voters in the case of new taxes, but here they sought to table this amendment. Kelda Helen Roys, a Madison Democrat, rose to oppose the tabling motion. "With this amendment we're giving one final chance to really listen to what the people are saying—all the people," she said.

Now Kramer spoke. "All those in favor of tabling will vote aye. All those opposed will vote no. The clerk will open the roll." He paused to wait for the votes to appear on the electronic board. "There are fifty-eight ayes and thirty-eight nays."

By then, Democrats had offered 128 amendments and still had about forty left that hadn't been taken up yet. After another Democratic objection on an obscure parliamentary question, Speaker Fitzgerald took the floor. "This issue has been very emotional for my caucus . . . because this bill affects people we know. It affects daughters who are teachers. My sister-in-law got her pink slip yesterday, who's a teacher, my brother's wife, the [Senate] majority leader's wife. This isn't easy stuff. But you know what? We're broke. We're completely broke and there's only two ways out of this. We can either cut spending, have everyone pitch in and try and solve this budget deficit without raising taxes, or we can do what was done two years ago," Fitzgerald said, referring to the tax increases passed by Democrats in 2009. "You guys know that's not going to fly.

"You know, my hometown's Horicon, Wisconsin. A lot of union folks. And I can tell you right now protests in my neighborhood this week—150 people—my neighbor who I've known for a long time let them do the protest on his lawn. . . . I'm not getting many waves any more from my neighbors. . . . This isn't easy, but it's the right thing to do. We don't have any other choices. Now we've been debating this bill for fifty-some hours. This is the longest in the history of the state Assembly that a bill has ever been debated. [But] in the end, you know we're going to have to take this vote. . . . I hope we can keep this civil, I think we have, and hopefully we can get out of here sometime." It was 8:10 p.m.

Democrats and Fitzgerald had several exchanges, jousting back and forth about whether Republicans would invoke an Assembly rule to cut off debate. Barca stood, saying that the last time such a motion was even made in the body was in May 1996, but it was withdrawn without being used. Barca repeated a request to take a break until the next morning or at least for a few hours. "We have a tradition in this body to allow people to speak if they're so moved on closing arguments on a debate on any bill—any bill—but especially given the historic nature of this debate," Barca said. "We're talking history. We're talking about the tradition of this state. . . . We're asking for a commitment from the speaker that you won't resort to [this] tactic."

Barca ended his speech at 8:47 p.m., and for an hour the Assembly stood idle as both sides talked quietly about what to do next. When they returned, Barca again asked for unanimous consent to recess until the next morning. Republicans objected and the speeches resumed. About half an hour later, Vos gave a speech dismissing Democrats' criticism of the cost curbs his party was seeking in state health programs. "No senior citizen is going to be hurt, Mr. Speaker. That's another lie," the tired and agitated lawmaker said. "They go on and on and on. In fact you got to the point where you said we're dismantling Medicaid."

Another Democrat, Louis Molepske Jr. of Stevens Point, stood up and asked to be recognized. "Mr. Speaker, obviously the effects of sleep deprivation on the brains and behavior of this body are affecting decorum, Mr. Speaker," he said.

Molepske, who was seeking a recess, sounded drunk because of the lack of sleep. At that moment, his incoherence was doing more to make his point for him than eloquence could have. "I've been asked by members of the body to rise and ask you as the presiding officer—as you can see, my speech is slurred," he said. "People have tempers. People have heart conditions in this room. We have members with many, many disorders."

There was laughter and applause from Vos, the other lawmakers, and the onlookers in the galleries at this bit of unintended humor from Molepske, who paused, shuffled a paper on his desk, and soldiered on. "We have people on medication. Sleep deprivation, Mr. Speaker, is a very serious problem. We have one physician in the body that can tell us that without rest over a prolonged period of time can lead to hallucinazations—I can't even say the word right now. I ask for a recess that you would control to allow us to close our eyes, get those neurons working right, the synapses connecting, the muscle regeneration that's needed, so when we finally press the button we are not doing so in a hallucinogenic state."

Kramer was having none of it. "We have been at this for a little over fifty-eight and a half hours, and with the exception of five of those hours, I have been in the chair," he said. "So as difficult as your job is, I do it standing up and I have to pay attention. I don't need a recess."

Vos again had the floor and went back to talking about the need to free the state from what he saw as the "death spiral" of unsustainable budgeting. "It's got to happen," he said. "The reason I rose under suspending the rules is because we cannot wait. The delay tactics on this side—I mean if you added it up of the fifty-eight hours, I have a feeling that fifty-six, if I'm generous, has been used by one side of the aisle. . . . Mr. Speaker, we need to suspend the rules. We need to get to a vote quickly. I hope we'll do that way before, way before, people get to the point where the earlier gentleman said we have to recess." Now Vos sat down and another Republican moved to bring the bill forward for the final debate on passage.

"No! No!" Democrats exploded, jumping to their feet as the vote was taken. "Mr. Speaker!" Barca shouted, demanding to be recognized. An unidentified Democrat yelled out an obscenity. Outside the chamber, the hundreds of protesters still in the rotunda surged up to the law enforcement line just a short distance from the chamber and screamed, "Kill the bill! Kill the bill!" Amid the uproar, Gordon Hintz, a Democrat from Oshkosh, was near Michelle Litjens. She represented a nearby district to Hintz's and had known him for years.

"You're fucking dead!" Hintz yelled at Litjens, making what she took to be a political, rather than physical, threat. Hintz later apologized but he wouldn't be the only one who lost his cool. After the vote, Kramer recognized Barca.

"This is what corruption looks like. This is just terrible," Barca said. "This is just flat-out wrong. You cannot refuse to recognize people, Mr. Speaker. I move for the removal of the presiding officer."

There was a debate over the motion, but Republicans easily beat it back, even gaining several Democrats who voted to keep Kramer in his chair. Democrats continued to press Republicans to allow all of their members to speak. At 10:51 p.m., Scott Suder, the majority leader, stood up and spoke. "We are at an impasse here, gentlemen," he said. "It seems clear that our side wants to vote and I challenge anyone watching to try to make the argument that we have not allowed for adequate debate. Now, some of you can laugh, some of you can yell but, look, we have been here fifty-nine hours. I don't know if that's the longest time period that we've had debate in this body. It is the longest time period for me and I've been here over a decade like you. But it astounds me that some people continue to try to say that we have stifled debate, that we are trampling democracy. My grandmother had a word for that: poppycock. My grandfather had a word for that that I won't use in this body."

The Democrats continued to debate both the bill and the idea of shutting down debate for the next two hours. One reporter later joked that the most dangerous duty of covering the chaotic Capitol was conducting interviews that night with the coughing lawmakers, who were now coming down with colds from their exhausting session in the middle of winter. As the time neared 1 a.m., many of the Republicans who had been absent from the floor came back to their seats. Another Democrat, sensing that something was coming, made a point of breaking into a colleague's speech to ask Kramer how many speakers were left in the queue. There were fifteen. Gary Hebl, a Democrat from Sun Prairie, had the floor. His voice was hoarse and he was breathing a little heavier than he should have been as he rambled through what would be the Democrats' last speech.

"Okay, I'll wrap it up, geez. Oh, how can I finish strong? Oh, I'll finish with what I said this morning," Hebl said, telling a story about what he had learned about politics from his father. "In Wisconsin, that's our heritage: We treat everybody like we want to be treated and, unfortunately, the reason there's people out in this Capitol lobby, in the rotunda, is because we are not treating people the way we would want to be treated. If that were true, this building would not be full of people at five after one on Friday morning. Thanks, Mr. Speaker."

Kramer then delivered a rapid-fire statement that was, in spite of the few tell-tale signs of the previous ten minutes, still a surprise to many in the room: "Having been read three times, shall the bill be passed? All in favor will vote aye, all opposed will vote no; the clerk will open the roll."

Assembly Chief Clerk Patrick Fuller and his support staff on the podium jumped into action to record the vote. Democrats erupted, leaping up and shouting, "No! No! Mr. Speaker! No!" They continued to scream as the votes were cast. Kramer had called for the vote even though lawmakers were in line waiting to speak. Under Assembly rules, a motion to end debate can be used if it's seconded by at least fifteen members and then approved on a roll call vote. Republicans did not seek to make a motion to end debate, to gather the number of seconds needed for the motion, or to take a roll call vote on ending debate. In the confusion, more than one-quarter of the body—twenty-eight lawmakers—didn't have or didn't take the opportunity to vote. Those included twenty-five Democrats and three representatives who supported Walker's bill—two Republicans and the body's lone independent lawmaker. Of those who did vote, all Democrats voted against the proposal along with four Republicans—Dean Kaufert of Neenah, Lee Nerison of Westby, Dick Spanbauer of Oshkosh, and Travis Tranel of Cuba City. "The clerk will close the roll," Kramer said. "There are fifty-one ayes, seventeen nays. The bill is passed."

A Republican made the motion to send the bill to the Senate and then adjourn. Republicans said yes in the voice vote, and Democrats continued to shout no. It was now 1:06 a.m. and the Assembly had been in session for sixty-one hours and fifteen minutes. "The ayes have it. The bill is in the Senate. The Assembly is adjourned," Kramer said above the din.

Chris Danou, a Democrat from Trempealeau, threw papers and a drink in the air as other Democrats erupted in an uproar of objections. To leave the floor the normal way through the large main doors of the Assembly, Republicans would have had to walk past the desks of angry Democratic lawmakers. Instead, they quietly walked out through a smaller side door into Speaker Fitzgerald's office. That took time and, as they exited, Democrats shook their fingers at them. "Shame! Shame! Shame!" Democrats shouted dozens of times.

A physical fight didn't seem likely. But the tension was high enough that a police officer stood in between the lawmakers of opposing parties as several Democrats—among them Danou, Brett Hulsey, and Nick Milroy—shouted at the Republicans from close quarters. "Cowards all! You're all cowards," Hulsey screamed as another Democrat tried to calm him down.

Republicans walked stoically into Fitzgerald's office and closed the door behind them. Many were escorted out of the building by law enforcement, who brushed journalists aside as they whisked Kramer and other GOP lawmakers into an elevator. The reporters blurted questions at them vainly as the doors closed. Litjens—worried more by the crowd than by Hintz's earlier outburst to her—didn't want to go out with the other Republicans even with the police. Forgetting her cell phone on her desk in her haste, she went to a room just off the floor used by the Assembly pages, changed from a sport coat into a sweatshirt, and pulled on a baseball cap. She also grabbed a protest sign with an image of a fist in the shape of the state of Wisconsin that she had taken earlier as a keepsake. She and another GOP lawmaker, Erik Severson, left the other way through the Assembly parlor and marched out amid the demonstrators.

In the rotunda, Jenni Dye was watching. During the nights of the marathon Assembly session, she watched the debate and then slept with blankets on the marble floors; she didn't yet own a sleeping bag. The final night of the debates, she climbed the stairs to the third floor to watch from the public galleries. When she got there, Dye ended up sitting next to a young woman and fellow high school classmate who was now working as a social worker. "A statistician should calculate how many people are opposed to this bill for me to randomly run into so many acquaintances," she tweeted later.

Dye watched the debate for a time, but as she did she knew that Twitter messages with questions for her were building up in her iPhone. She decided she would be more useful to the opposition if she went back to the rotunda. There, she could watch the debate on the television monitors and tweet about it to her growing group of followers. She couldn't do that in the gallery because visitors weren't allowed to use cell phones there. She left before the bill was moved to the third reading.

When the vote came, it was relatively quiet in the rotunda, with many people asleep. Dye was still awake and watching the televisions. But from outside the chamber it was even harder to catch the subtle signs of Republicans preparing to end the debate, so the vote took Dye by complete surprise. "They voted! They voted!" people around her screamed as they rushed to wake those who were sleeping so they wouldn't miss the climax of the debate. Others came running from the wings of the Capitol to the rotunda as quickly as they could. A man got on a microphone or bullhorn and told the crowd that "now is not the time to revolt." But looking at her fellow demonstrators, Dye wasn't worried about that possibility. The crowd didn't seem to her to want to revolt, just to be heard. For her, the Assembly vote had been expected eventually and with the Senate Democrats still in Illinois, there was still reason for hope. She tapped out a series of tweets:

"It is a shame that the Republicans couldn't let the remaining Dems speak. They had the votes. At least give people a voice."

"I sort of want to punch something. I'm guessing this marble wall would be a poor choice."

"I will never forget that I was here the day the Assembly Republicans voted to shut down the middle class."

By then, Dye wanted some sleep. The crowd around her began to sing "We Shall Overcome" and, later, the national anthem. As Dye watched from the ground floor, the Assembly Democrats came to a second floor walkway and raised their fists in a tired gesture of solidarity. One more tweet zipped out of Dye's iPhone.

"Dems come to balcony. We're cheering. I'm crying."

13

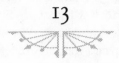

The Capitol in Lockdown

A LIGHT SNOW AND A SENSE OF TENSION fell on the Capitol square
on Saturday, February 26. The largest crowd yet swamped the side-
walks and lawn; official estimates put the number of the throng at
more than 70,000, though some said it was larger. Madison was seeing its
biggest sustained demonstrations since the Vietnam War. Outside the statehouse, the crowd was peaceful and triumphant. Near State Street, the statue
known as *Forward*, of a woman with outstretched arm clutching a flag, had
been blindfolded and garlanded with a "For Sale" sign around her neck.
"We're baaaack," one labor leader said to the crowd as a series of celebrities
and ordinary workers addressed them. The actor Bradley Whitford, a Madison native and former cast member of the political television drama *The West
Wing*, had traveled to the capital city with a message for Walker and the demonstrators. "This guy needs to understand Wisconsin is a stubborn constit-
uency," he said. "We fish through ice." Peter Yarrow of the folk group Peter,
Paul, and Mary performed for the crowd. Angela Aldous, a thirty-year-old
nurse from Madison, drew loud cheers when she scoffed at Walker's claim
that the protesters were largely from out of state. "Governor Walker, I'm not
faking this Wisconsin accent," Aldous said. "I was born in Wisconsin. I live
in Wisconsin. And I came back early from my ice-fishing trip to tell you, 'You
are not going to crush Wisconsin.'"

That day, the governor and his staff were trading e-mails about what they
might do to respond to the massive protests. "We need to get info out about
[what] Mitch Daniels did in 2005 in IN," Walker wrote to five of his top aides
that morning, referring to the Indiana governor's cancellation of collective

bargaining for state workers. "We need to show how household income went up in his first term, how property taxes were frozen and we need to show what happened to government workers."

"I have an idea, it may not be a good one," communications director Chris Schrimpf replied. "What if we reached out to Mitch Daniels, and asked him to join us at a [press conference] and walk everyone through what collective bargaining reform meant for his state?"

"I actually like a presser with him on the phone," the governor answered.

"Let's just remember, he just offered a compromise to the House Dems who fled," wrote Walker's deputy chief of staff, Eric Schutt, referring to Daniels's efforts to reach out to the Democrats who had copied Wisconsin Democrats and left Indiana to try to block union legislation there.

"If he's on the phone he just explains and says bye and we do the questions," Schrimpf wrote.

"Maybe he talks about his offer was to get folks back from [right-to-work legislation], but what we are doing is reasonable. Just want us to think it through," Schutt wrote.

Whatever the reason, no such news or phone conference happened.

Meanwhile, inside the statehouse, the demonstrators were again overwhelmingly peaceful, but a threat of confrontation loomed. The Walker administration was seeking to clear the Capitol of the demonstrators who had occupied it since the marathon budget hearings two weeks before. On Saturday, the police started blocking the public from bringing in sleeping bags and blankets. By 4 p.m. on Sunday, February 27, many of the demonstrators had left the building, but several hundred still refused. Facing one of their biggest dilemmas so far, Capitol Police Chief Charles Tubbs and UW–Madison Police Chief Susan Riseling trusted to a strategy of having demonstrators voluntarily comply with the rules rather than moving them out forcibly. The approach meant they didn't get everyone out of the building, but they avoided a potentially violent confrontation that night. The protesters moved their possessions so the cleaning crew could do its work, chanted "Thank you!" to the workers as they did, and then went to sleep on their customary bedding of stone floors. Much later, Dane County Sheriff Dave Mahoney argued that the tolerant approach by police established a "model for law enforcement moving forward." Had police approached demonstrators in the heavy-handed manner employed decades earlier during the protests of the Vietnam War, there might well have been confrontations, he said. "There undoubtedly would have been damage both to the reputation of law enforcement and to the

Constitution of the United States." But the next day, Monday, February 28, brought back the question of what to do with the remaining demonstrators. The Walker administration tried a peaceful siege in which they blocked new protesters going into the Capitol and tried to wait out the ones who were already inside. Still, the occupiers remained. The administration shut down all the public entrances to the building except the King Street doors, with a second entrance reserved for staff and the media. For the first time in long memory, the public was being kept out of the statehouse. At 9 a.m., protesters lined up outside the King Street entrance, waiting to be let in, as Capitol Police officers cordoned off areas inside and readied metal detectors that were about to be put into use at the entrances to the Capitol for the first time since immediately after the September 11, 2001, terrorist attacks. Just beyond the security area, a handful of the protesters who had spent the night in the building were singing the old union standard "Which Side Are You On?" Down the hallway, most of the Capitol elevators had been shut down. The police controlled every stairwell—and thus determined who could get to the upper floors.

At first, no one was let into the statehouse at all. Over the course of the day, a few people were allowed in if they had a meeting scheduled with a lawmaker or were going to a committee meeting like the ongoing informal public hearing being held by Democratic lawmakers on Walker's bill. But hardly anyone was getting in simply to demonstrate. Those with connections—such as community leaders and lobbyists—were now the main ones allowed into the building. Walker administration spokeswoman Carla Vigue said new demonstrators wouldn't be allowed back in "until police feel comfortable," but she wouldn't say who had the supposed concerns or why or what it would take to allay those concerns. Outside, opponents bristled. Assembly Democrat Kelda Helen Roys of Madison, who within months would announce she was running for Congress, declined to show her Capitol identification card and was turned away at several entrances by police. Inside, the clampdown left the Capitol more subdued than usual since the crisis began, but the rotunda still erupted regularly with drumming and chanting from the several hundred remaining demonstrators. At one point, a man not affiliated with the demonstrators climbed onto a first-floor balcony. After a short standoff, police safely lowered him to the ground and took him to a mental health evaluation.

Dye got to the Capitol at 8 a.m., the building's normal hour for opening for the public. The doors were locked and people were told that the opening time had been pushed back. Dye tweeted a photo of demonstrators bundled up against the below-freezing weather and carrying their signs as they milled in front of the door. The protesters were undeterred by the cold, with one telling Dye, "Honey, I'm from Superior, Wisconsin. This is tropical weather!" Dye posted a link to the administration's new policy on the building. "If I have to sleep on the Capitol steps, I will. And I will be really angry about it," she tweeted.

Dye had to go on to work for a deposition but fired off another tweet before she did. "Things I just said out loud: Someone should file an injunction," she wrote.

The Wisconsin State Employees Union had the same thought and quickly took the administration to court to challenge the virtual lockout. To handle the case, the unions brought in Peg Lautenschlager, a feisty Democrat and former attorney general who had headed the Department of Justice for four years before a drunk-driving incident got her voted out of office. She filed a motion for a temporary restraining order and several affidavits that Monday in Dane County Circuit Court. A hearing was scheduled for that next morning before the duty judge.

A fight loomed between an administration that felt it had the right to put basic controls on the building and demonstrators who believed the statehouse belonged to the people. Protesters wanting to enter or pass food to those inside had to do it surreptitiously through the windows of bathrooms or of Democratic offices on the ground floor. Some demonstrators removed wooden blocks from some ground floor windows that had been in place for years to prevent the windows from being raised more than a few inches. The building staff secured the windows again by driving in bolts and then snapping off the heads to make them tougher to remove. This episode inspired an AFL-CIO blog to claim that the windows were being "welded shut." In fact, the windows of the Capitol were made of wood, but that didn't stop the post from zipping through the Web on Twitter and Facebook.

Besides the fight over the building, the second major source of tension was the approaching deadline over the refinancing of state debt. The refinancing was key to the state balancing its budget and avoiding other, harsher means to do so, such as deeper cuts to state programs or tax increases. The plan to push back $165 million in principal payments was more important in the short term to balancing the state's books than the controversial savings from the cuts to benefits for its work force. But officials said the state needed to act quickly to restructure its bonds. The administration originally said that law-makers and the governor needed to approve the deal by that Saturday, February 27, to take it to market in time to realize the savings before the end of the budget period on June 30. As the stalemate dragged on, Walker said the deal could still happen if approved by Tuesday, March 1, the date he was to give his budget address. The governor warned that failing to pass the bill could lead to the layoffs of 1,500 workers, though his office wouldn't say exactly when. Longtime followers of Walker's career noted that he had made similar threats during his previous contract disputes with workers in Milwaukee County but didn't follow through on them there. Democrats also suspected Walker was leaving wiggle room in his deadlines, a common tactic in budget standoffs.

There was an irony to Walker, who presented himself as a fiscal archconservative, pushing a debt refinancing. The plan took a payment that was due on May 1 and spread it out over a decade, costing the state about $40 million in extra interest. The plan was a miniature version of past borrowing schemes that the governor had criticized throughout his campaign and vowed never to repeat. Democrats were happy to point that out but still generally supported it because the refinancing would give the state breathing room. Mark Miller and Senate Democrats presented their own plan to resolve the state's immediate budget shortfall—and avert layoffs—without restructuring the state's debt, but the plan hinged on holding the governor to a requirement to find $79 million in almost immediate cuts, something that the Walker administration had said it couldn't do in such a short time frame.

It seemed increasingly clear that the Democrats would not return from Illinois in time for the budget-repair bill to be passed by Walker's deadline. In the Senate, the efforts of the Republicans focused on a series of small punishments they futilely meted out on the absent Democratic senators and their staffs. On February 28 GOP senators took away from their Democratic colleagues the right to decide whether the Democrats' aides would get paid. The chamber's leadership committee passed the measure on a three-to-zero vote; the "no" votes cast by fax by the two Democrats on the committee were left uncounted.

Meanwhile, Walker's poll numbers were sinking. A Democratic-leaning polling firm released results showing that a majority of the state would now pick Walker's defeated opponent, Tom Barrett, if they were given a chance to recast their November vote. The survey by Public Policy Polling, based in North Carolina, showed that Walker's approval ratings were now upside down, with higher disapproval than approval from voters, and that more of those surveyed sided with the unions in the standoff than with the governor. Most alarming for Republicans, voters split evenly on the question of whether to recall the governor from office, with 48 percent on each side. Now not just the unions were fighting for their political lives—the governor was as well.

On Monday night, February 28, Jenni Dye lay down to sleep on the concrete outside the Capitol in the below-freezing weather in a sleeping bag that she had bought for the occasion. Above her loomed the great columns of the east wing of the Capitol that held up the great pediment and its classical sculpted figures representing Dye's profession, the law. She took an ant's-view photo of the Capitol, and the nighttime image took on an unreal quality in the poor light. Naturally, she tweeted the photo to her followers. "The view from my bed! This. Is. Amazing," she wrote.

Dye tagged her post and photo with the label "Walkerville," a reference to the "Hooverville" shantytowns built during the Great Depression. When demonstrators decided to set up the encampment on the square that night in protest of the shutdown of the statehouse, someone had taken an Ian's Pizza box, written "Hooverville" on it, crossed that word out, and then written "Walkerville." Before coming to spend the night, Dye went to a nearby bar to charge her phone and spirits, staying out as late as she could to avoid having to go out in the cold. A series of urgent tweets helped marshal blankets for the makeshift settlement and convince some wavering souls to commit to spending the night as well. The group was relatively small, as any group would have to be when its purpose was camping out in the city on a night when the temperature would dip to under 20 degrees. "For the record, I can't believe I'm doing this, either," she tweeted.

Her group laid down cardboard, then covered that with the blankets. Dye broke open a disposable heating pad, edged up to a friend for warmth, and settled in for the cold night. She woke on March 1 to news a Dane County judge had issued a temporary restraining order requiring the administration to open up the Capitol during business hours and official meetings until a hearing on the case could be held that afternoon before a different judge.

But the judge's order to open the Capitol seemingly had lost its force somewhere along the two blocks between the courthouse and the statehouse. Dye had to leave early for work, but she never stopped following the fight. Demonstrators brought copies of the temporary restraining order to the Capitol steps to show them to the law enforcement officers standing at the door. "Let us in!" the crowd shouted as protesters held up hand-lettered signs with passages from the Constitution. In one tweet Dye wrote, "Why in God's name are the doors still locked? When a court order means nothing, our system has failed." The building didn't open because Walker's Department of Administration stuck with a plan issued that morning that further restricted demonstrators' access to the building. This time visitors had to be escorted to committee hearings or lawmakers' offices—a time-consuming process— and limits were placed on the number of people who could enter the Capitol. Just before noon, a spokesman for the administration said that lawyers would review the restraining order but didn't say when the doors might be opened.

Up until that time, Dane County sheriff's deputies had been outside guarding the doors to the Capitol. But with access to the statehouse restricted in spite of the court order, Democratic Sheriff Dave Mahoney decided he'd had enough. He pulled his deputies away from the doors, saying they wouldn't act as "palace guards."

By that afternoon, a crowd had gathered in the waiting area outside Dane County Circuit Judge John C. Albert's courtroom on South Hamilton Street. Albert, a sixty-four-year-old judge who was appointed in 1999 by Governor Tommy Thompson, was now tasked with handling the standoff. The proceeding was watched by a packed courtroom, with a video feed in a basement overflow room where dozens more followed the action. In more than a decade on the bench, Albert had never seen so many people wanting to attend one of his hearings. He was intensely aware of his responsibility not only to uphold the law and the rights of the parties but also to preserve the fragile peace that had so far prevailed at the Capitol. Albert, who was up for election the next year, hoped he would not have to hold either side in contempt of court. "The emotions were running so high that such a finding and order could not have done anything but raise the flame," he remembered later.

At the hearing, the unions' attorney, Peg Lautenschlager, presented nine witnesses, all of whom said they were restricted from getting into the Capitol. But the lawyer for the state argued that "it's time for the Capitol to be back in business," with reasonable rules protecting the health and safety of those inside it. After more than four hours of testimony and arguments, the judge kept in place the court order issued by his colleague earlier that day that the Capitol be open to the public. But the case needed more than that to resolve it. "What we have is a disagreement over what an open Wisconsin Capitol means," said Albert.

The judge knew the statehouse wasn't open, but he was determined not to wade into what to do about it until he had heard fully from both sides. Near the end of the hearing, Lautenschlager alleged that even as Walker administration officials were shutting out demonstrators, they were using the tunnel to bring supporters into the Capitol for the governor's budget speech. The underground entrance, she said, allowed the administration to bring in guests without having them subjected to the taunts of the crowd locked outside. The following day in court, a Madison alderwoman testified before Albert about seeing some Republicans, including First Lady Tonette Walker, being taken to the tunnel ahead of the budget address to be led into the Capitol. But the Walker administration said that besides staff and officials, only the first lady and a group with her had come in that way. Video footage from a security camera released later showed the tunnel was used sparingly in the hours before the speech. The underground passage would, however, play an important role before much longer.

Senator Glenn Grothman, the conservative provocateur who had angered Dye and so many other union supporters on the night of the budget committee vote, walked through the crowd that afternoon. Grothman said afterward that he enjoyed coming to the Capitol through the demonstrators, whom he sometimes called slobs in media interviews. He also said he was comfortable around the crowds because, in his college days, "I used to be a liberal" and "I like to talk to people." That evening, shortly after Walker's speech, Grothman left the Capitol to give a talk at the Inn on the Park and then walked back across the street to the statehouse. In spite of his identification badge, the senator was turned away by police at the West Washington Avenue entrance and sent to the Martin Luther King Jr. Boulevard entrance, where he was unable to get in because of the crowds. As Grothman wandered about looking for a way in, protesters followed him, shaking their fingers at him and shouting, "Shame! Shame! Shame!" The senator tapped at the ground-floor window of his own office, but his aides had the shades drawn and didn't raise them, believing that he was just another protester. Meanwhile, the group around Grothman grew.

Nearby, a labor organizer and Democratic campaign strategist named Brennan Balestrieri was growing uncomfortable with what he saw. Balestrieri, who was then working as a consultant for the Wisconsin AFL-CIO, was walking back from a meal with Stephanie Bloomingdale, the AFL-CIO's secretary-treasurer. She was worried that if Balestrieri got involved in the scene, he might look like part of the problem. But as Balestrieri watched some of the demonstrators getting in Grothman's way, the twenty-nine-year-old felt he had to act. "If one person punches him in the face, this whole thing is over," he remembered thinking. "I didn't want to deal with all this energy diffusing."

Still holding a box of Thai leftovers, Balestrieri intervened to help Grothman get to another covered entrance at the Capitol. At six foot seven and with a thick beard, Balestrieri had an imposing presence that he used to Grothman's advantage. Nearby, Democratic representative Brett Hulsey of Madison—the gatecrasher from Walker's news conference on the fake Koch call—heard the shouts of "Shame! Shame! Shame!" and saw the crowd had surrounded someone. "Oh, this is not good. This is not what we need," Hulsey thought to himself as he also moved forward to help.

The appearance of Hulsey on the scene was almost poetic, as the spotlight-loving environmentalist is a kind of mirror image of Grothman. Both made regular appearances in the Capitol pressroom, talking up reporters and asking them, as Grothman often put it, "Does anybody need a quote?" The pair had even sparred from time to time on a Madison talk radio program. Now, the two became part of a very different kind of news story. Balestrieri and Hulsey got Grothman to the nearest doors, the covered entrance on the West Washington Avenue side of the Capitol, but they found those doors were locked, too, and the senator was then trapped by the people who had followed them. Balestrieri said later he wasn't worried about someone attacking the senator, but he was concerned that someone in the tight space might end up being crushed by the gathering crowd. Using his size to push back against the people and fiercely flashing a peace sign, the organizer helped open up space around the lawmakers. By then, Bloomingdale had gotten involved as well. Holding up her fingers in a peace sign, she stood outside the covered area and stopped newly arriving people from going any farther. The incident seemed surreal to Bloomingdale at the time and, to her, out of keeping with other parts of the protests. Grothman said afterward that he was not worried and, with the exception of one protester, did not feel threatened physically. For his part, Hulsey felt that the situation could have gotten out of control. "It was a tense deal," he said later.

Gradually the chants changed to "Peace!" and "Peaceful!" Two of the volunteer marshals who helped keep order at the protests showed up along with an aide to Grothman. The senator himself helped by remaining calm and for once not engaging the protesters around him. Finally, someone got a bull-horn to Hulsey and he spoke to the crowd. "Everybody, everybody. Hold up, folks, peaceful. Listen, listen, please. I know you're angry," Hulsey started.

"You're damn right," one man shouted.

"Listen, listen, please. I'm state Representative Brett Hulsey," he said. "The most important thing about this whole event is that it has been peaceful and respectful."

"That's right," a woman called.

"Glenn Grothman and I probably could not disagree on more things, but he's my friend."

"Stop destroying our families," a man shouted.

"We need to respect him," Hulsey said. "We need to respect him and keep this peaceful. It's very important."

"How is he respecting our—" someone shouted.

"It's not him. It's Governor Walker," Hulsey said, conveniently overlooking what was widely known—that Grothman actually wanted more cuts to union interests than Walker had proposed.

People started to echo the call to let Grothman pass. Balestrieri helped clear the way for a group of firefighters who showed up and ended up escorting the senator away. As they walked off and defused the situation, some cheered. Grothman, for his part, took the incident in stride and stuck with his gruff critique of the protesters as university students who were "sleeping on air mattresses with their girlfriends." "I don't hate these people for being slobs," he told the *Wisconsin State Journal* in an interview afterward. "I don't mind nice slobs. I really think five years from now most of these people will have a real job and be voting Republican."

Grothman wasn't the only official who was denied access to the Capitol. The firefighters who showed up during the senator's ordeal had come on an emergency call and were also turned away at that same covered entrance. Dave Trainor, a Madison firefighter, testified to the events two days later in court. He said that he was part of a crew dispatched to the Capitol to respond to a call, but the firefighters didn't know if it was a routine request or a life-threatening emergency. When Trainor's crew was refused entry at the West Washington doors, they had to make their way through the crowd of protest-ers outside the building and drive their hundred-foot ladder truck to the other side of the statehouse to get inside. In the process, they lost ten to fifteen minutes on a call that might have been life or death, Trainor testified. Fortu-nately, the problem turned out to be minor—a policeman was trapped in an elevator. It was possible the crew was turned away because the protesters at the Capitol included firefighters in uniform, but Trainor said he didn't think police officers would have mistaken the crew for protesters because they had their equipment and radios and had arrived in a fire truck. "They seemed to know we needed to get in, but not have the authority to let us in," Trainor testified of the police.

Throughout the day, Dye urged on the protests. Ever the lawyer, she tweeted that the state was "getting all Marbury v. Madison in Madison, with branches of government close to ignoring each other," referring to the landmark U.S. Supreme Court decision that established the ability of courts to review laws passed by Congress. When late afternoon and the time for Walker's speech arrived, Dye was among the thousands of demonstrators who crowded outside the State Street entrance. She took a photo of one man with a sign that read "I voted for Walker and I'm sorry." From the sidewalk, steps, and lawn, the crowd shouted up at the windows on the west wing's second floor. "I'm not a lobbyist or a Tea Partier, so I can't get inside. But I can stand here and yell like hell!" she posted.

In the Assembly chamber, the mood was as taut as a circus high wire. The vast room had much of the usual pageantry that accompanies a budget speech. The galleries were filled with cabinet secretaries and other Republican guests, the floor with prominent elected officials, and the side nearest the windows with an arsenal of television cameras. But even before the action of the day had begun, it was clear that much was amiss. Not only were there no Democratic senators on hand, but many of the Democratic representatives from the Assembly also appeared to be missing. The rest wore their usual mix of formal clothes and orange union T-shirts. In addition, the time of the speech was in the late afternoon and not at the formal evening hour that had been the custom of recent years. Then there were the police at the doors and the thunder of the thousands of voices outside. The administration later revealed that prior to the speech police received a threat that electrical service to the Capitol would be disrupted during the event. As a precaution, all but the essential personnel at the nearby plant were told to leave before and during the speech. In the end, the utilities never faltered.

For the Democratic lawmakers who were on the floor, Peter Barca was registering their objections. "We certainly do not want to delay these proceedings," the minority leader said on the Assembly floor before Walker's arrival.

"But I just want to make it clear to everybody in the body that many members of our side of the aisle had a very difficult time coming to the chamber today because there was a court injunction that was issued to open this building and the building is still not open. We're concerned it could be a violation of the open meetings law, which requires that the building be opened to the public."

This time, Barca kept his speech short and then sat down so Walker's address could begin. The Assembly sergeant at arms, Anne Tonnon Byers, stood in the center aisle just inside the grand entrance of the room and raised her voice to introduce "the Honorable Scott Walker." As the governor entered the hall, the contrast deepened between this budget speech and others that had come before it. In past budget speeches, governors could expect to be greeted warmly by lawmakers, no matter how unpopular they or their policies were. When Governor Jim Doyle entered the Assembly chamber in February 2009 to deliver his speech on a budget that was hated by Republicans, the Democratic governor got sustained applause and handshakes from legislators of both parties. Only one month before, Walker himself had received similar applause and smiles on all sides as he walked down the Assembly aisle to deliver his state-of-the-state address. At that time a Democratic senator had marched into the chamber along with the governor and other GOP lawmakers. Not so now. Republicans still rose, turned, and clapped for Walker, like wedding guests marking the arrival of the bride. But Democrats sat mute at their desks, not applauding or even looking at the governor as he passed. The Democratic senator who accompanied Walker before, Jim Holperin, was in Illinois and already looking to the prospect of a bitter recall election against him in his relatively conservative Northwoods district. The sole sign of bipartisanship that afternoon—unmarked by most—came when a GOP lawmaker trailing Walker tapped Representative Gordon Hintz on the shoulder to say something to him. It was Michelle Litjens, the representative whom Hintz had cursed at during the Assembly's last meeting. Hintz scrambled to his feet and the pair shared a brief hug. The two parties would not come together again that day on anything.

Walker stepped up to the rostrum. Senate President Mike Ellis presented the governor to the assembled group, and Walker began to speak, seeking immediately to strike a note of unity. "We all share something in common—an unrivaled passion for this state and the people who call it home," he said. "We all want Wisconsin to be the very best that it can be. Yet, because our experiences are unique and our beliefs diverse, our paths sometimes diverge as we tackle today's challenges. But even at the height of our differences, we can and must keep our promise to the people of Wisconsin that they will always come first."

The appeals in the speech to bipartisanship had little effect. Republican lawmakers stood and applauded, the first of many times that afternoon they would do so. Democrats didn't hide their unhappiness, but they didn't visibly react or boo Walker. At least one of them quietly took other measures though. Hulsey sent out a tweet to "make some noise outside" that was picked up by Dye and others. "They can hear us!!!!!! Keep it up!!!!" Dye tweeted to those who were standing on the square around her, then she posted another to those following the crisis from farther away. "Crowd roaring, someone waves American flag in the middle. We are Americans. Our freedom of speech & assembly shall not be abridged."

Early in the speech, Walker sought to make the case that the painful steps in the budget were not only needed, but they were unavoidable. "The facts are clear: Wisconsin is broke and it's time to start paying our bills today—so our kids are not stuck with even bigger bills tomorrow. This deficit did not appear overnight. Wisconsin got here through a reliance on one-time fixes, accounting gimmicks, and tax increases," he said, blaming past governors and lawmakers of both political parties.

Gradually, the governor warmed up and began to seem less nervous. He said his budget would avoid tax increases and accounting tricks, and in the process make a 90 percent cut in the state's so-called structural deficit, the shortfall that was normally pushed by Wisconsin leaders into the next budget. To do that, Walker had to deal with real challenges. From July 2011 to June 2013 the state had a roughly $3 billion budget gap to make up—more than 10 percent of the budget's main account. By one measure, the state's budget shortfall was actually smaller than the average one in other states, but it was still daunting. The state could have slashed every penny of its own spending on Wisconsin's twenty-six public universities and colleges and still not have had enough savings to cover the potential shortfall. To bridge it, the state would also have had to cut half of its spending on prisons. Walker was seeking to avoid accounting tricks and cut taxes rather than raise them. That meant making billions of dollars in spending cuts in some areas.

There were only a few places to do it. In the popular mind, state government is often seen as mainly composed of bureaucracy. But in reality, most of the money that taxpayers pay into Wisconsin's government simply flows out again in the form of aid to smaller units of governments and payments made to individuals or on their behalf. The state spent the vast majority of its funds on just five areas: schools, local governments, medical care for the poor, universities, and prisons. Even within those limited categories, the spending on education stood out, counting as one-third or two-fifths of the state budget depending on how it was counted. The medical programs for the needy counted for about 14 percent of state spending, much of it for the elderly and some for children—difficult places to skimp. The other three big spending categories counted for about 7 percent each of the state budget, or some 21 percent all together. There were other places to make cuts in the state budget, like its workforce and its bureaucracy, but those areas were too small to get the savings that Walker wanted. So to meet his goals of avoiding most tax increases but still ensuring sound state finances for future generations, Walker recommended cutting spending for schools being attended by children today. He would also have to cut or control spending on universities, prisons, and local services such as police and firefighters. The intimidating effects of cuts like that had long kept politicians from making them, but the governor told his audience that the time had finally come. Over two years he intended to cut more than $1 billion in state aid to schools and local governments. While making those cuts, his budget also expanded state programs providing taxpayer money for private voucher schools.

These cuts were among the highest in the nation, as measured by such groups as the National Association of State Budget Officers. For instance, the Center on Budget and Policy Priorities ranked Wisconsin second in the nation for dollars cut per student. Even with the decreases, the state would still outrank many others in education spending. In 2009—before the cuts—Wisconsin ranked seventeenth in the country for spending per pupil and the Milwaukee Public Schools outspent all other metropolitan districts in the nation except for those in New York City, Washington, D.C., and Baltimore, according to the U.S. Census Bureau. Walker also told his audience he had a plan to keep the cuts from affecting children and communities—by passing his union-bargaining changes to shift the cuts onto the teachers, snow plow drivers, and social workers across the state who provided those services. "As we decrease spending, we also increase flexibility so local government and state government have the tools to deal with reduced revenue. It's true we are reducing aid to local government by just over $1.25 billion, but we are providing almost $1.5 billion in savings through our budget-repair bill," Walker said. "Let me repeat that: despite the reductions in our budget, local governments would gain $150 million overall in the next biennium—but only if the Senate is allowed to act."

It was a controversial claim, and Walker made it at the time without conclusive supporting evidence. The savings for local governments—and the losses for their employees—clearly added up to more than $750 million statewide, and possibly a good deal more. But even more than a year and a half later, it couldn't be fully verified because the necessary data were only available for schools, not local governments. The best study available, done by the Wisconsin Taxpayers Alliance, found that Act 10 had made up for about two-thirds of the cuts to school revenues statewide and would have done more had they not been blocked in some places by union contracts. The savings cushioned but didn't eliminate cuts in teaching positions. The overall effects of the governor's policies, however, varied widely by school district and local government. In many areas, the savings weren't blocked by union contracts and more than made up for the state aid cuts, especially in communities where public employees hadn't previously contributed to their benefits. In other areas, the savings fell short—sometimes well short—either because the local government was already making employees pay more for their health insurance or because the local unions refused to reopen existing contracts that prevented the otherwise legally mandated cuts for a year or two. The different outcomes showed up both in Milwaukee County, a Democratic area with some desperately poor sections, and in neighboring Waukesha County, an affluent Republican stronghold. The cities of Milwaukee and Brookfield, a Waukesha County suburb, both saved more money in cuts to employee compensation than they lost in state aid. Waukesha County and the Hamilton School District, located in that county, saved about as much. Meanwhile, the city of Waukesha, Milwaukee Public Schools, and Milwaukee County—Walker's old charge—lost more than they saved, at least in the short term.

"It is impossible to definitively say at this point [fall 2012] whether the net impacts have been good or bad for local governments and schools. It depends," stated Rob Henken, president of the nonpartisan Public Policy Forum in Milwaukee and a former Walker appointee in Milwaukee County.

In the long term, there was a clear advantage for the budgets of Milwaukee County and the Milwaukee Public Schools, which faced problems funding retiree health care and pensions far in excess of the typical local government in Wisconsin. Their elected boards couldn't alter the benefits that workers had already earned but after Act 10 could unilaterally pare them back going forward. Milwaukee schools, for instance, later raised eligibility requirements for employees' retirement health benefits and changed the design of health coverage. An actuary found that the district lowered its projected obligation to retirees by a whopping $1 billion, or 42 percent, between 2009 and 2011.

In the short term, the budget picture wasn't so clear cut. Milwaukee schools lost $82 million in state aid and couldn't get the health and pension savings from employees because the school board had agreed to a four-year contract with the teachers union with some concessions in November 2010, before Walker took office. The union later narrowly rejected the school board's appeal to reopen the contract, and the district resorted to cutting programs and laying off more than 280 teachers and educational assistants as of March 2012. Class sizes swelled to forty students in some extreme cases. The Hamilton School District, on the other hand, used the employee compensation cuts and other tools to close a $2.6 million gap in the district's budget in the 2011–12 school year. The district saw a much higher than usual number of retirements but replaced the great majority of those employees and didn't have to cut services. Some districts also got savings from being able to take competitive bids from health carriers—previously many labor contracts had steered that business toward WEA Trust, an affiliate of the state teachers union that provided generous coverage. In one notable case, an Appleton school official said the district had saved $3.1 million, or more than 10 percent, and retained the same coverage when it switched away from WEA Trust. But even in districts and local governments that were, like Hamilton, in relatively good shape, many administrators acknowledged that they faced a tradeoff. Going forward, they would encounter growing financial pressures and the decision on whether to use their newfound ability to shift more of that burden to their workers. But they would also need to pay enough to keep their good employees and attract new ones. When Walker's bill became law, large numbers of both local and state workers retired, easing the budgets of the employers they left behind but taking with them decades of experience not easily replaced.

The cut in state aid also carried the possibility that school boards, county boards, and city councils would choose to raise property taxes to make up part of the lost state money. To prevent that, Walker's budget put in place state caps on property tax levies so local elected officials couldn't raise them. For municipalities, the bill froze tax levies, allowing increases only to reflect the construction of new homes or buildings or payments on debt. For schools, the governor's proposal went farther. In Wisconsin, schools are limited by law on how much money they can raise per pupil through property taxes and general state aid. The final version of the legislation cut that amount by 5.5 percent with certain exceptions. That meant that school districts would not only see their state aid cut, but many would also be required by law to cut their property tax levy. In all, schools ultimately lost more than $900 million over two years in the total amount they could raise through state aid or tax levy authority to teach students. Because of these forced freezes and cuts, the property tax levy for schools across the state fell slightly in December 2011. Overall property taxes factoring in other local governments statewide stayed roughly flat and actually fell just slightly for the median-value home in the state by 0.4 percent, according to the Walker administration.

The governor put an additional $1.2 billion in state tax money into Medicaid health programs. Enrollment in these programs—paid for by both the state and the federal government—had grown faster in Wisconsin in recent years than almost any other state in the country. The growth had helped make sure that most state residents had health coverage but at a steadily rising cost. The state budget officers' survey showed that Walker's increase in state spending on Medicaid ranked seventh in the nation. But, ironically, because of declining federal money, the overall health care spending in Wisconsin would still fall and ultimately lead an estimated 17,000 people to leave or be turned away from Medicaid. The number of those affected would have been even higher but President Barack Obama's administration rejected larger cuts proposed by Walker. For the state's universities, Walker made $300 million in cuts over two years. There again, the cuts were some of the deepest in the nation. Meanwhile, prisons saw much smaller cuts. Culminating a decade-and-a-half trend, the budget bill was the first to allocate more state money to the prison system and its inmates than to the university system and its students. Walker largely kept his campaign promise not to raise taxes on anyone. His budget included cuts to capital gains taxes and taxes on multistate corporations over the first two years, and then ramped those up to higher levels in future budgets in which state officials would have to find ways to pay for them. But in a move that went unmentioned in his speech, Walker did not keep his campaign pledge to the working poor. In his budget the governor proposed cutting the earned income tax credit by about $40 million over two years. Because the credit rewards work, President Ronald Reagan had called an equivalent federal program "the best anti-poverty, the best pro-family, the best job creation measure to come out of Congress." But Walker cut it and also froze another program, the homestead tax credit, which helps low-income homeowners and renters. When the proposal became public, outraged Democrats and advocates for the poor said that Walker had raised taxes on those who were least able to afford them.

Republicans countered that the credit was generous by national standards and was redistributing wealth to people who didn't owe income taxes in the first place, though they would owe other payroll taxes, such as those for Social Security. The GOP officials were right that the credits are refundable, which means that qualifying workers do not need to pay any income taxes to get the benefit. According to the Legislature's budget office, four in five of those who qualify for the earned income tax credit do not owe any state income taxes and get a check from the state. Republicans argued that for those residents Walker's action didn't amount to a tax increase. But for the remaining one in five people on the program, there was no debate. Those workers owed state taxes and overall would see their taxes increase because Walker had broken his no-tax pledge.

None of those arguments came out until days after Walker finished his speech. He sought to do that on a note that called up an optimistic, unifying vision for Wisconsin's next four years, one in which the state created his promised quarter of a million jobs. "Like every parent and grandparent in this state, I want my two sons to grow up in a Wisconsin at least, at least, as great as the Wisconsin I grew up in," he said. "Working together, I know we can do it. Thank you. May God richly bless you and your family. And may God continue to bless the great state of Wisconsin."

On the Assembly floor, the reality of a divided state remained unchanged. Republicans stood and clapped warmly; Democrats sat still. After greeting GOP lawmakers, Walker shook a few of the Democrats' hands as he walked out the door; none of them stood up from their seats to do it. The protests continued that day, but the governor did not dwell on them—or at least he tried not to. That evening, Walker sent a tweet to his followers about what he did with the rest of that day. "Had some chili w/Tonette as we watched @AmericanIdol," he wrote.

"Seven Thousand People in the Statehouse"

F OR THE TWO DAYS OF COURT TESTIMONY, Judge John Albert wore a black robe and a look that alternated between concern, exasperation, and bemusement to find himself at the center of a case that he called "the largest expression of free speech and addressing the government in the history of our state." As the case played out on March 2 and March 3 in Dane County's handsome modern courthouse, answers to even the simplest and most relevant questions sometimes eluded the skilled lawyers in the courtroom. "There's no beginning level course in what to do with seven thousand people in the statehouse in law school," Albert said in an interview a year later.

In the courtroom that first day, the judge was listening intently to Mike Huebsch, a former speaker of the Assembly and Scott Walker's top cabinet secretary. At the table to the judge's left sat Peg Lautenschlager and the other attorneys for the plaintiff, the Wisconsin State Employees Union. The defendants were Huebsch and the state. He was represented by lawyers from the state Department of Justice, and they were seated together at the table to the judge's right. Those attorneys included Steven Means, a thin, balding man who was Republican Attorney General J.B. Van Hollen's executive assistant. Means, a political appointee and able attorney, was putting a seemingly easy question to Huebsch. "Does the Capitol have a graded capacity for occupancy as to the number of people?" Means asked.

"It does not," Huebsch said.

"Have you come to a conclusion in your mind what would be an appropriate number of people that it would be permissible to allow into the Capitol?"

"I have not," Huebsch said.

The administration secretary explained that to him the real answer depended on the number of police that the state could find and afford to pay to provide security. The effect had been made for the audience: unlike other buildings in the state, there was no normal regulation of the Capitol by a fire inspector. Just as it had been for UW–Madison Police Chief Susan Riseling, this was a disappointment to Albert, who was expecting to get an objective standard for determining whether too many people were in the statehouse to be safe. "I was very surprised to find I had no baseline to make that determination," he said later.

A few blocks away, the Capitol was open but tightly restricted, with about one hundred protesters still camping inside in what they began to call the "rotunda community." A couple of Democrats hauled their desks onto the Capitol grounds that day to hold office hours, meet with members of the public, and draw attention to the fact that people could no longer enter the statehouse as they pleased. The desks were eventually ordered back inside the building.

In the courtroom, the case had started that day with several witnesses taking the stand for the plaintiffs. Among them, Representative Kelda Helen Roys and another Democratic lawmaker told the court about how the shifting rules at the Capitol had made it difficult to do their jobs. The witnesses for the union testified that the demonstrations had been overwhelmingly free from violence and that protesters had mostly gotten along well with the police. The Walker administration's new policy, the witnesses said, was stifling peaceful dissent.

Then Huebsch came to the stand to give a different view. Like Walker, Huebsch was an affable and articulate conservative who rose to prominence at a young age. As Walker's secretary of administration, Huebsch's many duties included overseeing state buildings and the Capitol Police. Huebsch, then forty-six, laid out the costs of the sizable police force assembled at the Capitol over the past two weeks. Normally, there were just a handful of officers in the Capitol during business hours, but lately there had been anywhere from 160 state and local officers to more than 400. So far, Huebsch said, the state had paid more than $2.1 million for the wages and overtime of the officers brought in to help the state, not counting their meals and lodging. The final costs, he said, could reach well beyond that, and in fact they did— later accounting put them at more than $9 million. The main argument that emerged from Steven Means's questions to Huebsch was simple: for reasons of safety, cost, and public welfare the administration was trying to get the statehouse under control. As long as demonstrators remained camped in the rotunda, the administration had the right to squeeze them out through peaceful means.

Now Lautenschlager cross-examined Huebsch. Though her manner sometimes came across as scattered, Lautenschlager was shrewd enough. Besides formerly serving as attorney general, she had been both a district attorney and a lawmaker who had just missed serving alongside Huebsch in the Assembly. Lautenschlager pressed the secretary on the effect of the Capitol restrictions, questioning whether the state was punishing thousands of law-abiding demonstrators on account of some one hundred people practicing civil disobedience. Then it was Judge Albert's turn to pose questions to Huebsch.

"Can you think of any other time in your sixteen-plus years of going in and out of the Wisconsin State Capitol that access has been as restricted as it has been Monday, Tuesday, and today?" he asked.

"I can think of no other time when we have seen the crowds that we have seen in the Capitol," Huebsch responded. "And so my answer, my direct answer to you, Judge, would be no, but I have also never seen the situation that we have endured in the last couple of weeks as far as some of the pictures indicate of the number of people and the activity and the signage that's in the Capitol."

Next on the stand was Riseling, the chief in charge of the Capitol's interior during the protests. Having arrived too late to catch the earlier testimony, Riseling had no chance to tell the court of her own earlier calculation of the Capitol's maximum occupancy. Riseling described her concerns about safety in the Capitol, noting that police had observed several kinds of people among the group of five hundred to eight hundred who were previously staying overnight in the building: demonstrators, homeless people, and criminals looking for something to snatch. Police had confiscated some potential weapons like box cutters and knives from people inside the statehouse; at one point counter-protesters had shown up outside on the Capitol square openly carrying holstered handguns, a legal practice in Wisconsin that police had to accept.

Riseling noted the toll that the duty at the Capitol was taking on hundreds of police officers. She herself had worked sixteen-hour days for more than two straight weeks with the exception of a single day off. Officers, she said, were standing for days on end on stone floors, out in the cold, putting plugs in their ears to muffle the sounds of voices, drums, noisemakers, loudspeakers, and vuvuzelas—all reverberating against the stone walls. She said the efforts of those officers had been key to helping keep the protests peaceful. "I don't believe you can bring those police resources together again and again and again every day," Riseling said.

Riseling made clear how impressed she was by the conduct of both law enforcement and the demonstrators. She noted the dozens of signs that protesters had posted around the Capitol to remind others in the crowd to remain peaceful. "I've never experienced anything like this in my life," she testified. "This has been exceptional. I mean, to have this many people with this much emotion be part of something historical and, as it stands today, eleven arrests from the interior branch [inside the Capitol], none since Sunday night. I just think it's unprecedented. I don't think there's another place in the country that can say they've gone through what we've gone through with this. The crowds have been exceptional. They've been polite. They've been respectful. . . . I've never been thanked so many times in my career as I have in the last two weeks."

The next witness, Glenn Grothman, struck a different note. The Republican senator described his harrowing encounter with the angry crowd the day before in his matter-of-fact way. "They bang their drums. They chant their slogans and they tape up their signs," he said. "Usually the people are okay but sometimes they aren't. . . . I think there's people there who do want to create a confrontation and it's an uncivil situation."

Judge Albert urged Grothman to leave with a bailiff "for your own safety, sir," and the next witness came to the stand. Ed Wall, the head of criminal investigations for the Department of Justice, described the more than fifty threats that had been made against the governor, the first lady, and other officials. At least a few of these threats were "very viable," Wall said, though he gave no specifics and acknowledged that the threats had played no part in the decision to close the Capitol. Wall described the crowds of demonstrators as reasonable but said he couldn't rule out "lone-wolf attacks." "There comes a point where we've got to maintain control of the building for a variety of reasons," he said.

Wall was the last witness of the day, and the judge took a few minutes to talk with the lawyers from both sides about his next step. He made clear that the protesters camped in the Capitol could expect no help from him. "If and when I enter an order in this case, I can guarantee you that one of the reasonable restrictions that I will validate on the part of the respondents is that you can't sleep in the Capitol," Albert said. He mused about the possibility of sending a written order to the rotunda community that, in order to help the building return to normal, they leave it after closing hours. But the lawyers for both sides voiced reservations about imposing an order on a group not represented in the courtroom. The judge sighed and gave up on the idea. "It's now a moot point," he said. "We are now adjourned until one o'clock tomorrow and I will, I think, probably be less than my usual patient person so that we can get done with the testimony tomorrow."

The next day, Thursday, March 3, dawned with an odd and troubling discovery on the Capitol square. Dane County deputies patrolling the grounds outside the statehouse found rounds of small-caliber ammunition by the State Street and King Street entrances and other spots. The forty-one cartridges were all identical .22 Long Rifle hollow points, a caliber better suited to a rabbit hunt than a gunfight. In the end, the person responsible for planting the rounds was never discovered, and his or her motives remained a mystery. When the court case resumed early that afternoon, the lawyers for the Walker administration used the finding to argue for a plan to reopen the Capitol that suited them. Chief Riseling returned to the witness stand to describe the discovery. "I don't like to see live ammunition outside when I have significant crowds, obviously," Riseling said. "You can't do much with live ammunition without the gun. But the presence of it doesn't thrill me. Usually it's one in partnership with the other."

Lautenschlager was unimpressed, saying it would be an "overreaction" to reduce access to the Capitol because of the stray cartridges. After all, she pointed out, people had already openly carried handguns around the square. "For all we know, somebody planted them there," Lautenschlager said of the rounds. "We don't know if it was a protester. We don't know what it has to do with. Just finding some live shells when there were people carrying weapons. . . . It's silly."

Next, the Walker administration laid down another card—a whopping new estimate on the possible damage done to the Capitol by the demonstrators. A lawyer for the Department of Administration told Judge Albert that a staffer at her agency had estimated the costs of removing the tape from the ubiquitous protest signs on the walls inside the Capitol and repairing other damage. The adhesive from the tape, she said, had to be carefully removed and then the walls cleaned to avoid leaving residue that could eventually stain and damage the stone. She put the cost of removing the adhesives, restoring the building's interior, and fixing up the building's exterior and grounds at $7.5 million. "These are estimates not from the government, your honor," she said. "These are estimates that we received from a vendor."

"I trust you're not willing to stipulate to that offer," Albert said dryly to Lautenschlager.

"I would perhaps make an offer to do it myself for half the price," Lautenschlager said to laughter from the courtroom.

Outside the courtroom, the figures produced a similar uproar of disbelief, with even some Republicans at the Capitol privately chuckling over them. In later testimony, Huebsch backed the damage estimate, calling it "true and accurate." He said he was relying on an estimate done by a state architect, Dan Stephans, in consultation with a contractor involved in the prior renovation of the Capitol. On the day the figure first came out in court, an attorney had asked Stephans what restoring the Capitol could cost and gave him just an hour to come up with a figure. Stephans's top concern was not tape residue but paintings and furniture, including desks and chairs that in some cases had cost tens of thousands of dollars apiece to restore more than a decade earlier. Stephans consulted with two knowledgeable architects that day but in a later and more thorough deposition made clear how rough he had to be on his hurried estimate of just the interior damage. "I took what I suspected may have been affected, being about 240,000 square feet of public space, and threw $25 a square foot on it and that came out to $6 million," he said.

The documentation for the damage figures was paper thin—one sheet, to be exact. A request under the state's open records law by the *Milwaukee Journal Sentinel* later turned up only a single handwritten page of notebook paper from Stephans—dated the day of the testimony—to back up the figure. By the next day, the Walker administration was sharply backpedaling from the estimate and acknowledging that no one had a clear idea yet how much the cleanup would cost. Meanwhile, in the Capitol itself, there was little if any sign of deliberate damage after the protesters left and the signs were taken down. The large crowds did cause some accidental wear and tear to the building—chipped paint, nicked stone, and stains left from the oils of hundreds of hands brushing walls. Outside, the lawn and some shrubs had been trampled and would need replanting. One year after the protests, the administration had paid just under $200,000 to do cleanup work specifically due to the demonstrations: reseeding the grass, replacing bushes, cleaning tape residue from the walls, and replacing a few patches of damaged stone. That was real money to be sure, but it was also less than 3 percent of what Huebsch had claimed.

The millions in overtime for police officers represented the real cost of the demonstrations.

In the courtroom, the lawyers cycled through several more witnesses under the impatient eyes of Judge Albert, and then gave closing arguments. Lautenschlager went first and asked that the Capitol be opened to the public without restriction, preferably within the next forty-eight hours. She also asked Albert to rule that the state was in violation of constitutional provisions protecting individuals' rights to free speech and assembly and to petition their government. The state constitution, Lautenschlager said, "doesn't diminish in extraordinary times." "Access has been limited and it is limited in a way that makes no sense, that has no historic parallel, and that tends to be limitations that quell the voices of those who want to speak," she went on. "In this case, [the Department of Administration] already has rules that I believe are sufficient to address the alleged issues of concern. But because DOA has chosen not to enforce existing powers, it cannot then create and adopt what are draconian policies that virtually eliminate the constitutional rights of individuals to come into the Capitol."

The courtroom was then handed over to Means. He argued that the state Capitol was a "limited public forum" that under the law was subject to reasonable time, place, and manner restrictions on the exercise of free speech. Essentially, Means argued that there was nothing in the state constitution that prevented the state from locking up the statehouse when its business was done for the day. If the state was being blocked from doing that, some temporary limits on access were needed so state officials could ensure public safety, conduct the people's business, and protect the building itself, he said. "We've heard opinions from people who have a vested interest in protest . . . but we've also heard from professionals. . . ." Means said. "You've heard testimony from Chief Riseling; she knows what she's doing. You've heard testimony from Ed Wall; he knows what he's doing. They've been trained on how to keep people safe. They've been trained on how to identify risk. They've been trained to make sure the building is safe and accessible."

Then the moment came for Albert to rule, and he quickly made clear he would grant the union a temporary restraining order and force the Walker administration to open up the Capitol while the case was being decided in the coming months. The judge commended all sides—the demonstrators, police, and staff at the statehouse—on their conduct and restraint. He quoted at length from the transcript of Chief Riseling's testimony on the "extraordinary" behavior of the peaceful protestors. But like Riseling he also pointed out that at times the crowded Capitol posed an inherent danger of a stampede in the event of a fire or other emergency. Likewise, the judge said testimony on how the Madison firefighters were turned away from one Capitol entrance was troubling. Finally, though Albert said he believed the administration had sought to act in good faith, he pointed to Huebsch's testimony that in recent years the Capitol never had been as tightly closed as it had been in recent days. The administration, he said, had violated the state constitution and infringed on fundamental freedoms that demonstrators elsewhere in the world—an indirect allusion to the protests then going on in Arab countries—were dying for at that moment. Finally, Albert found that the remaining demonstrators in the rotunda were violating state law and administrative rules.

In his order, the judge told the Department of Administration to enforce the law and "remove unauthorized materials and people remaining in the state Capitol after 6 p.m. today." But he added that the state on the following Monday had to make the building as open as it had been prior to the introduction of Walker's bill. For the second time, Albert considered sending a letter to the demonstrators still in the rotunda respectfully asking them to leave the Capitol and "do your part to adhere to the principles of nonviolent protest that have characterized these events." And again, he dismissed the idea. "We're adjourned," Albert said.

The judge couldn't return home right away as he normally would have because law enforcement was taking extra security precautions for him. But Albert's main concern was what would happen to the police and protesters in the Capitol now that he had given his order. "I was holding my breath, absolutely holding my breath," he said later. Outside the courtroom, Huebsch stated that the judge had given the Walker administration a "fair hearing" and a reasonable order. Lautenschlager called the ruling a victory showing that the administration had violated the state constitution.

As Albert had been considering his order in the courthouse, the tension had risen at the statehouse, so much so that a lawmaker and a police officer did in fact have an altercation. Representative Nick Milroy, a Democrat from South Range, tried to get into the Capitol to retrieve some clothes but was stopped by the officer at the door. Frustrated that the electronic key cards issued to him and other lawmakers had been disabled, Milroy held up a Capitol identification card and came up close to the policeman's face. The two tussled and the officer, brought in from Two Rivers a hundred and fifty miles from Madison, pulled Milroy away from the door and brought him to the ground. The lawmaker scrambled up, clutching his identification card. "I need to get

clothes in my office!" he shouted. He was allowed into the Capitol a few minutes later through a different entrance. Afterward, he sought out the officer
to apologize, saying he was overly aggressive, but he also told reporters the
situation was the result of a palace-guard mentality.

Another, potentially more serious, confrontation loomed when a group of
about one hundred protesters—most of them college age—entered the previously restricted and quiet Capitol after someone let them in at the State Street
entrance. Chanting, "Our house, our house," the protesters entered just as
Walker was about to start a news conference in a separate part of the building. A phalanx of police officers stopped the group on the ground floor of
the west wing, which prevented them from reaching the rotunda and joining
the group of protesters who had been spending the night in the Capitol. The
protesters and police—both of whom would soon afterward be singled out for
praise by the judge for their restraint—appeared at risk of a clash.

Capitol Police Chief Charles Tubbs, a bear of a man with a thin mustache,
gentle demeanor, and gravelly voice, calmly approached the newcomers. In
equal measure he pleaded and persuaded, and the new crowd slowly dis-
persed, until most of those who had entered through the security breach had
left. That still left the most determined protesters in the rotunda. The judge
had ordered them to leave the statehouse. If they refused, police would be
compelled to make them go, and a physical confrontation would finally come.
There was still some hope, however, that it could be avoided. Lautenschlager
brought a copy of Albert's order to read to the protesters who clustered around
her. "The thing for me is we've won this battle," she told them.

Not all the demonstrators were ready to declare victory and head to their
beds. They mulled the question of leaving and talked with volunteer legal advisors about what might happen to them if they didn't. The tension ratcheted
upward now that the 6 p.m. closing time had passed and the police had asked
the group to leave many times. The protesters defiantly sat and stood in the
empty space in the rotunda. Police surrounded that circular area, standing in
the spaces between the stone pillars that ringed the rotunda on the ground
floor. Television cameras filmed it at close range, sometimes shining spot-
lights on the already edgy group of demonstrators.

Throughout this crisis, Tubbs's status as one of the few African American
police chiefs in the state was an unspoken asset to him. The demonstrators
saw their battle for labor rights as echoing earlier struggles in American history, such as those during the civil rights era. But not even those who saw
similarities between the times could mistake Chief Tubbs for Bull Connor,

the infamous segregationist and commissioner of public safety in Birmingham, Alabama. Tubbs could sympathize and connect with intransigent young demonstrators, perhaps in part because his own sons had had troubles with the law. The protesters around him may not have known that, but the chief himself was well aware of what it meant to be young and suddenly acquire a criminal record. In the coming months, the relationship between the police at the Capitol and some habitual protesters would sour. That night, however, due in great part to the efforts of Tubbs, Riseling, and countless other officers, the police still held some legitimacy for demonstrators in the rotunda even though Walker did not.

None of this prevented the mood at the Capitol that night from darkening as the time for a resolution neared. For her part, Riseling remained sure that a clash could be avoided, but not everyone shared her confidence. Peter Barca, the Assembly Democratic leader, was worried as he walked the floor of the rotunda, doing what he could to make sure there was no confrontation. "I felt like one of my obligations was to keep the calm and keep people safe and make sure they respected law enforcement," Barca said later, remembering the respect he had then for the police and their work over the previous weeks. During those tense moments, Barca and Huebsch, Assembly colleagues, texted each other and shared information about the standoff and the judge's order to help keep the peace. "He just said, 'Can I help?'" Huebsch remembered.

For the first time during the crisis, the police guarding the stairs looked uneasy and told passing reporters to be careful. Down on the ground floor, the cops ringing the rotunda put on black leather gloves and stretched their arms and backs. A confrontation seemed just minutes away, but the chief patiently held it back, talking and pleading with the people around him not to resist. Tubbs waded into the group of demonstrators so that he was surrounded by them like a coach in a huddle; at six foot five and 300 pounds, he towered over the protesters as he talked to them calmly and at length. Rather than appearing menacing, Tubbs's height and bulk helped to emphasize his restraint. "We have to get back to normalcy," he told the group. "I'm asking you tonight to please leave."

Tubbs didn't speak eloquently but was as dogged as he was polite, repeatedly asking the demonstrators to leave. He also listened as the informal spokespeople for the group shared their distrust about whether the building would truly be opened up again. And many of the demonstrators responded to Tubbs, even as they condemned the governor. "We respect you, chief," some of them said. "Then do as I ask," Tubbs responded. And gradually, they did. Giving the group time to talk through the situation allowed some of the older demonstrators the chance to make their own appeals to their younger cohorts. The main group of remaining protesters left around 9 p.m., ending the fears of a free-for-all. The more than two-week occupation of the Capitol ended not with billy clubs or even a scuffle but with a group hug and a final chorus of "Solidarity Forever." At 9:58 p.m., about an hour after the main group left, the last five protesters exited the building. No one had been hurt and not a single arrest had been made. The struggle in Wisconsin avoided the worst moments of the Occupy Wall Street protests that, in the months to come, would see clashes between the demonstrators and police and some serious injuries.

That following Monday, March 7, the Capitol reopened to the public. It was still far from normal; just two of its eight entrances were open, and as visitors came in they were checked with metal-detecting wands. The statehouse had been thoroughly cleaned, and the thousands of signs removed and taken to the basement of a state building two blocks away. That week the public was allowed to come there and search for their signs to take home as a keepsake. Workers from the Wisconsin Historical Society picked through the rest looking for choice specimens to save along with photos, blog posts, documents, and tweets—a record of the struggle. A curator from the Smithsonian National Museum of American History came from Washington and returned with two dozen signs for the collections there. History was being made in Madison—and peacefully so.

15

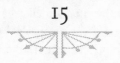

No Deal

THE ABSENT DEMOCRATS IN ILLINOIS were meeting daily at constantly changing locations as they sought to stay ahead of the media scrum and Tea Party activists. On February 26 they were told to meet at an unusual spot—the Illinois Education Association office in Libertyville, about ten miles away from their hotel in Gurnee. Mark Miller, the Senate minority leader, welcomed the free use of space from the sympathetic teachers union. During his three weeks in Illinois he spent thousands of dollars in personal funds on meeting space, food, and hotel rooms for himself and others. The location was also supposed to provide the Democrats with a video hookup so they could greet the throngs of protesters at the Wisconsin Capitol, but computer problems ultimately prevented that from happening.

Jim Holperin, a Northwoods senator targeted for recall four days earlier, understood the benefit of the venue but he and some others were surprised when they arrived to learn they wouldn't be meeting with just their fellow senators. Also attending the meeting were three labor officials: Rich Abelson, executive director of the AFSCME local that represented county and municipal workers in Milwaukee County; an unidentified person; and John Stocks, the incoming executive director of the National Education Association, which with some three million members was the largest union in the country. Stocks wasn't an outsider—he knew most of the Democrats from his fourteen years as a former top official and lobbyist with the Wisconsin Education Association Council, the in-state affiliate of the national teachers union. A New Orleans native and former Idaho state senator, Stocks still had a home in the Madison area and was among the union officials who had been consulting with Miller

throughout the Democrats' time in Illinois. As a sign of his frequent contacts, Stocks had to register with Wisconsin ethics officials as a lobbyist for
the NEA on February 22, 2011—five days after the Democratic senators left
the state—and then turned in his lobbyist's license several months later.
Stocks was the NEA's only registered lobbyist in Wisconsin and the only one
for any national union office turning up in state records during that time.
The NEA reported that Stocks spent twenty-six hours talking to lawmakers
and their aides about Walker's bill and that NEA staff spent 207 other hours
on lobbying activities on the bill such as research or communicating with
other union members, for a cost of $67,600 in total. Not all of those hours
would have been with Democrats. Stocks also reached out to Republicans
he knew from his time with WEAC. The NEA lobbying was small change
when put in the context of the millions of dollars in total that in-state unions
and business groups spent on lobbying on the bill, but the NEA contacts were
significant because of Stocks's national profile.

Senator Bob Jauch had been among those talking to Stocks, but he considered it inappropriate for the caucus to meet privately with any interest
group and thought it might eventually create public relations problems for
the Democrats if the news came out. Subway sandwiches were available for
the senators at the union hall, and Jauch asked, "Who's paying for lunch?"
He was comforted when he was told that Miller, not the unions, had provided
the food. He asked to speak with only his fellow Democrats and told them
he wouldn't participate in the meeting with union officials, warning them it
wasn't in their best interest to do so either. He went to another part of the
building, found a desk, and made a few phone calls. Unlike Jauch, Senator
Tim Cullen decided to stay in the meeting in spite of his own concerns about
it. "I was interested in one question and my question was, 'How long are you
expecting us to stay and what's your strategy for us coming home?'" Cullen
remembered, saying he suspected Miller was taking cues from labor leaders.
"I wanted to hear their answers. And I got no answers from them."

Others were untroubled by the meeting. Senator Julie Lassa, who as caucus chairwoman ran the Democratic get-togethers in Illinois, said there was
nothing unusual about hearing out people directly affected by the legislation.
Just because the Democrats talked with the union officials didn't mean they
did whatever they wanted, she said.

By the time of the meeting with Stocks and Abelson, the Democrats had
agreed several times to return to Wisconsin but had not finalized when to
do it. The union officials stressed a different strategy. Cullen described the

meeting as a pep rally in which the union officials argued that the senators' absence was working and would indeed block Walker's bill. Holperin gave little credence to what the union officials presented because he felt they were only feeding the senators information that they believed would persuade them to stay in Illinois. "The undercurrent message was, 'You're winning; stay out,'" Holperin recalled.

The meeting was just part of what could be seen as encouragement—or pressure—on the fourteen senators from their allies. State and national labor leaders, as well as other Democrats, made regular calls to the senators in Illinois to boost their morale and their resolve to fight just as Republicans were being encouraged by their backers. Calls to Democrats also came from civil-rights leader and Georgia Congressman John Lewis and U.S. Senate Majority Leader Harry Reid of Nevada. Whenever a rumor arose that a senator might be considering returning to Wisconsin, the calls from union leaders intensified. One labor official said later that there was "a lot of drama" involved in keeping all fourteen of the senators on the southern side of the border. "I think some of the union leaders didn't care if we stayed in Illinois for the rest of our lives," Jauch said later.

Many of the Democrats were more content to remain where they were, believing that staying in Illinois would force Republicans to engage in meaningful negotiations or find a way to pass the measure without them. Holperin, Cullen, and Jauch, however, believed the Democrats could not wait out the Republicans. If both sides held firm, the Democrats might have to stay away from the Capitol for months, which they considered impossible and politically suicidal. Meanwhile, Republicans ratcheted up the pressure any way they could. They sent state troopers to the homes of the Democrats whom they suspected were most likely to return for a visit, such as Lassa, who was seven months pregnant and had two young daughters at home. Other efforts were less intimidating and seemed to only strengthen the resolve of Democrats. But some threats had to be taken seriously, such as the filings made days earlier to recall most of the Democrats. The senators in Illinois knew that most of those efforts would come to naught, but they were also aware that Holperin and others in competitive districts were vulnerable to recall.

Republicans faced similar difficulties. Messages from union supporters deluged the GOP senators seen as most likely to change their position. Over the course of the four-week struggle, Senator Robert Cowles of Allouez alone received some 82,000 e-mails from around the country, Canada, and Europe, with a majority of them urging him to vote against the bill. Cowles had a staff of four people who struggled to respond to them, narrowing them down to the 4,500 that were clearly from within his district and replying to those. The phone in the senator's Capitol office rang constantly, often overwhelming the staff's ability to answer it. At his home, Cowles had an answering machine that could hold fifty messages. Whenever he returned home, he always found it full of messages from both opponents and supporters of the bill. In the face of this wave, the senator found he couldn't keep up with his usual practice of returning calls from his constituents. "Eventually, I just gave up," he said. Many of the Democrats knew the targeting by protesters included camping out near Republicans' front lawns but also that conservative activists were hinting they would run primary opponents against them if they caved to the unions. "My reaction was that was the stuff that will harden someone's position," Tim Cullen said later. "I thought there was no chance they were going to change."

Some in the caucus held fast to the idea that their absence would force the Republicans to compromise. To Cullen, simply waiting in Illinois for a breakthrough didn't seem like much of a strategy. He had been surprised ten days earlier when he'd met his Democratic colleagues at the Clock Tower in Rockford to discover they had never discussed a plan for returning to Wisconsin before they drove to Illinois. When they left Wisconsin, Cullen had the impression that Democrats and Republicans alike believed they would return after just a few days. Now both sides were dug in, with no end to the conflict in view. Cullen and Jauch—like many senators of both parties—also worried about the Senate as an institution. Although both believed that the Democrats had made the right decision in going to Illinois, they were concerned that it would worsen the already poisonous partisan divisions in their house and set a potentially harmful precedent. Would the Senate be able to take on tough fiscal problems in the future without one party leaving the state? "I felt we accomplished our purpose—to slow [the bill] down and let the public be heard," Cullen said later. "So I started to push in the first seven to ten days, 'What was our exit strategy?'"

Despite a lifetime in politics, nothing had prepared Cullen to operate in such a divided environment. Cullen was a former Democratic Senate majority leader who was long accustomed to working across party lines. He once helped a Republican senator get a lawyer after a drunk-driving incident rather than skewering him in the press. And after his first stint in the Senate, he went to work for Republican Governor Tommy Thompson. Still, as majority leader he had been viewed as both effective and liberal enough to be dubbed the

"Prince of Darkness" by an anonymous opponent in a *Milwaukee Magazine* article. When he returned to the Senate in January 2011—almost a quarter of a century after he left it—he found a place that had become so hyperpartisan it was unrecognizable. At sixty-seven, Cullen was a skilled deal-maker in a situation where no compromise seemed possible or even wanted. He felt that Thompson, his old boss, would have never put forward a bill like Walker's and that even if he had, Thompson still could have found a way to end the stalemate. At the same time, some Democrats viewed the former leader as well meaning but naïve about what could be gained from negotiating with GOP senators and Walker. "He's trapped in a time bubble, believes it's the same fraternity as thirty years ago," one prominent union figure said about Cullen.

Along with Jauch, Cullen tried to ignite a spark of those old fraternal feelings of bipartisanship. He talked to a number of Republicans he knew, including Thompson and Michael Grebe, the Bradley Foundation president who had chaired Walker's campaign and led his transition team. "I was just trying to find somebody who had access to the governor who might encourage us to work out some deal," Cullen said.

Others in the caucus were making similar calls, but it was Cullen's contact with Gerald Whitburn that helped arrange a phone call between Miller and Scott Fitzgerald hours before the Democrats' meeting at the Illinois teachers union headquarters. The call did not go well. Miller started off by saying something like, "I understand the governor has asked us to call you." Walker had not in fact requested the call be made, and that mischaracterization was off-putting for Fitzgerald, who felt Miller didn't recognize that Senate Republicans were likewise essential to any deal on the Democrats' return. "The conversation went downhill from there," recalled Jauch, who was in the room with Miller when he spoke to Fitzgerald. That call highlighted the inability of the two Senate leaders to trust each other or effectively communicate, Jauch said. Throughout the Democrats' absence, Miller and Fitzgerald talked almost daily, but only briefly and without true progress.

Jauch and Cullen had better luck with Fitzgerald. The next day, Sunday, February 27, Whitburn called Cullen and told him that Fitzgerald would be calling him soon. A Walker supporter, Whitburn was a veteran of handling volatile political situations who had served under Tommy Thompson as labor secretary and—like Cullen—health secretary. He considered Cullen, Jauch, and Holperin friends, and he had talked with all of them shortly after the Democrats left the state. He started the conversations by telling them they shouldn't have gone to Illinois, but then talked with them about ways to resolve the standoff. At the same time, he was having a series of conversations with Walker, and he encouraged having the two sides get together to resolve the crisis. "I was a nudger," Whitburn recalled a year later.

When Fitzgerald called Cullen that evening, they discussed the importance of resolving the impasse. Cullen suggested they meet the next day at a McDonald's situated at the crossroads of Interstate 94 and Highway 50 in Kenosha, just fifteen minutes from the Democrats' hotel in Gurnee. Cullen and Jauch were not concerned about meeting with Fitzgerald in Wisconsin, even though Fitzgerald had talked about having state troopers commanded by his father bring back any Democrat who was caught on the wrong side of the state line. In the first days, Cullen and other Democrats believed they had to stay in Illinois to make sure they would not be forced back into session, but Cullen soon talked with the police chief and sheriff from his area and determined Democrats were indeed able to return to Wisconsin as long as they didn't enter the Capitol.

Cullen and Jauch had concerns about what Democrats might say about the meeting. All fourteen Democratic senators had agreed early on that none of them would break ranks and return to the Capitol alone; the group as a whole was opposed to going back unless Walker agreed to significant changes to the bill. Other Democrats said later that they supported the talks and hoped Cullen and Jauch could help frame up a deal. But none of them trusted that the Republicans were serious about working with the Democrats, and some Democrats feared Cullen and Jauch would not adequately represent the caucus' negotiating stance. Marty Beil, the executive director of the Wisconsin State Employees Union, said later that he backed the talks but also said he fretted that Cullen and Jauch were not familiar enough with collective bargaining law to understand all the implications of a deal. Beil's worry was that revisions might be brokered that would appear to help labor but still allow the administration to largely dispense with bargaining. Beil trusted Cullen and consulted with him, but steered clear of Jauch because the two clashed.

Cullen and Jauch believed their meeting with Fitzgerald was well timed because the situation was going badly enough for both sides that a deal seemed possible. The poor poll numbers for Walker for his hard line and for the Democrats for remaining in Illinois; the looming deadline on the debt refinancing; the threat of recall attempts against both sides—all combined to give Cullen and Jauch a little optimism. What's more, Cullen and Jauch had only a modest goal. They wanted to restore as much collective bargaining as possible, but they were not seeking a bill that they would support, just one that would allow the Democrats to agree to return to the Capitol to cast "no" votes. What now passed for bipartisanship wasn't voting the same way; it was simply agreeing to be in the same room together. Cullen and Jauch's approach had not been approved by the caucus, and they would have to sell whatever deal emerged to skeptical colleagues demanding dramatic changes to the bill. Once Cullen, Jauch, and Fitzgerald started talking, it became clear how difficult achieving even modest changes would be.

By that time, the bill had already passed the Assembly in its bitter, marathon session, and Fitzgerald said he would not accept any changes to it. In what was either a tactical error or a gambit to shut down negotiations—or both—Assembly Republicans had essentially walked the plank by approving the bill as passed by the Joint Finance Committee. In the process, Republicans in that house had rejected Democratic amendments with some of the very changes that Cullen and Jauch were now seeking to make. That created a dilemma for Scott Fitzgerald, who felt obligated to back Jeff Fitzgerald, his younger brother and the Assembly speaker. Any changes, Scott Fitzgerald told the Democrats, would have to be passed months later as part of the state budget. That was a difficult proposition for Democrats, because it meant they would have to come back to Wisconsin with nothing but a promise that GOP lawmakers would hold up their end of the bargain—a notion that would be all but impossible for some Democrats to accept. The approach also might have been illegal because under Wisconsin's anti-"logrolling" statute, lawmakers cannot pledge to offer influence on one bill in exchange for a vote for or against another one. Despite the difficulties, the meeting got the two sides talking. Cullen and Jauch presented several ideas; Fitzgerald rejected some of those and later made a counteroffer that was no good to the Democrats. Still, the talk was friendly. "There was never any fist-pounding or demands," Cullen said.

Scott Fitzgerald had come because he thought if nothing else he could get a handle on the chances of the Democrats returning. He thought they had boxed themselves in politically and now saw no means of getting out of Illinois. "I asked those guys point blank, 'Are the unions keeping you out of the state or could you come back?' And they didn't answer real quickly. They kind of tap danced," Fitzgerald said. After the meeting, Fitzgerald forwarded the Democrats' ideas to the governor's office, but he did not believe Democrats as a whole would be serious about reaching a deal.

Back in Madison, Republicans kept up the pressure. They had already launched efforts to collect recall signatures against the eight Democratic senators who were more than a year into their term and thus eligible for recall. On

March 2, the Senate, with only Republicans present, voted to fine the absent Democrats a hundred dollars each time they missed a session day without a valid excuse. The Republicans also voted to make the Democrats responsible for repaying the state for the costs of seeking to force them to show up for Senate business. Fitzgerald considered firing all the aides of the Senate Democrats but stopped short of that, instead assigning Republican senators to oversee the Democratic staffers while their elected bosses were away. The Democrats responded that such efforts only galvanized the caucus. "They're taking copying privileges away from us. What's that supposed to do, scare the hell out of us?" Jon Erpenbach later deadpanned. Fitzgerald discussed his talks with Democrats publicly but gave little indication to the press that they would go anywhere. "The items that they brought up were items that could never make it into the state budget," he told reporters. "At this point, I'm not sure why I'd reach out to them again."

The Republicans, however, had their own pressures. That same day, opponents of Walker's bill filed paperwork launching recall efforts against eight GOP senators. In all, efforts were made to recall all sixteen senators who were eligible for recall at that time—eight from each party. Republicans controlled the Senate nineteen to fourteen, and so far they were holding firm in spite of the opposition from labor groups. Democrats needed to win over three GOP senators to stop the bill, and one of them, Dale Schultz, had already criticized the legislation and was widely assumed to be a "no" vote. "All I know is, we're not talking," Schultz told a local radio station on March 1. "We're wasting valuable time on collective bargaining, which I don't remember being a part of the last election whatsoever. But most of all, you know, to me, this just looks like the classic overreach we see every two years."

If Schultz was a "no," only two more Republicans were needed to block the bill, and there were several possibilities. Scott Fitzgerald was confident he had the votes, but privately, Republicans continued to explore their options. Many Democrats were routinely talking with GOP contacts, with Miller touching base at some point with all of the Senate Republicans he considered moderate and potentially open to compromise. But it was Cullen and Jauch who came closest to a concrete deal, even if it might never have been acceptable to the rest of the caucus. Late in the day on March 2, Whitburn called Cullen to tell him talks could get back under way soon. "You're going to get a call from the governor's chief of staff," Whitburn told Cullen.

Now there was at least a chance at headway. The talks with the administration had taken nearly two weeks to start, partly because Walker's administration was so new, filled with aides and cabinet secretaries who had been appointed less than two months before the Democratic senators split for Illinois. Both sides had to try to make contacts and build trust in the midst of the tensest political standoff in the state in more than a generation. Around 6 p.m. Walker's chief of staff, Keith Gilkes, called Cullen. He said he and the deputy chief of staff, Eric Schutt, would like to meet with the two Democrats that night. They decided to do it at the same McDonald's in Kenosha at 9 p.m., and Cullen figured they must be serious because the governor's aides were willing to drive to a meeting two hours away. He thought he ought to bring Miller to the meeting as well.

Cullen had not met Gilkes before and did not know Schutt well. But the two aides understood the workings of the Senate. Before running Walker's 2010 campaign, Gilkes had overseen the campaigns of all Senate Republican candidates. He had also worked stints as a legislative staffer, though he preferred working on campaigns rather than in the Capitol. Schutt had been involved with everything from the state budget as a top Assembly staffer to a statewide ban on smoking in bars and restaurants as a lobbyist for the American Cancer Society. Now, the two young aides and three older senators sat down over coffee and hot cocoa.

The meeting showed potential for a deal. Walker's aides talked for the first time of making some changes to the bill itself, and it appeared at least possible that the two sides could bridge the gap between them enough to allow the Democrats to return. Cullen and Jauch's focus was on preserving collective bargaining as much as possible. The Republicans were willing to listen but said they wouldn't negotiate on the question of allowing the automatic deduction of dues from the paychecks of public employees. That would be a difficult proposition because of the sharp effect it would have on unions' financial health, and some Democrats later said that showed Walker wasn't interested in a true compromise. Miller talked mostly about why the bill was bad, focusing on why the Republicans should abandon it. Cullen saw this as a waste of time, since Walker had made clear he wasn't dropping his bill. He felt it was better to concentrate on negotiating the best deal possible. Gilkes viewed Miller's stance as politically naïve because he did not seem to recognize that the out-of-power Democrats had little negotiating leverage. Cullen and Jauch, by contrast, knew how to negotiate and were proposing ideas that could lead to a deal, Gilkes thought.

The McDonald's meeting lasted about two hours. It went well enough that afterward Gilkes and Schutt called to wake Walker just before midnight to brief him on it and establish the parameters of any future talks. As the three Democrats drove back to Illinois, Cullen and Jauch felt they had made good progress as well. Miller didn't say much to them in the car and spent much of his time on his cell phone. At a caucus meeting the next morning, Miller told the other senators the governor was making a minimal offer. Most of the Democrats in turn reacted coldly to it, to Cullen's disappointment. Gilkes soon heard about how Miller presented it to his caucus and called him about it. "You're not interested, so we're done," Gilkes later said he told Miller, though a year and a half afterward Miller said he did not recall the exchange. The two sides wouldn't meet again until that weekend. The time to find a deal was slipping away.

The next day, March 3, the Republicans voted to find the Democrats in contempt of the Senate and issued orders to Wisconsin law enforcement to detain them if they crossed into Wisconsin. Fitzgerald signed for each missing senator an "order to detain" and said that anyone who saw the absent Democrats in Wisconsin could report them to police. Fitzgerald himself said he couldn't believe the situation had come to this, admitting publicly that Republicans were initially nervous about taking such a step but saying that Democrats had created a "constitutional crisis." "The minority party has forced our hand," he said. "They're insulting the very fabric of our representative democracy."

The idea for the contempt resolution came from longtime GOP lawyer Jim Troupis. Two days earlier, Troupis had brought a lawsuit against Holperin on behalf of the chairman of the Oconto County Republican Party in an attempt to force Holperin back to Wisconsin. The lawsuit was funded in part by the Wisconsin Club for Growth, one of the conservative outfits running ads in favor of Walker's plans. On March 2 a judge there ruled that Holperin appeared to be violating Senate rules but that only the Senate could enforce those rules. Troupis also had the Senate as a client, and he cited the Oconto County case as evidence that the Senate could find its absent members in contempt and issue warrant-like orders to police demanding their return. For the contempt question, Troupis and his firm were paid as much as $375 an hour by taxpayers, with the total bill for five days of work coming to $26,955. In spite of the money paid for the legal strategy, it was questionable whether the Senate had any power to have Democratic lawmakers detained and brought by force to the Capitol. The state constitution says that lawmakers can be compelled to attend legislative sessions but does not spell out how that can be enforced. The constitution also says legislators can be arrested only for crimes, treason, or breach of the peace. Well-known Democratic attorneys produced

their own legal memo and arguments that the Senate had no such authority, calling the Republicans' posture mere "chest thumping." Now, Fitzgerald
said that Republicans would also consider disciplining Democrats by repri-
manding them, censuring them, or expelling them from the Senate. Expelling the Democrats was impossible for the GOP majority because they fell
short of the two-thirds margin needed for that action. Nonetheless, the Republicans had the votes to reprimand or censure senators if they chose to do it.
All these threats, however, seemed to do little besides make the Democrats
more defiant.

Despite the back-channel talks, the stalemate held. The Democrats debated
constantly about what to do. Cullen, Jauch, and Holperin pushed for a compromise while others—particularly Miller, Chris Larson, Jon Erpenbach, and
Lena Taylor—argued for staying put because they believed Republicans were
weakening. Larson, who was new to the Senate, liked the idea of Cullen and
Jauch talking with the administration but also warned the caucus that he
knew from his two years on the Milwaukee County Board that Walker couldn't
be trusted in negotiations. "The thing that I did know was that Scott Walker
tends to push the edges and he tends to push until people push back," Larson
said later. The Democrats agreed to return several times, but final decisions
kept being put off. For instance, the Democrats scuttled plans to come back
when the Republicans withheld their paychecks, fearing that if they returned
it would appear they cared only about getting paid. They also put off plans to
return when the prank phone call to Walker came out because many in the
caucus believed it changed the dynamic enough that they could win concessions on the bill. "It seemed every couple days longer we stayed out, they did
something stupid," making it easier for Democrats to stay away from Madison, Erpenbach recalled. He was one of the most reluctant to return to the
Senate chamber unless Republicans caved. "We'd be breaking everybody's
heart and I didn't want to walk into a situation like that," he said.

The caucus meetings were often tense. Being away from home and being
bombarded with calls put everyone on edge. The close quarters—at one point,
the senators squeezed themselves around two beds in a small hotel room for
a caucus meeting—didn't help. The group supported, sometimes grudgingly,
Cullen and Jauch's efforts but felt they needed a strong deal that would provide enough of a reason to return, particularly for those most vulnerable to
recall. Despite the competing views on what to do, the internal discussions
were always civil, Holperin and Lassa remembered. Regular closed-door meetings in the Capitol can grow heated, but the absent senators said that happened

less frequently in Illinois because they were united by their support for collective bargaining—and the knowledge that one defector would provide Republicans with what they needed. "Our whole strategy depended on this cohesiveness of the caucus," Holperin said. "We understood from the beginning that one person could end the cohesion."

On Friday, March 4, Walker followed through on his promise to send layoff notices to 1,500 state workers, saying the state would have to cut their positions if the debt refinancing wasn't done on time. That got no immediate response from Democrats, who maintained they still had time to compromise as well as develop a plan for balancing the budget without the debt deal. The Walker administration itself had acknowledged that even financially stressed programs like the state's health plans for the poor had enough money to run for weeks to come. So in spite of the supposed deadline for the refinancing, the state's budget wasn't demanding immediate action from either side.

On Saturday, March 5, Jauch telephoned Gilkes to set up another meeting for the next day, this time in South Beloit, Illinois. "We had a good conversation the first time," Jauch remembered saying. "We would like to bring this to resolution because each day this thing is building. It's becoming more politically tense and it's not in anybody's interest to keep the conflict going."

Jauch rented a motel room in South Beloit for the rest of the week and met with Cullen that Sunday to plan. That afternoon, the governor's two aides showed up at the Best Western and had a three-hour conversation with the senators. After the meeting, the two sides had an exchange of e-mails that captured the state of the negotiations. That same day, Walker met with Scott and Jeff Fitzgerald to keep the two legislative leaders up to date on where the negotiations were headed. To help refine the proposal, Schutt went to Bob Lang, the respected head of the Legislature's nonpartisan budget office, sending a proposal to Lang just after 6 p.m. Lang, who had served as the Legislative Fiscal Bureau director since 1977, was one of the few people trusted by both the governor's office and the senators in Illinois, and had been asked at times to serve as a liaison between the two sides in conveying the proposals as well as helping review them. The proposal that Schutt discussed with Lang included a number of changes to Walker's bill: public employee union bargaining over wages would no longer be limited to the rate of inflation, and no referenda would be required to raise wages; labor contracts would be good for two years instead of one; unions could bargain over issues of physical health and workplace safety for at least some employees; unions would have to vote every three years to recertify and retain their official status with the state, instead of voting every year; and, if employers agreed, unions would be allowed to bargain over certain economic issues, including mandatory overtime, performance bonuses, hazardous duty pay, and classroom size. The bill remained disastrous for unions. But in these negotiations, in which the two senators' expectations were already low, the proposal that was shaping up seemed like progress—especially considering they were firmly in the minority and negotiating from out of state. "To me that was a substantial package of improvements that would have meant a lot to public employees," Cullen said. "I left there feeling, 'Wow that's pretty good.'"

The two kept the talks to themselves for the moment. Jauch planned to fill in his colleagues at a caucus meeting the next day, but that would prove to be too late. For starters, Republicans were getting anxious to move forward. That evening, Cullen talked again to Whitburn, his Republican friend. "You've only got a couple days left," Whitburn told him.

Cullen understood. He didn't know what the Republicans might do to pass the bill on their own, but he knew they wielded the tremendous power of the Legislature and with that came options. Republicans needed to move. So far they had held together, but they faced a real risk that two more of their colleagues might join Schultz in opposing the bill. GOP Senators Van Wanggaard of Racine and Luther Olsen of Ripon said they supported the bill, but both had also expressed concerns about it. Olsen, one of the senators facing a serious recall effort, said that he favored some negotiation with Democrats and had passed along some ideas to the governor. "They're in the minority but they're holding some cards, so you've got to negotiate. You can't give up the whole ship," Olsen said on Monday, March 7.

Both sides waited for an opportunity or excuse to act. Early that Monday morning, Miller sent a letter to Walker and Scott Fitzgerald, before Jauch or Cullen told Miller and the other Democratic senators about their meeting with Walker's aides the day before. In his letter, which he quickly made public, the Democratic leader offered to meet with Republican leaders in person to seek a solution to the crisis. "I assure you that Democratic state senators, despite our differences and the vigorous debate we have had, remain ready and willing to find a reasonable compromise," Miller wrote. "To that end, I would ask that you or your authorized representatives agree to meet with us near the Wisconsin-Illinois border to formally resume serious discussions as soon as possible."

Cullen quickly concluded the letter "was not intended to be helpful." It conveniently overlooked the fact that Walker's "authorized representatives"

had met with Miller the previous week. Cullen also thought it was preposter-
ous to ask a governor to meet at the border. For his part, Miller feared Walker
was stringing them along and needed to be engaged in a public way. But
Cullen believed that Republicans had been looking for a way to cut off the
time-consuming talks and that Miller's letter gave them an excuse to do it.
Indeed, the letter drew a sharp response from Republicans. Over the lunch
hour, Walker called a meeting with the media. Flanked by Scott and Jeff
Fitzgerald, Walker indignantly held up Miller's letter and called it ridiculous.
The governor then laid out the three talks that had happened between Jauch,
Cullen, and Republicans, and went on to blame Miller for the lack of progress
in them. Walker claimed that Scott Fitzgerald and his aides had been reach-
ing out to these "reasonable" Democrats who had wanted to come home.
"Time and time again, the person standing in the way of this is Senator Mark
Miller," Walker said.

The governor stuck to the line that he had been negotiating in earnest
and hinted repeatedly that unreleased e-mails between his office and the
Democratic senators would show that. The Democrats watched the press
conference on a computer, and many of them were thunderstruck to find
out what the talks entailed. "If stares could kill, I would have been buried by
my colleagues then and there," Jauch said. When Jauch explained what he
and Cullen had been trying to do, the others' attitudes became less chilly,
though some remained concerned because they sought a much better deal.
The governor and Miller still had not talked, and they would not do so before
the crisis was over. Now, Walker's tentative relationship with the moderate
Democrats was also hurt. Jauch said later that day he believed talks could still
go forward but acknowledged the day's exchange was a setback. "I was furious when he suggested that Tim and I were willing to cut a deal to find a way
to go back," Jauch said of Walker. "There was no agreement. We were just
trying to build that staircase."

Labor groups remained aggressively opposed to Walker's bill—the modest proposed changes discussed by Jauch, Cullen, and the governor's aides
hadn't changed that at all. For instance, the proposal didn't alter the parts of
the bill dealing with union dues—some of its most hated provisions for labor
leaders. The plan would still end the requirement that all employees make fair
share payments to unions if they chose not to belong to them. The governor's
legislation would also prohibit the state and local governments from collecting
dues on behalf of unions. Those two provisions struck at the ability of labor
to raise the kind of money that was needed to make an impact in elections

through television ads and in the halls of the Capitol with lobbyists. Cullen and Jauch also hadn't sought any changes to the provision in the bill that required state and local employees to pay more for their health and pension benefits. The two knew there were limits to what they could achieve, and they concentrated on getting what they saw as the best deal possible for rank-and-file public employees. But faced with the possibility of losing so much, union officials and most of the Democratic senators preferred to focus on stopping what they considered the most onerous parts of the bill in the Legislature or seeking recall elections against Republicans for supporting it. "The majority of the caucus viewed this as a larger fight and they were not willing to come back as half-winners," Cullen said.

Quietly, Republicans turned to other ways that they could move their plan through the Senate without the missing Democrats. On Tuesday, March 8, Walker's office released e-mails between Jauch and Cullen and the governor's top two staffers to the *Milwaukee Journal Sentinel* in response to a request under the state's open records law—providing them within hours instead of the days, weeks, or months that state officials usually take to fulfill such requests. The governor's spokesman said in a statement that the e-mails showed that "the lines of communication have been open and negotiations have been ongoing for more than a week." But Jauch and Cullen criticized both the release of the e-mails and the way the governor's office described them. Jauch cautioned that the two sides had never reached a deal; Cullen stressed that the pair of Democrats had not been authorized to speak on behalf of others in their caucus. "I've never seen negotiations be done successfully in public," a disappointed Cullen said at the time. "I thought they were bargaining in good faith."

The two sides were done talking with one another. Now Republicans were moving forward with a secret plan to end the standoff and pass the bill.

16

End Game

HOURS AFTER MARK MILLER SENT HIS LETTER asking to sit down with Governor Walker, top Republicans and nonpartisan staff of the Legislature met privately across the street from the Capitol at the Legislative Fiscal Bureau office. In attendance on Monday, March 7, were Scott and Jeff Fitzgerald, Fiscal Bureau Director Bob Lang, Walker's budget director, and the chief clerks of both houses. Also present was Eric Schutt, Walker's deputy chief of staff who had negotiated with Tim Cullen and Bob Jauch in Illinois the day before.

The Fitzgeralds were looking for a way to pass the union bargaining bill without the Democrats, but they were hampered by the section of the state constitution requiring a three-fifths quorum of lawmakers to approve a bill that "imposes, continues or renews a tax, or creates a debt or charge, or makes, continues or renews an appropriation of public or trust money, or releases, discharges or commutes a claim or demand of the state." One solution was to remove the elements in the bill that triggered the requirement that twenty members of the Senate be present to vote on it. Scott Fitzgerald had been pushing the idea, but some Senate Republicans resisted it because such a move would suggest that the collective bargaining limits were not sparked by the state's budget woes. Nonetheless, the group discussed that possibility, and the Republican officials asked Lang to meet with attorneys from the Legislative Reference Bureau and the Legislative Council to determine which items of the bill could come to a vote without requiring the three-fifths quorum. It later became clear that the parts of the legislation that needed to be removed included additional spending to make up deficits in areas like prisons and health care, and another section authorizing the debt refinancing. GOP Senator Rob Cowles of Allouez, an old hand at utilities issues, teamed up with his ally Senate President Mike Ellis to also yank the provision allowing the no-bid sale of state power plants. The collective bargaining changes remained in place, as did the requirement that public workers pay more for their benefits. That provision had a financial effect for the state as well as its workers, but it didn't trip the higher quorum requirement because it saved the state money instead of costing it. The plan was kept quiet the next day, Tuesday, March 8, as Walker's office released the e-mails detailing the talks with Cullen and Jauch to make the case that negotiations had failed.

Meanwhile, unions continued to press the governor. A representative of the Wisconsin Professional Employees Council, a union of white-collar workers, wrote to the Walker administration asking a series of pointed questions about the budget and requesting that bargaining on contracts start up again. As long as the state employee unions remained certified, the administration had a legal obligation to sit down with them and discuss contracts. That Tuesday, Cindy Archer, Walker's deputy administration secretary, e-mailed a copy of the union letter to a number of Walker's other appointees. "This is the second letter we have received like this," she wrote. "We discussed it yesterday with the governor and he agreed that we should hold off responding in any way to these letters until later next week. The pressure is mounting and I am sure you all know, the sooner we can get resolution (the bill past [sic]) the better . . . for now, we are just sitting tight."

The following morning, March 9, the Capitol was comparatively quiet. The Republican senators met briefly to pass a routine bill, as well as resolutions carrying through, for the first time, on the threat of fining the absent Democrats one hundred dollars each for missing the day's session. Democrats scoffed at the resolutions, saying they were as unenforceable as the warrants issued against them the week before. Despite the drama of the vote, Ellis seemed not to take the issue seriously either—though the public didn't know it, the Senate president never signed the resolutions. After the morning session, the Republicans went behind closed doors, and Walker met with them for about half an hour. After Walker left, Scott Fitzgerald again urged his caucus to split the bill so they could pass it without the Democrats. This time, his previously wary colleagues readily agreed to the notion, deciding to take a committee vote and then a Senate vote that night. "Everybody was like, 'This needs to end,'" Fitzgerald recalled. Fitzgerald had discussed the idea with the governor's office from time to time but cautioned that he didn't have the full support of the caucus. Now he had the votes, but he didn't inform Walker's aides right away, and they didn't learn of the plan until later in the afternoon. He relied on an axiom of lawmakers—when you have the votes, go to the floor. "I didn't feel there was an obligation to run down the hallway and tell the governor what we were going to do," he said later. That afternoon he went on Fox News to talk about the importance of the legislation. For weeks, Walker and the Fitzgerald brothers had insisted that the collective bargaining changes were about the state's finances and not politics. But in the Fox News interview, Scott Fitzgerald highlighted how weakening the unions would help defeat President Barack Obama in Wisconsin in 2012. "If we win this battle, and the money is not there under the auspices of the unions, certainly what you're going to find is President Obama is going to have a much more difficult time getting elected and winning the state of Wisconsin," he said.

Around 2:15 p.m., the Fitzgeralds sent for Bob Lang, who was in a caucus briefing with Assembly Republicans going over the provisions of the separate two-year budget bill. Lang left that caucus and met with the Fitzgeralds in the Legislative Fiscal Bureau's small office off the Joint Finance Committee's hearing room. The Republican leaders told Lang that a conference committee would be meeting at 6 p.m. to amend the collective bargaining bill and remove the financial elements requiring a larger quorum and that Lang would need to issue drafting instructions for an amendment to do that. Lang called his staff and told them to meet with bill-drafting attorneys from the Legislative Reference Bureau in the Fiscal Bureau's main office. Hurrying to the meeting, Lang gave the group the instructions he had received from the Fitzgeralds and told the staffers to pound out an amendment to that effect and a summary explaining its provisions. Normally, lawmakers formed conference committees when control of the Legislature was split between the parties so they could work out differences in a state budget or other contentious piece of legislation. Now, Republicans were forming a conference committee so they could pass their plan without the presence of the Senate Democrats. During this time, a series of informal bull sessions on strategy were held in Ellis's office, with the core pair of Ellis and Scott Fitzgerald being joined sometimes by other GOP senators like Cowles and Senator Luther Olsen of Ripon as they wandered in. Ellis aide Mike Boerger said he couldn't remember who first raised the idea of convening a conference committee to amend the bill but thought it came out of those meetings rather than from an outside source like Walker's office. Fitzgerald noted that one part of using a conference committee was especially helpful—the bill would come out of the committee and be subject to a strict up or down vote. That would block Democrats in the Assembly from stalling by offering scores of new amendments.

At 4:03 p.m., the Senate Republicans abruptly returned to the floor and created the conference committee so the bill could be sent to it. Shortly afterward, the Assembly took the same action in a so-called skeletal session—a relatively common form of legislative action in which only a few lawmakers take part and which is usually for mundane business. In the Senate parlor, staff set up twenty chairs for the public, making accommodations for just a handful of those who wanted to attend. The chief clerk's office sent an e-mail to all lawmakers at 4:18 p.m. alerting them to the meeting. Around the same time, notices were also posted on bulletin boards outside the Senate and Assembly chambers. This meant that the official notice of the meeting was made about an hour and forty minutes beforehand—a fact that would soon be the focus of a legal challenge.

The protests inside the Capitol had died down in the days before the vote because of tightened security, leaving relatively few demonstrators on hand when the Senate convened to form the conference committee. Activity in the statehouse was so slow that some police officers were sent home that afternoon by their still uninformed senior officers. Once the conference committee was ordered, journalists and smartphone-packing protesters quickly reported the news through their websites and social media, and the bill's opponents rushed to the Capitol. Only two of the building's eight entrances had been open that day, and the police closed one of the two around 5 p.m. to strengthen the security for the committee, leaving only one entrance open just before the size of the crowd surged. Hundreds lined up, anxious to get in, as others circled the building.

The conference committee vote was to be held in the Senate parlor, the narrow room behind the chamber. The sergeant at arms' staff counted off twenty people and denied entry to the rest of the public. Chanting slogans, the remaining protesters packed into the area outside of the Senate chamber. A page unlocked the door for legislators, aides, and reporters with the proper identification while the demonstrators circulated a spontaneous petition to show that they were barred from getting into the meeting. When they were done, they dropped off papers with 2,967 names on them in the Assembly minority leader's office.

Republicans had not thought to warn the police about their plans, and Fitzgerald said more than a year later he wished that someone had. "I didn't anticipate the rush of students up State Street and the crush of people," he said. The evening of the conference committee vote, Chief Susan Riseling of the UW–Madison police was working on paperwork in her campus office, unaware of the action that GOP lawmakers were about to take. On Monday of that week, she had returned to her regular job, satisfied that the statehouse was under control and that she was no longer needed there. After nearly a full month of working overtime hours at the Capitol, many of her officers had also gone home to get some much-needed rest. At about 5:40 p.m., Riseling's phone rang—it was Deputy Chief Dan Blackdeer of the Capitol Police and he sounded worried. "Bring everybody you have and get up here," he urged her. Surprised and now concerned herself, Riseling quickly assembled the five officers she had available, had them grab riot gear, and headed to the statehouse. When they arrived, Riseling saw at a dispiriting glance that all her efforts to restore order to the building had been undone within minutes. "The whole place is like a sieve," she remembered later. "People are coming in windows. People are coming in doors."

Dane County Sheriff Dave Mahoney also showed up with about a dozen deputies, ready to respond to the urgent request for help from the Capitol Police but resolved not to remove demonstrators. "We were there to ensure safety and security," Mahoney said later. The situation was certainly tense. Law enforcement officers were becoming so desperate that at one point they slapped handcuffs around some door knobs to keep the entrances closed to protesters outside—a move that meant that people inside could no longer exit through those doors if need arose. Riseling left her officers at the King Street entrance and went to the Capitol Police's fourth-floor command center. There she found Blackdeer looking stunned for reasons that the newly arrived Riseling didn't understand. According to several sources familiar with that night, Blackdeer had called the Madison Police Department and asked for the city's officers to also come and help his officers handle the sudden influx of demonstrators. But although Dane County and UW–Madison both sent officers, the Madison police had refused to help, according to the sources. A year and a half later, Madison Police Chief Noble Wray acknowledged that the city officer in charge had received a call from the Capitol Police but maintained that the officer hadn't understood Blackdeer to be making an urgent call for help in the way that Riseling instantly had on her own call. Wray could offer no explanation for the misunderstanding, stressing instead that he and his department had given large amounts of aid during the crisis and would have responded that night too if they had realized how desperately the Capitol

Police wanted help. "I think there was probably some kind of miscommuni-
cation but I don't know what happened," Wray said. The exchange between
Madison police and Blackdeer later led to speculation that the Madison police
had refused help because of their political objections to the bill and the Republicans' method of passing it. That charge stung—cops are honor bound to
back one another—and Wray denied it.

That night, Riseling had no time to worry about that dispute. "How many
cops do we have and where are they?" she asked Blackdeer. He wasn't sure
but he knew one thing. "We have as many cops as we're going to get," he
said. Riseling didn't know what had happened at the Capitol to so agitate the
crowd, just that it was something big. She made a quick decision—the police
didn't have enough officers on hand to try to hold the doors of the Capitol
against the flood of angry protesters. Trying to force them back could lead to
fights and injuries on both sides, and she didn't want that. She decided to cede
most of the Capitol, with the exception of the upper floors and the second-
floor Assembly and Senate chambers, where she was still confident lawmakers could be kept safe.

"You're going to get all the cops to come up to the third floor and hold,"
Riseling said. "We're not defending the doors. You can't, there's not enough
cops. . . . These people are really angry right now." Riseling went back to the
King Street entrance to check on her officers. By avoiding resistance and reassuring the demonstrators that they would be able to get into the Capitol, they had calmed down the crowd at that entrance enough to get them to
line up to be searched for weapons. Some state troopers had started going
through the protesters' bags and Riseling told them not to waste too much
time on exhaustive searches. "A gun or a bomb—that's all you care about," she
said. Just outside the statehouse, Secretary of Administration Mike Huebsch
was standing at the top of Wisconsin Avenue, watching as the Capitol Police
that he oversaw lost control of the building. Huebsch was still embroiled
in the lawsuit over access to the Capitol, which had been continuing in the
days after Judge Albert's interim order clearing the building and which
would go on for several months yet. But the statehouse had been under control for days, and Huebsch now had a sinking feeling as he watched that fall
apart. Demonstrators were milling around the covered northwest entrance of
the building and Huebsch saw someone inside the building open a ground-
floor window that Huebsch afterward identified as belonging to Democratic
Representative Cory Mason of Racine. A couple of protesters climbed inside.
"Oh, this could be bad," Huebsch thought, as more people joined them in a

movement he later described as being like "sand going into an hourglass." He grabbed his cell phone and called Deputy Chief Blackdeer in the command center; they had two separate conversations over the next several minutes.

"You're about to lose the north wing," Huebsch told him.

But Blackdeer had more bad news for Huebsch, explaining that the over-whelmed police were already mostly pulling back to the third floor, where there was no open rotunda, just hallways, and it was easier to hold ground. Huebsch, realizing that the command post was just one floor above that, had a vision of the police losing control of the entire building.

"Don't give up the command post!" Huebsch cautioned, as Blackdeer assured him that they wouldn't.

By then, some of the demonstrators still outside the Capitol had noticed the state official in a suit and long dress coat who was talking on a cell phone behind them. They approached Huebsch, with one of them asking him, "Who are you?" Huebsch thought it best to move along. For the open window, Mason took abuse afterward from conservative bloggers, with one labeling him a "Benedict Arnold." Mason responded that he wasn't in his office at the time but acknowledged that during the crisis he had allowed his staff to let in lawmakers, journalists, and ordinary protesters, saying that they had a con-stitutional right to observe official business as it was happening and that it had been wrong to shut them out.

Among the opponents of the bill streaming into the Capitol were Tim Gehrke and Benjamin Taft, who learned of the conference committee meet-ing a little after 5 p.m. They hurried to the statehouse after they got off work, cleared security by about 5:40 p.m., and headed to the Senate galleries so they could observe the senators after the conference committee met. At a security checkpoint just outside the galleries, an officer told Taft he couldn't bring his laptop and shoulder bag inside. Taft stepped out of line and hid his bag behind a desk in the hall while Gehrke proceeded into one of the galleries. Taft got back in line behind several people. Once he got to the security check-point again, an officer checked him with a metal-detecting wand. Cleared, he stepped toward the double wooden doors of the gallery, but an officer came through the doors at that moment and told Taft to stop. A second officer then told the group that no one else would be allowed in for the time being, and they formed a line in front of the doors. Inside the viewing gallery, a staffer told Gehrke no one else would be allowed in because of a security breach. The staffer locked the doors, and they remained locked for the next forty min-utes—throughout the conference committee meeting and the Senate session that followed. While waiting for the proceedings to begin, Gehrke counted twenty-four people in the galleries, or less than a third of the eighty-six seats. Just outside the galleries, Taft couldn't get an answer from officers about why he wasn't allowed in. He saw no legitimate security reason for keeping him out, and he believed as a citizen he deserved to witness what his government was doing. "It sort of summed everything up," he said later. "We were powerless to stop it. We did everything we could and they pulled every dirty trick to put us down." As the Capitol filled, law enforcement told the public over an intercom that the building would close at 6 p.m., an announcement that should not have been made because a committee of the Legislature was about to meet.

Barca was the first member of the conference committee to come to the Senate parlor. He showed up a few minutes early to make sure that Republicans did not try to vote before the starting time, as they had on the Assembly floor. He had been provided no details about the changes to the bill despite repeatedly asking for them from Republican offices over the previous hour and a half. He would be the only committee member present to challenge the Republican plan because Miller, the committee's only other Democrat, was still in Illinois. The Republicans on the committee—Scott Fitzgerald, Mike Ellis, Jeff Fitzgerald, and Scott Suder—soon filed in and sat at a table in the middle of the stately room. Packed around them were reporters, photographers, television crews, fellow legislators, and aides. Much of the room remained dark, but the bright lights of the television crews shone on the lawmakers and camera bulbs flashed.

Across the street from the Capitol, Bob Lang and his staff had finished the summary of the amendment and sent copies of it to the Fitzgerald brothers. Lang hurried to the meeting with more copies of the summary and sent word to the Reference Bureau staff that they needed to send the text of the amendment as soon as possible. He was prepared to serve as the clerk of the committee and to give an explanation of the amendment to the committee members and to take their questions—a common part of budget deliberations. As soon as Lang arrived at the table, the meeting was called to order. Reading from a paper, Scott Fitzgerald told the committee that he and his brother had prepared a new version of the bill. Barca raised his hand to ask a question. "Mr. Chairman," he cut in.

Fitzgerald ignored him, and Barca piped up again, "Mr. Chairman." Now Fitzgerald glanced up at him. "Let me read this statement," Fitzgerald said.

He explained the amended bill would not require the three-fifths quorum, and he moved to adopt it.

"Wait," Barca said, his hand aloft, a pen wedged between his fingers. "Excuse me, Mr. Chairman, excuse me. I have a question about the open meetings law, whether the open meetings law has been violated."

"Is there a second?" Fitzgerald asked.

Ellis gave Fitzgerald his second as Barca continued to yell. Someone from the crowd bellowed over them. "Take a moment," the citizen shouted. "Take a moment. Step back from the abyss. Think about what you're doing here!"

Massed on the other side of the Senate's locked doors, a growing crowd thundered, "Shame! Shame! Shame!" Their cries were so deafening they could be heard through the three marble walls between the protesters and the legislators. Hundreds if not thousands of citizens now stood outside the locked doors demanding to get in. A line of officers kept them at bay, even as the crowd grew. Scott Fitzgerald finally told Barca he could speak, and Barca asked to hear a summary of the changes to the bill.

"It's the same bill you debated for sixty hours," Fitzgerald said.

"Oh, there's nothing different?" Barca asked, his eyes blinking rapidly.

"Nah, they just removed items from it," Fitzgerald said.

Barca said he wanted a fuller explanation of the changes—the sort of details that Lang had at the ready—and said he'd like to offer amendments to the bill.

"No motions," Fitzgerald said flatly.

Barca noted that offering amendments was standard procedure for committees. "But before we get to that," he said, "I want to say that this is a violation of the open meetings law." He began reading from a recent memo by J.B. Van Hollen, the Republican attorney general, about the requirement that twenty-four hours' notice must be given before most government meetings.

"Representative Barca," Fitzgerald interjected. Barca kept reading from the memo. "Representative Barca! Representative Barca!"

"Yes?"

"Clerk, call the roll," Fitzgerald said.

"No! No!" Barca cried as he stood up. "Excuse me! Listen, it says, 'If there's any doubt as to whether good cause exists, the governmental body should provide twenty-four hours' notice.' This is clearly a violation of the open meetings law."

Amid Barca's shouts, the Republicans one by one muttered their "ayes."

"This is a violation of *law*," Barca said. "This is not just a rule. It is the *law*." Fitzgerald slammed down the gavel. "We're adjourned," he said as he and the other Republicans stood and walked out.

The meeting lasted a little over four minutes. Barca never voted, refraining from doing so because of the confusion and because he believed the meeting was illegal. Lang, who had not given any explanation of the bill, now gave copies of the summary of the amendment to the Senate sergeant's staff to be delivered to the desk of every senator. The few opponents in the room who had been allowed in began to chant, but Barca raised his hands and told the crowd to stop. He gripped the top of a giant Quiznos cup and sucked on its straw as reporters and demonstrators surrounded him. "The people of this state have a right to come to this building and attend a meeting," he said. "In this case, we saw a violation of the law." He noted that the bill putting limits on collective bargaining and increasing workers' benefit contributions had been stripped of many of its other provisions. "The gig is now up," Barca said. "The fraud on the people of Wisconsin is now clear. They now are going to take up a bill to take away people's rights."

Ten minutes later, the Republicans took their seats in the outer row of desks in the Senate chamber. The inner ring, where the minority party sits, remained empty. Senate Chief Clerk Rob Marchant read the title of the bill. No one spoke for or against it, and Marchant called out each senator's name. Eighteen "ayes" and one "nay" came back. "Shame on you!" protesters cried from the viewing galleries.

The "no" vote came from Senator Dale Schultz, who issued a statement later that evening explaining his dissent. He said the two sides should have been able to broker a compromise and that collective bargaining should have been kept in place because it had fostered labor peace for decades. "I've had the honor and privilege of representing folks in southwest and south-central Wisconsin for twenty-eight years, and where I come from 'compromise' isn't a dirty word," Schultz said.

In Illinois, Mark Miller learned an hour or more before the Senate ordered the conference committee that Republicans were likely to use the ploy to advance the bill, but Miller and his colleagues were unsure what to do. With Democrats absent, Republican leaders could let their most vulnerable members vote against the bill because all that was needed to pass it was a majority of those present. Some Democrats also saw an advantage to being there so they could argue against the bill on the floor, but others contended their absence would help expose to the public that the Republicans were going to extreme lengths to attack workers. The Democrats also were not sure that they could get there in time in rush-hour traffic. Miller told the Democrats to start driving toward Madison as they made up their minds on what to do, but before long Miller called them off when many had answered that they wanted to caucus on their strategy. Chris Larson didn't heed that request and continued driving toward Madison, in part because he felt helpless about what to do. He stopped in Johnson Creek, about thirty-five miles from Madison, to fill his tank and check his e-mail. There, he discovered the bill had passed and then drove back to Illinois to rejoin the other Democrats.

After the vote, the crowd outside the Senate chamber seethed. "You lied! You lied! You lied to Wisconsin!" they chanted. By 6:30 p.m., the Republicans were done for the night. But the thousands inside the building weren't going anywhere. They yelled, blew horns, and banged drums. Locked outside, some hurled snowballs at the Capitol. As the throng continued to grow, troopers escorted the senators out of the chamber, down the stairs, and into the underground tunnel that led across the street to the Department of Justice's headquarters. In the parking lot behind that building was a city bus that was being used to ferry law enforcement between the statehouse and a parking lot a few miles away, where officers kept their vehicles while on duty. Charles Tubbs, the Capitol Police chief, stepped onto the bus and told the driver he needed it to drive the senators away from the Capitol. Once the senators boarded the bus, Tubbs positioned himself by the driver and directed him where to go. The bus lurched through downtown streets amid protesters who banged on its sides and shouted at the Republicans. The senators watched warily.

Once the bus broke free of the crowd, the mood on the bus turned light-hearted. The senators chatted and laughed as they headed down East Washington Avenue. When the bus neared the Avenue Bar—a favorite tavern for some of the veteran lawmakers—Senator Rob Cowles asked if the bus could stop so he could get off. Tubbs agreed, but then said the bus was being followed. "There are people following us?" Cowles asked. "Forget it then." The bus took the senators to the Wisconsin National Guard's headquarters about five miles away. None of the protesters who had followed the bus bothered the Republicans once they arrived at the security facility, according to Scott Fitzgerald. Some of the senators had parked their personal vehicles at the National Guard offices, and others waited for their staffs to come pick them up and then drive them back downtown so they could get their own cars.

❖❖

While the senators were returning to their homes, hotels, and apartments, a panicked Michael Brown was working frantically. When the conference committee vote was taken that evening, people flooded his United Wisconsin website to sign the petition to recall the governor. The site and the United Wisconsin Facebook page had been growing by startling degrees since their launch on February 17, the day the Democratic senators left the state. By the morning of March 1 when Walker delivered his budget address, the site's database had 46,300 names. By the next morning, it had 70,300. On March 4, Brown registered his group as a political action committee, which allowed it to raise money and advance its advocacy work. The then-volunteer task of running the site was an all-consuming job for Brown, who was getting little sleep and neglecting his web business that paid the bills for him and his son. The site had already crashed once because traffic had grown too large to handle. By the evening of March 8, the site had 113,900 names. The evening of the conference committee vote, the site's traffic increased again as angry citizens sought to show their support for a recall. "People flew to our website," he remembered later. "I've never seen anything like it and I'll probably never see it again. They jumped!" The site was down for about five hours, and Brown eventually had to switch it to a different server to make sure it wouldn't go down again. He realized that his effort was growing so big that he could no longer manage it on his own. He needed help.

Meanwhile at the Capitol on the night of the Senate vote, protesters continued to surge into the building. Cars circled the square and beeped their horns, and the crowd inside grew to an estimated eight or nine thousand, Chief Tubbs later said. Over the intercom, police stated that the building was closed and the public needed to leave. "Hell no, we won't go," the crowd replied. Law enforcement did not know how long the occupation would last, and the head of the state Division of Criminal Investigation that night told all his agents to report the next morning for duty. "Please pack enough clothes for a couple of days," Ed Wall, administrator of the division, wrote in his e-mail to agents. "As you have probably heard, the situation is very tense."

Department of Administration officials grew worried that the walkways on the upper levels of the Capitol could collapse because of the number of people. "We are concerned about the structural integrity of the bridges," Capitol Police said over the public address system. "Please do not be on the bridges." They repeated their pleas, to little avail. Tim Donovan, a spokesman for the department, explained to reporters that the marble walkways were only held up by hidden timber support beams that were a century old. This, however, would turn out to be wrong. The walkways were well reinforced with steel, not timber, and were never in danger of collapsing.

Mark Miller's wife thanked the crowd for its support early on, and later tried to get them to voluntarily leave the Capitol. "If we can evacuate, we can win this battle," Jo Oyama-Miller told protesters in the Assembly's antechamber. "We won't if we break the law." But many remained, with more than two hundred spending the night and some bedding down in the Assembly vestibule and in front of Jeff Fitzgerald's office in an effort to stall the vote scheduled for the next day in that house. The building did not open to the general public at its normal 8 a.m. time. Outside the King Street entrance to the Capitol, several hundred people gathered, along with the Reverend Jesse Jackson, and demanded to be let in. Huebsch, Walker's administration secretary, said he wanted to open the building but the overnight demonstrators would first have to gather on the ground floor and be checked with metal-detecting wands. Only those with appropriate badges—lawmakers, staff, members of the media—were allowed inside, but even they encountered difficulty. A number of Assembly Democrats and at least one Republican were barred for a time from getting into the building. Democrat David Cullen of Milwaukee and Republican Dick Spanbauer of Oshkosh tried to show their IDs to police, were turned away, and ended up climbing through a window together. Some Democrats later joked that it was the lone bipartisan act of the day, but getting briefly shut out wasn't funny to Spanbauer, who saw something sacred in lawmakers' work representing the people. Spanbauer was a born-again Christian, a former volunteer assistant to a prison chaplain, and head usher at his church, and he was prepared to vote a second time against Walker's bill. As he walked the statehouse halls, he was deeply disturbed by the division on display. Looking at the protesters and Walker supporters, the show of police force, and the bitter air of conflict, he said later that he saw "the devil in physical form that day."

"I had tears in my eyes. . . . That was a very, very, very black day for everybody, for both sides, for the Capitol," said Spanbauer, who later decided to end nearly four decades of service as a local and state official rather than run for re-election.

That same morning, Barca set off three months of intense legal wrangling by filing a complaint with the Democratic Dane County district attorney, Ismael Ozanne. Three other opponents to the bill filed similar complaints that day. Barca's complaint made the same argument that he had made to the conference committee—that lawmakers had to give twenty-four hours' notice before convening the committee under the open meetings law. The meetings law says government bodies can meet with two hours' notice in emergencies, but Barca said there was no emergency in this case and, anyway, less than two hours' notice had been given. He also pointed to the fact that the chamber was locked at the time of the meeting, making it impossible for most people to attend. Republicans shot back that the Legislature was in special session at the time and that Senate rules allowed them to hold meetings with little notice as long as they posted them on a bulletin board outside the chamber. In short, Republicans and Chief Clerk Rob Marchant argued the lawmakers had followed legislative rules and that those rules trumped the open meetings law—a policy noted in the meetings law itself. The district attorney now had to decide whether to formally allege in court that Republicans had violated the open meetings law.

The Assembly's 11 a.m. start time was pushed back, and state troopers marched into the occupied antechamber. Chief Riseling ordered the foyer cleared so the lawmakers could meet, and Lieutenant Brad Altman of the State Patrol was sent to handle the removal of the protesters. Altman ordered some troopers into riot gear; they were then positioned in a stairwell near the Assembly where they could be used if needed, though they never were. Altman told his captain about his order but not Riseling, who didn't know until much later that officers had donned what they called their "hard gear." If she had known, she might have descended to the Assembly from her command post to check out the situation for herself and overruled the order—at the least she would have kept the troopers off the stairway, where their presence provoked both concern and defiance from some protesters before the officers were quickly moved out of sight again. "Just the sight of them raises tensions," Riseling said later. Barca saw the riot police in the stairwell near his office and said later he would never forget it. "That was a very imposing sight. That was one that had me worried," he said.

The troopers not in riot gear led demonstrators individually out of the narrow antechamber as the crowd chanted, "Shame!" and one protester yelled, "You're helping to bust unions!" About a dozen demonstrators sat down and locked arms as Charles Tubbs crouched down and in soft tones asked them to leave to avoid arrest. One of the women watching the encounter sobbed, wiping her eyes with a tissue as her shoulders shook. "Chief Tubbs, I respect your position, but we gotta do what we gotta do," one of the sitting protesters said. The troopers moved in. One put his hands under a protester's armpits, lifted him, and hauled him out of the antechamber as his heels dragged on

the marble floor. "Union forever!" he shouted. The troopers removed protesters one by one as observers recorded the scene with their smartphones.

At 11:30 a.m., three entrances to the Capitol were opened. Jeff Fitzgerald
told Democrats he would allow about two hours of debate, and a little after
12:30 p.m. the Assembly came to order. Representative Michelle Litjens went
to the podium to deliver a prayer but she was repeatedly interrupted by Barca
and the Democrats shouting to get the attention of Speaker Pro Tem Bill
Kramer. The Democrats had wanted Jesse Jackson to deliver a prayer, which,
after Litjens's words and a brief hesitation by Republicans, Jackson was
allowed to do. He took to the dais, asked Republicans and Democrats to join
hands, and then prayed for unity. That moment didn't last, and soon Barca
called for Fitzgerald's removal as speaker because of the way the conference
committee was handled. "Your Speaker's judgment is impaired," he repeatedly told lawmakers as he ticked off his complaints against Fitzgerald for violations of Assembly rules and state law. "Our democracy is out of control in
Wisconsin. You all know it. You can feel it."

Fitzgerald stood to respond to Barca. He stated that he saw the attempt to
remove him as a delay tactic and scoffed at the notion that Republicans had
trampled on the legislative process, saying the Assembly's earlier debate was
the longest in the state's history. Assembly Republicans had campaigned on
fixing the state's finances once and for all without gimmicks, and they were
now delivering on that promise, he said. "This is a pretty big political move for
us as well, and it's a gamble," he said, pressing his fingers against his chest.
"But you know what? We feel it's the right thing to do to get this state on
the right track. We feel it. As passionate as you are about this argument, we
are on this side as well, that this is the right move for Wisconsin, that we are
going to solve the deficit by cutting spending and not raising taxes."

Fitzgerald said he had security concerns, suggesting that that issue had
warranted the limits he was putting on the debate. He read from an e-mail
he and other Republicans received the night before. "This is how it's going to
happen: I as well as many others know where you and your family live, it's a
matter of public records," Fitzgerald read. "We have all planned to assult [sic]
you by arriving at your house and putting a nice little bullet in your head."

A twenty-six-year-old woman from Cross Plains with a history of mental
problems but no criminal record later pleaded guilty to making the threat.
Both Democrats and Republicans had received death threats in those weeks,
with some coming from out of state. Most were found by police to carry little
risk and no violence occurred, but a few threats led to arrests.

A number of Democrats made the case for removing Fitzgerald as speaker, including Mark Pocan, a savvy Madison representative who the following year would win a run for Congress. He said he felt like he was living in a third-world nation that he dubbed Fitzwalkerstan. The phrase took off, immediately becoming a trending topic on Twitter. Supporters embraced the idea across the web, deeming the state beverage to be "Koch" and the state bird a "cuckoo," and designing a state flag that replaced Wisconsin's traditional miner and sailor with a pair of cartoon tycoons from the game Monopoly. The Fitzgeralds embraced the dig, and aides to Scott Fitzgerald later hung in his office a T-shirt with a map of Fitzwalkerstan and cities such as "Milwalker" and "Prairie du Fitz."

The Assembly then voted fifty-seven to thirty-seven to reject stripping Fitzgerald of his post. Within three hours, Republicans forced a vote on the bill itself. It passed fifty-three to forty-two, with Republicans Dick Spanbauer, Dean Kaufert, Lee Nerison, and Travis Tranel again joining all Democrats in opposing it. The Democrats stood and raised their hands in opposition to the abrupt vote. Barca pulled a megaphone from under his desk. "Mr. Speaker, I demand to be recognized," he called out, but Republicans ignored him. The galleries exploded with chants of "Shame! Shame! Shame!" and the Republicans silently filed into the speaker's office, where law enforcement met them to escort them from the building.

As the Republicans left, the Democrats joined the protesters in denouncing them, pointing at them as they called "Shame!" After the vote, Barca continued to talk through his megaphone. "We think this vote will not stand," he said. "We believe it violates the law." Several hundred protesters stayed in the Capitol after it closed that evening. Chief Tubbs pleaded with them to leave. "All I'm asking you to do, from the bottom of my heart, is leave cooperatively," he said. Within thirty minutes, dozens of them had. Then, police walked one man out of the building and carried two women away. No one was arrested.

At 9:30 the next morning, Friday, March 11, Walker signed the bill in private and rescinded the layoff notices that had been sent to 1,500 state workers. That afternoon, with members of his cabinet and four lawmakers at his side, he held a ceremonial signing in the governor's conference room before a crowd of reporters and photographers. When he was done, he handed a pen he'd used to sign the bill to Scott Fitzgerald and shook his hand as camera

lights flashed. "For us, we're doing this to lead the way in our own state, to get Wisconsin working again," Walker told the crowd. "But if along the way we help lead a movement across the state to pass true fiscal reform, true budgetary reform, to ultimately inspire others across this country, state by state, and in our federal government . . . I think that's a good thing and a thing we're willing to accept as part of our legacy."

That same day, Kathleen Falk—the acting Dane County executive who would seek to challenge Walker in a recall race a year later—went to court seeking a temporary restraining order to prevent the law from being published. She and other county officials argued that the conference committee had violated the open meetings law in passing it and that the bill still contained enough fiscal elements to require a three-fifths quorum. Amy Smith, the Dane County circuit judge who heard their arguments that day, declined to issue the restraining order, saying they had not shown that the county and its workers would suffer irreparable harm if the bill were published.

Walker's office quickly delivered the signed bill to Secretary of State Doug La Follette, a Democrat who had served in that position for all but four years since 1975. A quirky figure often seen walking the streets of Madison wearing a wide-brimmed hat, La Follette had held onto his low-profile job in part because of his famous last name. (His great-grandfather was the brother of Fighting Bob La Follette.) Wisconsin's secretary of state has few duties but is responsible for designating a date for publishing laws and notifying the public of them in the official state newspaper, the *Wisconsin State Journal*, within ten business days of the governor signing them. Walker aides asked La Follette to publish the notice about the new law right away, but La Follette decided to wait the full ten days because of the controversy over the legislation and the legal questions over how it was passed. Under his plan, the law would appear in the newspaper on March 25 and take effect the next day. La Follette said that was both prudent and routine, but Republicans said that it would give local unions time to reach labor contracts that would exempt them from the new law for two years or more.

With the bill passed, labor unions scheduled a rally—their biggest yet—for Saturday, March 12, to welcome back the Senate Democrats as they returned from Illinois. According to an official estimate, about 85,000 gathered on the muddy Capitol lawn and the surrounding streets on a windy, cloudy day. Susan Riseling, the chief of the UW–Madison police, estimated the crowd outside the statehouse at 125,000. Farmers opposed to Walker brought tractors to the demonstration and circled the Capitol before the main rally. One of them posted above a manure spreader a sign that read "Walker's bill belongs here." The rallies weren't just in Madison, though. That night in tiny Washburn on the shore of Lake Superior, some two thousand protesters gathered outside a Lincoln Day fund-raiser where Walker appeared. At a Republican Party event featuring Walker the next day in Howard near Green Bay, thousands again showed up to express their opposition. In Madison the crowd passed around recall petitions for Republican senators and took down the names of those who wanted to sign petitions against Walker in the fall when he became eligible for recall. The demonstrators—many of them wearing T-shirts with the number fourteen stamped across an image of the state—hailed the Democratic senators as the Fabulous Fourteen. They cheered as the Madison firefighters' bagpipe troupe led the senators to the stage. "This is not the end," Senator Fred Risser told the crowd. "This is the beginning of phase two."

Many of the Democrats reveled in the reception. "There were people with tears in their eyes welcoming us back because of the powerful emotions that had been aroused by this assault on basic fairness in Wisconsin," Mark Miller said later. "People wanted to express their appreciation for the role that we played in that. It's like nothing I've ever been part of before." Tim Cullen felt differently as he walked with his fellow senators through the demonstrators to the podium on the Capitol steps. "It was an amazing experience. . . . It was an amazing walk to take," Cullen said. "But as I am looking at these people, they really don't know how close we were to actually—not fixing the bill, but making it a lot less horrendous than it is today."

Within days, Cullen tried to reach across party lines by proposing an amendment to the state constitution that would prevent lawmakers from leaving the state to halt action on bills. The proposal helped ease Republicans' fears that Democrats would again leave Wisconsin to prevent adoption of the state budget, but the proposal was never adopted. Some of Cullen's fellow Democrats immediately rejected it, seeing it as an implicit criticism of their departure to Illinois or a further sign that he was too willing to give in to Republicans. The Democrats' reception at the rally enraged Scott Fitzgerald, though. Just before the event, he issued a statement saying the Democrats were "going to pretend they're heroes for taking a three-week vacation. . . . Their appearance at the Capitol today . . . proves their absolute disregard for the institution of the Senate and the constitution they took an oath of office to serve." The end of his statement addressed the Democrats directly. "When you smile for the cameras today and pretend you're heroes, I hope you look at that beautiful Capitol building you insulted," it said. "And I hope you're embarrassed to call yourselves senators."

Still angry two days later, Fitzgerald told his caucus that Democrats could attend committee meetings but not vote in them because they had been found in contempt of the Senate. But a day after that, under pressure from Ellis, Fitzgerald backed off. The two leaders held a news conference to announce they would not enforce the contempt finding, the hundred-dollar fines on Democrats for missing sessions, or any of the other punitive provisions passed while the Democrats were in Illinois. "The name of the game is moving this state forward, putting this stuff behind us," Ellis said. "We have serious problems facing this state and this is our good-faith effort to say, 'Let's get on with the people's business. Let's stop all the bickering.'"

Relationships in the Senate, however, would remain in tatters as recall elections moved forward against lawmakers from both sides, and the legal challenges to Walker's legislation were launched. The case brought by Falk, the acting Dane County executive, faltered over the coming weeks, but that Wednesday, March 16, the Dane County district attorney filed his suit over the conference committee meeting. His suit named the four Republicans on the committee and La Follette, who was included to block publication of the law. Ozanne was seeking ultimately to void the measure and fine the Republicans on the committee three hundred dollars each for knowingly violating the open meetings law. He argued they broke that law by giving too little notice for the meeting and by holding it in a room with limited public access. That lawsuit landed with Maryann Sumi, a trial court judge who would soon deliver an explosive ruling in the case.

17

Rebukes and Recount

JUDGE MARYANN SUMI, A RED SHIRT poking out from beneath the neckline of her black robes, took her seat at the bench. Although Sumi is short, her raised seat gave her both height and authority. As she spoke to the lawyers in her courtroom, she occasionally glanced down at her notes and a book of statutes. She slipped on a pair of reading glasses when she did so, taking them off again when she looked up to address the courtroom. After hearing a little more than an hour of arguments from the attorneys, she was ready to issue her first judgment on the way lawmakers had passed the collective bargaining law. At this initial hearing she was to determine whether Ismael Ozanne, the relatively new district attorney, was likely to succeed with his argument that lawmakers had violated the open meetings law. Ozanne, a stocky lawyer who went by "Ish," had received four verified complaints about the conference committee action and passage of Walker's legislation, and had acted on them quickly. He had expected his office to be drawn into the events at the Capitol two blocks up South Hamilton Street—what he called "the stuff on the hill"—but he was still surprised by the degree. "I don't think anyone expected it to unfold the way it unfolded," he said later.

None of the Republican lawmakers appeared in the courtroom, and that was a calculated decision. The state constitution provides lawmakers immunity from civil suit during the legislative session, and the state Department of Justice quickly invoked that clause in its defense of their actions. Early on in the hearing, Assistant Attorney General Steven Kilpatrick asked to stop the proceeding because of that immunity, but Sumi ruled that the case could continue because Doug La Follette, the Democratic secretary of state, had also been named in the lawsuit.

Issuing her ruling, Sumi found that Ozanne was likely to prevail in the case and granted a temporary restraining order barring La Follette from publishing the official notice of the law that would allow it to take effect. The ruling stunned some. Sumi had said at the beginning of the hearing that she wanted to listen to arguments from the attorneys before determining whether she needed to take testimony from witnesses. Now, after a ten-minute break, she was reading from a written order. The judge said the Department of Justice had not pointed to any legislative rule that would supersede the notice requirements of the open meetings law. Justice Department lawyers also failed to give a reason that would allow lawmakers to meet with two hours' notice, rather than the usual twenty-four hours, she said. She noted that some might view the failure to provide appropriate notice as something that was not significant enough to stop the law from going into effect. "And my answer to that is, it's not minor," Sumi said. "It's not a minor detail. . . . We are entitled by law to free and open access to governmental meetings, and especially governmental meetings that lead to the resolution of very highly conflicted and controversial matters. That's our right. And a violation of that right is tantamount to a violation of what is already provided in the [state] constitution—open doors, open access, and nothing in this government happens in secret."

She stated that she was not weighing in on the merits of the collective bargaining law and reminded the attorneys that lawmakers could restore the law whenever they wanted by simply meeting again with the proper notice and passing the measure anew. As soon as Sumi issued her ruling, Department of Justice officials signaled they would appeal. "The reason they have appellate courts is because circuit court judges make errors, and they have in this case," said Steven Means, the executive assistant to the attorney general who had also represented the state in the lawsuit over access to the Capitol.

Sumi had served as an assistant attorney general and had held a top position at the state Department of Natural Resources before she was appointed to the bench in 1998 by GOP Governor Tommy Thompson. Once she issued her ruling on the open meetings law, she was quickly vilified by conservatives and received scores of letters and e-mails criticizing the decision, with some suggesting she deserved imprisonment or even death for it. Bloggers accused her of bias and cast about for ways to prove it, lighting on the fact that her son had once worked for the Service Employees International Union and the AFL-CIO. Sumi took the rare step for a judge of issuing a statement about the matter. "My kids are adult, they are independent, and they lead their own lives," the statement read. "I do not consult my family about my decisions."

On Monday, March 21, the first business day after Sumi issued her order, the state appealed. The Department of Justice argued that Sumi could not prevent a bill from becoming law and that she had the power to strike down Walker's legislation only after it was published and took effect. The argument rested in part on a 1943 Wisconsin Supreme Court decision in a case in which Governor Walter Goodland sued Secretary of State Fred Zimmerman. Goodland had vetoed a bill creating the State Bar of Wisconsin, but the Legislature overrode his veto. Goodland argued that lawmakers had not followed the dictates of the state constitution and sued Zimmerman to prevent him from publishing the law. The Supreme Court ruled that it could not block a bill's publication because setting the laws of the state was the purview of the Legislature alone. "If a court can intervene and prohibit the publication of an act, the court determines what shall be law and not the Legislature," the justices wrote. "If the court does that, it does not in terms legislate but it invades the constitutional power of the Legislature to declare what shall become law. This it may not do."

The Department of Justice also argued that Sumi's order should be vacated because legislators were immune from lawsuit during the session and because of a 1983 decision that said that laws could be struck down only if lawmakers violated the state constitution in passing them, rather than violating state statutes or legislative rules. While the Department of Justice had cited two cases to bolster its position, two other cases helped Ozanne's side. In 1976 the Supreme Court ruled that a different version of the open meetings law then in effect did apply to the Legislature. And in 2009 the Supreme Court—consisting of the same seven justices now on the bench—found the high court could review the Legislature's internal procedures as it interpreted the state constitution in a lawsuit over access to public records.

Three days later, on March 24, the appeals court passed on making its own ruling in Ozanne's case and asked the Supreme Court to take up the case because of conflicting past decisions. The next day, a Friday, Scott Fitzgerald asked to talk with Stephen Miller, chief of the nonpartisan Legislative Reference Bureau. The meeting was arranged so hastily that it wasn't until after it started that Miller learned that Fitzgerald wanted to talk about publishing the law on collective bargaining. Under state law, the secretary of state must publish notices of laws in the *Wisconsin State Journal* within ten business days of the governor signing them. Separately, the Reference Bureau is required to publish the law, which consists of posting it on its website and making printed copies of it available to the public. In short, the secretary of state identifies the date the law is to be printed in the newspaper and published by the Reference Bureau.

Before Sumi issued her initial ruling, Doug La Follette had told the Reference Bureau to publish the collective bargaining law on March 25, the last possible day it could be published under the ten-day limit in the law. When Sumi issued her first decision, on March 18, La Follette sent a letter to the Reference Bureau rescinding his order that the law be published on March 25. He also canceled plans for a notice about the law to be published in the *State Journal*.

Sumi's order named only La Follette, however, not the Reference Bureau. In the meeting with Stephen Miller, Fitzgerald contended that the Reference Bureau was still required to publish the law within ten days, and at the meeting he urged Miller to call Deputy Attorney General Kevin St. John, the top aide to Van Hollen, about whether to publish the law. Miller called St. John, who argued that the Reference Bureau had a duty to publish the law and risked a lawsuit if it didn't.

In twelve years heading his well-respected, nonpartisan agency, Miller had never before published a law without the secretary of state designating a date to do so. In fact, the Reference Bureau had already decided it would not publish it because of the court order. But after meeting on March 25 with Fitzgerald and reviewing the law, officials at the Reference Bureau changed course and published the measure by posting it on the Web and distributing copies of it. Fitzgerald "is our boss, so a request from him would be at the level of insisting," Cathlene Hanaman, the bureau's chief deputy, explained days later in court. The official copy of the act included a footnote explaining the restraining order, but Fitzgerald and the Department of Justice argued the law would now go into effect the next day. "It's published," Fitzgerald declared. "It's law. That's what I contend."

Both the bureau's director and La Follette believed, however, that the law would not go into effect until the secretary of state acted. The Legislative Council, the nonpartisan agency providing legal advice to lawmakers, issued a memo that day agreeing that the law wouldn't yet go into effect. The Department of Justice backed up Fitzgerald's reading of the law, but few independent legal authorities appeared to do so. Republicans had a strong case for overturning Judge Sumi's decision on appeal, but rather than waiting for a higher court ruling, they had sought to make a controversial end run around the judge.

Walker's administration secretary, Mike Huebsch, issued a statement that he would "carry out the law as required" now that the Reference Bureau had published it. Ozanne sought a new temporary restraining order, saying the bill had yet to become law. He released a statement that he was surprised by the Reference Bureau's action and the news that it had been sought by Fitzgerald, who was named as a defendant in the lawsuit. On Sunday, March 27, Huebsch said his Department of Administration had taken steps to charge employees more for their insurance and pensions and stop collecting dues on behalf of unions starting with paychecks that would be issued in less than a month. Van Hollen asked to withdraw his appeal of the Sumi decision because the Reference Bureau had published the law, but the appeals court said it did not have the power to do so because it had already certified the matter to the Supreme Court.

Days after Van Hollen first appealed Sumi's ruling, Ozanne amended his complaint to argue lawmakers had violated the state constitution, not just the open meetings law. The constitution says "the doors of each house shall be kept open except when the public welfare shall require secrecy," and Ozanne argued that lawmakers had failed to follow that mandate. In amending the complaint, he also listed the Assembly and Senate as defendants, specifically naming the minority leaders, ostensibly because they served on the conference committee. More important, Peter Barca and Mark Miller were willing to waive their immunity from lawsuits, thus helping Ozanne keep his case alive. After five hours of testimony on March 29, Sumi reminded the attorneys of her earlier order. Her arms crossed, she reread the part of her March 18 order restraining carrying out the collective bargaining law. Ignoring the order could lead to court sanctions, she said. "Apparently that language was either misunderstood or ignored, but what I said was the further implementation of Act 10 was enjoined," she said, pointing at her new written order. "That's what I now want to make crystal clear."

She reminded the litigants that lawmakers could simply pass the law again if they wanted. "I am dismayed at this point given the relative easy fix for this that thousands and thousands of dollars are being spent," she said, raising her finger, "all being footed by the taxpayers of this state to pursue this litigation."

Republicans were dumbfounded. The Legislative Reference Bureau and the Walker administration were not parties to the case, but now the court's orders were being extended to them. The brief written order did not say whether the law had been put into effect by the Reference Bureau's action, but in an impromptu news conference outside the courtroom, Steven Means of the Department of Justice insisted that it was. "It's our position and the position of those who control state government that we believe the law has been published and is in effect," he said. Barca listened to Means from off to one side and then spoke to reporters himself. "It's just startling that the attorney general believes you should not follow court orders anymore," Barca said. Republicans were scathing in their response to Sumi's latest order. "It's disappointing that a Dane County judge wants to keep interjecting herself into the legislative process with no regard to the state constitution," read a statement issued by Jeff Fitzgerald. "Her action today again flies in the face of the separation of powers between the three branches of government."

Two days later, on March 31, Sumi issued a written ruling that was now explicit in saying the law had not been published and, thus, was not in effect. From the moment Sumi issued her first order, the case appeared certain to go to the Supreme Court, and the April 5 election for a seat on that panel was fast approaching. Sumi herself had considered running for the Supreme Court that spring against Justice David Prosser but decided against it because her seat on the circuit court was also up for election that year. Collective bargaining had shaken up the once-quiet contest between Prosser and his challenger, JoAnne Kloppenburg. Signs for Kloppenburg—until then a little-known assistant attorney general who handled environmental cases—began popping up at Capitol rallies, and demonstrators passed out flyers urging people to vote for her. They referred to Prosser, a former Republican Assembly speaker and district attorney, as a proxy for Walker, noting that earlier in the race Prosser's campaign manager announced—in a statement Prosser hadn't approved—that the justice would serve as a "complement" to the governor. The surging anti-Walker sentiment emerging in the state at the moment gave Kloppenburg a chance to win, an opportunity that the political novice otherwise wouldn't have had.

"There are a lot of very angry people out there," Prosser said just before the election. "They are very easily mobilized, and if you can get them to focus their anger on a particular target, namely me, my tenure on the Supreme Court may be very brief."

Kloppenburg insisted that people were supporting her simply because they perceived her as impartial, but some of her supporters had a different take. "The makeup of the Supreme Court is currently four-three in favor of antiunion justices," said a letter from the union that represented teachers at Milwaukee Area Technical College. "A Kloppenburg victory would swing the balance to our side. A vote for Prosser is a vote for Walker. It's time to get even. Vote Kloppenburg on April 5."

The race was the first chance voters had to express their views at the ballot box on Walker's legislation. The court would decide the fate of that law, but the election results weren't likely to affect the ruling because the winner's ten-year term on the court wouldn't begin until August. On election day, turnout hit 34 percent of the voting-age population—a huge increase over the usual voting rate in Supreme Court races. That night, returns showed a freakishly tight race.

Shortly after 1 a.m., Kloppenburg greeted a small crowd that had been watching results at Madison's Edgewater Hotel. She announced that the Associated Press had told her the race was too close to call because a few precincts had not yet reported their results. "It's not over and we are still hopeful," she said. At the Seven Seas restaurant in suburban Milwaukee, Prosser's campaign manager, Brian Nemoir, said a recount appeared inevitable. He said he'd been through ten or so local recounts, but nothing like the one that was about to unfold on a statewide basis. "There's no playbook for this," he said.

The next day, the Associated Press reported its unofficial tally of the votes—740,090 for Kloppenburg and 739,886 for Prosser. That put the challenger and political novice ahead by 204 votes, or 0.014 percent. Both campaigns were preparing for a recount, but Kloppenburg seized on her edge to claim victory. "Wisconsin voters have spoken and I am grateful for, and humbled by, their confidence and trust," she said in a statement.

Then came the "Brookfield bombshell." On April 7, Waukesha County Clerk Kathy Nickolaus went before the television cameras at a hastily called press conference to say that due to a computer error she hadn't included 14,315 votes from Brookfield in the tally she'd given to the media on election night. Waukesha County is a conservative stronghold, and Prosser had won a lopsided victory in Brookfield. Once those votes were counted, he had a lead of 7,582 statewide. That meant the race was still close—less than half a percentage point—but Kloppenburg was now almost certain to lose. Republicans celebrated and Democrats questioned whether the election had been stolen.

Given the unusual events, state officials conducted an investigation of the uncounted votes. They found the clerk hadn't complied with election laws but had not actually committed a crime because the error appeared to have been accidental. Nickolaus's sloppy performance frustrated Republicans as well as Democrats, and county officials tried to limit her role in running future elections. Nickolaus resisted calls for her to resign but did not seek re-election in 2012. Meanwhile, Kloppenburg also requested what was only the third statewide recount in Wisconsin history, following ones in 1858 and 1989. When it was completed a month later, Prosser was declared the winner by 7,006 votes. But there was still more controversy to come for the Supreme Court over Walker's law—and Prosser would be a key figure in it.

18

A Court Divided

B Y THE TIME SCOTT WALKER ARRIVED before a congressional committee on April 14, he needed no introduction to its members or the country. During his short tenure as governor, Walker had become a national figure, both loved and loathed. Now he had a chance to make his case to the nation before the U.S. House Oversight and Government Reform Committee as the panel explored the debt facing state and local governments. Walker continued to draw support from conservatives around the country—in just two days, former GOP vice presidential nominee Sarah Palin would rally supporters on the lawn of the Wisconsin Capitol—but it was one of Wisconsin's own that introduced Walker to the committee. Congressman F. James Sensenbrenner Jr. told members that Walker had a Republican pedigree but still managed to win election three times as the leader of one of the country's most Democratic counties. "His political success has been based upon the fact that he tells people where he stands and once elected implements that," Sensenbrenner said. He noted that Walker had come to national prominence only recently, but argued those who knew him best were not surprised by his changes on collective bargaining. "He's a very polarizing figure, but those of us who love him in Wisconsin really thank him for the job that he's done," the congressman continued.

Also appearing at the hearing was Peter Shumlin, the Democratic Vermont governor. After their introductions, Walker and Shumlin were sworn in, shook hands, and sat down. Walker ran down Wisconsin's budget problems and noted most other states were dealing with their fiscal woes with mass layoffs or major tax hikes. "In Wisconsin, we have a different option, a progressive—

in the best sense of the word—a progressive option," he said, jabbing liberals who saw his proposal as a betrayal of the state's Progressive history. "For us, we're giving state and local governments the tools they need not just to balance the budget this year or for the next two years, but for generations to come."

Walker concentrated his opening comments on making public employees pay more for their benefits, rather than limiting collective bargaining. The Vermont governor also stressed the difficult economic times facing all states and highlighted the need to work together. He handed a small bottle of Vermont maple syrup to Walker, who smiled broadly and held it aloft to a smattering of applause. Shumlin said that he had negotiated pay cuts and higher retirement ages for workers "without taking on the basic right of collective bargaining." "We get more with maple syrup than we do with vinegar," Shumlin said.

Walker advocated a different tack. "I believe more important than working together is that people want results," he said. In his written testimony, he went even farther, saying, "Sometimes, bipartisanship is not so good." Members of the committee spent the next two and a half hours peppering the governors with questions. The Republicans praised Walker, thanking him for making tough choices. The Democrats grilled him. Congressman Dennis Kucinich of Ohio questioned how requiring unions to hold annual recertification votes would save the state money. Walker conceded there were no savings but said he wanted to "give the workers the right to choose." Bruce Braley, an Iowa Democrat, noted that Walker's campaign had focused on bringing people together. "I think if Dr. Phil were here, he'd say, 'How's that working for you?'" he said. Walker said that he believed he had brought people together by getting bipartisan votes on earlier legislation. Braley cut him off, and Walker responded, "If you want to do a political stunt, go ahead."

Virginia Democrat Gerald Connolly asked Walker why he did not highlight his ideas for collective bargaining in his run for governor. Walker acknowledged he was not explicit about his ideas on the issue in the campaign. "I didn't run an ad saying I'm going to do exactly this," he said. But he also stated that people should not have been taken aback by his actions given his campaign themes and his actions as county executive.

"So from your point of view, nobody should have been surprised?" Connolly asked.

"That's correct, 100 percent correct," said Walker.

In the back of the crowded room, the young Fitchburg lawyer Jenni Dye stood and watched the exchanges. She was in Washington as part of a previously scheduled visit for a Wisconsin delegation of the American Bar Association. Because Dye was active in the association, she had had her expenses paid to come lobby the state's U.S. senators and representatives on legal issues. On break, she walked to the hearing room to catch part of Walker's testimony to the committee. There, she had the bizarre feeling that the controversy in Wisconsin was following her across the country. She listened as the legislators gave Walker and Shumlin easy questions or tough ones, depending on whether the governor was in their party. She wasn't impressed. It seemed to her that the members of the committee were more interested in getting a sound bite for the news than in solving states' problems. "This is not what people want," she thought to herself.

After watching for perhaps twenty minutes and sending off a couple of tweets, Dye headed to her next meeting. In the previous weeks, she had begun to think that there could be more to being a citizen than just demonstrating. If elected leaders weren't living up to her standards, she thought, maybe she had an obligation to do more to change that. She tweeted that she was thinking about running for public office and got encouragement from her many Twitter followers, including from a family friend who was on the Dane County Board. The board was a good fit for Dye because it was possible to run as a relative newcomer to politics and because the veteran supervisor representing her area was more conservative than Dye—someone she wanted to see replaced. With the help of the friend, Dye landed a meeting with the liberal County Board chairman, Scott McDonell, to talk about a run. McDonell had been watching out for candidates like Dye. "We were looking for people energized by the protests who wanted to run," he said.

McDonell wanted Dye to run in an easier, adjacent district where she wouldn't face a veteran incumbent. But she planned to campaign in the tougher district, and McDonell and others saw that she got training. Dye started focusing on local issues where she felt she could make the most difference.

She still found some time for state politics, showing up at the Capitol to demonstrate against the bill requiring voters to show photo identification at the polls. Republicans said the bill would cut down on voter fraud. The concept received relatively strong support from voters in public opinion surveys, although there was no evidence of widespread fraud that the bill would specifically address. Like many Democrats, Dye believed the bill would end up preventing some students, senior citizens, and minorities from voting. On May 11, 2011, the day of the Assembly vote on the bill, she was disheartened to see that relatively few demonstrators showed up to oppose it. The bill passed easily, sixty to thirty-five, and as on other occasions at the Capitol that year, Dye ended up sitting down and crying, this time at the King Street entrance.

The protests inside and outside the Capitol had grown much quieter since they peaked in the spring. In the weeks after Walker's union legislation was signed, many of the governor's opponents had shifted from trying to stop the proposal to trying to recall some of the Republican senators who had voted for it. A few demonstrators still continued to show up regularly. The Solidarity Sing Along participants, for instance, still belted out their protest music at noon in the rotunda. In the days before the Legislature's budget deliberations, the demonstrators also built a small tent city, which they once again called Walkerville, across the street from the Capitol, a precursor to the Occupy Wall Street encampments that would soon spring up around the country. Dye, who had helped create the original Walkerville sleep-in on the square in late February and early March, came back for the second round of political camping and stayed three different nights.

In the coming months, Dye had a first-hand chance to compare the Wisconsin demonstrations to the Occupy protests on the East Coast. In the first week of October 2011 she and a friend traveled by train to New York to visit Zuccotti Park, the site of the Occupy Wall Street encampment. She had been deeply moved by the support that the Wisconsin protests had received from around the country, and she wanted to return that favor. The pair of friends stayed at a hotel and spent time in the park, and on October 5 they marched with thousands of union members from Foley Square to the encampment. The two continued on to visit the Occupy Boston demonstration in that city, and Dye also participated in an Occupy Milwaukee event later that month. She was struck by both the similarities and differences that she found between the Occupy demonstrations and the ones in Madison. Both sets of events were motivated by the feeling that the wealthy and corporations had hijacked the political process. Both sought measures that the demonstrators felt would return power to ordinary people. But whereas the Madison demonstrations had a laser focus—killing Walker's union legislation—the goals of the Occupy Wall Street movement were amorphous. In Zuccotti Park, Dye didn't feel the same sense of single purpose she felt in the protests in Madison. "I didn't get that sense of community that I felt in Wisconsin that we were all heading in the same direction," Dye recalled later.

But during the labor unions' march to the park and later at Occupy Boston, she did feel that same unity and kinship. The day of the march in New York, she wore a Wisconsin T-shirt and received thanks and congratulations from many demonstrators who said they had been inspired by the Madison protests. To Dye, it appeared as if more of the Occupy Wall Street protesters had been inspired by the Arab Spring uprisings than by those in Wisconsin, but the protests in Madison seemed to her to have been the moment in which that energy of democratic dissent had first taken hold in her own country. She noticed one other major difference. In Madison, the demonstrations had been free from any violent confrontations with police, and in fact the protesters generally had a strong relationship with the police.

During the late spring and early summer, a small group of demonstrators in Madison began to rack up several arrests or more apiece, introducing a different feel to some of the protests. Sometimes they were cited for innocuous behavior, like holding up signs or filming the proceedings in the Assembly gallery while lawmakers were in session. A long-standing rule prohibited signs being displayed in the gallery, though Republicans weren't shy about changing another long-standing rule to allow concealed firearms to be carried into the viewing area. Protesters sometimes harangued Republican lawmakers in hallways and committee hearings to an extent that even Democrats and union members occasionally objected to the tactics. One protester, twenty-two-year-old Jeremy Ryan, tooled around the building on a Segway taunting lawmakers and journalists and toting handmade signs, including one that provided Administration Secretary Mike Huebsch's cell phone number and urged people to call him. One of the most notorious and disheveled protesters, William Gruber, was dubbed "Bad Babies" by reporters because of his frequent rants in which he referred to union backers as "good babies" and Walker and Republicans as "bad babies." He gave his most memorable monologue when he grabbed a microphone during a break at a Joint Finance Committee meeting in early June. "Walker sucks," he said in a raspy baritone. "Bad babies are going to hell right quick. Good babies are taking hold. Worldwide baby union. All good babies are in. Bad babies go to hell forever. And now is the time and good babies know. The good babies make us safe. The good babies put out the fires. The good babies take care of you when you're ill. The good babies are hooked up and not faking any more. That's right. We're not going to take it. Sorry. Sorry, babies." Gruber ended the tirade as someone moved him away from the microphone he was using.

During a late-night debate on the photo identification bill, Gruber got past security and stormed onto the Senate floor shouting "No!" and had to be escorted away by Democratic senators. On a different occasion, another demonstrator, Miles Kristan, confronted Randy Hopper, one of the Republican senators targeted for recall, as they crossed paths in a Capitol stairwell. Seizing on reports that the senator had been engaged in an affair, Kristan asked for the telephone number of Hopper's "girlfriend," saying he believed she would welcome his advances. Demonstrators like Ryan and Kristan said that civil disobedience was the only tool left to oppose what they saw as a harmful GOP agenda and that there was generally no basis for their citations. Ozanne, the district attorney, stated later that such tactics departed from the restraint shown by the early, massive crowds. "The energy changed," he said of the group of young protesters who were repeatedly arrested. "There was a shift in some of those people and the actions they took."

On September 14 Kristan approached Representative Robin Vos and two of his Republican colleagues in the bar at the Inn on the Park. "You're not going to get away with this," Kristan said and then poured a beer on Vos's head, splattering the two other GOP lawmakers as well. Kristan later pleaded no contest to a misdemeanor disorderly conduct charge. Early on, many of the charges of criminal and ordinance violations against habitual demonstrators like Kristan were dropped by Ozanne. As of August 2012 Ryan had only two convictions so far out of thirty-five separate charges and citations. Outraged, Republicans sharply criticized the Democratic prosecutor. Ozanne responded that many of the charges wouldn't have held up in court.

On December 1, 2011, the Walker administration sought to control the protests with an enforcement plan that could hold demonstrators at the Capitol liable for the cost of extra police or cleanup and repairs after protests. The policy stated that groups of four or more people inside the Capitol and groups of one hundred outside normally had to obtain permits for all demonstrations and displays, and needed to apply for those permits at least seventy-two hours in advance. The rules drew immediate criticism and threats of lawsuits from civil liberties groups and received national attention in the news media. In many respects, they weren't unusual, however; all but a handful of states around the country either prohibit protests inside their capitols or require a permit to hold a small demonstration. The Walker administration bowed to the pressure for a time, first tweaking the rules and then declining to enforce them. The Solidarity Sing Along group never applied for a permit or missed a single lunch-hour performance. The administration didn't crack down on the protesters until after the recall and the resignation of Charles Tubbs, who was replaced as Capitol Police chief by David Erwin, a former state trooper and Marine who had overseen security for Walker and before him Democrat Jim Doyle. In September 2012 the administration started enforcing the permit requirement and citing the leaders of the sing-along when they declined to get one. The administration also installed hundreds of wireless panic buttons around the Capitol, as many as several to a single office, at a cost of $103,000. Protesters said they would fight for what they saw as their free-speech rights, and the daily standoff continued. As of November 2012 more than 275 citations had been issued by the Capitol Police following the signing of Act 10 on March 11, 2011, compared to fewer than 30 written during the four weeks of massive protests prior to that.

Meanwhile, the John Doe investigation into Walker's aides and associates crept forward. The first charges of the probe were filed in April 2011 against William Gardner, the chief executive officer of the Wisconsin & Southern Railroad Company, for illegal campaign donations. Gardner the same day pleaded guilty to two felonies—one for exceeding campaign contribution limits, the other for passing personal and company money onto associates so they could donate nearly $53,000 to Walker, as well as lesser amounts to other politicians. Gardner was later sentenced to two years of probation. The railroad company, which for years had relied on millions of dollars in state grants and loans to stay afloat, also paid a civil forfeiture of nearly $167,000, the largest ever imposed by Wisconsin election officials.

The sideline investigation of Gardner seemed to create few worries for Walker, but other aspects of the John Doe probe did. Prosecutors had been gathering ever larger amounts of evidence from raids on county offices, Walker's campaign headquarters, and the homes of his associates. They were getting more testimony, too. Three days after the Gardner charges, on April 14, 2011, Walker's official spokesman, Cullen Werwie, was quietly granted immunity in another aspect of the investigation. Werwie had been the campaign manager for Brett Davis, the state representative who lost the 2010 GOP primary for lieutenant governor. He worked closely with Davis's fund-raiser Kelly Rindfleisch, who was later found guilty of doing extensive campaign work out of Walker's county office while drawing a paycheck from taxpayers. Walker stayed publicly neutral in the four-way primary for lieutenant governor, but those involved in Walker's campaign privately helped Davis. After Davis lost the primary, Werwie joined Walker's campaign, and then later his administration as press secretary. His immunity deal, however, didn't become public until September 2011. In spite of the blinding spotlight on Walker, the John Doe probe remained largely in the shadows.

The legal challenges to Act 10 got much more attention. On April 7, the same day of the surprise release of vote totals putting Justice David Prosser ahead in the Supreme Court race, the Walker administration petitioned the high court to review Judge Sumi's decisions in the case. The filing said the justices should stay proceedings in the Dane County court and vacate Sumi's rulings. Republicans had been taken aback by Sumi's series of decisions, and now they saw a chance to get the case before a court that was more amenable to their point of view. "I was always very, very, very comfortable with where we were legally, guardedly optimistic that things will go smoothly through the court system," Attorney General J.B. Van Hollen said months after the case concluded. "I don't think I'm ever shocked by what judges do anymore. I don't believe there was enough of a legal issue for this to go very far, but not surprised that we did have to take it to the point we did." In early May the high court scheduled oral arguments for June 6, and on May 26 Sumi issued her final order, a thirty-three-page ruling that voided the collective bargaining law because she found that lawmakers had violated the meetings law. Sumi's decision said judges have an obligation to issue rulings even if they are seen as "controversial or unpopular." She noted the state constitution's requirement that the doors of the Legislature remain open during session, and said lawmakers had incorporated those constitutional provisions expressly into the open meetings law. "The Legislature and its committees are bound to comply with the open meetings law by their own choice," she wrote. "Having made that choice, they cannot now shield themselves from the provisions that give the law force and effect." Her decision surprised Republicans because they did not expect Sumi to take any more actions now that the Supreme Court was contemplating taking the case.

Walker and Republicans in the Legislature said they were now focusing on the Supreme Court. If their efforts there failed, they would include the collective bargaining changes in the state budget they planned to adopt by the end of June. Ozanne called Sumi's decision a victory for the moment but acknowledged the case's fate now rested with the Supreme Court. "It's not over yet. I'm positive of that," he told a reporter. "The Supremes are the Supremes. They can do what they want."

The court was deeply divided—not just ideologically but also personally. In the minority were Chief Justice Shirley Abrahamson and Justice Ann Walsh Bradley, the court's liberals. Justice N. Patrick Crooks often ruled with the majority in criminal cases, but he aligned with the liberals on many civil cases and on the issues that most bitterly split the court. The conservatives held the majority and were led by Patience Roggensack, who one well-connected lawyer called the court's de facto chief justice. The other conservatives were Prosser, Michael Gableman, and Annette Ziegler. The divisions on the court had been exacerbated by increasingly expensive campaigns that saw an outpouring of special-interest money from both sides. Over the previous three years, the court disciplined one of its own members for the first time in its history and had come close to punishing another one. The high court reprimanded Ziegler in 2008 for ruling as a Washington County judge on loan default cases involving a bank where her husband was a director. Next, the court—without Gableman's participation—deadlocked three to three in 2010 on whether Gableman violated the ethics code with a misleading 2008 ad against his opponent, then-Justice Louis Butler.

But it was Prosser who had some of the most contentious interactions with his colleagues on the court. His opponents said he had an explosive temper, while he and his allies claimed he was frequently goaded by Abrahamson and Bradley. More than a decade earlier, Prosser had aligned himself with Chief Justice Abrahamson as Crooks and three other justices tried to take power away from the chief justice. In an argument over the issue, Prosser called Crooks a viper, stormed out of the room, and slammed the door behind him. Crooks said such blowups happened a couple of times a year, though Prosser said that was overstated. In February 2010 Prosser grew angry at Abrahamson as the justices discussed whether Gableman had to recuse himself from criminal cases. Prosser called the chief justice a "total bitch" and said he would "destroy her," adding "It won't be a ground war." He explained later that what he'd meant was that if the chief justice tried to destroy him, he would do the same to her, by which he was saying that he would try to damage her politically—not physically attack her. The exchange prompted Crooks and Bradley to meet with the director of state courts and the court's human resources director in an attempt to get Prosser to address what they considered his abusive behavior. They were told little could be done because Prosser was an elected official. The "bitch" incident came to light in a *Journal Sentinel* article less than three weeks before Prosser's April 2011 election. Prosser offered no evidence that Bradley was involved in the leaking of that story, but he viewed Bradley's decision to speak to a reporter for that article as an attempt to damage him politically. Prosser's public comments about the chief justice during his campaign raised concerns for Bradley, and she discussed them with the court marshal. The marshal in turn spoke with the Capitol Police and then provided Bradley and Abrahamson with all of Capitol Police Chief Charles Tubbs's phone numbers.

The pressure from the legal challenge to Walker's legislation overwhelmed the last vestiges of civility on the court. The June 6 oral arguments highlighted the stakes involved. Arguments before the court usually last about an hour, but in this case they went on for five and a half hours—making them the longest in memory.

"Hear ye, hear ye, hear ye," the court marshal called as everyone in the packed hearing room stood. "The Supreme Court of Wisconsin is now in session. Your silence is commanded." The seven justices filed into the hearing room, four from the left, three from the right. The chief justice made her way to the middle of the long, mahogany bench and sat in her oversized leather chair. The other justices—the most junior ones on either end—lined up alongside her. Above the justices was an expansive mural depicting the signing of the U.S. Constitution. The other walls each displayed an equally large painting concerning the law—of the signing of the Magna Carta, of Augustus Caesar hearing the trial of a soldier, and of the 1830 murder trial of Chief Oshkosh of the Menominee Indians. The large, marble-lined room had poor acoustics, so the crowd maintained utter silence.

During the arguments, Roggensack peered at Ozanne over the glasses perched halfway down the bridge of her nose and made clear where she stood on the case. Ozanne argued that the legislators had to follow joint legislative rules because the conference committee consisted of lawmakers from both houses. The senators had relied on a Senate rule, rather than a joint rule, in determining whether they had to give twenty-four hours' notice for the meeting. Roggensack questioned why it mattered what rule they used, given that the Legislature was a separate branch of government that could chart its own course for its proceedings. "Why do we look further, if that's the rule they relied on?" she asked. "Why should we be looking at something else? There clearly is a rule under the statutes that says you don't have to give notice if you've got a body rule. And a finding of fact [from the lower court] says, hey, that's what they relied on. Now, you can say they relied wrongly on that rule, but that's questioning their own application of their own rules. . . . If we're going to say, hey, if they relied on their own rules"—she shrugged and spread her arms— "that's the end of the story, unless there's a constitutional violation."

The increasingly anxious GOP lawmakers called on the justices in public comments to rule before the Legislature took up the two-year budget bill even though the court normally takes weeks or months to render decisions. To the Republicans, no immediate decision was almost as bad as a ruling against them. They needed to ensure the collective bargaining changes—and the requirement that public workers pay more for benefits—were in place before they cut aid to local governments and schools. If the court didn't provide a ruling in their favor, they would have to amend the budget to include the collective bargaining changes. Assembly Speaker Jeff Fitzgerald said so explicitly on Monday, June 13, and drew prominent coverage from the news media. Privately, many Republicans acknowledged they were not looking forward to voting on the union measure again because it could bring back thousands of protesters and nonstop floor debate.

The justices had agreed among themselves on Friday, June 10, to complete their decision that Monday, June 13. When the day arrived, the minority justices were surprised to learn Prosser was writing an extensive concurrence to go along with the short per curiam order prepared by Roggensack. The three dissenting justices considered themselves to be rushing to respond to Prosser's concurrence in their opinion, while the four majority justices detected nothing but more delay. The situation was all the more frustrating for the conservatives because of their long-standing belief that Abrahamson used her position as chief justice to manipulate court processes to her advantage. By the time Jeff Fitzgerald said the Legislature might take up collective bargaining anew, the majority justices were agitated.

The four gathered in Roggensack's office to discuss what to do. Gableman, Roggensack, and Ziegler wanted the group to go over to the court clerk's office across the street from the Capitol and force staff to release the opinion, but Prosser rejected the idea. The group decided instead that the court should issue a statement saying the decision would be released the following day. Around 6 p.m., Prosser and the others went to see Abrahamson and found her in Bradley's chambers, a suite of three rooms. They entered the first of those, where Bradley's secretary worked, and gathered near the entryway to Bradley's personal office. Bradley was at her desk reading a draft of the dissent, with Abrahamson sitting across from her. The chief justice walked over to the others near the threshold, and Ziegler told her the majority wanted to issue a press release saying the decision would come out the next day. Abrahamson said that wasn't possible; the court staff had already gone home for the day, and, anyway, she did not know when the final version of the decision would be ready. Bradley, still sitting at her desk, put in that they needed more time because they hadn't known Prosser was writing a separate opinion. Prosser, his voice rising, responded that he had worked all weekend without the help of a clerk, and Bradley told him she wouldn't put up with yelling. He quieted. Abrahamson said she would circulate the dissent the next day and asked Prosser whether he could guarantee he would not want to make changes to his concurrence to respond. "I expect you to call me a fascist pig, but I will not revise," he said, according to one account.

Bradley remained at her desk reading the draft opinion for a time, but then came over to Abrahamson. She and the chief justice were on one side of the threshold, with the conservatives on the other. Bradley asked why the others saw the need for a press release and discounted talk by pundits about when the decision would come out. "We work on court time, not the Legislature's time," she said. Roggensack said the majority justices had expected to issue the decision that day and a press release would serve as a consolation prize for them. Prosser told Abrahamson she was holding up the case and that he had lost confidence in her leadership. Bradley, who had long been seen by other justices as protective of the chief, had grown increasingly intolerant of Prosser's behavior when he was angry. Now she just wanted him out of her office, and she moved quickly toward Prosser, who was perhaps five feet away. She locked eyes with him and deliberately got in his face, much like a coach gets in a player's face, she said later.

Here, the accounts of the justices—told to detectives two weeks later—diverge most sharply. Prosser, Roggensack, and Gableman said Bradley charged Prosser with her fist raised; Roggensack and Gableman said they believed that she was going to hit him. Bradley and Abrahamson said Bradley's fist was not raised, but that she pointed to the door as she told Prosser to leave. Ziegler could not recall where Bradley's hands were during the incident.

Neither justice was large—Bradley was five foot three and Prosser was five foot nine—but they were now face to face about a foot apart. "Buddy, get out of my office," Bradley remembered saying. Prosser, in what he later called a reflex, raised his hands and put them around Bradley's neck. He felt its warmth and thought, "Oh my God, I'm touching her neck." Bradley felt no pain or pressure, but Prosser's action struck her as eerie and she cried out in shock for him to never put his hands on her. Roggensack inserted herself between the two justices and separated them. "Ann, this isn't like you," she said several times. Roggensack said Bradley had charged at Prosser, and Bradley responded, "I didn't touch him at all." Prosser felt limp at the realization that his hands had been on Bradley's neck, and he and Gableman quickly left the suite. Bradley returned to her computer and started typing up notes about what had happened. Ziegler and Roggensack resumed discussing with Abrahamson the need for a press release but soon left. That night, Bradley spoke with Justice Crooks by phone and left messages for Charles Tubbs, the Capitol Police chief, as well as the Supreme Court marshal. She tried to continue to work on the dissent but left the office about two hours later.

Just before 5 p.m. the next day—Tuesday, June 14—the court issued its opinion, which came just in time to save GOP lawmakers from having to vote again on Walker's bill. In a four-to-three decision, the court upheld Act 10, voided Sumi's decision, and opened the way for the law to be published and put into effect. The short main opinion said Sumi's court "exceeded its jurisdiction, invaded the Legislature's constitutional powers . . . and erred in enjoining the publication and further implementation of the Act." Lawmakers had not violated the state constitution because the Legislature remained open to the press and at least some members of the public, the decision said, noting the proceeding was broadcast live by the public affairs network WisconsinEye. The Legislature determines how it operates and the Supreme Court would not second guess it here, the decision said.

The majority opinion was brief, but Prosser's lengthy concurrence expounded on the majority's rationale. He stressed that the public knew about the meeting and what was happening in it and included in his concurrence a photocopy of the *Wisconsin State Journal*'s front page coverage of the meeting that bore the headline "CAPITOL SHOCKER." Prosser's opinion said the court would abdicate its responsibility if it delayed making a decision while waiting for the "perfect appeal." As it turned out, Prosser was the one who determined that the law had not yet taken effect and would not take force until the secretary of state acted. The other conservatives had wanted to go farther and say that the law had already been published and taken effect, but Prosser wouldn't go along with them.

In her sharp dissent, Chief Justice Abrahamson said the majority opinion amounted to naked partisanship and opened the court to accusations that the majority had "reached a predetermined conclusion not based on the facts and the law, which undermines the majority's ultimate decision." The conservatives "make their own findings of fact, mischaracterize the parties' arguments, misinterpret statutes, minimize (if not eliminate) Wisconsin constitutional guarantees, and misstate case law, appearing to silently overrule case law dating back to at least 1891," she wrote. Her opinion, joined by Bradley and Crooks, was labeled as a partial concurrence and a partial dissent, but there was almost nothing in it that agreed with the majority.

Abrahamson also took issue with the way the court had accepted the case, saying that the justices should have allowed it to rise to the court through an ordinary appeal rather than weighing in before that process had played itself out. "Faced with no record, they conjure their own facts," she wrote of the majority justices. In a separate dissent, Crooks focused on those procedural issues. "Those who would rush to judgment on these matters are essentially taking the position that getting this opinion out is more important than doing it right and getting it right," he wrote. The case had become a "procedural morass" in which the justices did not have the complete record of the proceedings, and as a result, the majority's conclusions were "based on facts that either conflict with or are not found in the limited record before this court," he wrote. Abrahamson and Bradley also signed onto his dissent.

Republicans praised the Supreme Court decision and savaged Sumi. "You think of all the chaos and discord and acrimony that's gone on in this Capitol as the result of her decision and just doing what she wanted, which she had no cause, no basis, no rule of law," said Senator Alberta Darling, one of the nine senators facing recall in the months ahead. "She just did what she wanted for political reasons. To me, it was despicable." Barca said Democrats would try, over the course of coming years, to amend the state constitution to make legislators subject to the open meetings law. "The majority of the Supreme Court is essentially saying that the Legislature is above the law. It's now clear that unless the constitution is amended, the Legislature is free to ignore any laws on the books," said a statement he issued. Democrats, stuck in the minority, made no progress on changing the constitution during the rest of the legislative session.

The day the opinion was released, Bradley sent an e-mail to all the justices saying she had arranged for the Capitol Police chief to meet with them at 8:30 a.m. the next day. At the meeting, Tubbs told the justices that he would not take notes because they would become public record. He stressed that a man could not place his hands on a woman's neck in the workplace and asked the justices to commit to avoiding any abuse. Bradley told the other justices her husband wanted her to seek a restraining order against Prosser but that she instead wanted the court to deal with the issue internally and asked for Prosser to seek counseling. Roggensack agreed harassment could not be tolerated but also said, "You, Ann, went berserk. He wasn't putting pressure on your neck." Roggensack said she did not believe the court could order counseling, and, if it could, she believed Bradley also needed it. "Stop enabling him," Bradley responded. Abrahamson at one point tried to reconstruct the incident, approaching Tubbs with her hands outstretched as if she were Prosser and he were Bradley. In her own description, Bradley said Prosser had put her in a chokehold, and Roggensack responded that she hadn't been choked. "That's because you stopped him," Bradley responded. Roggensack said she had stopped Bradley from hitting Prosser. Tubbs again sought agreements from everyone that there would be no threats or violence in the workplace. "Not all of the facts are out and no judgment should be made," Justice Gableman told him.

Bradley viewed the meeting as a failure, and by the end of the following week she began to see a police investigation as inevitable and told Tubbs she was no longer refraining from having him investigate. Tubbs soon turned the matter over to Dave Mahoney, the Democratic sheriff of Dane County. Sheriff's investigators turned their findings over to Ismael Ozanne, the same district attorney who had brought the open meetings case that the justices were arguing about at the time of the altercation. To avoid a conflict of interest, Ozanne had a Dane County judge appoint a special prosecutor to handle the case. The job went to Patricia Barrett, the district attorney in neighboring Sauk County. A Republican planning to retire in a little more than a year, Barrett had long favored making district attorneys nonpartisan because she did not believe politics should play a role in their jobs.

Ten days after receiving the case, on August 25, Barrett determined that charges were not warranted for either Prosser or Bradley and declined further comment. That didn't end the matter, though. Shortly after the incident, Chief Justice Shirley Abrahamson discussed it with the Wisconsin Judicial Commission, which enforces the code of conduct for state judges, and in March 2012 the commission filed ethics allegations with the Supreme Court against Prosser. The commission accused the justice of violating provisions of the ethics code that say judges must be "patient, dignified, and courteous" to those involved in the court system; that judges must cooperate with one another; and that judges should maintain high standards of conduct to ensure the integrity of the judiciary. The case was to be reviewed by a special panel of three appeals court judges, but only Prosser's colleagues on the Supreme Court could impose discipline. Prosser asked all the justices to recuse themselves because of their involvement in the matter. Roggensack, Gableman, and Ziegler all withdrew from the case, and Prosser said he was not participating, as is standard for justices when their own disciplinary cases are pending. At least four justices are needed for the court to take most actions, and Prosser argued the recusals ended the case. The commission disagreed and said the special panel should be formed to hear the matter. Before all the conservatives removed themselves from the case, Crooks announced he was staying on it because he was not present during the altercation and because of a legal rule that allows judges to remain on cases they would normally have to step aside from if doing so meant the case would go unheard. Eight months after the allegations were filed, Abrahamson and Bradley had yet to say whether they would participate in the case, and the matter remained open at the time of this book's writing.

The legal battle over Act 10 also continued. Ozanne asked the Supreme Court in December 2011 to reconsider the case after learning one of the law firms working on the case for the state, Michael Best & Friedrich, had not charged Justice Gableman for the two years of work it did on his ethics case. Ozanne said that meant Gableman could not ethically hear the case and that the court should take it up anew. Gableman said he would not step aside, and in July 2012 the court determined it would not rehear the case. More significantly, a federal judge in Madison found in a case brought by seven unions that parts of Act 10 violated the equal-protection clause of the U.S. Constitution. District Judge William M. Conley in March 2012 enjoined the sections of the law that required the unions to recertify annually and that barred the state from deducting wages from the paychecks of employees who chose to be in unions. He found that there was no good reason for the majority of public workers to be treated differently than police and firefighters in those two ways. He kept in place, however, the major elements of the law. The unions argued the equal-protection clause also meant general employees could not be barred from negotiating anything but wages while public-safety workers still have full-scale bargaining. But Conley said the state had sufficiently argued that it could provide more collective bargaining powers to the public-safety workers because it wanted to avoid disrupting core government services through work stoppages. Five months later, a different set of unions had much better success with similar arguments before a Dane County judge who struck down significant aspects of the law for school and municipal workers. Both the state and federal cases were appealed, and it was clear a final ruling on collective bargaining in Wisconsin could take months or years to resolve. In June 2011, though, these decisions dealing new blows to Act 10 were months away and only distant hopes for the unions. For the moment, opponents of the law were increasingly focused on a different way to reverse it: efforts to recall state officials began at a level unmatched in the nation's history.

19

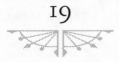

Recalls

RICHELLE ZIMMERMAN'S LEFT HAND gripped the blue plastic tub as she and another recall volunteer marched down East Washington Avenue, each carrying half the load. A throng of supporters cheered them on as they neared the offices of the state Government Accountability Board. Zimmerman raised her right fist in the air, then headed inside the elections agency. There, more backers greeted her, along with a line of television cameras. She and her colleague heaved the tub of some three thousand petition pages onto the counter and handed over a form declaring that they had gathered enough signatures to recall Republican Senator Dan Kapanke of La Crosse. Zimmerman and her cohorts had had sixty days to gather the 15,588 signatures called for by a formula written into state law. But they collected far more than that—22,561—in half the time allowed.

Zimmerman had taken time off that morning from her job as a La Crosse County social worker so she could deliver a speech and see the petitions sent off to Madison. At the last moment, someone asked her to come along to personally hand in the petitions to the Accountability Board. She explained the situation to her boss and asked for additional time off, nervous that he wouldn't allow it. To her surprise, he asked if there was still time to sign a petition, signed one, and gave her the time off. Zimmerman had spent the previous weeks immersed in the recall, often spending her lunch hour with two others collecting signatures along the roadside. Her involvement was no surprise. She was active in the La Crosse County Democratic Party and held strong views on social justice shaped by her Catholic upbringing. Her father had been a union steward at the post office, and he assisted her with Kapanke's recall.

A union member herself, Zimmerman was horrorstruck by the Republicans' move against collective bargaining, and driven to tears at one point by a radio ad that she believed vilified civil servants. She felt conservatives were unfairly making her out to be a public enemy. "I get paid twenty-two dollars an hour to go into crack houses. There's nothing luxurious about my life," she said. She went to the protests in Madison a half dozen times, as well as to local rallies. When the recall effort against Kapanke began she didn't know if it would succeed, but she welcomed the chance to throw herself into it. "It was some place we could put our energy in," she said.

Kapanke was a popular senator, but his grip on his increasingly Democratic district was tenuous. Though the senator had hung onto his seat in 2008, Barack Obama had captured 61 percent of the vote in Kapanke's western Wisconsin district that year. Of all the Republican senators now facing the threat of recall, he was the most vulnerable, and that fact was highlighted by the ability of recall organizers to turn in signatures against him before any other senator. At this point, Democratic Representative Jennifer Shilling was emerging as a likely challenger to Kapanke. Democratic leaders in past election cycles had twice tried to recruit her to run for the Senate, but she had rejected the idea, in part because she had been able to work closely with Kapanke on some issues, and she found that constituents loved the notion of a Democrat and Republican collaborating. She felt, however, that Kapanke had taken a rightward turn with his unsuccessful 2010 run for Congress, and the night of the collective bargaining vote in the Senate she knew the recall would happen. "I think at that moment I knew I was going to do it," she said more than a year later. "History found me. I was not looking to run for the Senate."

As Zimmerman marched into the Accountability Board office, the enormity of what she and others were doing sank in. Observers knew the petitions were just the first of many. Signatures were being gathered in efforts to recall sixteen senators from both parties—every member of the Senate who was eligible at the time. A conservative Utah group with a national focus on recalls filed papers against seven Democrats. Separately, homegrown operations started up against some of those Democrats, sometimes more than one, meaning that some Democrats had multiple petition drives going against them at once. The efforts against the Republicans were better controlled, with all of them started the same day with the help of the state Democratic Party. By that spring, petitions would be turned in to recall six Republicans and three Democrats, triggering the biggest wave of recalls against state lawmakers in

the nation's history. At the time Wisconsin's recalls were launched, just thirteen state lawmakers from around the country had ever been removed by
recall. No other state in history had seen so many legislative recall attempts
at once, and no such battles had ever included simultaneous efforts to recall
both Democrats and Republicans over the same issue. And never before had
attempts to recall state lawmakers taken on such national dimensions, with
powerful interests outside the state investing so heavily in the outcome.

Wisconsin was one of nineteen states that allowed recalls of elected officials,
and one of just five that had actually removed lawmakers using that process.
In 1926 Wisconsin citizens narrowly voted to amend the state constitution to
allow recalls, but the first successful one against a lawmaker didn't happen
until seventy years later, in 1996, when George Petak, a Republican senator
from Racine, was removed for switching his position and voting for a local
sales tax to pay for a stadium for the Milwaukee Brewers. Then in 2003 Democratic Senator Gary George of Milwaukee was ousted, just a month before
he was indicted for accepting kickbacks. Enough petitions had been filed to
force recalls against Wisconsin lawmakers on just two other occasions, and
both attempts had failed. In 1932 Senator Otto Mueller faced recall for breaking with his fellow Republicans, and in 1990 Representative Jim Holperin,
a Northwoods Democrat, faced a recall election because he did not oppose a
federal court ruling on spear fishing rights for Ojibwe tribes as strongly as
his political foes wanted. After surviving the recall, Holperin was elected to
two more full terms before leaving office in 1995. He went on to serve as
state tourism secretary for four years and rejoined the Legislature after being
elected to the Senate in 2008. In 2011 he became the only state lawmaker in
the country's history to twice face (and survive) a recall election.

Holperin saw few parallels between his two rounds of recalls because the
issues prompting them were so different. He held a focus group during the
1990 recall and quickly concluded that his constituents did not support re-
calling him over a federal issue over which he had almost no control. During
the 2011 recall, his advisers conducted another focus group, but nine months
after the election he still hadn't watched video of it. The briefing of it was
sufficient for him to get the message. "They came in and said, 'You're in trouble, buddy,'" Holperin remembered. He believed he ended up winning in
large part because Republicans selected a flawed candidate immersed in Tea
Party politics.

In the first days of the protests in February 2011, homemade signs demanding Walker's recall popped up, and recall chants became increasingly common.

Under Wisconsin's constitution, officials can be recalled only after serving a year of their terms, so Walker could not be targeted right away. Unlike some other states like Ohio, Wisconsin also had no method of challenging a new law directly through a voter referendum. Thus, protesters and union officials turned their anger on senators last elected in 2008—the only Republicans immediately eligible for recall. But in 2011 it was the Republicans who first filed recall paperwork against Democrats, in an effort to draw them back to the state.

The stakes in the elections were high. Wisconsin's past legislative recalls had been over unique issues and aimed at specific lawmakers. Now, many lawmakers from both parties were facing recalls for their stances on the same bill, and control of the Senate hung in the balance. Republicans wanted to keep their power over all of state government, and Walker's opponents wanted to gain a majority in the Senate to repudiate the governor's early agenda and give them veto power over the rest of it. Democrats had only fourteen seats to the Republicans' nineteen and needed to net three seats from the recalls to take the Senate.

To force a recall election against each senator, organizers had sixty days to gather signatures equal to 25 percent of the total votes cast for governor in that senator's district. That requirement had normally been an almost un-achievable burden, but not now. Inflamed passions, the power of social net-works, outsized fund-raising, and a seemingly endless base of volunteers gave both sides an unprecedented ability to gather signatures. In the weeks after the Kapanke signatures were submitted, petitions against other senators rolled in. They easily surpassed the required minimums. The Government Accountability Board—created in 2007 in reaction to the caucus scandal that saw five lawmakers charged for using state offices and state staff to cam-paign—now had the unenviable job of reviewing those signatures. The new board, which combined the state's ethics and elections boards, was meant to be both aggressive and fair. To ensure this, the Accountability Board was run by six former judges. The agency had wide support in the beginning—every Republican member of the Legislature voted to create it—but as the recalls mounted in 2011, GOP officials angrily accused the agency of helping Democrats. In turn, Democrats said the agency took too long to review recall petitions, making plain that the Accountability Board pleased no one.

The sheer number of signatures filed proved a challenge for the Account-ability Board. The task was made even greater by the fact that the thousands of signatures arrived in the midst of the Supreme Court recount—the first statewide recount in the better part of a generation. Under state law, the board had thirty-one days to determine whether each election should take place, but the agency asked for and received an extension from a Dane County judge because of the scale of the work. The Accountability Board wanted to rule on all petitions at the same time to make sure the elections occurred on the same date, but the judge told them they had to make rulings as soon as they were able because of the state constitution's guarantee of holding recalls if enough signatures were submitted. The Accountability Board had first received petitions against five Republicans, then against three Democrats, and then against a sixth Republican. Republicans believed the board should deal with the petitions in that order, but instead the board took up all the petitions against the Republicans first because the challenges to them dealt with questions of law that were relatively easy to resolve. The petitions against the Democrats drew challenges that alleged fraud and raised factual questions that took longer to answer. On June 3 the board ordered that elections be held for the Republicans, and a week later, on June 10, it ordered that elections be held for the Democrats. Republicans howled over the board's approach because it meant the recall elections would be held a week apart—with the Republicans facing recall one Tuesday, and the Democrats facing recall the following Tuesday.

Convinced that they needed more time to campaign, Republicans took advantage of a clause in the state constitution to delay their recall elections. The constitution requires a recall to be held six weeks after election officials determine enough signatures have been filed. But if more than one member of any party runs, that election becomes a primary, with the general election following four weeks later. So the Republicans set to work to ensure there were primaries by recruiting their own supporters to run as Democrats. Now it was the Democrats' turn to be outraged. Holding the unnecessary primaries cost taxpayers $475,000 on top of the already sizable $2.1 million cost of holding the recall elections.

While primaries in the recall elections for Republicans were held because of the fake Democrats, true primary contests were expected in the recalls where Democrats were targeted. One didn't materialize when Republicans embarrassed themselves by failing to gather enough valid signatures to get their preferred candidate on the ballot. The developments created a confusing set of election dates: on July 12 there were the six primaries featuring the fake Democrats; on July 19 there was a general election in the Green Bay area between a Democratic incumbent and a flawed Republican challenger with a criminal record; on that same day, two more primaries were held to choose the Republicans who would take on the other two Democratic incumbents. Then on August 9 the six Republican incumbents faced their general recall elections, with the two remaining Democrats facing their general recall elections a week later, on August 16. With the national implications clear, outside groups from both sides poured previously unseen amounts of money into the legislative races, and total spending reached an estimated $44 million. The spending was more than double the money spent on the 116 legislative seats that were up in 2010. The biggest spender was We Are Wisconsin, a coalition of unions that threw $10.7 million into this round of recalls. Second place went to the Wisconsin chapter of the conservative Club for Growth, which spent an estimated $9 million. In spite of their homegrown names, these groups took significant money from out of state. We Are Wisconsin sounded local, but it had sister groups such as We Are Ohio and We Are One Illinois, all of which received considerable sums from national labor unions. We Are Wisconsin, for instance, received more than 90 percent of its money in 2011 from national unions. The Wisconsin Club for Growth didn't disclose the money it took as readily as We Are Wisconsin, but two donations to the group that were disclosed came from out-of-state corporate interests: $250,000 from Trevor Rees-Jones, the wealthy founder of the Texas firm Chief Oil & Gas, and $150,000 from the international asset management and securities firm Citadel. The Club for Growth also took $1 million from an offshoot of the state Realtors association, according to the Wisconsin Center for Investigative Journalism.

The spending climbed so high that six of the nine recall races topped the previous record of $3 million spent on a Wisconsin Senate race. The unsuccessful recall attempt against Senator Alberta Darling alone cost the campaigns and outside groups an estimated $7.9 million. A quirk in state law helped drive the extra spending. Normally, the most someone can give to a state senator is $1,000, but that limit is lifted for costs incurred from the time recall petitions are first circulated until state officials decide whether recall elections should be held. This unlimited fund-raising is open only to incumbents, not their challengers. That provision in state law was added in the 1987 state budget through a unanimous and, by definition, bipartisan vote on the budget committee, and it was made at a time when Gary George and another state senator had recently had to mount court challenges to stave off recall attempts. That had left George with $60,000 in legal debts, and the law was written in such a way to give him the opportunity to use unlimited contributions to pay off those debts. This maneuvering didn't ultimately save George from the successful recall in 2003, but it helped Republicans in 2011 and 2012. Darling, the co-chairwoman of the Legislature's budget committee, took in $30,000 from one donor, or thirty times the normal limit, as well as several other five-figure donations. Those contributions foreshadowed the unprecedented sums that Walker would be able to raise eight months later.

Ironically, the recall campaigns included little discussion of collective bargaining, the issue that gave rise to them. Democrats focused on issues with wider traditional resonance for voters, such as Walker's cuts to education and health care. Republicans were no more eager to broach the subject of their controversial action, talking instead more generally of their efforts to hold down taxes and spending. The recall efforts took on the tint of ordinary, albeit unusually expensive and slick, campaigns. Voters were engaged, turning up in numbers well above normal elections that lacked a strong top-of-the-ticket race like that of governor or president. When the contests were over, Democrats came up just short of their goal of gaining three seats. They netted two, narrowing the Republican advantage in the Senate to seventeen to the Democrats' sixteen seats. Democrats didn't lose any of their own seats, but they beat only the most vulnerable GOP incumbents—Kapanke and Senator Randy Hopper of Empire. Hopper, whose district was packed with state correctional officers, had received unwanted attention because his estranged wife said the forty-five-year-old senator had started an affair the year before with a twenty-six-year-old and was now living in Madison instead of the Fond du Lac area he represented.

Although they fell short of their goal, Democrats picked up enough seats to block parts of Walker's remaining agenda. For instance, the Senate would later reject legislation sought by the governor to ease mining regulations when they were joined by Dale Schultz, the one Republican senator who had voted against Act 10. But so far they weren't even close to restoring unions to their former place. Already, Act 10 was sapping the strength of labor groups. Just before the elections, the state stopped collecting union dues out of members' paychecks and forwarding them to the unions. Most significant, public employees no longer had to contribute any union dues if they chose not to belong. The unions were able to persuade some of their members to keep paying their dues, but many of the unions wouldn't disclose those numbers—a signal they didn't have a retention rate they could brag about. The changes drained the money that was the unions' lifeblood. In August, the Wisconsin Education Association Council sent layoff notices to about forty of their one hundred workers. AFSCME in Wisconsin also had to tighten its spending and not fill some vacant positions.

Unions soon lost even more than workers. The Act 10 clause requiring re-certification votes for unions to keep their official status kicked in. The standard for winning those votes was getting 51 percent of all eligible employees in unionized workplaces, whether or not the workers voted—a higher standard than elected officials ever have to meet. For large unions with workers in locations around the state, organizing such an effort would require considerable work and expense, and it would have to be done not just once but every year. If a large union lost an election, as was distinctly possible under the difficult rules, Walker could claim victory. If the unions put in the work and won, they would be able to bargain over cost-of-living salary increases but nothing else. Under those circumstances, many of the largest unions chose not to recertify. By September the major state employee unions covering tens of thousands of employees had declined to hold votes and thus lost their official status, meaning that the government no longer had to recognize them as representatives of the employees. A federal judge in March 2012 ruled the recertification procedures were unconstitutional, but the decertified unions remained unrecognized while the case was being appealed. Dane County Circuit Judge Juan Colás in September 2012 struck down even more parts of the law, but that ruling affected municipal and school workers, not state employees, and was also immediately appealed. For the moment, only six small unions for state employees were officially intact. Statewide, more than two hundred public employee unions at the local level decided to hold elections, and nearly 90 percent of them succeeded in keeping their official status. But it was a largely empty victory—the recall election against Walker was their only hope of returning to their former relevance. For that, Democrats hoped that the John Doe investigation might play a role.

On a crisp September morning just a month after the Senate recalls, a contingent of FBI agents and other law enforcement officers appeared at the Madison home of longtime Walker aide Cindy Archer. The agents removed a box of material from her home and also seized from a neighbor a computer that Archer had sold at a garage sale. Archer had served as the head of Walker's Department of Administration in Milwaukee County and helped on his campaign for governor, and after Walker was elected she became the state's deputy administration secretary. She had a reputation as a straight talker but also a fierce bureaucratic infighter with a gift for making enemies, even among people who might be expected to be allies. As deputy administration secretary, she was closely involved with planning Walker's repeal of collective bargaining, and developing response plans for expected work stoppages and protests.

Shortly before the raid, Archer had gone on leave and then been transferred to a much less important policy job in another agency. On what was to be her first day on the new job, Archer changed her leave time to medical leave, and she was still absent for that reason when the federal agents came to her door sometime before 7 a.m. on September 14, 2011. In the weeks afterward, the public also learned about the immunity granted to Walker spokesman Cullen Werwie and low-level Republican operative Rose Ann Dieck over the previous months. Suddenly, the long-ignored John Doe probe began to catch the attention of the news media. Walker said he had not known anything about the immunity deals and was not concerned about the ongoing probe. "I know that throughout my career—first in the Legislature, then as county executive, and now for the last ten months as governor—I live by the standards I got from my parents," he said then. "Certainly, they got me to the rank of Eagle Scout, and I continue to have that kind of integrity."

Around that time, in the fall of 2011, prosecutors planned to give immunity to Andrew Jensen Jr., a broker who had worked on county real estate deals. Immunity grants are the one part of John Doe proceedings that happen in open court, though they are often done quietly. Jensen asked that his immunity be granted in secret, but judges rejected that request, first in the Doe proceeding and then on appeal. On December 13, 2011, authorities arrested Jensen for declining to cooperate. The next day, prosecutors released Jensen without charges, but those following the probe now felt certain that more charges were coming—and probably soon. By April, Jensen's attorney released a statement—on Milwaukee County District Attorney John Chisholm's letterhead—that said Jensen and his firm were not targets of the Doe and would not be charged. Such a statement of exoneration, released with the permission of Chisholm and the John Doe judge, was unusual and appeared to signal that Jensen's cooperation was extensive.

There was movement in other aspects of the Doe probe as well. On January 5, 2012, prosecutors accused Tim Russell, Walker's longtime aide and former deputy chief of staff in Milwaukee, and Kevin Kavanaugh, a Walker appointee to a veterans board, of separately embezzling a total of more than $50,000 from a fund for veterans and their families. A year after taking office as Milwaukee County executive in 2002, Walker created and hosted Operation

Freedom, an event at the county zoo that provided free food and admission to veterans. In 2006 Walker turned bookkeeping duties for the event over to a veterans group and Kavanaugh, its finance officer. Prosecutors alleged that Kavanaugh, sixty-one, had embezzled $35,000 that had been designated for Operation Freedom. He was charged with five felonies for theft and fraudulent writings by a corporate officer.

By February 2009 county officials noticed some of the missing funds and turned Operation Freedom's finances over to a different veterans group, which performed its duties appropriately. In spite of that success, in October 2009 Walker again transferred the bookkeeping responsibilities—and about $19,000—this time to the Heritage Guard Preservation Society, a group run by Russell. Prosecutors charged that Russell, who had money trouble, began improperly withdrawing money from Heritage Guard just months after taking in money for Operation Freedom. He pulled out more than $10,000 from Heritage Guard for trips to the Caribbean and Hawaii and for a meeting in Atlanta in December 2010 to help launch Herman Cain's campaign for president. Altogether, he stole $21,000 from the group in 2010. Russell was also accused of skimming money from the campaign accounts of two conservative candidates for the Milwaukee County Board. In all, he was charged with two felonies and one misdemeanor for embezzlement. (In October 2009, the same month Russell's Heritage Guard took control of Operation Freedom, Russell formed a consulting firm that conducted opposition research on Walker's 2010 primary opponent, Mark Neumann; Walker's campaign manager was a client of the firm.)

On January 26, 2012, prosecutors charged two more former aides from Walker's time as county executive—Darlene Wink, his former constituent services coordinator; and Kelly Rindfleisch, another former deputy chief of staff. In a deal with prosecutors, Wink agreed to plead guilty to two misdemeanor counts and provide information about the destruction of digital evidence. The criminal complaint alleged that Wink had not just been posting online comments about Walker during her work day, as had been reported a year and a half earlier by the *Journal Sentinel*; she had also arranged fundraisers and a phone bank for Walker while on county time. Rindfleisch had started with the county in January 2010 as a policy adviser and soon after replaced Russell as deputy chief of staff. She was charged with four felony counts of misconduct in office for allegedly working on the county clock on the failed lieutenant governor campaign of state Representative Brett Davis, who went on to direct state health programs for Walker. Rindfleisch also helped Walker's campaign, exchanging more than a thousand e-mails with campaign officials during normal business hours in early 2010 using the private router set up in her office. Shortly after she took the job with the county, she told a friend in an Internet chat that "half of what I'm doing is policy for the campaign." Rindfleisch had been granted immunity by prosecutors more than a decade earlier as part of the caucus scandal, in which lawmakers from both parties had been convicted for campaigning on state time. She apparently hadn't learned from that episode. The latest charges brought the investigation much closer to Walker—some of the acts alleged in the complaints happened within yards of his county executive's office. Within weeks the governor acknowledged he had hired two high-priced defense attorneys and would be meeting with the district attorney. On March 10, 2012, he announced he had set up a legal defense fund that could accept money from his campaign, which outside election attorneys said was a tacit acknowledgment that he or his campaign was under investigation for violations of state election law.

20

Recalls Redux

BY THE EVENING OF MARCH 11, 2011—the day that Walker signed the union legislation—the United Wisconsin website had 142,200 signatures of people who said they would sign petitions to recall Scott Walker and his lieutenant governor, Rebecca Kleefisch. The wild success of the website was creating an immense amount of work, and stress, for Michael Brown. He was just a young web developer and marketer with a sometimes contrarian political outlook; now he had the responsibility of representing the views of a group nearly twice as large as the population of his home city of Appleton. He also disliked the time he had to spend away from his son, and he needed help. To get it he put out an invitation to a meeting on March 15 at the Wil-Mar Neighborhood Center on Madison's liberal east side. He got hundreds of responses, so many that he ended up limiting attendance. Scores of people packed the meeting room as Brown explained that he wanted a field presence for what had been an online-only organization. To recall the governor, opponents would have sixty days to gather 540,208 valid signatures— one-quarter of the number of voters in the 2010 governor's race. To guarantee that there were enough legal signatures, Brown was seeking to gather more than 700,000 because inevitably some signatures would be found invalid. "We want to be aggressive with this, we want to be on the ground," Brown told the group. Brown was approached after the meeting by a reporter from the *Capital Times* and found himself a little panicked by the idea of getting broader exposure. "Now it's starting," he thought to himself. "We're not ready for this yet." Brown increasingly found himself in the public eye, sometimes uncomfortably so. Twice, strangers showed up at his duplex to harass him about

starting the recall and ask him why he had done it, prompting him to threaten
to call the police.

At the meeting, Brown met four others who would become board members
of United Wisconsin by the end of the month. One of them, Kevin Straka,
soon became the chairman. Brown served as a simple board member, scaled
back his involvement, and within seven months left the group. By April 1 the
group had 176,700 pledges, but the real work was just beginning. In the
coming weeks the board and organization had to branch out, drawing in volunteers and eventually paid staff that could send mass e-mails, field media
questions, and organize the public. Board members began to establish a delicate relationship with the Democratic Party as Brown, Straka, and other political independents in the group learned to work with the partisan operatives
and union activists who were crucial to reaching their shared goal. United
Wisconsin clearly had its own profile. By the time the recall signatures were
filed early the next year, the group had 44,200 "likes" from Facebook users—
more than half again as many as the state Democratic Party's page had. When
Brown talked by phone for the first time with Mike Tate, the state Democratic
Party chairman, Tate started the conversation with a question. "How did you
do this?" he asked. Tate said later "it was pretty goddamn incredible" that
Brown had developed his database in such a short time without any significant spending or advertising. But the movement also seemed inevitable. "If
United Wisconsin hadn't hit that moment in time, . . . it would have been
somebody else," Tate said. Brown, too, knew it hadn't been him, though he
had the technical know-how and the stubborn belief that the cause was right
and the time was ripe. It was the reckless enthusiasm of Walker's opponents—captured in a historic moment—that made it happen.

Not everyone saw right away that the recall would occur. In early April,
Tate and others from the Democratic Party met with United Wisconsin and
indicated to the group that the national unions were not on board with re-
calling Walker. United Wisconsin's leaders made clear that they couldn't be
swayed. "We said, 'We're going to do this whether you like it or not,'" Lynn
Freeman, a United Wisconsin board member, remembered. "We said, 'We
are doing this. United Wisconsin will make this happen. Are you in or are
you out?'" While committed to the cause, United Wisconsin faced challenges
that political professionals would not have. The group early on sent a mass
e-mail to people who had pledged to sign recall petitions, but its database of
supporters needed to be cleaned up and so far no one had done it. United
Wisconsin's e-mail vendor quickly dropped the group because too many copies

of the message were recorded as spam. The inability to communicate with its members constrained United Wisconsin's fund-raising, and in that period the group sometimes scraped by.

That spring, Tate convened a working group separate from United Wisconsin that consisted of about a half dozen political professionals to consider the issues. The group included Tate; Maggie Brickerman, executive director of the state party; Doug Burnett, an AFSCME political organizer and lobbyist; and Paul Maslin, a Madison pollster who had worked for California Governor Gray Davis when he was recalled. State law restricts coordination between groups that run independent ads in campaigns and political parties, but Burnett was able to talk with the others about a Walker recall because at that stage the recall was theoretical. When the discussion drifted to the ongoing legislative recalls, Burnett had to leave the room because AFSCME was active in them. The group met several times to consider "any number of questions, virtually none of which we had any ability to control," Tate said. The group discussed Walker's fund-raising ability, potential Democratic opponents, when to launch the recalls, and other issues.

As the date approached when opponents could legally launch a recall against Walker, Tate's group and United Wisconsin had to decide when to start the sixty-day stopwatch for gathering signatures. They could start circulating paperwork on November 4, 2011, but some wanted to wait until the summer so they could time Walker's recall with the November 2012 election, when President Barack Obama would be on the ballot and the Democratic turnout would be at its highest. There were arguments against this because there was no way to guarantee when the recall election would be held—no one knew how much time the Accountability Board would need to count signatures, and the Republicans could easily manipulate the election schedule with legal challenges. Others feared that the opposition to Walker would wane over time. United Wisconsin agonized over the issue, having long debates as a board and in conference calls with its one hundred county coordinators. In August 2011 the group finally decided it would aim to have the recall election along with the 2012 presidential election. That same month, United Wisconsin started having monthly meetings with representatives from labor and the Democratic Party so they could coordinate their efforts. Soon, members of that larger group revisited the question of timing and concluded an earlier recall might be more effective. Tate initially supported holding the recall in November 2012 but knew that the governor's opponents couldn't be held back. He worried that an individual or poorly organized group would launch a recall attempt that would fail to get the necessary signatures. The real recall effort would still be free to start up later, but in the meantime Walker would have gotten months of unlimited fund-raising. Moving up the recall was a bitter draught for United Wisconsin's board members because doing so would take away months of their preparation time and would also mean they would have to tell their county coordinators they were reversing course just a couple of weeks after their earlier decision on a November 2012 recall. When the idea of an earlier start to the recall first came up, Straka felt nauseated—the chairman of United Wisconsin thought he might throw up or pass out. The Democrats and labor leaders were coalescing around the idea of seizing on the momentum of the moment and launching the recall immediately, but they told United Wisconsin they would abide by whatever decision its board members made. In September, United Wisconsin's board considered its options and voted three to two to start the petition drive right away. They settled on November 15—a week and a half after the first possible day. They would have to gather signatures over Thanksgiving, hunting season, Christmas, and the New Year's holiday, but they were confident they could get more than the necessary amount. In October, United Wisconsin hired an executive director and finance director and announced the start of signature gathering. Those actions improved its fund-raising tremendously—it raised more than $350,000 in the last half of 2011, the vast majority of it in the final three months of the year. Tate and others conveyed to national officials the importance of assisting the recall—even if they felt it was poor strategy—and stressed that it would happen no matter what. "This is a stampeding bull and if we don't figure this out it's going to run right over us," he told his colleagues.

That message was delivered in October at a private meeting on the south side of Madison in the once unassailable hilltop headquarters of the Wisconsin Education Association Council (WEAC), the teachers union wounded by Act 10. Jim Messina and Jennifer O'Malley Dillon, Obama's campaign manager and deputy campaign manager, respectively, attended the three-hour meeting, as did perhaps a half dozen others, including Tate; Burnett; Maslin; Dan Burkhalter, WEAC's executive director; and Brian Weeks, an assistant director in AFSCME International's political action division. They reviewed polling from the Senate recalls and discussed strategy and potential candidates, according to several participants. Messina was skeptical of the recall effort, and he warned the group that a Republican had told him Walker's side could raise $60 million to $80 million—sums that would hurt Democrats in the recall and could hurt Obama's re-election effort in a battleground state.

The eight to ten people gathered there explained the recall would happen no matter what, and by the end of the meeting Messina seemed to understand that. "The basic message to him was 'We have no way to stop this,'" one participant said. "He came to appreciate this train was leaving whether we liked it or not." Labor activists at the meeting also made clear they opposed a run by Tom Barrett, the Milwaukee mayor who had lost to Walker in 2010, despite support for him from Obama's team. The labor leaders didn't believe that he had backed labor strongly enough as mayor.

Brown and United Wisconsin also intended to recall Kleefisch, who had been elected with Walker on a joint ticket but who would have to be recalled separately. The lieutenant governor's job is largely meaningless—it has no constitutional duties—and some recall supporters did not want to burn up resources on that effort. Still, they feared that if they recalled Walker without trying to also recall Kleefisch, Republicans could argue in court that Kleefisch should ascend to the position of governor, rather than the Democrat who appeared on the ballot against Walker. As a result, they targeted Kleefisch for recall. Separately from United Wisconsin, the Democratic Party organized recalls against three freshman senators who had been swept into office during 2010's conservative wave—Pam Galloway of Wausau, Terry Moulton of Chippewa Falls, and Van Wanggaard of Racine. Lori Compas, a Fort Atkinson photographer politically awakened by Act 10, independently launched a recall effort against Scott Fitzgerald, seeking to oust a lawmaker who was safely entrenched in a solidly GOP district. At first, the party offered no help for the effort against Fitzgerald.

Just days before the Wisconsin recalls started, a vote in Ohio energized union supporters. Republicans in that state had passed a bill similar to the one in Wisconsin scaling back collective bargaining for public workers. Unlike Wisconsin, Ohio had a process allowing citizens to vote to repeal laws—and that's what they did. They submitted 915,000 valid signatures, forcing a November 2011 referendum to voters on the union measure. A convincing 61 percent of those at the polls voted to overturn the limits, dealing a setback to GOP Governor John Kasich. The vote didn't entirely stop efforts in other states to reduce unions' influence—Indiana passed its right-to-work law just three months later, and Michigan followed suit ten months after that. But the Ohio victory gave momentum to Walker's opponents, and for a time the efforts in both states slowed the progress of such legislation elsewhere.

Organizers launched the Wisconsin recalls in festive style. Around the state they held dozens of 12:01 a.m. events, some of them billed as pajama parties.

Many were out partying after that night's Green Bay Packers game and came to places like Hawk's Bar & Grill on State Street in Madison to sign the recall petitions. "It's great to be one of the first people to start the movement," UW–Madison student Amanda Lazzari told a reporter.

Walker had been preparing for the recall. In early October, his chief of staff and 2010 campaign manager, Keith Gilkes, left his post in the governor's office to return to overseeing the campaign. On the eve of the recall, Walker began his ad campaign during the Packers game. "Wisconsin's best days are yet to come," he told viewers. He and Wanggaard, one of the senators singled out for recall, announced the next day that a Racine manufacturer would add hundreds of jobs with a plant expansion. On November 15 the recall circulators were everywhere. They had filed paperwork electronically just after midnight with the Accountability Board, and then later that morning they paraded to the election agency's headquarters led by Kathleen Falk, the former Dane County executive; and Mahlon Mitchell, the president of the state firefighters' union. More than a thousand recall supporters marched outside Walker's Wauwatosa home, outraging conservatives who saw it as encroaching on the governor's private life. Some of the governor's neighbors encouraged the effort and allowed their driveways to be used to gather signatures. "Occupy Walker's Street" read one sign, a nod to the Occupy Wall Street movement that had started two months earlier.

In the weeks ahead, recall organizers sent people across the state to canvass houses and stand on street corners. They set up curbside operations so drivers could quickly sign petitions. Recall volunteers showed up at malls, at deer-registration stations during hunting season, even across the country at the stadium in Pasadena, California, when the UW Badgers played in the Rose Bowl in January. They passed out white petitions to recall Walker and yellow ones to recall Kleefisch. Recall volunteers were often greeted with waves and honks of support but also faced bitter complaints from Walker supporters. A small number of people harassed recall volunteers and tore up their petitions, which is classified as a felony under Wisconsin law. As the tensions rose, occasional death threats once again cropped up even for people only peripherally involved in the process.

While recall volunteers were on the street, Walker was on the air with more television ads urging voters not to support the recall. He had no trouble paying for the ads, thanks to his national notoriety and the provision in state law that allowed him to accept unlimited donations. In the seventeen months from the time Walker was sworn in until the recall election, he raised an

unprecedented $37.3 million, destroying past records in Wisconsin and reset-
ting the standard by which future races would be judged.

Prior to Walker, it was considered a respectable effort if a Wisconsin
governor raised a half-million dollars for his re-election campaign in six
months. Now, two donors were each giving Walker that amount. One was
Bob Perry, a Houston homebuilder who had been one of the primary backers
of the Swiftboat Veterans for Truth ads against John Kerry in the 2004 race
for president. The other was Diane Hendricks, the Beloit billionaire whose
video-recorded quizzing of Walker on right-to-work legislation was about
to take center stage in the recall campaign. Five others gave the governor a
quarter of a million dollars each—Sheldon Adelson, the casino mogul who,
along with his wife, propped up Newt Gingrich's 2012 presidential Super
PAC; Richard DeVos, the cofounder of the parent company of direct marketing firm Amway, who was active in the school voucher movement; Stanley
Herzog, the chief executive officer of a Missouri-based road and rail contractor; and David Humphreys and Sarah Atkins of Tamko Roofing Products,
another Missouri company. Liz and Dick Uihlein, founders of the shipping
supply company Uline, gave a combined $230,000. The Schuette family,
which owns Wausau Homes and helped fund Wisconsin's Tea Party movement, gave more than $175,000. Ten others gave $100,000 each, including Foster Friess, the Wyoming investor with Wisconsin roots who almost
singlehandedly funded the Super PAC supporting Rick Santorum's run for
president.

The Democrats were badly outspent in the race. The entire campaign cost
$80.9 million, with $58.7 million spent on the Republican side and $22 mil-
lion spent on the Democratic side, according to figures compiled and estimated
by the Wisconsin Democracy Campaign. (Independent candidate Hariprasad
Trivedi spent $300,000.) Walker's efforts were boosted by groups such as
Wisconsin Manufacturers & Commerce, the state's largest business lobby;
and the Republican Governors Association, which received $1 million from
the real David Koch in early 2012. "We're helping [Walker], as we should.
We've gotten pretty good at this over the years," Koch told the *Palm Beach
Post* in February 2012. "We've spent a lot of money in Wisconsin. We're
going to spend more." Spending on the Democratic side later ramped up, but
Walker's unprecedented fund-raising meant that he and his allies were able
to easily outspend the Democrats in this latest round of recalls.

❧ ❧

While the recall was getting under way, Jenni Dye was getting her own introduction to running for office. By chance, she officially kicked off her campaign for Dane County Board on November 16, 2011, the day after the effort
to recall Walker began. She had a challenging race in her unusual district,
which included low-income housing, suburban homes, and even a few farms.
Her opponent, Jack Martz, was a fiscal conservative and donor to Walker and
other Republicans; he had lived in Fitchburg for decades and had been on the
County Board for ten years. Martz might also benefit from the fact that the
election would be held on April 3 along with Wisconsin's GOP presidential
primary. But by the time she announced, Dye had built a following for herself
both on Twitter and around the area that included many public employees.
Naturally, Dye created a second Twitter account for herself, @JenniForDane,
to serve her campaign. The unions that she had spent the last year supporting also gave her help in return. She was endorsed by the Madison teachers
union, an AFSCME affiliate, the local firefighters union, and the AFL-CIO,
along with many individual union leaders, and she received donations from
union officials and labor political action committees. She also won support
from the county's top liberal elected officials and from groups like the Sierra
Club. The center-right editorial page of the *Wisconsin State Journal* even endorsed her, calling Dye a "fresh and effective voice," and she had garnered
the resources to do four mailings to voters and one robocall to get out the
vote. Act 10 had also given unions more of an incentive to participate in political races, first for school boards and increasingly for city councils and county
boards. No longer could public workers rely on their unions to bargain for
their interests before public officials who were indifferent or even hostile to
them. Now, elections were more important than ever for labor.

Still, the Dane County Board's chairman, Scott McDonell, was not expecting much from Dye's race. Martz had beaten a good challenger two years
before, and in the run-up to the election an internal poll showed Dye trailing.
But she had worked hard on her campaign, and the backlash against Walker
in Dane County had galvanized liberals beyond anyone's expectations. When
the results were in, she won with 55 percent of the vote to Martz's 45 percent.
Her convincing victory was matched by liberals in other parts of Dane County,
and their control of the thirty-seven-member board increased to twenty-eight
from twenty-three. "Scott Walker was my co-pilot," McDonell said on election
night. Dye's win, he said, was the "big exclamation point" that brought home
how well liberals had done. The win also showed that unions and their allies,
however embattled they were, would continue to be a force in certain parts of

Wisconsin. It gave Dye a chance and challenge as a leader: like some of the GOP lawmakers in the Legislature, she had been elected in a wave and would now need to represent voters who might be more centrist than she was. She wanted to keep Fitchburg affordable, but to maintain services there, she and other county supervisors could face difficult decisions in the coming months. She was learning that governing in the wake of a deep recession leaves few easy or good choices.

As Dye put together her campaign, the recall drive against Walker showed immediate signs of success. Two days after launching the effort, organizers had received 48,000 signatures to recall Walker, and in less than a week they had 158,000. By December 15—the halfway point—they had 578,000, according to United Wisconsin's internal figures. The group gave the public periodic updates of how the drive was going, but the leaders underreported how many signatures they had gathered, in part because they did not want to dampen the enthusiasm of those who were collecting signatures. By the January 17 deadline they had more than 900,000. That day, they parked a U-Haul truck a half block from the Accountability Board's office. The truck, draped with a banner declaring "Yes We Did," held stacks of banker's boxes containing the signatures, which together weighed roughly one and a half tons. Recall supporters filled the street, turning the event into a minifestival. A twelve-foot puppet of Walker towered above the crowd. Small bands played. Television cameras lined the sidewalk in front of the entrance. Then, one by one, organizers carried the boxes from the back of the U-Haul into the office, as a supporter called out the name of the county where each set of signatures had been collected.

The organizers also submitted 843,000 signatures against Kleefisch—making her the first lieutenant governor in the nation's history to face a recall—and more than 18,000 for each of the recalls against the four senators. In all, nearly 1.9 million signatures were turned in, well above the threshold of valid signatures to trigger the recalls. Organizers stacked their boxes up at the Accountability Board's office; state workers then loaded them into another truck and transported them to a nearby state building surrounded by barbed wire that housed printing facilities and a vehicle fleet. The location was kept secret for the next month as a team of agency staff and thirty temporary workers copied the petitions using high-powered scanners and began processing them.

As the recall petitions were filed, Walker was in New York City at a fundraiser hosted by Maurice Greenberg, the founder of the troubled financial services company American International Group. The media-friendly governor that day declined to do interviews with major mainstream outlets in Wisconsin, but he joined the programs of conservative radio hosts Rush Limbaugh and Charlie Sykes. On February 10 Walker took his case to the Conservative Political Action Conference in Washington, D.C., and told the attendees his ouster would hurt the national conservative movement for the long term. "Lord help us if we fail," he said. "I'm not planning on it, but if we were to fail, I think this sets aside any courageous act in American politics for at least a decade, if not a generation."

All the while, Walker and Republicans had been making legal maneuvers over the recall petitions. The month before the signatures were submitted, Walker's campaign sued the Accountability Board to force the agency to do more to ferret out illegible, fictitious, and duplicate names. The campaign brought the case in conservative Waukesha County—a move open to Walker because, just a few months earlier, the governor had signed a law allowing citizens to sue state government in any county. Republicans had pushed the law in part because they viewed judges in Dane County, the previous starting place for nearly all lawsuits against state agencies, as too liberal.

Walker's campaign argued that the Accountability Board's long-standing process for counting recall signatures was not rigorous enough. The elections agency had previously said state law was clear that the targets of recalls had the duty to identify improper signatures and formally challenge them before the board, which would then determine which signatures to count. For a judge, the Walker campaign drew J. Mac Davis, a former Republican state senator who quickly ruled that the Accountability Board had to more aggressively seek out and remove duplicate and problem signatures. The only way the board could do that was to build a database, which added to its time for reviewing signatures. In early February, a Madison-based appeals court vacated Mac Davis's ruling, but the Accountability Board stuck by its plans to create the database. The governor's campaign was supposed to submit its challenges to the signatures by February 27. A Dane County judge had given the governor thirty days to review the signatures instead of the usual ten in state law. But even with its vast financial resources and help from thousands of volunteers, the Walker campaign said it was unable to review the signatures in time and thus never submitted any challenges.

On March 30 the Accountability Board found that 900,938 of the signatures were valid and ordered an election against Walker. The primary would be held on May 8 and the general election on June 5. The recall elections for the lieutenant governor and state senators would be held on the same schedule, and the cost to taxpayers for holding the elections would come to more than $14 million. Two weeks earlier, as the legislative session ended, Senator Galloway resigned from the Senate rather than face recall, citing health concerns in her family. Republican Representative Jerry Petrowski of Stettin soon took her place on the ballot. The same day the recall elections were ordered, the federal court in Madison found parts of Act 10 unconstitutional because the judge found no rational reason for treating general public employees differently than police and firefighters when it came to recertification votes and dues deductions. But Judge William M. Conley kept in place all the other elements of the law, giving unions the most limited of victories.

Also that day, Milwaukee Mayor Tom Barrett announced that he was getting into the race, creating a four-way primary. In the contest with him were Falk, the former Dane County executive; Secretary of State Doug La Follette; and Kathleen Vinehout, one of the "Fab Fourteen" senators who left the state during the collective bargaining fight. La Follette and Vinehout were relatively unknown, and the contest was always a race between Barrett and Falk. The two had faced each other before, in the 2002 Democratic primary for governor; both came in behind Jim Doyle, the attorney general who went on to serve two terms as governor. Falk in 2006 lost a race for attorney general and Barrett came in behind Walker in 2010, meaning the recall race was the third statewide run for both Barrett and Falk.

The jockeying over which Democrat should challenge Walker began even before the signatures against him had been filed. The week before Christmas 2011, leaders of the state's largest public employee unions met privately with Barrett at the Milwaukee offices of the Wisconsin AFL-CIO, part of a series of meetings with candidates. The group, members of the We Are Wisconsin coalition, wanted to talk with Barrett about their concerns ahead of the looming recall. The union leaders included Marty Beil, executive director of the Wisconsin State Employees Union, an AFSCME affiliate; Mary Bell, president of the Wisconsin Education Association Council; and Dan Burkhalter, WEAC's executive director. Besides Barrett's loss to Walker a year before, Beil and Bell had other issues with the mayor. A local AFSCME affiliate had butted heads with Barrett over the effect of his budget cuts on their members in the city's workforce, and WEAC had opposed a failed plan by Doyle and Barrett two years earlier to put control of Milwaukee's troubled school system in the hands of the mayor. In Barrett's 2010 gubernatorial campaign, the statewide teachers group didn't run ads in support of him, giving Walker an easier path to victory. The week of the meeting, Bell was particularly angry about Barrett's recent comments at a news conference hedging about whether he would sign the petition to recall Walker—something he ultimately did do.

"Mayor Barrett has not signed a recall petition," Bell, a former librarian, wrote in an e-mail to members after the meeting with Barrett. "He said he might sign. 'In all likelihood' he will sign. REALLY? Wisconsin citizens—our members—are standing in the cold to gather signatures and Mayor Barrett is undecided?"

At the meeting, Beil of AFSCME had his own question for Barrett. He asked the mayor whether he would commit as governor to vetoing any budget that didn't restore the collective bargaining provisions lost under Act 10. Such a commitment would be potentially explosive, both as policy and politics. Unlike some states, Wisconsin would not be without a budget if a new one didn't pass by June 30, 2013, when the existing budget expired: funding levels and taxes would remain in place until updated by a new budget. But a veto might mean that the state wouldn't have enough money to pay for fast-growing costs for Medicaid health programs, prisons, and other services, and that could lead to layoffs of state employees and cutbacks in services. Whatever happened in the recalls, Republicans would almost certainly still control the Assembly in the years ahead, and they had vowed not to restore the unions in any circumstances. Blocking the budget was more likely to embolden them than persuade them to change their minds, especially because such gridlock would guarantee that there would be no tax or spending increases as long as the current budget remained in place. Politically, it was dangerous as well. Walker was already charging that Democrats were controlled by unions, and such a pledge could make the governor's argument for him.

Barrett told the unions he was committed to restoring collective bargaining and would call a special session of the Legislature to make that happen. If this didn't work—and it likely wouldn't—he said he would look at other means of accomplishing the goal without giving specifics. But the mayor wouldn't commit to vetoing the budget. The labor leaders and Barrett finished the meeting with handshakes but with a substantial difference of opinion as well. Later, both Beil and Bell denied that their rejection of Barrett was based mainly on his refusal to commit to the veto, pointing to other factors like their previous disagreements. "It wasn't the bottom line [that] we wouldn't support him if he wouldn't commit," Beil said. "That was one concern out of a lot of concerns about Tom Barrett's candidacy."

Falk, however, committed to the budget veto and soon after became the first candidate to jump in the race, getting in the day after recall organizers turned in their petitions in January. Within weeks, she received endorsements and heavy financial support from WEAC, AFSCME, and other public-sector unions. The endorsements were controversial even among some local members and leaders of those unions, with some in WEAC saying publicly that their umbrella union should have waited to see who else was running before endorsing Falk. Six months later, anger over the endorsement of Falk would be one of several factors that led a group of correctional officers to break off from AFSCME, which had represented them for decades, to try to form their own union. Those who opposed the Falk endorsement worried that the pledge could be damaging to her in the general election. When the commitment became public and Falk readily acknowledged it, it drew withering criticism from Republicans, who said it proved she was a mere tool of the unions. Falk responded that she was showing an openness about her agenda that Walker never did while he was campaigning.

Undaunted, the unions spent $4.5 million on behalf of Falk, mostly on ads promoting her and criticizing Walker. It did little for her, though, and Barrett beat her by twenty-four points—58 percent to 34 percent. In spite of his big win, the mayor faced challenges because of a steady dose of attack ads from Walker and his allies. After having poured all his money into beating Falk, Barrett had little available after the primary to use against Walker. Spending by unions on his behalf—the kind done for Falk—would help him in the general election, but their coffers weren't as full because of their spending for her.

There was another troubling sign for Barrett and his backers in the election results. Walker faced only nominal opposition in his primary from Arthur Kohl-Riggs, a liberal blogger and protester at the Capitol who campaigned wearing an Abraham Lincoln–style stovepipe hat to highlight his desire to bring the Republican Party back to what he saw as its roots. As they had in 2011, Republicans were again running fake Democrats in the recall races, and Kohl-Riggs's campaign was in part an effort to force conservatives to vote in the Republican primary instead of casting a ballot for fake Democrat Gladys Huber in the governor's race. Walker's victory over Kohl-Riggs was assured, giving little incentive to his supporters to come to the polls. Nonetheless, 627,000 of them voted for the governor—nearly as many as the 665,900 or so Democrats who turned out to vote for one of their four main candidates.

Restoring collective bargaining rights figured prominently in the primary race, but Barrett drifted away from that issue during the campaign against Walker. The governor announced a projected budget surplus that he said was a result of making tough decisions and argued that his changes to state law created more than $1 billion in savings for taxpayers, mostly because public employees were paying more for their benefits. Barrett focused on the ongoing John Doe probe of Walker aides, the lagging economy, and what he said was the likelihood that Walker would eventually enact right-to-work legislation if he remained governor. Walker insisted he had no plans to pursue such legislation but repeatedly dodged questions about whether he would veto a right-to-work bill if it got to him. His stance briefly put him in a difficult spot when the *Journal Sentinel* reported on the video featuring his "divide and conquer" comments made in January 2011 to Beloit billionaire Diane Hendricks. The video became public days after the primary, at a time when Walker was heading into the state Republican Party's convention in Green Bay. The evening the convention kicked off, Walker avoided addressing what he'd meant by his statements to Hendricks and declined to answer the veto question but said right-to-work legislation would not come to his desk. "I'm going to do everything in my power to make sure it isn't there because my focal point [is] private-sector unions have overwhelmingly come to the table to be my partner in economic development," he said.

More problematic for Walker was a string of monthly reports that said the state was losing jobs. They showed Wisconsin shedding 33,900 jobs in 2011, making it the worst in the nation. Barrett hammered on the point, saying that Walker took his attention off of creating jobs so he could engage in ideological warfare, and that the state's economy suffered for it. But Walker's administration saw other indicators that said the jobs outlook was not as dire as suggested by the monthly reports, which for reasons unclear to economists had diverged from the actual job creation numbers for northern states such as Wisconsin and Minnesota. State officials were compiling data for a quarterly census of employers and finding that the state was in fact gaining jobs, not losing them. The quarterly reports—made using extensive unemployment insurance data from most businesses in the state—are better trusted than the monthly estimates, which are based on a survey rather than a census. But the numbers for the final quarter of 2011 were not slated for public release until three weeks after the recall election, after the federal Bureau of Labor Statistics had reviewed the figures of all the states. Walker's team wanted those numbers out right away and saw a way to do it. Although the Bureau of Labor Statistics would not report the figures until June 28, nothing but precedent kept Wisconsin officials from releasing them when they sent the data to the federal government. At the GOP convention, Walker hinted that positive news was on the way and recommitted to his promise to create a quarter of a million private-sector jobs by 2015, even though the state was not on track to do that—no matter which jobs numbers were used.

Walker's team leaked the new figures to the *Journal Sentinel* so they could appear in the May 16 paper. They showed the state had gained more than 23,000 jobs in 2011. Within hours of the newspaper being printed, Walker was on the air with an ad that quoted from the story, overlooking the fact that the paper noted the release of such figures early was highly unusual, that they had not yet been verified by the federal government, and that they could not be compared with those of other states, whose numbers were still undisclosed. "I've got some bad news for Tom Barrett," Walker said in the ad. He then leaned into the camera and continued. "But good news for Wisconsin. The government just released the final jobs numbers. As it turns out Wisconsin actually gained—that's right, gained—more than twenty thousand jobs during my first year in office." Jobs figures flashed on the background under the *Journal Sentinel*'s logo.

"Mayor Barrett, you said this election's about jobs," he went on. He turned to his left and gave an exaggerated, skeptical frown. "I couldn't agree more. Our reforms are working and we're moving Wisconsin"—he pointed at the camera—"forward." Barrett decried the move as hyperpolitical and said Walker's numbers couldn't be trusted because they hadn't been checked. "In a move that is virtually unheard of, Scott Walker is suddenly trotting out an altogether new set of unverified numbers twenty days before the election to mask his economic failure," Barrett said.

By focusing on whether the figures were right or wrong, Barrett missed a chance to point out that even if true the numbers suggested poor job creation. Walker's administration that very day transmitted the figures—which were not final, as the governor had said in the ad—to the Bureau of Labor Statistics and made them available to news outlets, which guaranteed widespread coverage into May 17, when the next set of monthly jobs figures was released. That report said Wisconsin lost an estimated 6,200 jobs in April, but by then Walker had made clear to the public the flaws in the once-trusted monthly reports. The state was not creating jobs particularly well, but the governor had successfully shown that the state was probably not the worst in the nation, muddying one of Barrett's clearest messages. Three weeks after the election, the federal government released state-by-state numbers for 2011 that largely upheld what Walker had claimed. The Bureau of Labor Statistics agreed with Wisconsin on the total number of jobs the state had as of the end of 2011, although it came up with a smaller job gain—just under 20,000, instead of 23,000—because it used a different set of baseline numbers. The release of the federal numbers allowed the first comparison to other states, and Wisconsin did not fare well. It ranked forty-first in job creation and gained fewer jobs than all of its neighbors.

Barrett continued to talk about the jobs numbers during the final weeks of the campaign, but increasingly he also spoke of the John Doe probe, the other area of greatest weakness for Walker. Down in the polls by about five points, Barrett called daily for Walker to disclose e-mails that he and his aides had sent during his time as county executive and demanded that Walker release details on who was bankrolling his criminal defense fund. Barrett's ads hit the same themes that the ads by the union-backed Greater Wisconsin Political Fund did. Walker did not engage on the issue, insisting that the district attorney had asked him not to talk about it and that lawyers for his campaign had been told that he was not a target of the investigation—though he said he did not know who had told them that.

Barrett hounded Walker on the investigation during their second and final debate just five days before the election. Walker answered by bringing up a *Journal Sentinel* investigation that found the Milwaukee Police Department had misclassified hundreds of serious crimes as lesser offenses. Barrett said the errors were simply bureaucratic. "I have a police department that arrests felons," he said. "He has a practice of hiring them." That morning, Walker's former spokeswoman, Fran McLaughlin, became the thirteenth person to reach an immunity deal in the ongoing probe. And just hours before the debate, the *Journal Sentinel* reported on its website that the secret probe had begun because Walker's county office had been "unwilling or unable" to provide information and records about the missing veterans' money. Walker argued during the debate that his office had been unable, not unwilling, to provide what prosecutors were seeking. "My integrity has always been high," he said. "It will continue to be a high level of integrity long after all of this is done." He accused Barrett of focusing on the probe out of desperation. He also warned that if Barrett won, it would continue an unending series of recalls. "I think you start what I call 'recall Ping-Pong.' . . . We want to change everything to do with recall because people are just sick of it," he said, adding that he wanted to change the state constitution to put limits on when recalls could occur. In March 2012 the Assembly would vote to do just that, but the Senate wouldn't go along with the effort. Barrett called the governor's idea hypocritical because Walker himself had effectively come into the Milwaukee County executive's job because of a recall effort. Though Barrett landed some

punches in the debates, he was not able to close the gap between him and
Walker. Tellingly, President Obama never came to Wisconsin to campaign
for what appeared to be a losing cause, even though he made stops in neighboring Minnesota and Illinois four days before the recall election.

When election day arrived, the voters jammed the polls. Turnout topped
57 percent—well above both the turnout for the 2010 race for governor and
the turnout for every midterm governor's race in Wisconsin since at least
1950. Barrett easily captured the Democratic strongholds of Milwaukee and
Madison, and also won parts of south central Wisconsin, Kenosha County, La
Crosse County, and the far northern counties of Douglas, Bayfield, and Ash-
land. But the vast majority of the rest of the state went red. In a dozen counties, Walker increased his margin by six percentage points. Statewide, Walker
beat Barrett 53 percent to 46 percent, performing about one percentage point
better than he did in 2010. According to exit polls, 37 percent of those who
voted for Walker described themselves as moderates, 23 percent belonged
to union households, and 17 percent said they planned to vote for Obama in
his re-election bid in November—enough to give the president the edge if
the election had been held that day. The margin for Kleefisch was similar to
Walker's, making her the first lieutenant governor in the country to not just
face, but survive, a recall election. Republicans won three of the Senate races
with commanding margins—Scott Fitzgerald took 58 percent, Senator Terry
Moulton took 57 percent, and Representative Jerry Petrowski took 61 percent
to fill the seat that Pam Galloway vacated after recall paperwork was filed
against her.

Democrats earned one consolation prize in what was otherwise a dreadful
night for them. In Racine County, former Senator John Lehman unseated
Senator Van Wanggaard in a volatile district that had the habit of throwing
out incumbents. Nineteen months earlier, in November 2010, voters had
tossed out Lehman in favor of Wanggaard. Now, they were giving Lehmann
a second chance but by the slimmest of margins. The official tally showed
him winning by 834 votes, or just over one percentage point. Wanggaard
demanded a recount, but the result barely changed—Lehman won by 819
votes and took his oath of office in July. With Lehman's win came control
of the Senate. Ordinarily, that would be a significant victory for Democrats
because it would put a block on Walker's agenda. But their one-vote margin
came at a time when the Legislature was out of session and the regular fall
elections were just five months away—elections that, as it turned out, would
place the Senate back in GOP hands. Democrats knew they had tough odds

in holding onto the chamber in November, in part because Republicans had redrawn the boundaries of legislative districts to their favor for those elections. Lehman's district and a neighboring one had changed the most dramatically, turning his district from a swing seat into a solidly Republican one. He was not slated to defend it until 2014, but he was at risk of a 2013 recall, and the tougher boundaries drove home the difficulties Democrats faced.

Wisconsin allows those who arrive at a polling place by closing time to cast ballots, and an hour after the polls closed at eight o'clock, some voters were still waiting in line in Milwaukee and other urban areas. By then, the major television networks and the Associated Press had called the race for Walker. Democrats, buoyed by reports about heavy turnout, still believed they could pull out a win. "We're not going to let the media call this election," Mike Tate, chairman of the state Democratic Party, told supporters at Barrett's party at the downtown Milwaukee Hilton. "Stay around because we're going to make big news later." But by around ten o'clock, Barrett took the stage to tell the crowd that he had just talked to Walker and congratulated him. "No!" the crowd cried, as some booed and screamed insults.

"We agreed it is important for us to work together," Barrett said, as the crowd continued to yell in defiance. He thanked them to a smattering of applause. "This has been the most amazing experience of our lives," he said. "And what we have seen over the last sixteen months is we have seen this democracy come alive. . . . We are a state that has been deeply divided and it's up to all of us—our side and their side—to listen, to listen to each other, and to try to do what's right for everyone in this state."

Barrett waded back into the crowd to shake hands and thank his supporters. He was approached by a woman who was furious because she believed, incorrectly, that the mayor had conceded at a time when votes were still being cast. In fact, the campaign had already confirmed with the city election commission that the voting had ended. The woman asked Barrett if she could slap him, and he replied, "I'd rather you hug me." As he leaned down to do that, she whacked her open palm against his cheek. The mayor downplayed the incident the next day, saying, "That's life in the big city." But for Barrett loyalists, the slap served as a metaphor for the shabby treatment that the mayor had received from many in his own party throughout the campaign.

Jenni Dye sat with friends at the outdoor patio of a tavern near the Capitol on State Street watching the results come in on their smartphones. Dye wasn't hopeful heading into the elections—like everyone else, she had seen the polls. She had backed Falk in the primary and was less than enthusiastic about Barrett as a candidate. But the day of the election, she allowed herself a sliver of optimism when she saw strong voter turnout in Milwaukee. She was disgusted when media outlets called the race while some voters were still casting ballots in Milwaukee. What surprised her, however, was that Walker's victory felt bearable. She knew a large portion of the state had actually voted to recall the governor, just as she knew her side would have to reflect on why a larger portion of the state had not. The next morning, she e-mailed some labor contacts about ways they could keep working for the issues that mattered to them. "I expected to feel devastated by a Walker win but instead I felt the way I did before: You have to keep fighting for the things you believe in," Dye said.

At the overflow Waukesha Exposition Center, the mood was electric. Kleefisch greeted the crowd with the phrase that had been the central anthem for Democrats during the protests. "Now *this* is what democracy looks like!" she said. "Years from now they will say the campaign to save America began tonight in Wisconsin."

Walker was introduced by his wife, Tonette, as "the only governor elected twice in one term." Walker took the stage to hoots and cheers as the country music hit "Only in America" blared across the room. He hugged his wife and took his place behind a lectern decorated with a placard that read "Moving Wisconsin Forward." The state's motto is "Forward," and Walker had adopted it during the recall as his campaign slogan, recycling one that Obama was already using and that U.S. Senator Russ Feingold had used in his unsuccessful 2010 re-election bid. Walker thanked his supporters and they rang out in chants of "Thank you, Scott."

"Tonight we tell Wisconsin, we tell our country, and we tell people all across the globe the voters really do want leaders that stand up and make the tough decisions," he said. "But now it is time to move on and move forward in Wisconsin." He told the crowd he would meet with his cabinet the next day to focus on the economy. "Tomorrow is the day after the election, and tomorrow we are no longer opponents," he said. "Tomorrow we are one as Wisconsinites." He told his supporters he had talked to Barrett a few minutes before, and some booed at the mention of the mayor's name. "No, no, no, no," Walker admonished them, raising his index finger. "No, the election is over. I talked to the mayor and we had a good talk and I said I'm committed to working with you to help the city of Milwaukee and help the state of Wisconsin.

Tomorrow, the election is over. It's time to move Wisconsin forward." Walker hoped he could translate his victory into that kind of momentum. "I believe there is more that unites us than divides us," he said.

Ultimately, Wisconsin's voters proved less volatile than the state's politics. They affirmed Walker by almost the same margin as they had in 2010, with a little extra room that came either from approval of his policies or weariness of the recalls. All summer, the governor rode high and was received like a rock star at the Republican National Convention in Tampa. Ahead of him, Walker had problems enough to fill the remaining years of his term. The governor's promise to create 250,000 jobs, for instance, still appeared nothing more than a dream and a slogan. The puzzling John Doe investigation plodded on. In October 2012 Kelly Rindfleisch pleaded guilty to felony misconduct in office for doing campaign work out of Walker's office when he was county executive. She was sentenced to six months in jail and three years of probation pending her appeal. The day after Rindfleisch pleaded guilty, a jury convicted former Walker appointee Kevin Kavanaugh of stealing more than $51,000 from the veterans fund. Then on November 29, 2012, former Walker aide Tim Russell pleaded guilty to embezzling more than $21,000 from the same fund, and in January 2013 he was sentenced to two years in prison and five years of probation. But the John Doe probe seemed to lack an end, and direction, with no clues to what was happening.

At any time, these troubles might threaten Walker's governorship, but for the moment at least the challenges crouched in the shadow of his victory. He had held onto the support of a swing state while winning the outright adulation of conservatives nationwide. He had assembled a campaign apparatus allowing him to raise money around the country from both small donors and the very wealthiest. In doing so, he had raised sums that were as great as second-tier presidential candidates. He now had ties to billionaire donors, including those funding the super PACs that had sustained the poorly funded presidential campaigns of Newt Gingrich and Rick Santorum.

Walker downplayed the possibility of one day running for higher office, but did so in numerous interviews with national media outlets that further raised his profile. This popularity with conservatives might turn out to have more than the usual staying power because it was based not on his charisma as a candidate but on his record in office. The free-market group Americans for Prosperity featured Walker as its keynote speaker at its annual conference in the nation's capital in August 2012. Tim Phillips, president of the group, said of Walker that his recall victory "solidifies him as the leading governor in the country on doing the hard things to get a state moving again. He's not going to *be* a national leader. He is one."

Meanwhile, a friend of Walker's and fellow forty-something conservative from Wisconsin, Congressman Paul Ryan of Janesville, had been chosen as Mitt Romney's running mate. As Ryan was picked and ran for vice president, Walker texted back and forth with him to offer advice and encouragement. The two men had a striking similarity—both of them had won acclaim at a young age for advocating an uncompromising approach of spending and tax cuts as a way to boost the economy and balance budgets. Both had pointed to the other's success as a confirmation of the rightness of their creed. When Romney picked Ryan as a running mate, Walker and other conservatives confidently predicted that the Republican presidential bid would have a high-minded focus on the country's fiscal problems and a successful outcome. Walker, they said, had dyed the state a permanent red and Ryan and Romney would soon prove that by winning a presidential race in Wisconsin for the first time since 1984 and gaining the White House in the end. In Wisconsin, though, political fights aren't so easy to finish.

Conclusion

O N THE SUNNY AFTERNOON OF SEPTEMBER 14 Jenni Dye crossed the Capitol square to join a demonstration of the Madison teachers union to show solidarity for striking educators in Chicago—a reminder that even states retaining collective bargaining were not immune from labor unrest. Waiting for the 5 p.m. rally to start, Dye checked her Twitter feed. To her shock, she saw the news that a Dane County judge had struck down much of Act 10. Kerry Motoviloff, president of Madison Teachers Inc., soon showed up and confirmed the late Friday afternoon surprise on the lawsuit, which had been brought jointly by her union and another one representing city of Milwaukee workers. Judge Juan Colás, an appointee of Democratic Governor Jim Doyle, had ruled that the law violated workers' constitutional rights to free speech, free association, and equal representation under the law by capping union workers' raises but not those of their nonunion counterparts. Much of the law was struck down for city, county, and school workers in Wisconsin, though the ruling had no effect on state workers. For the moment, local workers and elected officials were likely once again allowed to bargain full labor contracts with one another. In disbelief, Dye called her father the teacher to tell him the news and he made her repeat it a few times before he would believe it. Dye also found a Madison school social worker she knew at the rally and gave her the news, moving the woman to tears of joy. When the rally started, Motoviloff announced the news to the whole group of teachers and their now celebratory supporters.

"Teachers fight, teachers win from Chicago to Madison!" the crowd chanted, invoking the Illinois strike.

More quietly, though, Dye and many others at the rally confided to one another that they were reluctant to get too excited. Within days, the attorney general appealed the decision, and it seemed destined to be heard eventually by the Wisconsin Supreme Court, where it would face a skeptical reception from the conservative majority. Dye wanted to use this unexpected opportunity for her county to start bargaining with its workers. But with county taxes still under state levy limits and the legal future cloudy, the young county board supervisor initially wanted to go slow. "I don't know what will happen ultimately but everyone should go into this with eyes wide open that we don't know," she said shortly after the court decision.

Just six days after the ruling came down, however, Dye sat down at her county supervisor's desk for a pivotal meeting in the downtown Madison City-County Building, her Apple laptop with its union sticker ready before her. "When I look at all the really important issues on tonight's county board agenda, I just keep thinking 'this is why I ran,'" Dye had tweeted earlier that afternoon. It was Thursday, September 20, and the Dane County Board was set to take up proposals to help provide shelter and assistance to homeless residents and domestic abuse victims. But above all, the board was voting on labor contracts that combined some concessions from 1,400 county workers with protections for their unions. To balance the budget, the contracts allowed the county to impose up to five unpaid furlough days. That would cut workers' salaries for that one year by up to 1.9 percent and save up to $5 million, a substantial sum. The contracts allowed for the possibility of further savings on employees' health care coverage. But even when combined with concessions negotiated with unions for 2013, the definite savings so far were significantly less than the permanent cuts that Walker had imposed on state workers through his legislation. The contracts also protected unions in the unlikely event that Act 10 was struck down entirely—in that case the agreements were voided and the unions could restart negotiations without givebacks.

The rushed county deals were made possible by the opening that the Colás ruling had created. The contracts' provisions would keep the county unions in place through 2015, potentially even if the judge's decision were overturned. The contracts could have extracted permanent givebacks from the union or the board could have likely imposed at least some, under both the law and the likely court decisions to come. If state aid stayed flat, or shrank even more, and the state kept limiting property tax increases, the decision could limit the options of the county for a year at a time of serious need. But for Dye the decision was clear. Wearing a gray sweater with black dress and visibly emotional, she spoke for the first time as a supervisor an hour and a half into the debate, arguing in favor of supporting the county's workers as partners in its work. "The deal that we're talking about today could achieve up to $5 million of savings if needed and doesn't promise these employees a dime in increases in either benefits or other types of compensation," she said. Dye cast her vote for the contracts and they passed easily, twenty-nine votes to eight. The agreements were praised by Democrats and unions that had backed Dye in the campaign and criticized by conservatives like Walker and longtime Dane County Supervisor Dave Wiganowsky, who saw them as mere payback. "They may end up killing programs so that we can repay their political favors," Wiganowsky said before the vote. After the vote, Walker's spokesman, Cullen Werwie, said that Dane County officials had failed to take full advantage of the savings that were available to them. For a year and a half, Dye had been criticizing the governor's policies and actions. Now he could return the favor.

Dye later acknowledged reservations about the speed of the approval, which limited the time both to consider the board's action and to get input from workers and the public. One of her chief criticisms of Walker had been the way he had pushed Act 10 through the Legislature so quickly. The contracts moved unusually quickly too. But she felt that she had clearly told voters where she stood on public unions, that the savings were enough, and that the county would do better in the long run by standing by its workers. As a new supervisor, Dye didn't get to set the timetable any more than rank and file Republican lawmakers had with Act 10—she had to choose. She cast her vote and later that night tweeted a photo of two cocktails—"a toast to democracy in WI." By the first week of October, she had something else to celebrate—a new job as the executive director of NARAL Pro-Choice Wisconsin, an organization that represented the political arm of the abortion rights movement in the state. Intrigued by the job opening, Dye applied for it, interviewed, and snagged it. Suddenly, just one month out from the presidential election, she was a soon-to-be registered lobbyist leading a group that endorsed and supported candidates for office, brought lawsuits, and advocated for bills. Of the two women who had held the job before her, one had gone on to serve in the state Assembly and run for Congress and the other was leading United Wisconsin. Dye, the woman who had protested being locked out of the Capitol the year before, now had real access to the statehouse and a seat on the county board.

In spite of labor victories like the Dane County contracts, it was still difficult for now to see how public unions in the state could ever fully recover their many lost members and staff and their ability to bargain and reliably raise large sums of money within Wisconsin. The courts certainly provided challenges—in January 2013, a panel of the U.S. Seventh Circuit Court of Appeals reversed a lower court opinion and upheld Act 10 in its entirety. That ruling did not affect the decision by Judge Colás that struck down parts of the law because he served on a state court, not a federal court. Nonetheless, the Seventh Circuit's ruling dealt a blow to unions and reminded them higher courts could eventually overturn Colás as well and fully reinstate the law. The unions had been unable to exact recall retribution on the governor who had led the charge against them and, equally telling, had even failed to get their preferred candidate through the Democratic recall primary. To try to overcome its setbacks, the American Federation of Teachers-Wisconsin, a union of varied white collar public workers, sought to merge with the larger Wisconsin Education Association Council. Some members of the Wisconsin State Employees Union went a different direction, with correctional officers seeking to break away and form their own union out of frustration with their parent union. That schism grew so heated that an official with the parent union drilled out a safety deposit box at a bank to seize funds from one prison local, leading the local leaders to call the police in an unsuccessful attempt to bring criminal charges. Republicans also had drawn favorable political maps for themselves in the state for the five fall elections through 2020. Following the November elections, the GOP retook the state Senate with an eighteen-to-fifteen majority, beating a Democrat elected only a year before in the first Senate recalls, and expanded their margin in the Assembly to sixty to thirty-nine. Unions like WEAC were once again shut out of the offices of greatest influence in the Capitol, perhaps for the rest of the decade.

There were a few points of light for unions, though. They had won outright victories in the Ohio referendum and the Wisconsin state Senate recall races, and had some success with the courts. The week after the November elections, WEAC's executive director played a role in helping thirty-two-year-old liberal state Senator Chris Larson of Milwaukee beat out a rival for the Senate minority leader spot in a bit of intraparty intrigue that left the losing Democrats fuming. Unions would still be influential in some parts of Wisconsin and the rest of the country, and would continue to help elect pro-labor candidates from county supervisor to president in Democratic areas and states. Politicians in swing states and liberal strongholds had been reminded that they could not ignore or strike out at public employee unions without a fight. Walker had refused to negotiate with unions during the height of the crisis in February 2011, insisting that local governments needed the certainty of being able to set their budgets without union interference. But a year and a half later, that certainty hadn't fully solidified for mayors, city councils, and school boards. For the moment, at least, the best-placed local governments appeared to be the ones able to reach an understanding with their employees and their much weakened unions.

The November 6 elections also gave liberals hope. President Obama won in Wisconsin by a seven-percentage-point margin, 52.8 percent of the vote to 45.9 percent, less than his 2008 margin of nearly fourteen points but still convincing. Just below him on the ballot, Madison Democrat Tammy Baldwin won election to the U.S. Senate as the first openly gay candidate ever to do so, beating political legend Tommy Thompson and helping retain for the president a Democratic majority in the upper house of Congress. Five months after electing for the second time a conservative governor who abhorred tax increases on the wealthy or others, Wisconsin voters had re-elected a president who was a Democratic icon for insisting on that. Two years after electing Ron Johnson as one of the most conservative members of the U.S. Senate, voters had chosen Baldwin, one of the most liberal members of the U.S. House of Representatives. As Obama and Baldwin were elected, however, state Republican lawmakers were winning the victories already mentioned, and Reid Ribble and Sean Duffy, freshmen GOP congressmen from Wisconsin, were being re-elected. What had happened? The answer has three parts, two obvious and one mysterious.

The first answer is that presidential elections turn out Democratic voters, such as minorities and the young, who simply don't show up for midterm elections for governor such as the one in 2010. Republicans tend to vote in both sets of elections. More than 3 million people in Wisconsin voted in each of Obama's presidential elections, compared to 2.5 million in Walker's June 2012 recall and 2.2 million in his 2010 election. That turnout difference is a powerful predictor of outcomes—Republicans have won six of the past eight races for governor in Wisconsin but lost the last seven presidential races. The second answer is that Republicans' redistricting legislation made it easier for them to win congressional and legislative races. But turnout and redistricting alone don't explain the outcomes of elections in Wisconsin, a state that as much as almost any other helps decide how America is run. Exit polling showed that the more Republican group of voters electing Walker in his June recall still favored Obama over Romney, and that a majority of the more Democratic group re-electing Obama in his race just months later approved of Walker. Polling from throughout 2012 by Marquette University Law School showed this trend of a small number of Obama-Walker voters making up about one-tenth of all registered voters. They tended to be rural white workers who identified themselves as moderate independents, paid less attention to the news and politics than other voters, and had a better view of the economy, even though they themselves earned relatively little income. These voters still like who they like and vote accordingly, helping to pull the state along with them.

There were also signs, however, that the vaunted independence of Wisconsin voters might be eroding. Thompson had been counting on Obama-Thompson ticket-splitters to help him win his first ever statewide race in a presidential election year, but they didn't materialize. It was perhaps no surprise. During the campaign, Thompson twice backtracked after calling himself a "moderate conservative," then in separate later remarks returned to that self-description again as if nothing had happened. The word "moderate" had become so tainted in some circles that a GOP candidate, even one in a tight general election race with Thompson's history of appealing to the center, wasn't sure whether to use it. Small wonder if some moderates weren't sure about voting for him.

That increase in partisanship was a reminder of the last great challenge facing Walker, Obama, and every other elected official who wants to improve life in Wisconsin and the rest of the nation. Voters and the leaders they elect have been on a trend toward increasing polarization. The day before Walker's recall election, a national survey by the Pew Research Center on the People and the Press found that the gap between the values of the voters in the two parties was widening. The survey found that nearly two in five Americans identify themselves as political independents—the largest share in seventy-five years and a clear rebuke to the two major parties and their increasingly extreme positions. The fight over Act 10 accelerated that trend of polarization in the state, as did the flood of national money into its campaigns. One tally estimated the spending in Wisconsin on 2012 campaigns alone at $310 million or more, enough to make up for the state's large cuts to its public universities over the two-year budget. The renewed fight over the Colás ruling promised to extend the battle and bitter feelings for months to come. Could some of those effects be undone, at least enough so that the people of Wisconsin would once again see it as safe to discuss politics with one another?

One encouraging sign is the engagement that voters on both sides showed for the struggle over Act 10 and the recalls. They demonstrated that they would fight for what they believed in, for what they saw as their rights and believed to be the best future for their children. Debate and struggle, even when explosive, can be healthy in a democracy, serving as the combustion that drives its engine and steers it down the best road. As the country as a whole dealt with the biggest economic difficulties since the Great Depression, Wisconsin and other states naturally faced more heated arguments about how to overcome these challenges. But anger alone cannot solve problems; unchecked, it can worsen them. For nearly two years the state's civic energy was focused more on confrontations than on meeting the numerous challenges facing its citizens. Now that the fight had ended, Walker, Democrats, and everyday citizens had to contemplate a question: Would they work together for a shared vision of Wisconsin, and if so, how?

The first test came when Walker decided not to implement an online insurance marketplace called for in the newly re-elected president's health care law. On November 16, 2012, Walker chose instead to let that insurance exchange be run by the federal government rather than the state, saying the risk of costs to the state outweighed the benefits that might have come from taking control of how the health care expansion would be handled in Wisconsin. With Obamacare, at least, there was no common ground. Walker's own agenda going forward had a somewhat better chance of yielding some agreements, and he began filling in some new details on that agenda. The same day as the announcement on the health care law, Walker opened up about his plans not in Wisconsin but outside Los Angeles in Simi Valley, California, the site of the Ronald Reagan Presidential Library and Museum, a forum for Republicans with national aspirations such as the presidency. The crowd of 1,000 had bought up the $45 tickets in advance and that Friday they packed the library's two-level auditorium decorated with red, white, and blue bunting. Walker was excited too—earlier in the day he had gotten to meet Nancy Reagan. The governor sat in front with his wife, Tonette, to his right. To his left was Diane Hendricks, the billionaire Wisconsin donor to both his campaign and the Reagan library who had spoken on video the year before with the governor about right-to-work legislation.

Stepping onto the stage to appreciative applause, Walker strode to a lectern embossed with a presidential seal and spoke for an hour on his past two years as governor and the future of his party. His voice swelling with pride and confidence, Walker predicted that the future of his party now lay in the thirty Republican governors who would be leading states around the country. Without putting forward in his speech any policies specially aimed at minorities besides voucher schools, Walker also predicted that his party already had the right values to win back the votes of these growing demographics.

"Our core beliefs aren't the problem. What we say, how we say it, and where we're willing to go to say it is the problem, at least at the national level. In the sense that we have a compelling message to young people, to young women, to young entrepreneurs, to young African American leaders, to young Hispanic leaders, we're just not doing an effective job of articulating it. We need to make sure that whomever our nominee is four years from now is someone—he or she—someone who's willing to make the effort to go out and speak to people where they're at in ways that we've never found possible to do before in places we historically have not gone to before."

In an interview that day with a local newspaper, Walker went farther in his criticism of failed Republican presidential nominee Mitt Romney. "Our future nominee needs to do a better job in articulating the views that we commonly hold as Republicans and to talk more optimistically about freedom and about prosperity, and the fact that we want every American to be able to live his or her piece of the American dream," he said."I don't think [Romney] did an effective job, nor did his campaign of communicating that with the majority voters in my state and others."

During the speech, which was frequently interrupted by applause, Walker spoke often of helping all citizens but not of bipartisanship and not of the sort of compromises that would be needed in Washington, D.C., to avoid an approaching fiscal cliff of federal tax increases and spending cuts. In response to a question afterward, Walker laid out an agenda of "massive tax reform," including an income tax cut; requiring the public schools from K-12 institutions to technical colleges and the University of Wisconsin System to meet performance-based targets to receive more state money as other states such as Florida and Pennsylvania were doing; expanding voucher schools; and cutting business regulations. He also talked of ending same-day voter registration, a practice that had given Wisconsin some of the highest voting rates in the country, to cut down on problems and lines on election day. The largely older, white audience stood and applauded for the man who had arguably achieved their party's best win at the ballot box that year. Men buttoned up their sport coats or suit jackets as the audience filed out. Walker still had to repeat his recall victory in a regular state re-election in just two years. But as his visit made clear, part of his work going forward would remain on a national stage. He would have two more years to remake Wisconsin according to his conservative vision. After that was the unknown.

Notes

Chapter 1. "Put Up or Shut Up"

This chapter, like the rest of the book, draws deeply on the authors' years of work as reporters in the statehouse for Wisconsin's largest newspaper. In the case of the November 2010 meeting between Walker and the GOP senators—as for most of the official events in this book—at least one of the authors was present. They exhaustively chronicled the coming events day by day in an ordeal that for journalists, as for the politicians and the most committed protesters, often seemed more like a physical contest of endurance than an intellectual exercise. In interviews, documents, hallway gossip, long acquaintance with state leaders, and direct observation, the writers had access to the events topped only by the few actors directly involved in them.

To recount those events, the authors drew on a number of sources besides their contemporaneous interviews and notes. First, they consulted their own *Milwaukee Journal Sentinel* articles as well as reports, videos, and photos by colleagues at the newspaper, including those listed in the acknowledgments. A major help was a retrospective article on the crisis and extensive interviews done by Bill Glauber, Dave Umhoefer, and Lee Bergquist that ran on June 4, 2011. The authors also reviewed stories by the Associated Press, the *Wisconsin State Journal*, and a variety of other media outlets, plus blog postings, Twitter updates, videos, photos, and other Internet postings. Important *Journal Sentinel* stories are noted along with all the items from any other outlets that furnished pertinent facts. The authors reviewed wherever possible the footage from the WisconsinEye Public Affairs Network, a wonderful historical record that captured the Walker meeting with the GOP senators in this chapter as well as all legislative sessions and most committee hearings and news conferences. Second, they reviewed thousands of pages of official documents: budget papers, calendars of state officials, e-mails, memos, and bill drafts. Third, throughout the events they spoke regularly to all elected officials involved and to most of the other main actors many times. In addition, they re-interviewed every significant actor who agreed to be questioned, often more than once. Last, they consulted with academics, experts at nonprofits, and other *Journal Sentinel* reporters about specific subject areas; their contributions are noted. All speeches and dialogue in official meetings broadcast by WisconsinEye have been checked against their archived video. Dialogue in private meetings was reconstructed by checking with all the parties to each conversation who would speak about it. If the opposing party would not discuss the conversation or if there is disagreement about the exchange, that is noted.

The descriptions of the lawmakers and their biographies come from several sources—the official Wisconsin Blue Books, *Journal Sentinel* stories, interviews with the lawmakers and their aides, and the authors' long acquaintance with the officials. The facts on the state Capitol come from official sources such as http://tours.wis consin.gov/. The information on the Milwaukee-to-Madison rail line comes from *Journal Sentinel* stories by the authors and Larry Sandler. The information and figures on the state economy come from newspaper stories and data from the federal Bureau of Labor Statistics and the Wisconsin Department of Workforce Development. The information on Jenni Dye comes from a number of interviews with her. The descriptions of the private briefings on Act 10 between the governor and GOP senators and representatives come from interviews with people in the room for those meetings. The information on the bill itself comes from the legislation, official summaries, analyses by outside experts, and many interviews with state and labor officials. The numbers on the financial effects on a worker from the bill come from the Department of Administration and the Legislative Fiscal Bureau. There is no reliable figure for the number of public workers affected by Act 10, and the number given is the best that nonpartisan state officials knowledgeable about unions could provide. Both authors were present when the Republican senators left their private briefing and when they returned to the Senate floor. A note on the Capitol: Visitors enter the building on what is officially called its ground floor, so that its first floor is actually what most would call its second floor; its fourth floor, the level where the Republican senators were meeting, is in turn what would be its fifth floor in common parlance.

Chapter 2. A Preacher's Son

The details on the 2006 campaign for governor and Walker's withdrawal come from articles in the *Journal Sentinel* as well as from the authors themselves, both of whom were involved in covering the race, one for the *Journal Sentinel* and the other for the *Wisconsin State Journal*. The details on the withdrawal announcement come in part from a March 25, 2006, *Journal Sentinel* article by Dave Umhoefer. The details on Walker's childhood, marriage, and personal life come from *Journal Sentinel* profiles, including a March 29, 2002, story by Steve Schultze and an October 16, 2010, article by Bill Glauber (http://www.jsonline.com/news/statepolitics/1051157 54.html). The information on Walker's time at Marquette and grade point average also comes from a July 31, 2010, *Journal Sentinel* article by Umhoefer and one of the authors (http://www.jsonline.com/news/statepolitics/99700384.html). The three governors in 2010 without college degrees were Jan Brewer of Arizona, M. Jodi Rell of Connecticut, and Gary Herbert of Utah.

Details on the worst-case scenario for payouts through the Milwaukee County pension lump-sum payments can be found in an October 1, 2010, story in the *Journal Sentinel* by Schultze (http://www.jsonline.com/news/milwaukee/104194024.html). Walker's opponent in the Milwaukee county executive general election race was Hales Corners Village President Jim Ryan. The numbers on the Milwaukee County property tax and workforce changes during Walker's tenure come from an October 21, 2010, *Journal Sentinel* story by Schultze (http://www.jsonline.com/news/statepolitics/105498198.html) and a calculation by the Legislative Fiscal Bureau. Walker's call for dismantling Milwaukee County government can be found in a July 20, 2009, *Journal Sentinel* article by Schultze (http://www.jsonline.com/news/milwaukee/51228407.html).

The data on Wisconsin's pension system and those of other states comes from two well-respected sources: a June 2012 report by the Pew Center on the States (http://www.pewstates.org/research/reports/the-widening-gap-update-85899398 241) and the most recent study by the National Association of State Retirement Administrators (http://www.nasra.org/resources/NASRACostsBrief1202.pdf). Rob Henken, a former Walker appointee in Milwaukee County and current president of the Public Policy Forum of Milwaukee, also answered questions about the county pension system. The forum's January 2010 comprehensive report on Milwaukee County government—"Should It Stay or Should It Go?"—discusses the factors that led to increases in the pension fund contributions (http://www.publicpolicyforum.org/pdfs/SectionI.pdf).

Chapter 3. "Open for Business"

After the election, one of Walker's first pieces of legislation limited the ability of the elderly and disabled to sue nursing homes for injuries and deaths. Democratic Representative Marlin Schneider was a forty-year veteran of the Assembly. The authors watched and covered political advertisements as part of the 2010 race for governor, and they turned back to that coverage and re-watched those ads for the opening of this chapter. Walker's decision to give back part of his pay—first $60,000 a year, later $10,000 a year—was detailed in a PolitiFact Wisconsin article by Tom Kertscher on October 28, 2011 (http://www.politifact.com/wisconsin/statements/2011/oct/28/blog-posting/bloggers-say-gov-scott-walker-taking-pay-raise-whi/). The Associated Press first pointed out that Walker's catering to high-end donors didn't fit his brownbag theme. The news service also first reported the campaign motif followed a similar one used more than a decade earlier by Ohio Republican George Voinovich.

Under Act 10, the pension contribution for Walker and other elected officials was both a little higher than what he promised on the campaign trail and higher than that required for rank-and-file employees. Governor Tommy Thompson's approval of a bill boosting the public workers' pensions was covered extensively by the *Journal Sentinel* at the time in stories such as "Pension Boosted, Pending Court Ruling," by Steven Walters on December 17, 1999. The details of Mark Green's strategy regarding public employee unions were confirmed with a knowledgeable source.

Various studies comparing the compensation of public- and private-sector workers were detailed in a December 14, 2010, article by Lee Bergquist and one of the authors (http://www.jsonline.com/news/wisconsin/111900074.html). The Economic Policy Institute report can be found at http://www.epi.org/publication/are_wiscon sin_public_employees_over-compensated/. Walker's campaign was most explicit about changing labor law when it provided details to one of the authors on his plan to allow schools to change which health care plans they offered teachers and other workers. The article ran in the *Journal Sentinel* on August 29, 2010 (http://www.js online.com/news/statepolitics/101771723.html). One of the authors covered Walker's pledge to have workers pay half the cost of their pensions and to put that much toward his own pension as soon as he took office (http://www.jsonline.com/news/ statepolitics/96578424.html). The Associated Press first reported on Walker not paying the higher pension amount until all workers were required to do so, despite his promise to do it as soon as he took office. The Dane County deputy was David Hopperdietzel, and his exchange with Ryan Murray is detailed in a June 1, 2012, *Journal Sentinel* article by one of the authors (http://www.jsonline.com/news/state politics/union-says-email-shows-walker-hid-bargaining-intentions-h45knhf-15643 6575.html). The video of Walker's visit to the *Oshkosh Northwestern* is on the newspaper's website (http://www.thenorthwestern.com/VideoNetwork/649759886001/ Republican-Gov-candidate-Scott-Walker-visits-editorial-board).

For the account of Tom Barrett getting attacked outside the Wisconsin State Fair, the authors relied on video of Barrett's testimony at sentencing, as well as a July 23, 2010, article by Crocker Stephenson (http://www.jsonline.com/news/milwaukee/ 99118074.html). Anthony Peters was sentenced to twelve years in prison and ten years of extended supervision. The calls to Barrett from Obama and Biden were reported in an October 25, 2009, column by Daniel Bice (http://www.jsonline.com/ watchdog/noquarter/65957092.html). Details of Barrett's background come from *Journal Sentinel* coverage and the Wisconsin Blue Book. Mark Neumann's entry into the race, and descriptions of his background, come from the authors' coverage of the 2010 race with Lee Bergquist. Walker moved to the right during the primary most notably when he switched his position on immigration and Wisconsin's recently enacted smoking ban.

Bice was the first to report on the John Doe investigation of Walker's aides, and he broke the major developments of the investigation. He first reported on some of the issues that emerged in the investigation before writing about the investigation itself, such as in his May 14, 2010, column about Darlene Wink (http://www.json line.com/watchdog/noquarter/93746099.html). Details of the investigation and what happened at the time come from his work and discussions with him, the authors' own reporting, and the work of other *Journal Sentinel* reporters, as well as public documents such as the criminal complaints against Darlene Wink, Kelly Rindfleish, Tim Russell, Kevin Kavanaugh, and William Gardner.

Walker's pledge to create a quarter of a million jobs in his first term and halt the Milwaukee-to-Madison rail line was drawn from the *Journal Sentinel*'s coverage of the campaign. Confirmation that the Wisconsin Education Association Council did not run ads to help Barrett in the 2010 race comes from an interview with a Barrett staffer. The performance of Republicans at the state level in November 2010 was drawn from a number of sources, including figures available from the National Conference of State Legislatures (http://www.ncsl.org/?tabid=21317), the *Washington Post* (http://www.washingtonpost.com/wp-srv/special/politics/2010-race-maps/governors/), and the *New York Times* (http://elections.nytimes.com/2010/results/governor). Dye's account of her attendance at Russ Feingold's election night party comes from interviews with her. Feingold's speech is archived on CSPAN's website (http://www.c-spanvideo.org/program/296383-1). The breakdown of votes in November 2010 comes from a November 3, 2010, *Journal Sentinel* article by Craig Gilbert (http://www.jsonline.com/news/statepolitics/106589258.html). The account of Walker's victory comes from video footage of his victory speech and *Journal Sentinel* coverage.

Chapter 4. "The First Step"

Details on the Bradley Foundation and the meal with Walker come from a piece that was written and researched by Daniel Bice, Bill Glauber, and Ben Poston of the *Journal Sentinel* and ran on November 19, 2011 (http://www.jsonline.com/news/milwaukee/from-local-roots-bradley-foundation-builds-conservative-empire-k7337pb-134187368.html). The article by Brian Fraley is available at the MacIver Institute website (http://www.maciverinstitute.com/2010/11/the-time-is-now-to-reform-labor-laws-which-threaten-our-states-future/). The December 3, 2010, budget analyst request on the bill draft is contained within the drafting file for Act 10 at the Legislative Reference Bureau, which is the official drafting agency for the Legislature, and the authors also interviewed Reference Bureau staff. The drafting file makes clear that by then the incoming Walker administration was also looking at changing state law on public employees' pension contributions as well. The request for the labor attorney to help the incoming Walker administration was recounted to the authors by two sources familiar with the matter. The *New York Times* article by Eric Lipton ran on February 21, 2011 (http://www.nytimes.com/2011/02/22/us/22koch.html). Governor Walker's denial of any outside involvement in Act 10 was made in a spring 2012 interview with Glauber. Details on the State Policy Network and Mackinac Center funding from Bradley come from *Journal Sentinel* research. Details on the group's activities come from their websites. The October 26, 2010, Bradley Working Group meeting is detailed on the website of the Sagamore Institute (http://www.sagamoreinstitute.org/article/lessons-from-the-bradley-working-group/), and a participant verified some details about it.

The account of Marty Beil's initial reaction to the governor's plan to crack down on unions comes from an interview with him. In the Assembly, the seventeenth labor contract, dealing with the Service Employees International Union, passed by a larger margin of forty-nine to forty-six votes because a Democrat, Peggy Krusick of Milwaukee, who had been voting against the contracts, voted for that particular one. Former Senator Russ Decker declined through a former aide to speak with the authors about his decision to vote against the contracts.

The meeting between Walker and Diane Hendricks comes from the video shot by Brad Lichtenstein and reporting by the authors, including interviews with Lichtenstein, Walker, and his campaign (Hendricks didn't agree to an interview). The authors' story ran on May 10, 2012, in the *Journal Sentinel* (http://www.jsonline.com/ news/statepolitics/in-film-walker-talks-of-divide-and-conquer-strategy-with-unions -8057h6f-151049555.html). The raw footage of the exchange has not been released publicly, but it was made available to the authors by Lichtenstein. The filmmaker had previously worked on Democratic campaigns and had given one hundred dollars in October 2010 to Milwaukee Mayor Tom Barrett, Walker's opponent that year in the governor's race. The figures on Hendricks's political giving come from the Federal Election Commission, the state Government Accountability Board, and the Wisconsin Democracy Campaign. The *Forbes* estimate of Hendricks's wealth can be found at http://www.forbes.com/profile/diane-hendricks/. The fact that right-to-work legislation was drafted by some conservative lawmakers in the Wisconsin Legislature comes from *Journal Sentinel* interviews with Assembly Speaker Jeff Fitzgerald and Representative Chris Kapenga, a Republican from Delafield (http://www.json line.com/blogs/news/151553505.html).

Chapter 5. "Dropping the Bomb"

The account of the behind-the-scenes debate between Walker and Senate Republicans comes from interviews with Senator Mike Ellis, his aide Mike Boerger, Senate Majority Leader Scott Fitzgerald, Representative Robin Vos, Walker Chief of Staff Keith Gilkes, and others. Along with police and firefighters, Walker and lawmakers also later exempted bus drivers from Act 10 after learning that changing labor law for them could cost the state its federal transit aid. Bill Glauber of the *Journal Sentinel* interviewed Jeff Fitzgerald in the spring of 2012, and that interview yielded the quotes on Walker mentoring him.

The information on the state budget comes primarily from Legislative Fiscal Bureau and state Budget Office documents, and from years of close coverage by the authors and extensive interviews with experts such as economist Andrew Reschovsky of the University of Wisconsin–Madison; Todd Berry, president of Wisconsin Taxpayers Alliance; the heads of the state Budget Office; and others. The authors interviewed Bob Lang, head of the nonpartisan Fiscal Bureau, to confirm the correct reading of the disputed January 31, 2011, LFB report (http://legis.wisconsin.gov/ lfb/publications/Revenue-Estimates/Documents/2011_01_31Vos_Darling.pdf). One of the authors published along with his former colleague Mark Pitsch an extensive look at the state's longstanding budget problems in the *State Journal* on February 1, 2009 (http://host.madison.com/news/article_15be467f-139a-5bec-8ff5-2771dbce 6f52.html). The calculations about the per capita size of the budget deficits were done by the authors.

When Walker took office, the potential budget shortfall through June 2013 was projected to be around $3.6 billion. That projection was dropped to $3 billion later that year.

The details on the appointment of Stephen Fitzgerald as the head of the State Patrol come from a February 8, 2011, story by the authors (http://www.jsonline .com/news/milwaukee/115560469.html). Walker gave the details on the meeting with his cabinet in a phone call with a blogger impersonating billionaire David Koch. That conversation is detailed in chapter 11. The *Journal Sentinel* interview with the governor in December 2011 was conducted by the authors. The comment by Senator Dale Schultz in the private meeting comes from knowledgeable Republican sources. The authors interviewed Representative Dick Spanbauer about the private Assembly GOP caucus with Walker and also confirmed his recollections with another source in the room. The notes to chapter 1 lay out where the details on Act 10 were found. The comments made by GOP senators exiting their private caucus with Walker come from interviews conducted at that moment by the authors.

Chapter 6. Laboratory of Democracy

Representative Peter Barca and Senator Mark Miller have talked on the record about the meeting with Walker, as have their chiefs of staff, Rich Judge and Jamie Kuhn. Walker and his aides have not, though a source close to the governor did answer some questions about it. The details on the lawmakers' upbringing come from interviews and the Wisconsin Blue Book. Robert W. Ozanne's 1984 book, *The Labor Movement in Wisconsin: A History*, serves as the basis of much of the Wisconsin labor and political history recounted in this chapter. Ozanne, as it turns out, was the grandfather of Ismael Ozanne, the Democratic Dane County district attorney who later sued to block Act 10. The authors also made use of the chapter on Wisconsin in the book *Public Workers: Government Employee Unions, the Law, and the State* by Joseph E. Slater, which provided figures on the growth in AFSCME membership in Wisconsin and nationally. Another book dealing with the labor history of the state and Walker's legislation is the short e-book *The Battle for Wisconsin*, written by the University of Wisconsin–Green Bay labor historian Andrew Kersten and published by Hill and Wang.

A history of Fighting Bob La Follette's role in instituting open primaries in Wisconsin can be found in a 1909 *Milwaukee Sentinel* article posted on the website of the Wisconsin Historical Society (http://www.wisconsinhistory.org/wlhba/article View.asp?pg=1&id=4187&pn=0). The figures on national and Wisconsin union membership come from the federal Bureau of Labor Statistics (http://www.bls.gov/ news.release/union2.nro.htm and http://www.bls.gov/ro5/unionwi.pdf). The details on Joe McCarthy's controversial career come mainly from the Wisconsin Historical Society (http://www.wisconsinhistory.org/whi/feature/mccarthy/ and http://www .wisconsinhistory.org/whi/feature/mccarthy/timeline.asp).

The figures on union donations to Democrats come from a February 28, 2011, article in the *Journal Sentinel* by Daniel Bice and Ben Poston (http://www.jsonline

.com/news/statepolitics/117078618.html). Analyzing records kept by the Wisconsin Democracy Campaign, the *Journal Sentinel* found that Senate Democrats had raised a total of $1.9 million in campaign money since the start of 2007. Out of that sum, public employee unions and individual government workers contributed at least $344,000. The figures on union donations also come from a March 7, 2011, story by Mark Pitsch in the *State Journal* (http://host.madison.com/wsj/news/local/govt-and-politics/article_87f6ba78-46c6-11e0-a5fc-001cc4c002e0.html). One Wisconsin Now's executive director Scot Ross acknowledges that his group takes union contributions, but the group does not disclose the amounts or specific donors. The National Guard visits to prisons were laid out in a February 22, 2011, blog post by one of the authors for the *Journal Sentinel* (http://www.jsonline.com/blogs/news/116672074.html). Governor Walker's timeline for passing what became Act 10 was included in an e-mail sent on the morning of Wednesday, February 9, by Ryan Murray, the governor's director of policy and legislative affairs, to several other top aides of the governor and was turned up in response to a request under the state's open records law made by the liberal Madison group Center for Media and Democracy.

Chapter 7. First Protests

The descriptions of the protests in this chapter come from the authors' coverage and impressions of that day and footage by WisconsinEye, news crews, and protesters, as well as interviews with Peter Rickman, Cullen Werwie, Susan Riseling, Noble Wray, Dave Mahoney, Marty Beil, Stephanie Bloomingdale, Attorney General J.B. Van Hollen, and Senators Scott Fitzgerald and Mike Ellis. The authors also relied on a February 27, 2011, article in the *State Journal* by Dan Simmons (http://host.madison.com/wsj/news/local/govt-and-politics/anatomy-of-a-protest-from-a-simple-march-to-a/article_3c7f9cd2-4274-11e0-8f25-001cc4c002e0.html). One of the authors was at Walker's news conferences mentioned in this chapter, and he and other reporters were led in through a side door of the governor's suite of offices on February 16 because of difficulty getting in through the main entrance. The authors also reviewed WisconsinEye footage of those news conferences for this chapter. A transcript of Rush Limbaugh's February 17, 2011, program on Wisconsin can be found at http://www.rushlimbaugh.com/daily/2011/02/17/union_thugs_turn_wisconsin_into_greece_as_the_freeloaders_protest.

Ellis's quotes that the Republicans had the votes to pass the bill come from a February 15, 2011, story by the Associated Press (http://host.madison.com/wsj/news/local/govt-and-politics/article_2d181172-391c-11e0-8a85-001cc4c002e0.html). The authors were present for both the Joint Finance Committee hearing and the vote the next day. They also reviewed footage of those days captured by WisconsinEye, as well as video shot by protesters. One of the authors was present for the impromptu 3 a.m. press conference after the Joint Finance hearing and reviewed footage of that event for this chapter. The detail on Sarandon stopping by Ian's Pizza comes from an April 23, 2011, article in the *State Journal* (http://host.madison.com/ wsj/news/local/ask/catching-up-with-protests-over-business-back-to-normal-at/article_6b2e6e82-6ddf-11e0-9a3a-001cc4c002e0.html). Details about the pizzeria's role in the protests also come from a February 22, 2011, column by Jim Stingl in the *Journal Sentinel* (http://www.jsonline.com/news/statepolitics/116709769 .html) and a February 25, 2011, article by Steven Greenhouse in the *New York Times* (http://www.nytimes.com/2011/02/26/us/26madison.html). One of the authors saw Vos jokingly sing protest songs in the Assembly speaker's office.

The details about how Senator Van Wanggaard switched his support to Walker's bill come from interviews with the senator and his chief of staff as well as a response to an open records request made by the authors for the governor's e-mails during that period. All of Dye's tweets from the budget crisis have now been purged from her account. But many of them have been preserved online, both on the site of the Madison weekly newspaper *Isthmus* (the outlet that created the #wiunion hashtag) and on an archive that was set up by Aaron S. Veenstra, a researcher at Southern Illinois University in Carbondale who has studied the protesters' use of social media. The information on the various hashtags used by the demonstrators and the number of tweets comes from Veenstra's research.

Chapter 8. The Interstate to Illinois

One of the authors observed both the Senate action in this chapter and Walker's press conference. The WisconsinEye footage was also reviewed in both cases, as was the extensive coverage by the *Journal Sentinel*. Interviews were also conducted with Senators Miller, Larson, Jauch, Cullen, Erpenbach, Holperin, Lassa, Fitzgerald, and Ellis, as well as Marty Beil, Miller aide Jamie Kuhn, Ellis aide Mike Boerger, Dave Mahoney, and Susan Riseling of the UW–Madison police. Dan Simmons of the *State Journal* was the first to report on how Ellis helped Cullen leave the Capitol in a February 27, 2011, article first cited in chapter 7.

The actions of the crowd come from a review of *Journal Sentinel* articles and blogs, numerous tweets archived on sites such as that of *Isthmus*, and the authors' own recollections. The exchange between Scott Fitzgerald and Mark Miller's staff was observed firsthand by one of the authors. The e-mail between Blaine Rummel and Mike Browne turned up in an open records request by one of the authors for the *Journal Sentinel*. The confrontation between Holperin and Tea Partiers at the Clock Tower is based on video posted on the Gateway Pundit blog. The story of Dale Schultz comes from interviews with him, his chief of staff Todd Allbaugh, Walker spokesman Cullen Werwie, and another source close to the Walker administration.

The account of Jenni Dye comes from interviews with her and a review of her archived tweets. The details on the start of United Wisconsin come from interviews with Michael Brown, *Journal Sentinel* stories, and records from the Government Accountability Board. A board staffer confirmed the detail about a Democratic complaint about Brown's Assembly website. The background on the Charles Benson interview with President Obama was verified with Benson. The quotes from labor leader Rich Abelson come from *Journal Sentinel* interviews with him. The e-mails to the governor started out overwhelmingly against Walker. On the day that the governor released his bill, the e-mails he received ran more than five to one against his proposal. Many of the e-mails came from government workers affected by the bill, including a large number of employees responding to an e-mail sent to them by Walker giving his justification for the legislation. The margin gradually narrowed but didn't shift to support of Walker until after the senators left the state.

Chapter 9. First Assembly Vote

One of the authors was present at the Senate and Assembly sessions and Walker's press conference. The WisconsinEye footage was reviewed as well as the *Journal Sentinel* coverage for the day, which supplies the quotes not otherwise attributed. The *Fox and Friends* interview can be found at http://video.foxnews.com/v/4545 226/gov-scott-walker-on-fox-friends/.

State Journal reporter Doug Erickson recorded the details about Erpenbach's morning in Chicago in a February 19, 2011, article (http://host.madison.com/wsj/ news/local/govt-and-politics/article_4a8of6de-3b8d-11e0-b61a-001cc4c002e0 .html). The video of the visit of the State Patrol trooper and Blazel to Miller's house was taken by *State Journal* reporter Patricia Simms (http://host.madison.com/wsj/ news/video/vmix_043d3490-3b96-11e0-96a5-001cc4c002e0.html). The We Ask America poll sampled Wisconsin residents rather than likely voters but also questioned 2,397 of them, an usually large number for a statewide poll. The survey found that a majority of Wisconsin residents disagreed with Governor Walker's plans, and the wording of that question was favorable to Republicans. It described the governor's bill as stripping unions of their "power" rather than their "rights" (http://weaskamerica.com/2011/02/18/weirdness-in-wisconsin/). The authors had one of the private interviews with the governor.

The official Assembly Journal for that day says the Assembly reconvened at 4:55 p.m. The timestamp on the WisconsinEye footage of the Assembly session, which can vary by a minute or two, shows the GOP lawmakers started at 4:54 p.m. The Republicans did not dispute the fact that they had started the session early. All the Democrats' seats were empty with the possible exception of one; some GOP lawmakers later remembered seeing Representative Peggy Krusick, a Democrat from Milwaukee, there. Krusick was an idiosyncratic lawmaker who often avoided her party's caucus meetings, sometimes voted with Republicans, and lost a Democratic primary challenge the next year. In an interview, she said she did not recall if she was present. If she was on the floor, she didn't show up in the video footage or speak up loudly. The details on the Capitol Police conversation with Jeff Fitzgerald come from interviews with him as well as Representative Robin Vos and a source close to Fitzgerald. Susan Riseling of the UW–Madison police and Keith Gilkes discussed in interviews the internal debate over clearing the Capitol that night. Charles Tubbs of the Capitol Police very briefly discussed the night.

Chapter 10. A State Divided

The details in this chapter come from *Journal Sentinel* stories, the authors' own recollections, and a number of other sources. Jack Craver's camel blog was posted on the *Isthmus* website, which was then hosting it, on February 21, 2011 (http://www.thedailypage.com/daily/article.php?article=32394). Craver also answered questions about the incident. John Oliver did not respond to an interview request by the authors but did talk to the Madison entertainment weekly *77 Squared* in a September 18, 2012, article (http://host.madison.com/entertainment/city_life/camel-or-no-camel-john-oliver-returns-to-madison/article_a355bd69-8536-5150-9cb9-0bc35 825d719.html). The details on the divided state and its citizens come from two *Journal Sentinel* articles: one on February 25, 2011, by Karen Herzog and Annysa Johnson (http://www.jsonline.com/news/statepolitics/116966938.html) and one on February 26, 2011, by Rick Romell (http://www.jsonline.com/news/statepolitics/11 6993638.html). Paul Ryan's comments on Cairo can be found in a PolitiFact Wisconsin article that ran in the *Journal Sentinel* on February 18, 2011 (http://www.poli tifact.com/wisconsin/statements/2011/feb/18/paul-ryan/us-rep-paul-ryan-com pares-madison-cairo-calls-prot/). The information on Riseling comes from interviews with her, and the figure of 40,000 demonstrators comes from a July 2012 filing in the Dane County Circuit Court by the state Department of Justice. John Nichols, associate editor of the *Capital Times* and author of the book *Uprising* about the Madison protests, noticed the protester badges describing Walker as the "Mubarak of the Middle West." The information on Walker's security costs comes from a November 8, 2011, *Journal Sentinel* article by the authors (http://www.jsonline.com/news/state politics/protection-costs-for-walker-kleefisch-more-than-double-sb2vipc-1334961 63.html). The information on the lobbying by unions comes from the state Government Accountability Board (http://gab.wi.gov/node/2025) and the *Journal Sentinel*.

PolitiFact Wisconsin reviewed Michael Moore's figures on the distribution of wealth in the country on March 10 and found they checked out (http://www.politi fact.com/wisconsin/statements/2011/mar/10/michael-moore/michael-moore-says-400-americans-have-more-wealth-/). Examples of Matt Wisniewski's work can be found at http://vimeo.com/mgwisni. *The Lamentable Tragedie of Scott Walker* was reviewed by Laurie Stark of *Isthmus* on July 30, 2011 (http://www.thedailypage.com/daily/article.php?article=34253). The Glen Shulfer songs "Stand with Walker" and the "Union Man" (definitely not a song in defense in labor) can be found at http://www.youtube.com/watch?v=rQIMDTjHB6A and http://www.youtube.com/watch ?v=3OUo2biBDxE. The Scott Walker Jedi rap can be found at http://www.youtube .com/watch?v=k8u9jhuVgIo. Tom Morello wrote about his trip to Madison in *Rolling Stone* on February 25, 2011 (http://www.rollingstone.com/politics/news/ frostbite-and-freedom-tom-morello-on-the-battle-of-madison-20110225). He made his comments to Nichols of the *Capital Times* in an August 23, 2011, article (http://host .madison.com/news/opinion/column/john_nichols/john-nichols-rage-against -paul-ryan/article_74ab71fa-ecb7-11e1-8023-001a4bcf887a.html). The Jimmy Fallon segment aired on March 3, 2011 (http://www.latenightwithjimmyfallon.com/blogs/

2011/03/slow-jam-the-news-wisconsin-protests-with-brian-williams/). The information on labor legislation in other states comes mainly from the *Journal Sentinel* and
the *New York Times*. The information on the vote on the general strike by the South
Central Federation of Labor comes from a February 23, 2011, story in the *State Journal* (http://host.madison.com/wsj/news/local/govt-and-politics/article_64c8d7a8
-3e8c-11e0-9911-001cc4c002e0.html). The information on the Badger Doctors group
comes from their disciplinary records and reporting and interviews by the *Journal
Sentinel*, the Associated Press, and the *State Journal*. The Solidarity Sing Along information comes from *Journal Sentinel* reporting and interviews with its leader. The
accounts of lactating mothers using Senator Risser's personal office to breastfeed
come from Sarah Briganti and other aides to Risser.

Chapter 11. The Beast from Buffalo

This chapter relies on the audio of the call Ian Murphy made available publicly, his
accounts of the call at the time and on its one-year anniversary, as well as other articles by Murphy. His account was supplemented with interviews with people close
to the governor and familiar with the call, as well as a spring 2012 interview with
Walker about the call by Bill Glauber of the *Journal Sentinel*. Details about spending
by Americans for Prosperity come from *Journal Sentinel* coverage. Madison Police
Chief Noble Wray's comments come from a statement released through the police
department. One of the authors was present for Walker's news conference on the
prank phone call, and the authors viewed WisconsinEye footage of it. The authors
also used the C-SPAN footage of Walker's testimony before a congressional committee, where he talked about the prank call. One of the authors also attended the
Senate Committee on Transportation and Elections described in this chapter. The
authors relied on coverage of the meeting by the *Journal Sentinel* and the Associated
Press as well as an audio recording of the meeting. The account of Senator Jon
Erpenbach's staff picking up his check from Senate Majority Leader Scott Fitzgerald comes from interviews with Erpenbach's staff and Fitzgerald.

Chapter 12. Lost Sleep and "Hallucinazations"

The authors witnessed large portions of the marathon Assembly session, and this
chapter draws on WisconsinEye footage of it, the official Assembly Journal, archived
records of the amendments and votes on the Legislature's website (https://docs.legis
.wisconsin.gov/2011/proposals/jr1/ab11), *Journal Sentinel* articles and blog posts, and
interviews with lawmakers. The details on the private Assembly GOP caucus come
from interviews with Representatives Al Ott, Robin Vos, and Michelle Litjens, and
several Republican aides as well as Walker's e-mails during that period released under
the open records law. The Knilans quote and some other details come from a piece
by Christian Schneider, which ran on March 17, 2011, on the website of *National
Review* (http://www.nationalreview.com/corner/262317/wisconsin-assemblys-bold
-leap-christian-schneider). That piece says this meeting happened on March 10—the
date of the second Assembly vote on Walker's bill, but those interviewed who could

remember a date believed the meeting happened on February 22, before the first vote. That makes the most sense, since the first vote on the bill would have likely provoked more deliberation than the second. The participants remembered the quotes vividly, though they differed somewhat in the wording. Ott provided the chapter and verse numbers of the passages he recited that came from the New King James Version translation of the Bible.

The information on the historic length of the session comes from a blog post by one of the authors on February 24, 2011 (http://www.jsonline.com/blogs/news/ 116836548.html). The details on Litjens's hasty exit from the Assembly chamber were given by her in interviews. She first shared the account with Steven Walters of WisconsinEye (http://wiseye.org/videoplayer/vp.html?sid=7882). Jenni Dye's actions come from interviews with her as well as a review of the tweet archive set up by Southern Illinois University in Carbondale.

Chapter 13. The Capitol in Lockdown

This chapter draws on the WisconsinEye footage of Walker's budget address, numerous *Journal Sentinel* stories about the budget, Legislative Fiscal Bureau documents, and other analyses by nonprofit groups, local governments, and the Walker administration. For the court case on access to the Capitol, see the notes to chapter 14. Jenni Dye's section comes from interviews with her and her archived tweets. The e-mails between Walker and aides were released to the authors through an open records request. The polling information comes from a Craig Gilbert blog post in the *Journal Sentinel* on March 1, 2011 (http://www.jsonline.com/blogs/news/1171 52958.html). Dave Mahoney was also interviewed.

The crowd and Senator Grothman were videotaped by Phil Ejercito, a local photographer and contributor to *Isthmus* (http://www.youtube.com/watch?v=9Cx77K8 e3WE). The authors also interviewed Grothman, Representative Hulsey, Balestrieri, and Bloomingdale about the incident. Some of the Grothman quotes come from a March 2, 2011, story by Mary Spicuzza of the *State Journal* (http://host.madison .com/wsj/news/local/govt-and-politics/article_970dc490-44ee-11e0-855c-001cc4c 03286.html). Local radio host John "Sly" Sylvester had had Grothman on his show on February 28, 2011, and had played clips of him over the weekend calling protesters "slobs" (http://slysoffice.blogspot.com/2011/02/glenn-grothman-protesters-at -capitol.html).

The video footage from a security camera in the tunnel was released to the authors through an open records request. It was too grainy to show faces well but recorded relatively few people moving through the tunnel in the hours before the speech. Mark Miller's budget proposal also would have cut a money-saving investment in the state's health program and lowered the minimum balance in state law for the state's main account. One of the authors looked at the studies by the National Association of State Budget Officers and the Center on Budget and Policy Priorities in a December 10, 2011, *Journal Sentinel* article (http://www.jsonline.com/news/ statepolitics/states-school-funding-gets-squeezed-studies-show-dc3cb0g-1353914

93.html). The Census Bureau study comparing Milwaukee Public Schools spending with that of the other fifty biggest districts was examined in a June 21, 2012, article by Erin Richards in the *Journal Sentinel* (http://www.jsonline.com/news/education/ mps-perpupil-spending-4th-highest-in-us-1u5rurq-159889555.html). The November 2012 Wisconsin Taxpayers Alliance study can be found on the group's website (http: //wistax.org/publication/after-the-storm-school-funding-in-2012). With much help from other *Journal Sentinel* reporters, one of the authors did a story on the effects of Walker's budget on local governments on March 4, 2012 (http://www.jsonline .com/news/statepolitics/has-walkers-budget-formula-worked-v14csp9-141385823 .html). The figures on the statewide property tax levy come from an April 16, 2012, memo from the state Department of Revenue. The figures on the savings from WEA Trust by the Appleton school district come from a PolitiFact Wisconsin article in the *Journal Sentinel* on May 21, 2012 (http://www.politifact.com/wisconsin/arti cle/2012/may/21/behind-rhetoric-wea-trust-and-school-health-care-c/).

Chapter 14. "Seven Thousand People in the Statehouse"

This chapter draws primarily on the WisconsinEye footage of the court testimony, *Journal Sentinel* articles written at the time, and interviews and fact-checking with Judge John Albert and several others familiar with the case. The authors were present during the standoff over access and observed the clearing of the Capitol by Chief Tubbs. The discovery of the .22 ammunition was described in court testimony. The details on the cleanup estimates and the actual costs come from *Journal Sentinel* articles, including one on March 30, 2011 (http://www.jsonline.com/news/statepol- itics/118951264.html) and another on April 4, 2012 (http://www.jsonline.com/ news/statepolitics/final-tab-for-capitol-cleanup-pegged-at-200000-jq4s1ia-1461309 85.html). The authors obtained access to a transcript of a deposition of state architect Dan Stephans, which provided the quote. The account of Representative Milroy's altercation comes from a *Journal Sentinel* blog post by one of the authors (http://www.jsonline.com/blogs/news/117413883.html) and video posted online of the incident (http://www.youtube.com/watch?v=YhQEJfaELdc). The background on some of the charges against Chief Tubbs's sons can be found in *State Journal* articles. The details on the texting between Huebsch and Representative Barca come from interviews with the two men and a Capitol access case deposition with Huebsch to which the authors obtained access. The details on the signs and the reopening of the Capitol come from *Journal Sentinel* articles, including Jim Stingl's March 10, 2011, column (http://www.jsonline.com/news/statepolitics/117780623.html).

Chapter 15. No Deal

This chapter relies on interviews with Senators Cullen, Jauch, Fitzgerald, Holperin, Lassa, Erpenbach, Miller and his aides, Gerald Whitburn, Keith Gilkes, and Marty Beil. It also draws on *Journal Sentinel* stories written during those days and on the June 4, 2011, retrospective article. It also relies on e-mails released to the authors by Walker's office through an open records request that detail the discussions with

Cullen and Jauch. Some of the information on Stocks and the National Education Association come from the union's website (http://www.nea.org/home/2580.htm and http://www.nea.org/home/47683.htm). Information on the lobbying by John Stocks and the National Education Association comes from the website of the state Government Accountability Board (http://ethics.state.wi.us/scripts/currentSession/oel.asp?PrinID=4443&start=N&start2=). The senator cited for drunk driving was Richard Kreul. As it happened, the former senator died while Cullen and the other senators had absented themselves from the Capitol, and Cullen decided he shouldn't attend the funeral, to avoid any uproar.

Chapter 16. End Game

This chapter comes from the authors' coverage, as well as testimony given in the court challenge to how Act 10 was adopted. One of the authors attended those hearings and reviewed video of them preserved on WisconsinEye for this chapter. Parts of this chapter also come from interviews with the senators listed in the notes for Chapter 15, as well as Keith Gilkes, Senator Chris Larson, Representative Dick Spanbauer, Mike Huebsch, Susan Riseling, Dave Mahoney, Noble Wray, and two protesters who rushed to the Capitol the day of the conference committee vote, Tim Gehrke and Benjamin Taft. Charles Tubbs declined comment. The sources for the call between the Madison Police and Blackdeer spoke on condition of anonymity. One of the authors attended the conference committee meeting and the Senate session that followed, and the authors also reviewed footage of those meetings for this chapter. The details on the protests that night come from *Journal Sentinel* coverage, as well as amateur video that was posted on YouTube. The description of what happened on the bus the senators took comes from interviews and standard video shot by a camera mounted in all city buses and obtained by the authors. The descriptions of the Assembly session the next day come from *Journal Sentinel* coverage, as well as footage by WisconsinEye and amateur videographers. Representative Pocan's column on how he coined the term "Fitzwalkerstan" ran on the website of the *Progressive* magazine on September 2, 2011 (http://progressive.org/fitzwalkerstan.html). One of the blog posts on Fitzwalkerstan can be found at http://www.uppitywis.org/blog article/welcome-fitzwalkerstan. One of the authors attended Walker's ceremonial signing of Act 10 and the court hearing in Kathleen Falk's lawsuit.

Chapter 17. Rebukes and Recount

This chapter is based primarily on articles by the authors in the *Journal Sentinel*. One of the authors attended the hearings before Judge Maryann Sumi and the news conferences held afterward, and for this chapter the authors rewatched the WisconsinEye footage of those events. Details about the letters sent to Sumi in response to her rulings come from information Bill Lueders published in *Isthmus*. On the day the law was published by the Legislative Reference Bureau, Scott Fitzgerald, in an interview with one of the authors, expressed his belief that the law would now go into effect. The authors covered the race between David Prosser and JoAnne

Kloppenburg—and the recount—with assistance from *Journal Sentinel* reporters
Larry Sandler and Laurel Walker.

Chapter 18. A Court Divided

The account of Scott Walker's congressional testimony comes from video of the
hearing maintained on the House's website, as well as a report on the hearing by
the *Journal Sentinel*'s Craig Gilbert. Jenni Dye's impressions come from interviews
with her. William Gruber's monologue during a Joint Finance Committee break
comes from a recording made by a reporter present for the speech and shared with
one of the authors, who was also present for that tirade. One of the authors was also
present when Gruber stormed onto the Senate floor and when Miles Kristan berated
Senator Randy Hopper in a Capitol stairwell. The quote from Jeremy Ryan comes
from a June 11, 2011, story by Emma Roller for the *Journal Sentinel* (http://www.json
line.com/news/statepolitics/123699094.html). Information on the permitting and
demonstration practices in other state capitols comes from several sources including the *State Journal*, which in a September 23, 2012, story by Nico Savidge surveyed
states around the country for their rules on demonstrations in their capitols (http://
host.madison.com/wsj/news/local/govt-and-politics/tighter-rules-for-capitol-pro
tests-not-unlike-many-other-states/article_aa208f9a-040a-11e2-a90b-0019bb2963
f4.html).The Walker administration also provided information on practices around
the country.

Details about the charges against William Gardner come from the *Journal Sentinel* and the criminal complaint. Madison lawyer Lester Pines referred to Justice
Patience Roggensack as the state Supreme Court's de facto chief justice during a
June 29, 2011, forum hosted by the Madison chapter of the Society of Professional
Journalists. The arguments before the state Supreme Court come from coverage at
the time and archived footage of them kept by WisconsinEye. The authors interviewed lawyers and parties involved in the case for the *Journal Sentinel* at the time
it was pending, and one of them also interviewed Attorney General J.B. Van Hollen
about it a year later. The descriptions of the murals in the hearing room are supplemented by information from the court and the Wisconsin Department of Administration. The descriptions of the altercation between Prosser and Bradley come from
Journal Sentinel coverage, interviews, the sheriff's report, and court records. The
heights of the justices come from the report. Prosser's quote about expecting to be
called a fascist pig comes from a description of the incident written by Bradley's law
clerk, Rachel Graham, shortly after it happened. Graham's memo is also the source
of Roggensack saying a press release would serve as a consolation prize. Prosser disputes Bradley told him to leave the office before he put his hands on her neck, but
other justices told detectives that she did say that. The incident in which Prosser
called Abrahamson a "total bitch" was first reported by one of the authors in a March
19, 2011, article (http://www.jsonline.com/news/statepolitics/118310479.html). The
details of the ethics case against Prosser comes from filings with the court and *Journal Sentinel* coverage.

Chapter 19. Recalls

The account of Richelle Zimmerman turning in signatures comes from press coverage of the event, video footage, and an interview with her a year later. Her comment about her wages somewhat understated her actual income, which was $25.42 an hour at the time. The six Republicans who faced recall in 2011 were Rob Cowles of Allouez, Alberta Darling of River Hills, Sheila Harsdorf of River Falls, Randy Hopper of Empire, Dan Kapanke of La Crosse, and Luther Olsen of Ripon; the three Democrats were Dave Hansen of Green Bay, Jim Holperin of Conover, and Bob Wirch of Pleasant Prairie. Kapanke lost to Jennifer Shilling, and Hopper lost to Jessica King; the other seven held onto their seats. Information on how many states allow recalls for state officials, and their success rate, comes from the National Conference of State Legislatures (http://www.ncsl.org/legislatures-elections/elections/recall-of-state-officials.aspx). The authors also relied on information from Joshua Spivak, a senior fellow at the Hugh L. Carey Institute for Government Reform at Wagner College, who runs the Recall Elections Blog at recallelections.blogspot.com. Some of the details on the history of the recall process in Wisconsin come from an April 2012 paper by Christian Schneider of the conservative Wisconsin Policy Research Institute (http://www.wpri.org/Reports/Volume25/Vol25No3/Vol25No3 .html) and from a rejoinder to that report by John D. Buenker, a professor emeritus at the University of Wisconsin–Parkside (https://www.box.com/s/51fc8a3b52cdac4 afd6c).

The story of how incumbents facing recall were allowed to raise unlimited money comes from a May 7, 2012, PolitiFact Wisconsin article by Dave Umhoefer (http://www.politifact.com/wisconsin/article/2012/may/07/behind-rhetoric-why-walker -was-able-raise-unlimite/). Representative John Nygren of Marinette came up short of getting on the ballot after Democrats challenged some of his signatures and the Accountability Board determined he had 398 valid signatures—two fewer than needed and an embarrassment for a party that had just finished gathering 15,540 signatures demanding the recall of incumbent Democratic Senator Dave Hansen of Green Bay. The Wisconsin Democracy Campaign, a tracker of political spending, estimated that in the 2011 recalls Democrats and unions spent $23.4 million, and Republicans and conservative groups spent $20.5 million—the estimate should be treated as a rough figure and not exact. The spending on the nine races topped the $37.4 million spent in the 2010 race for governor and was also more than double the $19.3 million spent in the fall 2010 legislative races, when 116 seats were up. We Are Wisconsin disclosed its spending; the Club for Growth did not, but its spending was estimated by the Democracy Campaign, which also provided the details on the two out-of-state contributions that did come to light. For the nine Senate recall districts combined, turnout topped 40 percent—about six points higher than for those districts in the April race for Supreme Court—and in one race reached 58 percent. In a district in northwestern Wisconsin, turnout was higher for the recall than it was for the 2010 race for governor.

Details of the John Doe investigation and charges come from court documents and *Journal Sentinel* coverage. Acting on a tip, one of the authors arrived in time to observe part of the FBI raid on Cindy Archer's home and was the only reporter there. During their investigation, authorities in December 2010 had also seized cell phones and computers from the Milwaukee home of Russell and his boyfriend, Brian Pierick. They found a series of chats, texts, and pictures exchanged by the two men with a seventeen-year-old Waukesha boy who had posted a salacious ad on Craigslist. Prosecutors charged Pierick with two felonies for child enticement and causing a child to expose himself.

The descriptions of the court rulings against Act 10 referenced in this chapter and the remainder of the book come from court filings and *Journal Sentinel* coverage of the decisions.

Chapter 20. Recalls Redux

Brown's quote about being "on the ground" comes from a *Capital Times* story. Accounts of United Wisconsin in the *Journal Sentinel*, *State Journal*, and the *Capital Times* as well as interviews with Brown and United Wisconsin board members Kevin Straka and Lynn Freeman helped to reconstruct the organization's rise. Mike Tate, chairman of the state Democratic Party, also discussed his impressions of United Wisconsin with one of the authors. The account of the meeting at WEAC's headquarters with officials from President Barack Obama's campaign comes from interviews with several participants. The David Koch article in the *Palm Beach Post* can be found at http://www.palmbeachpost.com/news/business/david-koch-intends -to-cure-cancer-in-his-lifetime-/nL4Fb/. The quote from Amanda Lazzari of UW– Madison was reported by the *State Journal*.

Details about the recall costs for the candidates and outside groups for their campaigns, as well as the costs to taxpayers for holding the elections, come from Government Accountability Board data and *Journal Sentinel* coverage. The move by some correctional officers to break away from AFSCME and form their own union was covered by the authors in a September 5, 2012, article (http://www.jsonline.com/ news/statepolitics/prison-officers-want-own-union-5c6ohmp-168692026.html).

The figures for turnout for the recall primaries come from the Accountability Board. In the two previous recalls for governor, North Dakota's Lynn Frazier was removed in 1921 and California's Gray Davis was removed in 2003. The account of the Barrett meeting with the unions, Bell's e-mail, and Falk's pledge comes from reporting by Daniel Bice and one of the authors for the *Journal Sentinel* as well as additional interviews with participants by the authors. Dye campaign details come from interviews with her, board chairman Scott McDonell, and Jack Martz. One quote from McDonell comes from an April 3, 2012, *State Journal* story (http://host .madison.com/news/local/govt-and-politics/elections/liberals-take-down-conserva tive-bloc-on-dane-county-board/article_404f1ada-7e06-11e1-9a9b-001a4bcf887a .html). The details on Walker's performance around the state come from a June 6, 2012, *Journal Sentinel* article by Craig Gilbert (http://www.jsonline.com/blogs/news/

157659025.html). The effect of the recalls on unions comes from a June 6, 2012, article by one of the authors (http://www.jsonline.com/news/statepolitics/unions -are-clear-losers-in-walker-victory-565lo9i-157377275.html). The details on the debate come from a June 1, 2012, story in the *Journal Sentinel* by one of the authors, Bill Glauber, and Don Walker (http://www.jsonline.com/news/statepolitics/barrett-foc uses-on-probe-of-walker-aides-in-final-recall-debate-9h5k6hr-156139325.html). The final accounting of how many jobs were created in Wisconsin in 2011 come from a June 28, 2012, *Journal Sentinel* story by Gilbert (http://www.jsonline.com/news/state politics/state-job-growth-lower-than-most-states-us-figures-show-i25ufs2-1606778 25.html). The point that Wisconsin's voters had proved less volatile than the state's politics in 2011 and 2012 was first made by Gilbert.

Conclusion

The details on the Madison Teachers Inc. rally come from interviews with Jenni Dye. Thompson made his comments about being a moderate to one of the authors and later at a news conference. The information on the Dane County union contracts and the board vote come from county briefing documents and contracts, an inter- view with county Department of Administration Director Travis Myren, an interview with Jenni Dye and a review of her tweets, and two *State Journal* articles by Steven Verburg published on September 20, 2012 (http://host.madison.com/wsj/news/local/ govt-and-politics/in-wake-of-act-ruling-dane-county-board-plans-to/article_877 d277c-02c1-11e2-b50f-0014bcf887a.html) and on September 21, 2012 (http://host .madison.com/news/local/govt-and-politics/dane-county-board-approves-new -union-contracts/article_1043b170-0385-11e2-841f-0014bcf887a.html). The quote from Dave Wiganowsky comes from the September 20 article and the Cullen Wer- wie quote from the September 21 piece. The County Board debate on the contracts can be found on the Madison City Channel website (http://media.cityofmadison .com/mediasite/Viewer/?peid=cb80da380c67487d9c38b06cb3856d671d). The effect of the recalls on unions comes from a June 6, 2012, article by one of the authors (http://www.jsonline.com/news/statepolitics/unions-are-clear-losers-in-walker-vic tory-565lo9i-157377275.html).

The interactions between Paul Ryan and Scott Walker during Ryan's vice-presi- dential bid were reported by journalists such as Mary Spicuzza of the *State Journal* in an August 15, 2012, article (http://host.madison.com/news/local/govt-and-politics/ first-walker-now-ryan-wisconsin-republicans-having-national-impact/article_ b304f1ec-e744-11e1-9497-0019bb2963f4.html). The analysis of the November 2012 election largely comes from a series of pieces by Gilbert in the *Journal Sentinel*, including a November 10, 2012, piece on the state's election swings (http://www .jsonline.com/blogs/news/178467801.html), a November 7, 2012, story on ticket splitting (http://www.jsonline.com/blogs/news/177673851.html), and an October 6, 2012, article on voters favoring both Obama and Walker (http://www.jsonline.com /news/statepolitics/approvers-of-obama-and-walker-are-indemand-swing-voters- nr74kio-172986401.html). Details on the Pew Center survey can be found at http://

www.people-press.org/2012/06/04/partisan-polarization-surges-in-bush-obama
-years/. The website WisPolitics compiled the figures on total spending in state and
federal campaigns in Wisconsin in 2012 in an article on November 29 of that year
by Jason Smathers (http://www.wispolitics.com/index.iml?Article=285155). Walker's
address at the Reagan Library can be found at http://www.youtube.com/watch?v=
4BSBckazR40. The *Ventura County Star* covered Walker's speech, and its interview
with Walker can be found at http://www.vcstar.com/news/2012/nov/16/in-simi
-visit-wisconsin-governor-reflects-on/.

Index

Governor Scott Walker (left) is interviewed in his statehouse office by *Milwaukee Journal Sentinel* reporters Jason Stein and Patrick Marley (right) on March 3, 2011, during the budget standoff. Also taking part in the interview is reporter Bill Glauber, obscured by Stein. (*Milwaukee Journal Sentinel*, photo by Mark Hoffman, © 2012 Journal Sentinel Inc., reproduced with permission)

JASON STEIN has reported on the Wisconsin Capitol and other news in Madison since 2002, working first for the *Wisconsin State Journal* and then the *Milwaukee Journal Sentinel*. He holds master's degrees in journalism from the University of Wisconsin–Madison and in linguistics from the University of Strasbourg in France. He served as president of the Wisconsin Capitol Correspondents Association from late 2010 to early 2012 and is also a past board president of the UW–Madison student paper the *Daily Cardinal*. He has received awards from the American Society of News Editors and the Society of American Business Editors and Writers.

PATRICK MARLEY has covered the Wisconsin Capitol for the *Milwaukee Journal Sentinel* since 2004. Before that, Marley covered local government for the *Kenosha News*. His work has been recognized by the Wisconsin Freedom of Information Council and the Wisconsin Newspaper Association. He holds a bachelor's degree in English from the University of Iowa and a master's degree in journalism from the University of Illinois at Urbana-Champaign.